HANDBOOK of DENOMINATIONS
in the United States

14th EDITION

Roger E. Olson

Craig D. Atwood

Frank S. Mead

Samuel S. Hill

 Abingdon Press™

Nashville

HANDBOOK OF DENOMINATIONS IN THE UNITED STATES
14TH EDITION

Library of Congress Cataloging-in-Publication Data has been requested.

ISBN 978-1-5018-2251-3

18 19 20 21 22 23 24 25 26 27—10 9 8 7 6 5 4 3 2 1

MANUFACTURED IN THE UNITED STATES OF AMERICA

In Memory of
Frank S. Mead (1898–1982)

CONTENTS

Contents

ALPHABETICAL TABLE OF CONTENTS
FOR DENOMINATIONS

PREFACE

This is the fourteenth edition of the *Handbook of Denominations* in the United States published occasionally by Abingdon Press. It contains many changes from previous editions but builds on the excellent work done by previous editors Frank Mead, Samuel Hill, and Craig Atwood. The most important changes are explained in the Introduction. The overall goal is to make the *Handbook* more usable by making it more streamlined and clearly focused. Entire categories introduced in previous editions have been eliminated; this edition includes only true denominations (a concept explained in the Introduction). A couple of new categories are introduced here including especially "Miscellaneous" for Christian denominations that do not fit any traditional category.

As with previous editions, this one attempts to include denominations in proper categories using historical and theological criteria. Common historical and theological roots bring together certain denominations that do not necessarily wish to be "lumped together." The editor and publisher apologize to denominations for any offense taken by that, but our defense is simply that categories are important to scholars, students, and people wanting to know the roots of denominations and how they are related to others, if at all.

Every attempt has been made to contact denominations and gain current information from them—especially about numbers of congregations and total adherents. Statistics can be problematic because many denominations simply do not keep such records or do not wish to share them. Also, some denominations include in their numbers congregations and adherents who also belong to other denominations. In other words, some denominations are not exclusive in terms of affiliation and membership. Many other challenges arise with counting congregations and adherents and gaining that information if it exists. Suffice it to say that we have done our best to obtain such information. When it was not forthcoming from a denomination we have relied on sources such as the *2010 Religion Census* compiled by the Association of Statisticians of Religious Bodies or the *2012 Yearbook of Churches in the United States and Canada*—the most recent edition of that reference volume. We have "fallen back" at times on other reference works such as encyclopedias of American religion and Internet sources.

Readers and users of this *Handbook* are encouraged to read the Introduction, which explains the meaning of "denomination" in a time when many people are uncomfortable with that term. We believe it is still useful when defined correctly. The Introduction also explains the criteria used for including a denomination here.

This editor thanks those who went before him. Earlier editions of the *Handbook* have been invaluable in my life of interest in American religion—going back to editions I first found and read in the 1960s in my father's pastoral library. I have attempted to remain faithful to the research and work done by previous editors while updating information and occasionally making corrections or helpful amendments. I also express appreciation to my two assistants Jared Patterson and Tyler Conway who helped with this revision project.

INTRODUCTION

The purpose of this *Handbook* is to provide especially non-scholars with a relatively simple, easy-to-use reference work for learning about the most significant Christian traditions and denominations in the United States in the second decade of the twenty-first century. It contains descriptions of over two hundred distinct Christian denominations that are "alive and well" in that decade as well as descriptions of the several major Christian traditions to which they belong—based on shared historical and theological roots and commitments.

The word *denomination* has fallen on hard times. According to many pundits we are living in a "post-denominational" age. Many churches have dropped their denominational affiliation from their names if not from their official (legal) papers. "Non-denominational" has become an increasingly popular self-description—even when someone with a keen eye can easily spot a denominational affiliation.

This writer, editor of this edition of the *Handbook of Denominations in the United States*, occasionally drives past a church called "Calvary Church." Nowhere on its exterior, including its sign, is any denominational affiliation displayed, not even any abbreviation. A deep scan of its website, however, reveals it to be an affiliated congregation of a major Reformed denomination. This is becoming the norm in many places in the United States.

Popular alternatives to "denomination" are "network" and "fellowship." One denominational executive referred to her "fellowship of churches" as a "denominet-work." One reader of this *Handbook* suggested that we retitle it—given the negative impression created in many people's minds when they hear the word denomination.

Ironically, in this allegedly post-denominational age, denominations, by whatever name, are proliferating and many are flourishing. Many especially educated, upwardly mobile young adults raised in allegedly "independent churches" are moving toward highly hierarchical churches with deep and even ancient roots. On the other hand, many of those are newer, eclectic denominations or networks that draw on several traditions.

One has to wonder about the roots of the negative popular image of "denomination." One theory is that it began with the publication of the classic American work on denominationalism entitled *The Social Sources of Denominationalism* by Yale University theologian and sociologist of religion H. Richard Niebuhr (1929). Niebuhr harshly criticized the so-called mainline Protestant denominations in America for identifying with middle-class American values and ignoring the poor and marginalized of society who went about creating their own "sects" mostly in obscurity.

The increasing negative valuation of "denominationalism," however, has led to something of a backlash among scholars of religion. Several scholarly defenses of denominations have been published in recent years including *American Denominational History: Perspectives on the Past, Prospects for the Future* (The University of Alabama Press, 2008), *Denomination: Assessing an Ecclesiological Category* (T and T Clark, 2011), and *Denominationalism Illustrated and Explained* (Cascade, 2013). In 2013 an evangelical publisher brought out a volume of essays by proud leading members of denominations entitled *Why We Belong: Evangelical Unity and Denominational Diversity* (Crossway).

Some wonder whether it is too late to rescue the concept "denomination" in its religious use. Apparently, to many people, "denomination" automatically implies an exclusivistic, superior-minded, divisive, and hierarchical religious group. That is certainly not its true meaning, however, and our intention here is to clear up that confusion and recover the word's true meaning.

Etymologically, *denomination* merely means *something named*. Over time, however, it has come to apply to two major phenomena that need to be distinguished within themselves: *types of money—especially paper money* and *religious bodies or groups*. For example, as most people know who've been to a bank teller to withdraw cash recently, an oft-heard question is "What denomination?" The bank teller is not asking about the customer's religious affiliation; the bank teller is asking about the types of paper money bills wanted—ones, fives, tens, twenties, and so on. For some reason nobody objects to that use of "denomination." Problems, wholly unnecessary ones rooted in misunderstanding, arise only when "denomination" is used in religious contexts.

Apparently, from what this writer can determine based on interviews, many people have come to think of a religious denomination as exclusivist and divisive. In other words, to their way of thinking, mistaken as it is, a denomination is a group of churches that believe they are spiritually superior to others. Of course, that may be true of some denominations just as it may be true of some independent churches. However, there is nothing inherent in the concept "denomination" that denotes a super-spiritual or superior attitude.

Then why do denominations exist? Very often the reasons have little or nothing to do with feelings of superiority and everything to do with ethnicity, geography, styles of worship, or someone's attempt to reform a particular Christian tradition. And very often a denomination came into existence simply because its founders wished to emphasize a seemingly forgotten dimension of the larger, older Christian tradition and were expelled for that. John Wesley, for example, did not intend to start a new denomination, but his Methodists, a renewal movement to emphasize "sanctification" within the Church of England, were expelled from it.

Let us state here and now the meaning of *denomination* for this *Handbook*'s purposes. For this *Handbook* a denomination is any group of churches, congregations, assemblies, or religious meetings with some affiliation among themselves however formal or informal it may be. A denomination does not have to have a headquarters to be included here; the affiliation, or connection among the congregations may be merely fraternal or even historical-theological. A denomination need not have bishops, although it may have one or more. A denomination need not have hierarchy, although it may have one. In other words, even "network" may be too "tight" a concept in some cases of denominations.

An example will illustrate and hopefully enlighten. The Churches of Christ is a denomination by our standards. Most sociologists of religion agree—even though the Churches of Christ (non-instrumental) has no headquarters or hierarchy or even formal connection. There is no "connective tissue" holding it together except fraternal association among the churches. As an unorganized group of a thousand or more congregations in the United States they look to certain publications and educational institutions as their alternative to traditional connective tissue. There is no authority over them all. And yet, without doubt, the Churches of Christ form a distinct denomination in the United States. For the most part, with a few exceptions, any Church of Christ member (or knowledgeable non-member) can predict with some degree of assurance what worship will be like on any Sunday morning in any Church of Christ.

A common habit has developed of new "networks" of congregations starting up and denying they constitute a denomination, and yet, sociologists of religion need a word for such networks. That word has long been and will continue to be *denomination*. Some observers have coined a new word for non-exclusive networks of congregations: *denominetwork*. This word will be used occasionally and cautiously here, especially when a network of congregations is evolving toward becoming a denomination but is still, at the time of this writing, non-exclusive.

In the past sociologists of religion tended to distinguish between "denomination" and "sect." Some even used the now-outmoded term *cult* for certain sects with a high degree of deviation from the standard orthodoxy of their own branches of a religion. Few sociologists of religion use the word *cult* anymore because of its pejorative connotations. Of course, the same could eventually happen with "denomination," but it is unlikely.

The distinction between "denomination" and "sect" derived from European societies with state churches—denominations given special recognition and privileges by the ruling authorities. The classical case of a state church is the Church of England, but at one time almost every European country had one or more state churches. "Church" was used to identify the denomination affiliated with the state; "sect" was used to identify religious groups with no affiliation with the state.

When that distinction was transferred to the New World with its separation of church and state, especially when certain "mainline denominations" began to lose their strong culture-shaping influence, it became increasingly problematic. Some sociologists of religion such as Niebuhr tried to hold onto the distinction in America by identifying certain especially older Protestant groups as "denominations" and smaller, less influential groups as "sects." The difference had to do with influence on the centers of political and cultural power. The language of "mainline Protestantism" came into use for the eight to ten "historic Protestant bodies" whose members tended to populate the halls of power in places like New York City and Washington, DC.

Overlooked, of course, was the fact that the largest church body in the United States in most of the twentieth century was the Roman Catholic Church, which was seldom, if ever, identified as "mainline" even when its influence on the political and cultural life of America increased. Also, the Southern Baptist Convention, the largest Protestant body in the United States throughout much of the twentieth century, was never identified as "mainline" even when a Southern Baptist was elected President (Jimmy Carter in 1976).

Sociologists of religion increasingly dropped the word *sect* as the distinction between "mainline" and "non-mainline" churches became obsolete; it no longer fit the religious situation in America's separationist and increasingly secular social milieu. Unfortunately, journalists have largely continued to use the word *mainline* to describe certain historic Protestant denominations even as they dwindle in numbers and influence.

A case could be made, and many are making it, that the very concept "denomination" is outmoded or has become so tarnished by negative connotations as to belong to the dustbin of history together with "sect." We disagree largely because there is no one term or concept to replace "denomination" as a way of naming church bodies, networks, fellowships, and so on. So for our purposes here, *denomination* will remain a useful term and category to include a wide variety of types of inter-congregational fellowships with or without headquarters, hierarchies, or formal connective tissue.

All that being said, however, the rise of truly independent, non-denominational churches must be acknowledged. Many observers take note of and mention the downsizing of American denominations. It would be wrong, however, to conclude from statistics of dwindling memberships that American religion is losing its vitality. Numerous truly independent, "unaffiliated" congregations have come into existence in the latter years of the twentieth century and first years of the twenty-first century in the United States. Especially in large urban centers in the South, for example, one sees numerous independent mega-churches with names like "Faith Family Fellowship." Sometimes these churches do have some affiliation with a denomination but hide it.

Often, however, they are totally self-sustaining and stand-alone in terms of lacking any affiliation with other congregations. This is a notable trend in American religion and difficult to measure.

Smaller and medium sized independent churches are popping up all over the landscape of America even in small towns and villages. It is common to see on the main street of a town in Minnesota, for example, a historic church building with "First Congregational Church" carved in the cornerstone but a new name such as "Faith Family Fellowship" on the new sign outside the front doors. Chances are it is Pentecostal and may be African American or Hispanic. This phenomenon makes the study of American religion extremely complicated. Simply counting up all the members of denominations, including "networks" and "fellowships," gives no clear picture of the total attendance in churches on Sunday mornings. There is simply no way to keep track of or count all the independent congregations started by an individual or family and not affiliated with any body of congregations beyond itself.

On the other hand, many of these independent, even entrepreneurial congregations, tend over time to discover similar ones and form some kind of connection among themselves. Thus new denominations arise—often unnoticed by those who study and pay attention mostly only to traditional denominations.

How many denominations exist in the United States? Nobody knows. Some sociologists of religion claim they number about twelve hundred, but much depends on the criteria used. Are five congregations in a county that share a summer camp and mutually support a missionary family a "denomination?" Who is to say?

For our purposes this *Handbook* uses several "rules of thumb" for deciding which of the numerous denominations in the United States to include here.

First, size matters. For the most part, with some exceptions, inclusion here requires approximately a minimum of one hundred congregations or five thousand to ten thousand members. The few exceptions are for historic churches with some unique characteristics or special influence.

Second, recognizability matters. There exist groups of congregations whose distinct identities and affiliation are so loose and tenuous that calling them a denomination does seem difficult. For example, some Baptist groups are little more than mission agencies.

Third, and finally, history matters. Some groups or networks of churches "pop up" for a time and then dissolve quickly. For the most part, denominations included here show evidence of "staying power." They may be of recent vintage but have nevertheless clear purpose and support and direction. Others of recent vintage seem ephemeral. If not, then they will no doubt find their way into later editions.

A few "complicating factors" need to be mentioned here. One fairly recent phenomenon in American religious life is churches populated exclusively by recent immigrants and pastored by missionaries from other countries and whose headquarters are located in their countries of origin. For example, observers report that Houston,

Texas, one of the most multi-cultural of urban areas in North America, contains numerous congregations founded and pastored by Brazilian evangelists and missionaries. The same is the case in the Northwest urban areas with Russian and Ukrainian congregations. For the most part these immigrant churches have not established US headquarters or centers; they tend to look back to their countries of origin for guidance and leadership. This makes it extremely difficult for scholars and students of American religious groups to study them. This is not a situation unique to immigrant churches, however. Some groups of churches that have existed in the United States for centuries such as the so-called Plymouth Brethren also lack any central, unifying "place" from which information about them can be gathered.

The reason the above "complicating factor" is mentioned, even though it is not totally new or unique to recent immigrant groups, is its seemingly sudden explosive rise in large urban centers of the United States: Houston, Los Angeles, Miami, Atlanta, Chicago, New York—all contain sometimes seemingly exotic churches that have little to no interest in integrating into or with the North American religious scene. They are not at all hidden from view but they are difficult to study—as groups of churches. An example is the many so-called Spiritual Baptists in the large urban centers of the Northeastern United States. Most are relatively recent immigrants from Caribbean islands. Their version of "Baptist" is so unlike any other in the continental United States that they are often overlooked or even shunned by other Baptists. Some of them integrate aspects of West African-Caribbean spiritualism into their worship. They may be studied by individual scholars, but looking "inside" is challenging for information-gathering purposes.

Another complicating factor that will take time and effort to study and integrate into handbooks such as this is the explosive rise of special interest churches. During the last decades of the twentieth century and first decades of the twenty-first century the United States has witnessed the rise of numerous congregations founded for the distinct purpose of bringing together people with interest or hobbies. These common interests may override doctrinal commitments. All over the United States "cowboy" or "Western culture" churches have popped up in recent years. Some are affiliated with a denomination; most are not. Some have found each other and formed informal networks, but for the most part they are independent and "free standing" Christian congregations with very little in common except a certain style of worship some might call "country-western." In almost any city of over one hundred thousand one can find so-called Hip-hop churches and Motorcycle churches. The only "connective tissue" among them may be on Facebook.

Again, people who decry or celebrate the alleged decline of church attendance in the United States, especially among the young, may be understandably overlooking these very non-traditional and totally unaffiliated special interest churches. Information-gathering about them is especially challenging.

Readers familiar with previous editions of the *Handbook* will notice a few changes here. Originally, and for many editions, the *Handbook* included mostly Christian denominations. One notable exception was the "Church of Buddhism" or "Buddhist Churches of America." Eventually that was dropped and only groups with some legitimate claim to be Christian, however unorthodox in other Christians' eyes, were included. Then an editor decided to include non-Christian groups that belong to "Abrahamic traditions." These included Jewish and Islamic groups in the United States and the Baha'i Faith.

This fourteenth edition returns to the tradition of including only denominations with some legitimate claim to be Christian without using any criteria of orthodoxy. In other words, if a group of congregations claims to be Christian and not only "compatible with Christianity," and if it meets the criteria stated above (size, stability, and so on), we include it here. The reasons for this exclusive focus on Christian denominations are several but will not be enumerated in detail here. Suffice it to say that there are enough Christian denominations to fill the book and broadening to include non-Christian "Abrahamic faiths" requires expertise and judgment calls with which this editor is not comfortable. Hopefully someone will write or edit a companion volume about non-Christian religions in America.

Some readers of this *Handbook* may be unhappy with our approach to categorizing and describing denominations. Here we will avoid treating certain denominations within categories as "canonical" or "orthodox" or "official" or "mainstream." These designations, however extremely important to the guardians of officialdom, are out of place in an even-handed treatment of diverse religious groups. When assigned by outsiders to a tradition they necessarily imply a lack of the neutrality a handbook such as this requires. Here we will simply provide subtle signals within descriptions indicating which groups are considered heterodox or unofficial by others without in any way "buying into" those judgments.

The editor acknowledges that *self-description is preferred description* by religious groups and therefore will use denominations' own sources as much as possible and make every attempt to describe them as they would describe themselves. Since no group considers itself a "cult" *and* the word has taken on a decidedly pejorative meaning that word will be strictly avoided. Similarly "sect" will be avoided as it has dropped out of use except as a negative value judgment.

The *Handbook* did not always use categories to organize and describe denominations, but that has long been its practice. That will continue in this edition although there will be some adjustments from previous ones. For example, a new category called simply "Miscellaneous" comes into existence here for those Christian denominations that simply do not fit any of the traditional ones. The traditional categories have to do with historical roots and theological similarities in terms of distinctives. Some denominations that would prefer not to be associated with others will, with apologies, be "lumped together" due to those shared notable features.

Finally, a few words are in order here about statistics. Many denominations claim that they do not keep records of membership. Others deny they are denominations in any sense of the word and therefore, even if they have some idea of membership, they do not reveal their numbers (of congregations or members). Yet others simply decline to respond to requests for information about statistics. This editor and his assistants have used many sources, including attempts at direct contacts with denominations, to determine the sizes of denominations. In some cases there are no headquarters or even central offices to contact. In other cases there are but they declined to respond to e-mails or phone calls. Almost all have websites; most do not give statistics.

So, the numbers of congregations and members (or adherents) in the United States provided for some denominations are educated guesses. In some cases they are taken from the *2012 Yearbook of Churches in the United States and Canada* (Abingdon) or the *2010 U.S. Religion Census* compiled by the Association of Statisticians of American Religious Bodies (ASARB). In a few cases they are taken from other sources.

RELIGION IN AMERICA

Craig D. Atwood and Roger E. Olson

Religion is one of the most powerful human forces. Religion lifts the heart, challenges the mind, and inspires great achievements. A disproportionate number of Nobel Peace Prize winners have been people whose religious convictions led them to confront injustice and seek to reconcile warring enemies. Religion plays a role in much that is noble and good in the world. It is impossible to understand American (or world) history and culture without knowledge of the religious fabric of our society.

In nearly every church, synagogue, and mosque in the United States similar things happen. Births are celebrated; children are taught to be virtuous and compassionate; adults learn to enjoy what is beautiful, good, and true; parents grow in wisdom and patience; the hungry are fed; the naked are clothed; and the lonely are redeemed from their isolation. Rabbis, imams, pastors, priests, and lay leaders bless marriages, bury the dead, comfort those who mourn, and challenge their flocks with a vision of a more peaceful and just society.

But there is a darker side to American religion. Some of the oldest houses of worship in the United States were built by Native Americans who had been subjugated by Europeans building global empires. No one knows how many tens of thousands of natives died during the conquest of the Americas, but we do know that in the 1690s some of the tribes in New Mexico revolted against their oppressors. They reclaimed their pueblos from the Spanish priests, and the only church they did not burn was that built by the Acoma people. It was spared, in part, because of respect for the dead who rested in the cemetery. Three centuries later, the violence of the Christian conquest and native revolt is a painful memory, and most of the Acoma people today are Catholics who live peacefully with relatives who prefer to worship in the traditional kivas. This is the history of American religion in a nutshell. Conflict and bitterness often yield to tolerance and mutual respect.

In an effort to avoid the religious violence that had plagued Europe for centuries, the authors of the United States Constitution guaranteed freedom of religion in the First Amendment. The great American experiment in religious freedom has always been a challenge, and the terrorist attacks on September 11, 2001, were a harsh reminder that

Americans have not escaped religious violence in the modern age. The terrorist attacks and events that followed challenged many Americans' tolerance of other religions. Religious beliefs, no matter how noble, can be twisted into tools of hatred and murder. No religion is exempt from the type of fanaticism that inspired 9/11.

A disturbing trend in the twenty-first century has been the increasing number of murders in the sacred spaces of America. Some of the murders in churches and synagogues were related to domestic disputes, but others were the direct result of religious fanaticism. People of every faith face the choice once presented by the prophet Moses: "I have set before you life and death, blessings and curses. Choose life so that you and your descendants may live" (Deut 30:19 NRSV). The path of life includes the pursuit of knowledge and understanding of others.

Reports of religious violence are so shocking and tragic that it is easy to overlook the fact that millions of Americans drew upon their faith after the 9/11 attacks and found the courage to reach beyond the boundaries of their own religious communities and embrace their neighbors in love. Across the country there were reports of Jews, Christians, Muslims, and others joining hands to protect mosques and synagogues. People of all faith traditions performed unheralded and heroic acts of mercy and charity. Millions of ordinary Americans discovered that people with different religious beliefs also love their families, work hard, care for their neighbors, love their country, and can be good friends.

One of the most interesting statistics from a 2005 study of American congregations was the dramatic increase in interfaith worship and service projects since 2001.[1] More than 20 percent of American congregations participated in interfaith worship, and nearly 40 percent joined in interfaith service projects in 2005, a dramatic increase from the year 2000. Countless numbers of ordinary people formed their own version of "The Faith Club," in which Muslims, Jews, and Christians get to know each other as people and as people of faith.[2] This *Handbook* is one of many tools to help people discover more about their friends, neighbors, and themselves.

Some people have responded to recent religious violence by rejecting religion itself. There has been an increase in unbelief and atheism in America in the twenty-first century. Almost every major religious body has reported a loss of members since 2000, and surveys indicate declining zeal among those who do attend worship. The trend away from organized religion is most pronounced among those under the age of forty, and there is a significant "graying" of American religion, especially among the clergy. About 16 percent of Americans in 2009 reported that they have no religious affiliation, but nearly a quarter of those under thirty have no affiliation.[3] These are the highest numbers in many decades.

[1] David Roozen, *American Congregations 2005* (Hartford, CT: Hartford Institute for Religion Research, 2007), 20.

[2] Ranya Idliby, Suzanne Oliver, and Priscilla Warner, *The Faith Club: A Muslim, a Christian, and a Jew—Three Women Search for Understanding* (New York: Free Press, 2006).

[3] *United States Religion Landscape Survey*, Pew Forum on Religion & Public Life (http://religions.pewforum.org/reports).

Americans remain more religious than people in Europe, but denominational loyalty continues to erode. Nearly half of Americans reported that they have changed their religious faith, either switching denominations or adopting a new religion.[4] This indicates both a significant level of religious interest and dissatisfaction with religious institutions. The religious groups that grew most in the past decade tended to be those that appealed to spiritual seekers.

Despite this apparent turning away from religion, the United States remains the most religious industrialized nation in the world, both in terms of personal profession of belief and the role that religion plays in public life. The 2008 Presidential campaign featured much discussion of the faith of the candidates. For a brief time, a preacher named Jeremiah Wright was the focus of media scrutiny, and many white Americans discovered "Black Theology" for the first time through cable news networks. The Catholicism of Joseph Biden and the evangelicalism of Sarah Palin helped frame the vice-presidential debate.

America is not only the most religious industrialized nation; it has become the most religiously diverse nation in history. Not only has the First Amendment made room for a bewildering variety of Protestant groups, it has provided shelter for many world religions to take root. America has also been the birthplace of more religions than any country other than India.

What is it that makes American religion so diverse, adaptable, and confusing? Why was it in the United States that the idea of "denominations" emerged so that we can speak of different religious groups without using the often-pejorative word *sects*? How does religion relate to social change and politics in America? In order to answer those questions, we need to take a step back in history and review some factors that are central to American religious experience.

First of all is the First Amendment. Until modern times—indeed, until the rise of the United States—it was assumed that civic harmony depended on religious conformity. There should be "one king, one faith, one law," in the famous phrase of Louis XIV, the king of France. Religion was seen as the warp of the social fabric, the glue that held different estates together and balanced conflicting interests. Religious diversity was equated with civic unrest and upheaval. The idea that a nation could tolerate not only different Christian churches but also radically different religions was considered lunacy until after the American Revolution. Modern Americans who have always lived under the Bill of Rights and its guarantee of freedom of worship have difficulty realizing what a truly radical experiment the First Amendment was when proposed by Madison and Jefferson.

Once the Bill of Rights was ratified, the federal government was forbidden to intervene in matters of personal faith. There have been notable cases in which local and national authorities have impinged this civil right, but for the most part the spirit of freedom of religion has prevailed in the United States for over two centuries. This means that no force other than popular opinion could prevent the formation of new religious

---

[4] Ibid.

organizations, new churches, and even new religions. Anyone who could gain followers could be the founder of a new denomination. Sometimes these new religions have been ridiculed by the public and have been termed cults, but some of them have developed into very popular and dynamic faith traditions.

Rather than leading to the demise of religion as many detractors (and a few supporters) of the First Amendment expected, this freedom of religious expression led to a marked increase in religious belief and practice in the United States. In contrast to other industrialized nations, the United States continues to have high levels of personal belief, membership in religious organizations, and participation in religious activities. It may appear ironic that the world's first completely secular government has fostered one of the most religious societies, but the reason is rather simple. In the free-enterprise system of American religion, religious bodies have always had to compete for the hearts and minds of the masses. Denominations in the United States have to present their message in a way that appeals to current and potential members. Even those churches that stress hierarchical and traditional values have had to adopt the methods of conversion-oriented churches in order to retain members.

Free competition has made American religion unusually responsive to changes in society as religious organizations adapt popular culture, especially music, for the purpose of attracting members. Each generation has seen the creation of new religious bodies and the transformation of older bodies as religious leaders have tried to address the anxieties of their age and offer hope for the perceivable future. This process of adaptation and change has often led to splits within denominations with one party embracing new techniques, such as revival meetings, and the other party promoting traditional approaches, such as the use of ancient liturgical forms.

New denominations may be innovative or traditionalist, but even the traditionalists have to "sell" members and potential members on the virtues of tradition. The pages that follow trace the way new churches develop out of older churches. The free-enterprise approach to religion has also encouraged experimentation with worship forms, doctrines, and even scriptures. Many of American denominations emerged during the heady days of the Second Great Awakening (1800–30), in the days of the early Republic when it seemed that the common person could achieve any dream. If backwoodsmen could serve in the Congress and farmers create a new government, why shouldn't an angel appear to an ordinary man and reveal a new scripture? Why couldn't a former housewife be the new incarnation of Christ?

Most of these new religious movements, like the Shakers and the Mormons, were radical variations on ancient Christian themes. Even among those that stayed closer to traditional Protestantism, there was a widespread sentiment that religious authorities could be ignored and that common people could recreate the church based on their own understanding of the Bible. Out of this conviction arose the denominations associated with Alexander Campbell and Barton Stone. Later Pentecostals, Adventists, and even the

Jehovah's Witnesses would also draw upon this idea of remaking the church according to one's own understanding of scripture. The old Reformation slogan of "scripture alone" produced a cornucopia of denominations in the United States as ordinary individuals took up the challenge of interpreting the Bible and judging religious authorities.

A **second** major factor in the diversity of American religion is immigration. Many churches began as ethnic churches as each wave of immigration brought different national churches. In fact, by the time the Constitution was written there were so many denominations that it would have been difficult, if not impossible, to have created a state church. Among the English colonists there were Congregationalists in New England, Quakers in Pennsylvania, and Anglicans in New York. There were Scots Presbyterians in Virginia and the Carolinas, and Roman Catholics were tolerated in Maryland. In addition, there were Dutch, Swiss, and German Reformed churches in the Middle Colonies living alongside Swedish and German Lutherans. French Huguenots, Dutch Mennonites, German Brethren, and Sephardic Jews added spice to the religious stew of colonial America. After the Revolution, the variety increased as Irish, Italian, and Romanian Catholics came through Ellis Island with Jews from Ukraine and Orthodox Christians from Greece and Russia.

Even within the same church, most noticeably the Roman Catholic and Lutheran churches, the United States has been home to an impressive array of ethnic communities that often posed a challenge to church hierarchies trying to maintain institutional unity. Italian and Irish Catholics shared a faith, but much of the day-to-day practice of religion was different in different ethnic parishes. Holy days, festivals, rituals, and especially language varied greatly within some churches. Hasidic Jews from Eastern Europe were not always welcomed in established synagogues in American cities, so they formed their own communities. Religion has provided each immigrant group with an identity in a foreign land. Religion has provided a way of being grounded in the old culture while adjusting to a new and confusing society. Ethnic culture in the United States is inseparable from ethnic religious tradition.

Over the decades, though, these ethnic denominations tend to adapt to the American setting as they struggle to win the allegiance of children and grandchildren who were born in the United States. The transition to English in worship is one benchmark of the Americanization process. Gradually immigrant churches grow to resemble their neighboring churches more than the national churches that gave them birth. Some denominations aggressively resist this process of assimilation, but in doing so they also adopt American techniques of marketing and organizational structure. Only in America do you see bumper stickers that say "Orthodoxy: Proclaiming the truth since AD 33."

In the second half of the twentieth century, immigration from Asia, Africa, and the Caribbean basin brought the religions of the world, including folk religions such as Santeria, to American shores. This dramatic increase in religious diversity will be one of the major factors of religious life in the United States during the twenty-first century. No longer will the symphony of American religion be composed of variations on the Abrahamic theme. Currently many denominations are struggling and even dividing over the issue of how to deal with other religions. The question of whether there can be truth and salvation in other religions is profoundly affecting the American religious scene.

Globalization is profoundly affecting American religion in another way in the twenty-first century. During the nineteenth and twentieth centuries, American churches contributed vast resources to the evangelization of the world, especially in Africa and Asia. For many decades that mission effort was hampered by being associated with colonialism, but after World War II indigenous churches grew rapidly in the non-industrialized world. Many of these growing churches were Pentecostal churches that required very little superstructure. Long before *globalization* became a buzzword in American business, American religion was establishing extensive global networks. Increasingly, American denominations report that they have more members outside of the United States than inside. Many Americans are in contact with Africans and Asians through their faith communities, often establishing close friendships across national and linguistic barriers. A famous example of this globalization of religion was when Malcolm X made his pilgrimage to Mecca and discovered that Islam is a world religion encompassing many races and tongues. When he returned from Saudi Arabia he led many African Americans out of the Nation of Islam and into Sunni Islam.

What is new in American religion is that immigrants are now bringing with them the faith that their parents and grandparents learned from American missionaries. Two of the largest congregations in the United States are Korean Presbyterian churches. Most American denominations are struggling with issues of language, culture, worship, and theology as immigrants from former "mission fields" seek inclusion in American denominations. The Abrahamic tradition in America has become a global tradition.

A **third** major factor in American religious diversity, including diversity among Christians, is theology. Here "theology" refers not only to doctrines but also to styles of church government (polity), spirituality, and worship. American Christianity is marked by a "blooming, buzzing confusion" of theologies—to borrow a description of nature from philosopher William James. Some distinctive theologies arrived with immigrants, but much of that variety developed in the United States itself. Without the legal controls imposed on churches in much of Europe (before the twentieth century), American Christianity became a fertile ground for new interpretations of the Bible, new types of worship, new doctrines, and new forms of polity—often hybrids of long existing ones. For example, although there were forerunners of Pentecostalism among the pietists of Europe, that particular style of Christianity "grew up," as it were, in the United States and then spread around the world. Its distinctive theology is that the supernatural "gifts of the Holy Spirit" mentioned in the New Testament (e.g., 1 Cor 12) were lost by ancient Christians, neglected by most Christians throughout history, but were being newly "poured out" on believers in these "last days" before the return of Christ. Especially speaking in tongues ("glossolalia") as the "initial, physical evidence" of being Spirit-filled became a uniquely

American contribution to world Christianity. Pentecostalism began in California in the first decade of the twentieth century but then spread as a revival movement and fragmented into numerous denominations each with its own "spin" on Pentecostal theology. During the 1960s and into the 1970s some aspects of Pentecostalism were taken up into so-called mainline denominations by people called "charismatics," many of whom eventually founded their own separate denominations. A movement scholars dubbed "Third Wave" was born in the United States in the 1970s—with emphasis on prophecy, speaking in tongues, divine healing, and a new kind of "contemporary revivalism."

Other Christian theologies that gave rise to distinct denominations were either imported or were born in the United States including "dispensationalism," new thought, fundamentalism, adventism, and restorationism. All have precursors in church history, but all took on the status of core beliefs and reasons for being in new denominations born in the United States. Especially during the mid-twentieth century many US denominations discovered their similarities and merged or formed cooperative organizations. "Ecumenism" did not happen only among the so-called mainline Protestant denominations; it also happened among more conservative, evangelical denominations. At the same time, however, fragmentation over theological differences occurred and gave rise to a plethora of distinctively American denominations. A mass movement of Christians to be "Christian only" without creeds and to unite all Christians in a restored New Testament fellowship of churches ("restorationism") was born out of the Second Great Awakening in the first half of the twentieth century. These people, inspired by the leadership of Barton Stone and Alexander Campbell, intended to be simple, Bible-only, non-creedal, non-denominational Christians with the goal of drawing all Christians back to a kind of generic New Testament fellowship of churches. A century later, however, the movement divided into three main branches over issues such as whether a New Testament church should use musical instruments in worship and whether it is proper for Christians to adjust theology to modern ways of thinking launched by the Enlightenment.

What is needed in order to understand American religion is a combination of sociological, historical, and theological acumen. Too often American religion, including denominational diversity, is looked at solely in terms of sociology or history. Theology tends to be left out of many treatments of the subject. One notable exception is the magisterial volume *Theology in America: Christian Thought from the Age of the Puritans to the Civil War* (Yale University Press, 2003) by scholar E. Brooks Holifield. Here, in this new edition of the *Handbook of Denominations in the United States*, an attempt will be made to inform readers about the theological distinctions of denominations even within the major categories (which are themselves largely theologically determined).

A **fourth** distinctive feature of American religion has been interchurch cooperation in the midst of competition. Again, one can use an economic analogy and point to the American penchant for large corporations and mergers. Interdenominational, parachurch, and cooperative ministries have brought together believers from different backgrounds throughout American history. In times of disaster it is not at all surprising to see Catholics, Protestants, Jews, and Muslims working hand-in-hand. The individuals helping are motivated by their religious values, which have been nurtured in a particular faith tradition. But in working together, they learn to respect other faiths. A special section on interdenominational agencies has been added to this edition of the *Handbook*.

Sometimes these cooperative efforts have led to the creation of new denominations, such as the United Church of Christ and the United Methodist Church. Such ecumenical efforts have generally increased religious toleration on the local level. This is the essence of denominationalism: diverse religious traditions and organizations openly compete for adherents while respecting other religious organizations as valid. It is rare, for instance, to hear a Presbyterian in the United States declare that Methodists are not really Christian. Furthermore, as the presence of world religions increases in the United States, one sees this sense of toleration being extended beyond Christian boundaries. Of course, as with every movement, the ecumenical trend has also led to the creation of new denominations that reject this perspective and insist on doctrinal or ecclesiastical conformity and exclusiveness.

Sociologists have noticed the strength of this ecumenism in American religion and have concluded that we are now in a "post-denominational" period when religious identity has lost its importance in individuals' lives. It is relatively easy for an Episcopalian to join a Lutheran church, for instance. Even the conversion from Catholic to Protestant or vice versa no longer carries the weight it did fifty years ago. There has been a tendency toward homogenization of religion as churches learn from each other and adopt successful practices. Most Americans have an eclectic faith stitched together from many different threads of tradition and contemporary ideas and attitudes. Even so, denominations remain vibrant because they provide a form of religious identity amid the pluralism of belief. They also provide needed resources for local communities of faith, such as facilities for training ministers, for publishing curriculum resources, and for overseeing certification procedures. However, churches freely share resources, and many theological schools are functionally ecumenical.

It is noteworthy that as denominations unite, splinter groups always form, thus acknowledging the usefulness of denominational structures even while they are rejecting the authority of the parent organization. It is interesting as well that many non-denominational churches gradually evolve their own denominational structures.

A **fifth** characteristic of American culture that affects religious institutions and belief is the close connection between politics, popular culture, public morality, and religion. The disestablishment clause of the Bill of Rights did not remove religion from the "public square." Throughout the past two and a quarter centuries people have been motivated by their faith to participate actively in the political process and in the social arena. This was most evident in the abolition movement, women's suffrage, and many campaigns for humane treatment of prisoners, human rights, voting rights, police reform, public education, and economic justice. Prohibition in the early twentieth century was one of the most successful "crusades" politically and least effective socially. Each of these campaigns was fought in the public square and in the pulpit. Each created new divisions in American religion and new alliances. Denominational identity became less important than political identity for many Christians, but by and large, the different denominations allowed for a diversity of political opinions among clergy and laity. It was rare for religious organizations to identify with a particular politician or political party. By the end of the twentieth century, there were signs that the old assumptions no longer held. Religious leaders established lobbying organizations, political action committees, and participated enthusiastically in campaigning for candidates who supported their positions on issues such as abortion, gay rights, and private schools.

Politics, they say, makes strange bedfellows, and that is particularly true when religious leaders enter the political fray. In the 1960s and 1970s radical Catholic priests shared jail cells with atheist political activists. In 2004, some Roman Catholic bishops urged Catholics to vote for a "born again" Southern evangelical Republican rather than a Roman Catholic Democratic senator because he had opposed efforts to outlaw abortion. It is likely that in the future denominational affinity and political opinion will grow closer together.

A **sixth** major factor in American religion is media. American religious leaders have always been adept at exploiting new communication technologies. George Whitefield used the popular press to advertise his evangelistic rallies in the 1740s, and Billy Graham used television to become the most famous preacher in the world in the 1960s. Some of the denominations in this *Handbook* evolved out of the radio and television ministries of popular preachers.

The new media today is the Internet. Religion is one of the major topics discussed in chat rooms and on websites, blogs, and Twitter. The Internet has even allowed for the creation of new denominations that gather primarily in "cyberspace." The factors discussed above all figure in the Internet's influence on American religion. Denominations use it to compete for followers; individuals use it as a resource in building their personal belief system; and immigrant churches use it as a resource to keep scattered members of the flock connected with the ethnic tradition. The Internet has also accelerated the globalization of American religion as people discuss issues of faith and morality across continents.

American religion is complex, and will grow increasingly so. This *Handbook* merely presents some of the more objective aspects of religion, such as membership statistics, to assist the reader in making sense of our world. It is no substitute for the lived experience of the different communities of faith where people find joy, strength, and hope day after day. If this book helps readers to get to know their neighbors, join a worshiping community, and better appreciate the intricate social fabric of America, then it has fulfilled its purpose.

SUGGESTIONS FOR FURTHER READING

Ahlstrom, Sydney E. *A Religious History of the American People.* 2 vols. New Haven, CT: Yale University Press, 1972.

Bowden, Henry W., ed. *Dictionary of American Religious Biography.* 2nd ed. Westport, CT: Greenwood Press, 1993.

Corbett, Julia Mitchell. *Religion in America.* 3rd ed. Upper Saddle River, NJ: Prentice Hall, 1997.

Eck, Diana. *A New Religious America: How a "Christian Country" Has Become the World's Most Religiously Diverse Nation.* San Francisco, CA: HarperSanFrancisco, 2001.

Gaustad, Edwin Scott, and Philip L. Barlow. *New Historical Atlas of Religion in America.* New York: Oxford University Press, 2001.

Hatch, Nathan O. *The Democratization of American Christianity.* New Haven, CT: Yale University Press, 1989.

Hill, Samuel S., ed. *The South and the North in American Religion.* Athens: University of Georgia Press, 1980.

Holifield, E. Brooks. *Theology in America: Christian Thought from the Age of the Puritans to the Civil War.* New Haven, CT: Yale University Press, 2003.

James, Janet W., ed. *Women in American Religion.* Philadelphia: University of Pennsylvania Press, 1980.

Lincoln, C. Eric, and Lawrence H. Mamiya. *The Black Church in the African-American Experience.* Durham, NC: Duke University Press, 1990.

Lippy, Charles H., and Peter W. Williams, eds. *Encyclopedia of American Religious Experience: Studies of Traditions and Movements.* 3 vols. New York: Scribner, 1988.

Marty, Martin E. *Modern American Religion.* 2 vols. Chicago, IL: University of Chicago Press, 1986.

Melton, J. Gordon. *Encyclopedia of American Religions.* 7th ed. 3 vols. Detroit, MI: Gale Research, 2003.

Moore, R. Laurence. *Selling God: American Religion in the Marketplace of Culture.* New York: Oxford University Press, 1994.

Noll, Mark A. *A History of Christianity in the United States and Canada.* Grand Rapids, MI: Eerdmans, 1992.

Noll, Mark A. *America's God: From Jonathan Edwards to Abraham Lincoln.* New York: Oxford University Press, 2002.

Porterfield, Amanda. *The Transformation of American Religion: The Story of a Late Twentieth-Century Awakening.* New York: Oxford University Press, 2001.

Raboteau, Albert J. *Slave Religion: The "Invisible Institution" in the Antebellum South.* New York: Oxford University Press, 1978.

Roof, Wade Clark. *Spiritual Marketplace: Baby Boomers and the Remaking of American Religion.* Princeton, NJ: Princeton University Press, 1999.

Ruether, Rosemary Radford, and Rosemary Skinner Keller, eds. *Women and Religion in America.* 3 vols. San Francisco, CA: Harper & Row, 1981.

Wuthnow, Robert. *The Restructuring of American Religion: Society and Faith Since World War II.* Princeton, NJ: Princeton University Press, 1988.

A WORD ABOUT CATEGORIES

Many denominations do not want to be "lumped together" with others in categories. However, this *Handbook* has long distinguished among the many included denominations that way. That is because it is helpful to readers to know which denominations have much in common with others in spite of some differences. No doubt, for example, many leaders within the Roman Catholic Church, the largest body of Christians in the world and in the United States, would prefer their church not be treated as a denomination at all and certainly not categorized together with other claimants to be "Catholic." The same is true of many denominations; they would prefer to be in a category all by themselves. We can only apologize for any offense given but argue that almost every church body and tradition in the United States shares some common roots and theological similarities with others. Including several denominations in one category by no means implies they are all the same.

So how have the editors of this *Handbook* made the often difficult decision about categories and which denominations belong in which of them? Often a single denomination could easily be located in two or more categories. And a few do not seem to belong in any category so they will be placed in a new one (for the *Handbook*) called "Miscellaneous."

First, it's important to explain that the categories are not "bounded sets" but "centered sets." They have no definite, recognizable boundaries because they have no membership; their location in a category with other denominations has to do with a common "center" which is an *affinity*. That affinity is here treated as historical-theological. Two groups that look very different are recognized by scholars of history and theology together as having a certain affinity with each other: common historical roots or common distinctive beliefs and practices. Of course all Christians form an affinity group; all have a common center: Jesus Christ as Lord and Savior. However, over the centuries of Christian history, for better or worse, they have divided into smaller affinity groups and then into denominations. A group of denominations that appears to have very little in common may be categorized together by historians, sociologists of religion, and theologians due to certain affinities.

An example is the category "Baptists." Some denominations in that category do not even use the word *Baptist*, but they are "baptistic" and rooted in Baptist history. They also share certain features, or affinities, with each other not shared to the same extent by others. A few groups that call themselves Baptists actually belong in another category (e.g., "Pentecostal") because of their strong difference from the majority of Baptists and their affinity with denominations in their category.

Without doubt this categorizing process involves some elements of subjectivity; judgment calls are made even though a coin is never tossed. There are reasons for placing a denomination in a category even if it could also be placed in another one. Some readers will think to themselves, about a certain denomination, "That should have been placed in a different category." That could be true and denominations have been moved between categories in various editions of the *Handbook*.

Readers should think of the categories not as "super-denominations" but as affinity groups and realize that some denominations within a category claim to have very little in common with others in the same category. However, we hope that readers and even denominations' members will see the rationale for inclusion of denominations together in categories.

ORTHODOX AND ORIENTAL ORTHODOX CHURCHES

With more than two hundred million members around the world, the Orthodox Church represents one of the three major branches of Christianity (the others being Roman Catholic and Protestant). Though there are over four million Orthodox in the United States, their churches remain mysterious to most Americans.

Unlike the Roman Catholic Church, the Orthodox Church (also known as the Eastern Orthodox Church) does not have a single hierarchical institution. Instead there are dozens of national bodies, each of which worships in its native language with its own independent (autocephalous) hierarchy. Each Orthodox church thus reflects its own national heritage and ethnic customs in its liturgy. Unlike the Protestant churches, which also demonstrate a wide variety of institutions and forms, most of the Orthodox churches are in communion with one another and hold to the same basic theology based on the ancient creeds of Christianity. A few Orthodox bodies are in communion with the Roman Catholic Church and are known as Uniate churches.

A few of the main Eastern bodies, however, reject the statements of the Council of Chalcedon (451 CE), in particular the phrase relating to Jesus Christ being one person in two natures, divine and human. These are known as non-Chalcedonian or Oriental Orthodox churches. Included among these bodies are the Armenian Church, the Coptic Church, the Ethiopian Church, the Eritrean Church, the Syrian Church of Antioch, and the Syrian Indian Church of South India.

Orthodox church services are elaborate, ritualistic, and beautiful. Virtually every architectural feature of the sanctuary, every movement of the priest's body, and every word spoken by the worshippers has symbolic value. The liturgy is an ancient drama that celebrates Christ's incarnation, crucifixion, and resurrection. Lighting, clerical vestments and altar adornments, icons, music, and consecrated bread and wine bring the kingdom of God into the present.

The word *orthodox* means true glory as well as straight teaching. "Giving glory to God is the purpose of life" is the keynote of this tradition. Praising God, giving God thanks, and receiving God's presence in the sanctified gifts capture the heart of worship. Through worship, and in God-informed relationships and responsibilities, these Christians mean to move toward sanctification. The Christian goal is *theosis*, "perfection" or "deification," living in genuine unity with God in the here and now and for eternity.

Extremely important to the Eastern Orthodox and Oriental Orthodox churches is the idea of "apostolic succession." This is not unique to them, but they place a special value and emphasis on it as the basis of their claims to be the contemporary expressions of the ancient church of the apostles. All of these churches are led by bishops; leading bishops are called "patriarchs." Each bishop claims to be able to trace his ordination "pedigree" back to one of the first century apostles. Priests must be ordained by a bishop in order to perform the sacraments and lead congregations. Also extremely important to these churches is tradition—a continuity of teaching, belief, and practice going back to the ancient churches. Each of them claims not to be a mere "restoring" of the ancient Christian church but its contemporary embodiment in unbroken succession.

History. What follows immediately here (in this introduction to the category) refers especially to a particular "family" of Eastern churches known especially in the West as the Eastern Orthodox Church; it is defined (in its various expressions) by the fact that it considers the patriarch of Constantinople (contemporary Istanbul, Turkey) "first among equals" and embraces as authoritative the first seven "ecumenical" or universal church councils (First Council of Nicea through Second Council of Nicea). It is sometimes called "the Church of the Seven Councils." It does not embrace as authoritative later councils called by popes of the Roman Catholic Church and emperors of the Holy Roman Empire. It stands out from other Eastern and Oriental ancient churches in embracing the doctrine of Christ promulgated at the fourth ecumenical council, the Council of Chalcedon in 451. That doctrine is known as the "hypostatic union" and proclaims that Jesus Christ was one person—the eternal Son of God, second person of the Trinity—possessing two distinct (not separate) natures divine and human. The other Eastern and Oriental ancient churches tend to reject that doctrine and the council that promulgated it.

Western history books will often state that the Eastern Orthodox Church separated from the Roman Catholic Church of the West, but that is not an accurate presentation. The Eastern Orthodox tradition claims direct descent from Christ and the apostles. For centuries, Christianity was primarily Eastern in orientation, with most of the episcopal sees of the early church being in Greece, Turkey, Egypt, and Syria. Greek, not Latin, was the language of the New Testament, early Christian liturgy, and early theology. The ecumenical councils that continue to define the beliefs of most of the world's Christians were held in the East and were attended primarily by Eastern bishops and theologians.

Of the five ancient patriarchal sees, or major jurisdictions (Rome, Alexandria, Antioch, Constantinople, and Jerusalem), only Rome was in the West. For centuries these five patriarchs, guided by councils of bishops, governed the worldwide Christian church. It is still the practice in the Orthodox Church that no one patriarch is responsible to any other patriarch. The bishops of the two capitals of the Roman Empire after 330,

Constantinople and Rome, had the greatest authority, but in 1054, the bishops of Constantinople and Rome mutually excommunicated each other along with their followers, creating a formal breach in Christianity that has only recently begun to heal. Long before the official schism between East and West, the two churches had already developed certain basic differences. The East was primarily Greek in speech and attitude, while the West was Latin and Roman. The transference of the imperial capital from Rome to Constantinople in the East meant a shifting of the center of political, social, and intellectual influences. As the Roman Empire decayed in the West and the Germanic tribes began pouring into Italy and Gaul, the bishop of Rome became a symbol of unity and stability for Westerners. When the pope crowned Charlemagne as Holy Roman Emperor in 800, it marked a clear break with the Roman Empire in the East (commonly called the Byzantine Empire). Conflict deepened between the pope at Rome and the patriarch at Constantinople. One major point of controversy was the addition of the words "and the son" (*filioque*) to the Nicene Creed in referring to the procession of the Holy Spirit.

The church in the East was integrally related to the Byzantine Empire, and the great cathedral of Hagia Sophia ("Holy Wisdom") in Constantinople was the center of both the church and the empire until it fell to the Turks in 1453. A number of the schisms in the East were both political and theological in nature, the most important of which involved the understanding of the person of Christ. In Syria, some churches embraced the views of Nestorius (ca. 351–451), who held that there were two separate persons in the incarnate Christ, one divine and one human. In Egypt and Armenia other churches accepted the teaching of Cyril of Alexandria (d. 444), as expressed in the phrase "one Incarnate nature of the Word." Most of the Eastern churches, though, remained in communion with the patriarch of Constantinople.

As the Byzantine Empire expanded to the west and north, Orthodox missionaries, such as the celebrated brothers Cyril (826–69) and Methodius (ca. 815–85), converted the Slavic peoples of Bulgaria, Serbia, and Russia to Christianity. The Divine Liturgy and holy books were translated into Slavic tongues, and monasteries and schools were established throughout Eastern Europe. As these peoples gained political independence, national Orthodox churches were gradually established, the first being the Bulgarian Orthodox Church.

Eastern Orthodox churches were profoundly affected by the dramatic rise and spread of Islam in the seventh century. Three of the ancient patriarchal sees (Antioch, Alexandria, and Jerusalem) quickly came under Muslim control and were effectively separated from Constantinople. Christianity in Muslim countries continued to exist as a minority faith living under severe restrictions. As a result, those churches were unable to grow numerically or exert influence on the surrounding culture. Relations with the Catholic Church in the West were nearly destroyed by the sack of Constantinople in 1204 by Latin crusaders in the Fourth Crusade.

The harshest blow to Eastern Orthodoxy came when the Turks captured Constantinople in 1453 and put an end to the Byzantine Empire. Hagia Sophia was converted into a mosque, and the ecumenical patriarch was forced to give allegiance to the Muslim rulers. For centuries the Orthodox churches in the Balkans struggled for existence under Turkish rule. During this time, the Russian Orthodox Church rose in power and prestige. Some considered Moscow to be "the third Rome." As the Ottoman Empire declined in the nineteenth century, other Slavic churches asserted their independence from Greek and Russian rule while still remaining in communion with the ecumenical patriarch.

The Russian Revolution of 1917 and the spread of communism to Eastern Europe following the Second World War led the Eastern Orthodox churches in Poland, Finland, Estonia, and Latvia to assert their independence. The Orthodox Church managed to survive communist rule despite persecution. After World War II, Estonia and Latvia were reintegrated into the Russian Orthodox Church.

Nearly all European and Asiatic bodies of this ancient church have established dioceses in the United States; some are governed by one of the five patriarchates, while others have declared themselves independent and self-governing (autocephalous). In the United States today, Albanian, Bulgarian, Greek, Romanian, Russian, Serbian, Ukrainian, Carpatho-Russian, and Syrian churches are under the supervision of bishops of their respective nationalities and usually are related to their respective mother churches in tradition and spirit, if not in administration. The patriarch of Moscow and of Alexandria each has jurisdiction over a few parishes. In recent years a number of churches of Protestant origin moved into the Orthodox orbit.

Beliefs and Practices. The Nicene Creed in its original form is central to the Orthodox faith in all its branches. It is recited whenever the Divine Liturgy is celebrated and is the heart of Orthodox theology and mysticism. For the Eastern churches a creed is "an adoring confession of the church engaged in worship"; faith is expressed more fully in liturgy than in a doctrinal statement.

It is the long tradition of the church, not the pronouncements of individual theologians or canon law, that defines orthodoxy. This tradition includes the decisions of the seven ecumenical councils as well as the tradition of the Divine Liturgy itself. Many of the doctrines and practices of the Roman Catholic and Protestant churches are rejected as inappropriate innovations. For instance, the dogma of the pope as the sole "vicar of Christ on earth" is rejected, together with that of papal infallibility. Members of Orthodox churches honor the Virgin Mary as *theotokos* ("the bearer of God") but do not subscribe to the dogmas of the Immaculate Conception and the Assumption. They show reverence to the cross, the saints, and nine orders of angels but reject the teaching of the treasury of merits of the saints and the doctrine of indulgences. Purgatory is denied, but prayers are offered for the dead. It is believed that the dead can and do pray for those on earth. Both faith and works are considered necessary for salvation.

Icons (consecrated pictures) of revered persons and events are central to Orthodox devotion. Orthodox Christians hold that since God became incarnate in Christ, God's human nature may be depicted in a sacred image. Refusal to venerate an icon is seen as denying the concrete reality of the incarnation; however, the Orthodox reject three-dimensional statues as being too close to "graven images" forbidden in scripture.

The mysteries, which are called sacraments in the Western church, are central in Orthodox life. These are physical items or actions that communicate spiritual reality. The seven that are definitive in the Roman Catholic Church (baptism, confirmation, the Eucharist, penance, extreme unction, holy orders, and matrimony) are important in the Orthodox tradition as well, but there is little disposition to restrict the number of mysteries formally to seven. Other rites have a sacramental character. In fact, for the Orthodox, worship itself is a mystery or sacrament. For some Orthodox theologians and mystics, even creation is a sacrament since creation communicates the presence of God to all people.

The Holy Eucharist, or Communion, is the "mystery of mysteries." It is the chief service on all Sundays and holy days, and it is treated with great reverence. All Orthodox churches teach that the bread and wine are the body and blood of Christ, but this is not described as transubstantiation (the doctrine that the bread and wine become the body and blood of Christ). Mysteries cannot be defined by human intellect.

Polity. The government of all Orthodox churches is episcopal and hierarchical to a degree. There is usually a synod of bishops over which an elected archbishop, metropolitan, or patriarch presides. In America each jurisdiction is incorporated, with a church assembly of bishops, clergy, and laity. The three orders of ministry are deacons (who assist in parish work and in administering the sacraments), priests, and bishops. Deacons and priests may be either secular or monastic. Candidates for the diaconate and priesthood may marry before ordination but are forbidden to marry thereafter. Bishops are chosen from members of the monastic communities and, therefore, are under lifelong vows of poverty, chastity, and obedience.

The history of the Orthodox in North America is primarily the story of immigration and ethnic identity. The church has been a way for immigrants to keep a connection with their homeland, their language, and their customs. Membership statistics are confusing and often unreliable, since membership is based on baptismal records rather than communicant status, but there are at least three and a half million Orthodox in the United States, and the number is probably growing.

After a century or so of "creeping disunity" within Orthodoxy, during the period of heavy immigration and the formation of various Orthodox communities of faith, there have been movements toward closer cooperation. One such movement was the organization in 1960 of the Standing Conference of Canonical Orthodox Bishops in the Americas, which has been composed of nine jurisdictions that represent the majority of the Orthodox in North America. Another was the formation of two pan-Orthodox seminaries. (As of 2014 this conference is called the Assembly of Canonical Orthodox Bishops of the

United States of America and includes thirteen bishops of Orthodox bodies in the United States who are in fellowship with the patriarch of Constantinople.)

There are a number of Orthodox churches in the United States that are not recognized as "canonically" Orthodox by members of the Assembly mentioned above. These "irregular" Eastern churches might be called autogenic, or self-starting, but they are not in canonical relationship with the patriarch of Constantinople and with one another. These autogenic churches are to be distinguished from the ancient non-Chalcedonian Orthodox Churches, such as the Coptic Church.

Which Orthodox groups should be considered "canonical" is a judgment call not rightly made by editors of handbooks such as this. The same can be said about the word *orthodox* with a small *o*, which simply means—in common language—theologically correct. In some senses of the words, every denomination thinks of itself as "canonical" and "orthodox." Therefore, the Orthodox denominations described here may be designated as in relationship with the Patriarch of Constantinople, the "pope," as it were, of Eastern Orthodoxy, or not in relationship with him. No evaluation of the "rightness" of their status is implied by that.

Little has been said so far, in this introduction to this category, about the churches, denominations, that are often lumped together (for lack of a better strategy) as "Oriental Orthodox." Generally speaking, these are very ancient families of Christians who did not accept the Chalcedonian Definition (of the person of Jesus Christ as a "hypostatic union") in 451. Some of them, however, existed completely independently and separately from the "Christianized" Roman Empire under Constantine and his successors, so their lack of affirmation of the doctrine did not cause a schism within ancient Christendom; they simply continued to exist almost unnoticed by Greek-speaking and Latin-speaking Christians for centuries. An example is the Mar Thoma church of India. These Oriental Orthodox churches are not in fellowship with the Eastern Orthodox churches that have fellowship with the patriarch of Constantinople. However, during the latter decades of the twentieth century and first decades of the twenty-first century a great deal of dialogue has happened between some of them and the Eastern Orthodox churches that look to that patriarch as their leader. Strides have been made toward eventual intercommunion as theologians on both and all sides have come to recognize that differences over doctrine may be rooted in misunderstandings.

In 2016 the Assembly of Canonical Orthodox Bishops in the United States of America and the Standing Conference of Oriental Orthodox Churches in America held a joint prayer service—a major step toward mutual acceptance if not reunion.

In brief, then, the denominations that follow here, in this category, do not all recognize each other as truly, fully Orthodox in the theological sense. All, however, have ancient roots or at least like to think of themselves (as in a few cases) as part of the ancient, apostolic Christian church, connected with it by apostolic succession, but not as part of the Western Catholic tradition.

Many attempts have been made by the editors of this *Handbook* to gain updated information from each of these Orthodox denominations; some such attempts have been unsuccessful. E-mails, letters, and phone calls have, unfortunately, gone unanswered in some cases. And in some cases the denominations' websites have not been as helpful for this *Handbook*'s purposes as the editor wishes. In a few cases responses such as "We are not they" have been received with "they" meaning a group with an identical name. Sorting out all the groups is extremely challenging; we have done the best we can while trying to be as inclusive as possible and not narrow this category down to a certain "slice" of Orthodoxy that considers itself "canonical" to the exclusion of others. That would make the task much easier, but it would result in exclusion of many American denominations that lay claim to being "Orthodox" in the "big O" sense of the word.

SUGGESTIONS FOR FURTHER READING

Constantelos, Demetrios J. *Understanding the Greek Orthodox Church: Its Faith, History, and Life*. Brookline, MA: Hellenic College Press, 1998.

Erickson, John H. *Orthodox Christians in America*. New York: Oxford University Press, 1999.

Fitzgerald, Thomas E. *The Orthodox Church*. Westport, CT: Greenwood Press, 1999.

Meyendorff, John. *The Orthodox Church*. Crestwood, NY: St. Vladmir's Seminary Press, 1981.

Roberson, Ronald. *The Eastern Churches: A Brief Survey*. 7th ed. Rome, Italy: Edizioni "Orientalia Christiana," 2008.

Ware, Kallistos T. *The Orthodox Way*. Crestwood, NY: St. Vladimir's Seminary Press, 1995.

AFRICAN ORTHODOX CHURCH

Founded: 1921
Membership: est. 5,000 (1999) in about 15 parishes

This denomination is not in communion with Eastern Orthodox churches generally; that is, it is not in communion with the patriarch of Constantinople. It claims, however, to be in apostolic succession, and thus truly ancient and orthodox, through the West Syrian Church of Antioch. It was established in 1921 by George Alexander Mc-Guire (1866–1934), who was an immigrant to the United States from Antigua. McGuire had served as a priest in the Protestant Episcopal Church but left that body because of racial prejudice. This quest for equality led him to Marcus Garvey's (1887–1940) Universal Negro Improvement Association. Once McGuire founded the African Orthodox Church, Garvey used his periodical, entitled *The Negro World,* to disseminate news about the denomination throughout Africa. The periodical also carried the story of McGuire's consecration by a white bishop named Joseph Rene Vilatte (1854–1929). In 1924, the church was established in South Africa, where it became a potent force among the black population.

The church puts strong emphasis on the apostolic succession and historic sacraments and rituals; it celebrates the seven sacraments of baptism, confirmation, Eucharist, penance, extreme unction, holy orders, and matrimony. Its worship is a blend of Western and Eastern liturgy, creeds, and symbols, though the liturgy is usually Western with a mingling of Anglican, Greek, and Roman patterns. The common creeds, Athanasian, Nicene, and Apostles', are used. Bishops are in charge of dioceses, or jurisdictions; and groups of dioceses form a province, each led by an archbishop and a primate. The primate, in turn, presides over the provincial synod. At the head stands a primate archbishop metropolitan, general overseer of all the work of the church, which now extends over the United States into Canada, Latin America, and South Africa.

One of the most unusual African American churches in the United States is Saint John Coltrane African Orthodox Church in San Francisco, which is named in honor of a famous African American jazz musician and specializes in celebrating his music and the contribution of jazz music generally to African American culture.

For more information: www.netministries.org/see/churches.exe/ch26904 and www.pitts.emory.edu/Archives/text/rg005.html

Headquarters: 122 West 129 Street, New York City, NY 10023

ALBANIAN ORTHODOX ARCHDIOCESE IN AMERICA

Founded: 1919
Membership: est. 40,000

The Albanian Orthodox Archdiocese in America has been part of the Orthodox Church of America* since 1971, but its bishops and clergy continue to minister to the special needs of the Albanian community. The history of the church in Albania is complex, filled with a series of persecutions and changes in the religious and political struggles of the Balkans. Christianized by both Latin and Greek missionaries, Albania, as part of Illyricum, had both Latin- and Greek-rite Christians and was at various times under the authority of the patriarch of Constantinople and the pope. When the Turks conquered Albania in 1478–79, half of its people became Muslim. The Christian minority remained divided between Latin-rite Christians in the North and Greek-rite Christians in the South.

When Albania became an independent nation in the twentieth century, its people demanded a liturgy in their language rather than in Greek. They turned to the Russian Orthodox Church for assistance, and in 1908 the Russian Orthodox Church in America set up an Albanian diocese under an Albanian archimandrite-administrator, Father Theophan S. Noli (1880–1965), who translated the liturgy into Albanian.

With the outbreak of the Russian Revolution, the ties with the Russian Church were severed, and Noli was consecrated the bishop in 1923 at the Korche Cathedral in Albania as the Archbishop and Metropolitan of Durres. In doing so, he became the first bishop of a completely independent Albanian Archdiocese, a "mother church" that, strangely enough, spread its influence back into Albania. Noli returned home to establish a metropolitan throne with its see in Boston. Because of the official closing of all religious institutions in Albania in 1967, communication between the American church and the Albanian church was not possible until the collapse of communism.

Another body, the Albanian Orthodox Diocese of America, was established in 1950 under the authority of the ecumenical patriarchate of Constantinople. It has two parishes with about three thousand members.

For more information: www.orthodoxalbania.org

Archdiocese Office: 523 East Broadway, South Boston, MA 02127

AMERICAN CARPATHO-RUSSIAN ORTHODOX CHURCH

Founded: 1938
Membership: est.10,500 in 79 parishes (2010)

The Carpatho-Russian people derive their name from the Carpathian mountain region of eastern Europe, where they have resided for centuries. For many years the mother church endured strife between Orthodoxy and Roman Catholicism. Under political pressure in the seventeenth century, it became a Uniate church, with Eastern rites and customs, but recognized the supremacy of the Roman Catholic pope.

The struggle to separate from Rome and become completely Eastern was transferred to North America when large numbers of members immigrated to the United States, especially to the coal-mining and industrial areas of the Northeast. In 1891, Alexis Toth, a Carpatho-Russian Uniate priest, led his Minneapolis parish back to the Orthodox Church. Along with several other pastors and parishes they were absorbed into the Russian Orthodox Church in the United States.

In 1938, a new American Carpatho-Russian Orthodox Greek Catholic diocese was established and canonized by Benjamin I, the ecumenical patriarch of Constantinople. Orestes P. Chornock (1883–1977) became its first bishop. Both the diocesan headquarters (Christ the Saviour Cathedral) and Christ the Saviour Seminary are located in Johnstown, Pennsylvania. The diocese maintains a youth camp, a retreat, and a conference center in Mercer, Pennsylvania.

The American Carpatho-Russian Orthodox Church is part of the Assembly of Canonical Orthodox Bishops of the United States and is in communion with the patriarch of Constantinople.

For more information: www.acrod.org

Headquarters: 312 Garfield Street, Johnstown, PA 15906

ANTIOCHIAN ORTHODOX CHRISTIAN ARCHDIOCESE OF NORTH AMERICA

Founded: 1975, with roots to 1895
Membership: est. 75,000 in 249 parishes (2010)

Antioch, in Syria, was one of the first cities to be evangelized by the apostles and its church was one of the most important ancient patriarchal sees. The faithful managed to maintain the existence of the church through centuries of Muslim rule, even adopting Arabic as a liturgical language, but as the Ottoman Empire collapsed in the late nineteenth century, thousands of Antiochene Christians immigrated to North America. Their spiritual needs were first met through the Syro-Arabian Mission of the Russian Orthodox Church (now called the Orthodox Church in America). In 1895, a Syrian Orthodox Benevolent Society was organized by Antiochian immigrants in New York City, with Dr. Ibrahim Arbeely, a prominent Damascene physician, serving as its first president.

Arbeely convinced Raphael Hawaweeny, a young Damascene clergyman serving as Professor of the Arabic Language at the Orthodox Theological Academy in Kazan, Russia, to come to New York to organize and pastor the first Arabic-speaking parish on the continent. Hawaweeny was consecrated as a bishop in New York in 1904, making him the first Orthodox bishop of any nationality to be consecrated in North America. He crisscrossed the United States and Canada, gathering the scattered immigrants into parish communities. He founded *al-Kalimat* (*The Word*) magazine in 1905, and published many liturgical books in Arabic for use in his parishes, in the Middle East, and in immigrant communities around the world.

The mission suffered because of the early death of Hawaweeny in 1915, the disruptions of the First World War, and the Russian Revolution. The Syro-Arabian Mission fell into divisiveness until 1975, when jurisdictional and administrative unity was restored with the merger of the Antiochian Orthodox Christian Archdiocese of New York and the Antiochian Archdiocese of Toledo. The resulting Archdiocese is divided into four chancelleries located in New Jersey, Ohio, Kansas, and California. The General Assembly, the largest legislative body of the Archdiocese, consists of all the pastors and representatives of every parish and mission. It meets in convention every other summer.

There are nearly four hundred priests and deacons who minister at the local level. Candidates for ordination complete an undergraduate program and then receive their theological education at either St. Vladimir's Orthodox Theological Seminary in New York or St. John of Damascus Orthodox Theological Academy near Tripoli, Lebanon. Their program is augmented by specialized courses offered annually by the Antiochian House of Studies, held for two weeks at the Heritage and Learning Center in Ligonier, Pennsylvania. Twenty-four established departments and commissions deal with specific needs of the Archdiocese, such as communications, translations, clergy education, and parish development.

A pioneer in the use of the English language in the Orthodox churches since the 1930s, the church has translated and published liturgical and devotional works into English. The Antiochian Village, a two-hundred-eighty-acre property located in southwestern Pennsylvania, serves as a retreat center and popular summer camp that attracts children and young adults from throughout North America. The St. John of Damascus Sacred Art Academy is also headquartered at the Village.

The Antiochian Orthodox Christian Archdiocese is part of the Assembly of Canonical Orthodox Bishops of the United States and is in communion with the patriarch of Constantinople through the patriarch of Antioch.

For more information: www.antiochian.org

Headquarters: 358 Mountain Road, PO Box 5238, Englewood, NJ 07631

APOSTOLIC CATHOLIC ASSYRIAN CHURCH OF THE EAST, NORTH AMERICAN DIOCESE

Founded: ca. 35 CE
Membership: 35,118, in 19 parishes (2000)

This church claims that it was founded by the apostle Thomas shortly after the resurrection of Jesus, and it claims a close connection to the apostles Thaddaeus and Bartholomew as well. Saints Mari and Addai were key figures in the founding and spread of this church in the Persian Empire, and one of its great scholars was Theodore of Mopsuetia, who was head of the school of Antioch in the fourth century. The church sent the first Christian missionaries to India, and it has a long relationship to the Syrian Orthodox community in India. This was the first church to establish Christianity in China, during the Tang dynasty (seventh and eighth centuries), especially in the city of Xian, but the Mongol invasions of the thirteenth century decimated the church. The Nicene Creed is central to this church's liturgy and theology.

Erroneously called the Nestorian Church, the Assyrian Church of the East rejected the Council of Ephesus and the monophysite theology of Cyril of Alexandria. The church insists that Christ had two natures (human and divine). Whether this church regards Christ as one divine person or two persons sharing a union of wills is debated by outsiders. It rejects the phrase *Theotokos* or "Mother of God" for the Virgin Mary. Instead, they pray to the "Ever Virgin Blessed Mary Mother of Christ" or *Christotokos*. During the Nestorian controversy, the Persian emperor gave refuge to Nestorius and others condemned by the patriarch of Constantinople. The school of Edessa was moved to Nisibis in Persia.

In the nineteenth and twentieth centuries the church suffered a schism between patriarchs and was persecuted for supporting the British during the two world wars. The current Catholicos Patriarch, Mar Dinkha IV, resides in Baghdad, Iraq. The church has three dioceses in the United States: Eastern, Western, and California. With the US invasion of Iraq, thousands of Iraqi Christians have sought refuge from persecution in the United States, many of them members of this church.

The church's worship is similar to other Eastern churches, but the liturgy is based on the ancient Liturgy of Saints Mari and Addai. The cross is particularly important to the Assyrian Church, and making the sign of the cross is seen as a sacrament.

This church is not in fellowship with the patriarch of Constantinople or any other patriarch of the Orthodox churches. It is jurisdictionally independent.

For more information: www.news.assyrianchurch.org

Media Contact: 7201 North Ashland, Chicago, IL 60626

APOSTOLIC EPISCOPAL CHURCH

Founded: 1980s
Membership: est. 12,000 in 200 parishes (2006)

The Apostolic Episcopal Church is one of the many bodies that separated from the Episcopal Church* because of changes in the 1928 *The Book of Common Prayer* and the admission of women to the ordained ministry. Like many of the Continuing Churches, the Apostolic Episcopal Church (AEC) moved more toward Eastern Orthodoxy than toward Roman Catholicism because of the Orthodox Church's policy of autocephalous national bodies. In 2000 the AEC signed concordats with several Orthodox bodies in the United States and became a Western Rite Orthodox Church under terms first established by the Holy Synod of Saint Petersburg in 1905. This denomination also calls itself the Holy Eastern Catholic and Apostolic Orthodox Church. It is not part of the Assembly of Canonical Orthodox Bishops of the United States.

According to the current Presiding Bishop (2016) John Kersey, this denomination emphasizes ecumenical cooperation and seeks to serve all God's people who have need of its ministry, whether they are exclusively associated with it or are seekers from elsewhere. It does not discriminate between adherents to itself and any others who may benefit from its ministry on a temporary or short-term basis. The denomination's 255 affiliated clergy minister with other churches and recognize and cooperate with traditional clergy in other denominations.

For more information: www.apostolicepiscopalchurch.org

Headquarters: 8046 234 Street, Queens, NY 11427-2116 (The denomination's website lists the following address: 46 Extons Road, King's Lynn, Norfolk PE305NT, England, UK.)

ARMENIAN APOSTOLIC CHURCH OF AMERICA
ARMENIAN APOSTOLIC CHURCH, DIOCESE OF AMERICA

Founded: 301; came to the United States in 1887
Membership: est. 1,010,000 in 108 parishes (2007)

Armenia, a mountainous country sandwiched between Turkey, Georgia, Azerbaijan, and Iran, is generally recognized as the first nation to become Christian when Christianity became the state religion in 301. Tradition holds that the apostles Thaddeus and Bartholomew first brought the message of Christ to Armenia. Saint Gregory the Illuminator became the first head of the national church in 314 and was given the title Patriarch Catholicos of All Armenians. A translation of the scriptures by St. Sahag and St. Mesrob and their students in the early part of the fifth century is accepted as the authoritative Armenian version of the Bible. The translators created an Armenian alphabet in order to give the Armenians the scriptures in their own language.

The Armenian Church administers seven sacraments: baptism, confirmation or chrismation, Eucharist, penance, matrimony, ordination, and extreme unction or order of the sick. Baptism, ordinarily of infants, is administered by immersion. Chrismation (anointing with oil) and Communion follow immediately after baptism. The Eucharist is offered on Sundays and on special feast days of the church. At the conclusion of the Eucharist, fragments of thin unleavened bread, simply blessed, are distributed to those not receiving Communion.

The hierarchical organization of the Armenian Church consists of the Catholicos, the supreme head of the church, who resides in the ancient city of Etchmiadzin, Armenia, and the Catholicate of Cilicia, located in Antelias, Lebanon. The two patriarchates are Jerusalem and Constantinople. There are three major orders of clergy, according to the tradition of all ancient churches: deacon, priest (presbyter), and bishop. Parish priests are ordinarily chosen from among married men, but bishops are chosen from among the celibate clergy. Widowed priests may be promoted to the episcopate. Clergy are trained in seminaries attached to Etchmiadzin, Jerusalem, and Antelias.

One of the most important aspects of the Armenian Church administration is its conciliar system. The administrative, doctrinal, liturgical, and canonical norms are set and approved by a council through a participatory decision-making process. The Council of Bishops (or the Synod) is the highest religious authority in the church.

The Armenian Church has sustained its people throughout a history marked by tragedy. It suffered in the conflict between the Byzantine Empire and Persia and sustained persecutions by the Turks, culminating in the genocide of 1915. Thousands of Armenians escaped to North America before World War I, but the bulk of emigration occurred after the war. The first Armenian Church in the United States was established in Worcester, Massachusetts, in 1891. The Armenian Diocese of America was organized in 1898, headed by a primate appointed by the Mother See of Holy Etchmiadzin in Armenia, under whose jurisdiction the diocese functioned.

In 1933 a dispute over matters related to the church in Soviet Armenia led to a split in the church in the United States. One group of churches, the Armenian Apostolic Church of America, chose to remain independent until 1957, when these churches placed themselves under the jurisdiction of the Holy See of Cilicia in Antelias. The other group, the Armenian Church of America, remained within the jurisdiction of the Mother See of Etchmiadzin. Dogma and liturgy were not affected by the division. Deacons, priests, bishops, and archbishops are ordained and elevated by the hierarchical authorities of the respective jurisdictions. The Armenian Church of America has seventy-two churches; the separated Apostolic Church has thirty-eight.

The Armenian Church is in communion with the Oriental Orthodox Church but not with the patriarch of Constantinople. It is therefore not part of the Assembly of Canonical Orthodox Bishops in the United States. Also known as monophysites ("one nature of Christ"), these are churches that did not ascribe to the doctrinal statement (the hypostatic union of Christ) adopted at the Council of Chalcedon in 451 CE. It should be noted that the Armenian Church accepts the decisions of the first three ecumenical councils. It affirms the christological formula of St. Cyril of Alexandria (d. 444): "One is the nature of the divine Word incarnate. The union of Godhead and the manhood are without confusion, without change, and indivisibly." In 1990, the theologians and official representatives of both Eastern and Oriental Orthodox churches agreed in a formal statement that their theological understanding, especially their Christology, is "orthodox." The statement called for unity and communion among the Eastern and Oriental Orthodox churches, which is an ongoing process.

For more information: www.armenianchurch-ed.net

Headquarters: 630 Second Avenue, New York, NY 10016

BULGARIAN EASTERN ORTHODOX CHURCH

Founded: 1938
Membership: 2,212 in 2 parishes (2010)

Christianity was introduced to the Bulgar peoples in the ninth century during the reign of Tsar Boris. The church is similar to other Orthodox churches in theology and worship. For centuries, the church struggled for independence from Constantinople, an independence won for brief periods. There was a schism between the Bulgarians and the ecumenical patriarch until the end of World War II. After the war, Bishop Boris was assassinated by the communists and other church leaders were imprisoned. Eventually the church came to an accord with the government and was allowed to function. With the collapse of communism in the 1989, the church has been free to operate in Bulgaria.

Before the outbreak of the Macedonian Revolution in 1903, very few Bulgarians emigrated to the United States. In 1940, there were still only about sixty thousand residents. They brought with them memories of the church's long struggle for independence from Constantinople. The first Bulgarian Orthodox Church in the United States was built in Madison, Illinois, in 1907. In 1922 the Bulgarian Orthodox Mission of the Holy Synod of Bulgaria began attempts to organize the Bulgars. It established a bishopric in 1938.

Attached directly to the Holy Synod of Bulgaria, the membership of this church is made up of descendants of immigrants from Bulgaria, Macedonia, Thrace, Dobruja, and other parts of the Balkan Peninsula. Services are in the Bulgarian and English languages, and doctrine is in accord with that of other Eastern Orthodox churches. The American Church is part of a larger diocese, the patriarchate of Bulgaria, which includes Canada and Australia. It is part of the Assembly of Canonical Orthodox Bishops of the United States and in communion with the patriarch of Constantinople.

For more information: www.bulgariandiocese.org

Headquarters: Diocese of the USA, Canada and Australia, 550-A West 50th Street, New York, NY 10019

COPTIC ORTHODOX CHURCHES

Founded: 60 CE; first American diocese founded in 1993
Membership: est. 300,000 in 100 parishes (2002)

The Coptic Church is one of the oldest Christian churches in the world, tracing its origins to the time of the apostle Mark who, according to tradition, brought Christianity to Egypt. The word *Coptic* refers to both the native people and language of Egypt before the Arab conquest in the seventh century. Alexandria in Egypt was one of the original patriarchal sees, and it produced some of the most significant theologians and bishops of early Christianity. Centuries later the works of Origen, Clement, Athanasius, and Cyril are still studied by Orthodox, Catholic, and Protestant theologians. Egyptian or Alexandrian theology was instrumental in the formation of the Nicene Creed recited weekly throughout the Christian world.

The hierarchy of the Egyptian church in Alexandria was primarily Greek, but by the year 500 Christianity had spread to the native peoples up the Nile. Coptic missionaries brought Christianity to Nubia and the Sudan over a thousand years before the great period of Protestant missions to the tribes of Africa. The story of Mary and Joseph's flight into Egypt to escape Pharaoh captured the popular imagination, and an elaborate pilgrimage route developed so worshippers could honor Jesus and the Blessed Virgin. Pagan shrines were converted to Christian worship, and the Copts developed a distinctive liturgical calendar based on the ancient Egyptian calendar.

The greatest contribution of the Egyptian church to Christianity came out of the desert. Two hundred years after Christianity was brought to Egypt, there were a few devout souls who felt that the urban churches were too comfortable with the sensuous culture of the pagan world. One of these was a wealthy man named Anthony who heard Jesus's call to "sell all you possess and give it to the poor." He did so and retreated in the desert to the mountains where he lived alone in a cave. His is reputed to be the first such monk (from the Greek word for solitary), and his story inspired hundreds of men and women to do likewise. Monasticism and its spirituality gradually spread to the whole Christian world and was the mainstay of Christianity until the Protestant Reformation. The desert monasteries provided much of the stories of saints and miracles that nourish the Coptic faithful today.

The Coptic Church was caught up in the political struggles of the Byzantine Empire in the fifth century, and many of the bishops believed that the Council of Chalcedon was more about imperial politics than theology. The iconography, liturgy, veneration of relics, and theology of the Coptic Church is very similar to other Orthodox churches, but the Coptic Church emphasizes the unity of Jesus Christ as both God and human but not two natures—as declared by the Council of Chalcedon in 451. Traditionally Coptic Christians have been labeled "monophysites" by both Roman Catholic and Eastern Orthodox Christians because of their belief in the "one nature" of Jesus Christ.

Despite their similarities, the Egyptian Church split between the Greek hierarchy in Alexandria (Greek Orthodox) and the Coptic-speaking church of the people who were persecuted by the Empire. The monastic caves became the centers of the opposition movement. The oppression of the native population was so severe that many people actually supported the Arabic conquerors in the seventh century since they broke the yoke of Constantinople. Initially the Muslim rulers were tolerant of Coptic Christianity, but the church faced many obstacles, including the prohibition of converting Muslims. At times, though, persecution could be severe; the age of martyrs in Coptic Christianity lasted longer than in other churches.

Coptic Christianity came to America with Egyptian immigration in the twentieth century. The American Coptic Church is part of the worldwide network of Copts who continue to worship in the language of their ancestors and honor their saints and martyrs. Like most immigrant churches, the Coptic Church enjoys the freedom of worship and evangelism America offers while it tries to help its people negotiate the permissiveness of American culture. The church in America is closely connected to the worldwide Coptic Church led by Pope Tawadros II, Pope of Alexandria, and the See of St. Mark. There is one monastery in the United States. Ecumenical dialogue with other Catholic and Orthodox churches has helped heal the old theological division over the nature of Christ.

For more information: www.coptic.org and www.copticchurch.net

Headquarters: There is no single headquarters of all Coptic Christians in the United States. The websites mentioned above provide much information about the various branches of Coptic Christianity in America. One center is at 427 West Side Avenue, PO Box 4397, Jersey City, NJ 07304.

ETHIOPIAN ORTHODOX CHRISTIANITY IN THE UNITED STATES

Founded: 1959, first diocese in the United States
Statistics unavailable

By most accounts Ethiopian Christianity is one of the oldest national forms of Christianity. In the West it is generally referred to as the Ethiopian Orthodox Church and was the state religion of the African country of Ethiopia (Abyssinia) for many centuries. Its headquarters is in the Ethiopian capital of Addis Ababa where resides the church's archbishop who is not in communion with the Orthodox patriarchs of Alexandria or of Constantinople. Ethiopian Orthodoxy is generally considered monophysite (like the Coptic Church of Egypt) due to its rejection of the doctrine of the hypostatic union of two natures of Jesus Christ declared by the Council of Chalcedon in 451. However, it does affirm the Nicene Creed, which is widely considered the canon of orthodoxy by Christians. The Ethiopian Orthodox (Tewahedo) Church of Ethiopia is in communion with other Oriental Orthodox churches such as the Coptic Church of Egypt and the Armenian Orthodox Church. (It should be noted that all non-Chalcedonian Orthodox Oriental churches reject the label "monophysite.")

The patriarch of Ethiopian Orthodoxy in Addis Ababa sent the first Ethiopian Orthodox bishop to the United States in 1959. He left and returned after a period of communion with the Rastafarians in Jamaica who considered Ethiopian Emperor Haile Salassie the embodiment of the return of Jesus Christ. The history of Ethiopian Orthodoxy in the United States since 1959 has been checkered at best with church leaders denouncing the patriarch in 1992 because he was appointed by the new Ethiopian military junta. Later, however, union was restored.

There exists no headquarters of Ethiopian Orthodoxy in the United States; individual congregations network with each other in two dioceses (Washington, DC and New York) led by archbishops appointed by Patriarch Abune Mathias who resides at the Holy Trinity Cathedral in Addis Ababa, Ethiopia. There are no reliable statistics for this form of Christianity in the United States but some observers estimate there are approximately thirty to forty major congregations and several thousand members.

For more information: www.ethiopianorthodox.org

GREEK ORTHODOX ARCHDIOCESE OF NORTH AMERICA

Founded: 1922
Membership: 476,878 in 545 parishes (2010)

The Greek Orthodox Church is one of the largest Orthodox bodies in the United States due to the massive immigration of Greeks to the United States between 1890 and 1929. Greece was one of the earliest and most vital centers of Christianity, but the capture of Constantinople by the Turks and the subjugation of the patriarch to Muslim rule was a severe blow to the Greek Orthodox Church. In the nineteenth century, the church in Greece established a Holy Synod independent from (but in communion with) the ecumenical patriarch. Orthodox priests were sent to the United States either by the Holy Synod of Greece or by the ecumenical patriarchate of Constantinople.

In 1864, the first Greek Orthodox Church in the United States was founded in New Orleans, Louisiana. By 1910 there were approximately thirty-five congregations in various parts of the country. A period of confusion existed from 1908 to 1922, during which time the jurisdiction of American churches shifted from the ecumenical patriarchate of Constantinople to the Holy Synod of Greece and back again. This was finally resolved with the Founding Tome of 1922, which established the Greek Orthodox Archdiocese of North and South America.

Archbishop Athenagoras Spyrou of Corfu was appointed to head the Greek Church in America in 1931, and under his leadership the church increased to two hundred and eighty-six parishes. In 1948, Athenagoras was elected patriarch of Constantinople and was succeeded by Archbishop Michael Constantinides of Corinth, who was enthroned in the New York Cathedral of the Holy Trinity. Since 1999, Archbishop Demetrios, appointed by Constantinople's ecumenical patriarch, has led the Greek Orthodox Archdiocese of North America. He oversees work in nine dioceses, each headed by a bishop. Worship, doctrine, and polity follow historical Orthodox patterns, with the service of worship being the center of congregational life. In the 1980s and 1990s the church began attracting Protestants and Catholics, some of whom felt their churches were too accommodating to modern culture, others who were attracted to the artistry and depth of Orthodox worship.

The Greek Orthodox Archdiocese of America is a full member of the Assembly of Canonical Orthodox Archbishops of the United States and is in fellowship with the patriarch of Constantinople. Many people in the United States mistakenly refer to all Eastern Orthodox churches as "Greek Orthodox" because this denomination is one of the oldest and largest of them.

The church supports eighteen parochial schools; nine summer camps; a school for orphans and children from broken homes; Hellenic College and Holy Cross Greek Orthodox School of Theology, both in Brookline, Massachusetts; three homes for teenage boys; and a home for the aged.

For more information: www.goarch.org

Headquarters: 8 East Seventy-Ninth Street, New York, NY 10021

MALANKARA ORTHODOX SYRIAN CHURCH AND MAR THOMA ORTHODOX SYRIAN CHURCH (INDIAN ORTHODOX)

Founded: 1978 in the United States; 1988
Membership: est. 70,000 in 154 parishes (2006)

These are the two major bodies of independent Indian Christian churches in the United States. Both bodies claim descent from Thomas the apostle, who legend says went to India as an evangelist after the resurrection of Christ. The Malankara Church was named for a town where Thomas is believed to have arrived in India in 52 CE. It uses the liturgy, calendar, language, and traditions of the Syrian Orthodox Church.

The church in India is indeed ancient and historically had close ties to the Syriac Church in Persia (see Apostolic Catholic Assyrian Church of the East), which was rooted in the theological tradition of Antioch and rejected the agreement of Chalcedon in 451 that declared Christ to be one person with two natures—one human and one divine ("hypostatic union"). The Persian (or Syrian) church is often called "Nestorian" because of its adherence to the doctrine attributed to the fifth-century theologian Nestorius of Antioch that such a strong distinction should be made between the divinity and humanity of Christ that he constituted a "union of wills." This idea contrasted strongly with the Alexandrian theology (see Coptic Orthodox) that Christ is a single person with a single nature ("monophysites"). Symbolic of the difference between this view and that of the Eastern Orthodox churches is that the Syrians and Indians never refer to Mary as "the mother of God." Instead, they call her "mother of Christ" (*Christotokos*). Missionaries from Persia established the church in India, and the ancient Indian churches used Syriac rather than one of the Indian languages in worship.

In 1599, under the influence of Portuguese missionaries, most Malankara Christians, who lived in southwest India, rejected Nestorianism. Many united with Rome as a Uniate church. Others, however, turned to the Syrian Orthodox Church for guidance. The Mar Thoma Church was established to preserve the native Indian church from forced Latinization by the Portuguese colonizers of the Malankara region. It is in communion with the Syrian Orthodox Church of Antioch and uses the Orthodox liturgy and calendar. In the nineteenth century, Christianity in India experienced further fracture during the period of British rule as Anglican and Protestant missionaries poured into India.

The American Diocese of the Malankara Syrian Orthodox Church was established in 1978 to serve Indian immigrants to the United States and their children. It includes about thirty thousand members in eighty parishes. The Mar Thoma Church is independent and is in communion with the Anglican churches worldwide. The American diocese was organized in 1988 to serve members in the immigrant community. It has about twenty-five thousand members in seventy parishes.

Neither of these India-based denominations is a member of the Assembly of Canonical Orthodox Bishops of the United States or in communion with the patriarch of Constantinople. Nor are they in communion with each other.

(Neither of these denominations should be confused with the Malankara Orthodox Syrian Archdiocese of Antioch, which is within the jurisdiction of the patriarch of Antioch and in communion with the patriarch of Constantinople. It is not a separate denomination but a sub-jurisdiction of the Antiochian Orthodox Christian Archdiocese of North America [in the United States].)

For more information: http://malankaraorthodoxchurch.in; http://marthomanae.org

Headquarters: Malankara Diocesan Center, 270 Whippany Road, Whippany, NJ 07981

Sinai Mar Thoma Center, Merrick, NY 11566

ORTHODOX CHURCH IN AMERICA
(RUSSIAN ORTHODOX)

Founded: 1970, with roots to 1794
Membership: 100,000 in 800 parishes (2016)

The Eastern Orthodox faith came to the New World shortly after the American Revolution by way of Alaska rather than from the East. This was because Alaska was part of Russia until 1867. Eight Russian Orthodox monks entered Alaska in 1794, and established headquarters at Kodiak. Orthodox monks and bishops created an alphabet and printed a grammar in the Aleutian language, translated portions of the Bible, and built a cathedral at Sitka.

Russia itself joined the Orthodox fold with the baptism of Grand Prince Vladimir of Kiev in 988 CE. The church was ruled at first by metropolitans appointed or approved by the patriarch of Constantinople, but eventually an independent patriarchate was established in Moscow, which came to be regarded by Slavs as "the Third Rome." Russian Orthodoxy was modeled on the church in Constantinople, but over the centuries it developed distinctive qualities. Russian iconography is greatly valued by art collectors, but is valued even higher by the faithful for whom the saints provide a connection to God and history. As with many churches, Russian Orthodoxy is closely connected with Russian patriotism, and many saints are national heroes. For centuries the Russian Church was governed by a Holy Synod rather than a patriarch.

Early in the nineteenth century, a chapel was built at a Russian trading post near present-day San Francisco. The Episcopal See was transferred to that city in 1872, but moved to New York City in 1905 as waves of immigration brought thousands of Slavs to the eastern states. For many years, the Russian hierarchy in the United States cared for immigrants from other Orthodox countries, such as Serbia, Syria, and Bulgaria. Many Eastern-rite Catholics from the old Austro-Hungarian Empire also transferred to the jurisdiction of the Russian Orthodox Church rather than accept the administration of Irish and Italian Catholic bishops.

Bishop Tikhon, who later became patriarch of the Russian Church, founded the first Russian Orthodox Theological Seminary in Minneapolis, Minnesota, in 1905. Bishop Tikhon also transferred the Episcopal See and its Ecclesiastical Consistory from San Francisco to New York City, where the Russian Orthodox headquarters for this hemisphere are still located. Under Tikhon, St. Nicholas Cathedral in New York was built in 1901. In 1919 the Russian Church in America held its first Sobor, or general council, at Pittsburgh.

The history of the church in the United States has been tied to political events in Russia. In 1917 the Bolsheviks took over the government of Russia and instituted restrictive religious policies. The patriarch and the Holy Synod resisted, but the government found some priests and bishops ready to support the new regime. These officials held an assembly that deposed the patriarch, endorsed communism, and declared itself the governing body of the Russian church.

Calling itself the Renovated, or Living, Church, this group changed the ancient disciplinary rules and instituted liturgical reforms. With the support of Soviet authorities, who hoped thus to divide and weaken the church, that body held control for several years but was never recognized by the great majority of clergy or people. The government considered opposition to the Living Church a civil offense and, on this basis, banished thousands of bishops, clergy, monks, and laypersons to labor camps.

The Living Church faction in Russia, supported by the communist government, sent an emissary to secure control of Russian Orthodox Church property in the United States; through action in the civil courts, it gained possession of the cathedral in New York City. In 1924, an assembly of the Diocese of North America, in an attempt to prevent further seizures, declared that, on a temporary basis, it was administratively, legislatively, and jurisdictionally independent of the church in Russia. But this independence was not recognized by the patriarchate of Moscow or by the Russian Orthodox Church outside of Russia, headquartered at that time in the former Yugoslavia.

In 1927 the Soviet government prevailed upon Metropolitan Sergius, the *locum tenens* (that is, temporary substitute) of the then-vacant patriarchal see, to submit the policy of the church totally to the Soviet regime. Stalin engineered the meeting of a small group of bishops to elect Metropolitan Sergius as patriarch of Moscow and all of Russia. Sergius called upon his people to support the government in the defense of their country during World War II, and this marked a turning point in the Soviet policy toward the church.

The Living Church was discarded, and the patriarch's authority was recognized by the state. Many surviving clergy and bishops who had been banished were permitted to return, and gradually the patriarchal administration became again the sole authority in the Orthodox Church of Russia.

A body of Russian émigrés, though, formed the Russian Orthodox Church outside of Russia* in 1920 under the authority of the ecumenical patriarch. They hold that the Moscow patriarchate forfeited its right to be considered a true Orthodox church because it adopted a position of submission to the atheistic Soviet regime, not only in regard to politics and external matters but also with respect to its internal policies and affairs. In 1950 this church came to the United States. It has about a hundred and seventy-five parishes dedicated to the traditions of the pre-Soviet Russian church.

Despite the conflicts in the church in Russia, the main body of believers in the United States maintained their institutional life and worked to bring other Slavic peoples together into a vibrant Orthodox Church. On May 18, 1970, a delegation of hierarchs, clergy, and laity of the Russian Orthodox Metropolia in America, headed by Bishop Theodosius went to Moscow to receive the Thomos of Authocephaly, the document of independence, from the head of the Russian Orthodox Church. Since that time, the Orthodox Church in America (OCA) has been independent.

Relations between the Orthodox in the United States and Russia have improved greatly since the collapse of the Soviet Union and restoration of the authority of the church in Russia to govern its own affairs and doctrine. In recognition of this, one of the most venerated Russian icons, which had been smuggled to the United States for safekeeping during the Soviet era, was returned to Saint Petersburg in 2004. Throngs of the faithful greeted the icon as it made its procession through Russia before being enthroned in the cathedral.

From administrative offices in New York City, the primate of the Orthodox Church in America oversees the work of eleven dioceses, which are in turn headed by bishops. The primate and bishops make up the Holy Synod of Bishops, which is the highest decision-making body in the church. Church ministry units include education and community life ministries, mission and stewardship ministries, pastoral life ministries, witness and communication ministries, and church order ministries. The church administers three theological seminaries: St. Tikhon's in Pennsylvania, St. Vladimir's in New York, and St. Herman's in Alaska. The church also operates several monasteries throughout the United States.

This church's relationship—as to its political autocephaly (autonomy)—with the patriarch of Constantinople and with some of the other Eastern Orthodox churches is unclear. Yet it is a full member of the Assembly of Canonical Orthodox Bishops in the United States. The patriarchs of Constantinople have disputed the authority of the patriarch of Moscow to grant "autocephaly" (autonomous status) to any church. Without doubt the precise jurisdictional status of the OCA depends on whom one asks. Its doctrinal status as orthodox is not in dispute; the only question is its status with regard to the patriarch of Constantinople. Patriarch Bartholomew, who convened the Holy and Great Council of the Orthodox Church in Greece (2016), did not invite the bishops of the OCA. Nevertheless, the OCA is in communion with the patriarch and most of the Eastern Orthodox churches, including the Russian Church outside of Russia, in the United States and throughout the world.

For more information: www.oca.org

Headquarters: PO Box 675, Syosset, NY 11791-0675

THE ROMANIAN ORTHODOX EPISCOPATE OF AMERICA

Founded: 1929
Membership: 10,635 in 64 parishes (2012)

Christianity came to Romania in the fourth century. Originally Western and Latin in orientation, the church there gradually came under the authority of Constantinople and adopted Greek liturgical practices and customs. In 1859, the church declared itself independent of Constantinople as a national church, a move that was officially acknowledged twenty-five years later. The church in the United States was organized at a congress convened in Detroit, Michigan, by clergy and lay representatives of Romanian Orthodox parishes in the United States and Canada. It remained under the canonical jurisdiction of the Romanian Orthodox patriarchate in Bucharest until political conditions forced its separation. It is now a diocese under the autocephalous Orthodox Church in America. The archbishop is a member of the Holy Synod of the Orthodox Church in America, and the diocese is recognized as an administratively self-governing body.

For more information: www.roea.org

Headquarters: PO Box 309, Grass Lake, MI 49240

THE ROMANIAN ORTHODOX ARCHDIOCESE IN THE AMERICAS

Statistics unavailable

The Romanian Orthodox Archdiocese in the Americas is the Romanian Orthodox body under the jurisdiction of the patriarchate of Romania and is a member of the Assembly of Canonical Orthodox Bishops of the United States. Its leader, Archbishop Nicolae Condrea, was appointed by the Romanian mother church headquartered in Bucharest. It is in communion with the patriarch of Constantinople through the Romanian patriarch.

For more information: www.romarch.org

Headquarters: 5410 North Newland Avenue, Chicago, IL 60656

RUSSIAN ORTHODOX CHURCH OUTSIDE OF RUSSIA

Founded: Unknown
Membership: 480,000 in 190 parishes (2008)

The Russian Orthodox Church outside of Russia is spread throughout the world as a kind of Orthodox diaspora of Russians. It is divided into dioceses led by bishops appointed by the patriarch of Moscow. In the United States it exists in three distinct dioceses with bishops in New York, Chicago, and San Francisco. It is a full member of the Assembly of Canonical Orthodox Bishops in the United States and is in fellowship with the patriarch of Constantinople through the patriarch of Moscow. For a brief history of Russian Orthodoxy outside Russia see the earlier entry about the Orthodox Church in America.

For more information: www.synod.com/synod/indexeng.htm

Headquarters: (Diocese of New York and Eastern America): 79 East Ninety-Third Street, New York, NY 10128

SERBIAN ORTHODOX CHURCH IN NORTH AND SOUTH AMERICA

Founded: 1921
Membership: 67,000 in 68 parishes (2012)

Saints Cyril (826–69) and Methodius (815–85) were sent by the patriarch in Constantinople to strengthen and spread Christianity among the Slavic peoples. One of their great achievements was creating the first Slavic alphabet, which they used to translate the Orthodox liturgy and the Gospels into the old Slavonic language. Most famous for their work in Moravia (the Czech Republic) and Kiev, they were also instrumental in establishing Christianity among the Serbian people.

From the seventh century until the thirteenth, the church in Serbia was under the jurisdiction of the patriarchate of Constantinople. It became the independent National Serbian Church in 1219 during the Western occupation of Constantinople. The church made notable contributions to art and architecture during the glory days of the medieval Serbian Empire until the defeat to the Turks at Kosovo in 1389. The Ottoman Turks governed their Christian subjects in part through church officials, most notably the ecumenical patriarch in Constantinople (now Istanbul); therefore the Serbian Church, like other Orthodox churches, became a symbol of national identity as well as religious faith. It played an important part in the Serbian struggle for independence, which was won in the nineteenth century. In 1879 the church also achieved independence from the patriarch of Constantinople following the freedom of the nation from Turkish control.

Through the close of World War I, the ecclesiastical and political situation in the Balkans was turbulent and complicated. Attempts were made to unite several Orthodox groups into one church. The fruit of the effort came in 1920 when the union of five autonomous bodies was proclaimed. Metropolitan Dimitriji of Belgrade was appointed patriarch, uniting in himself the historic titles of archbishop of Ipek, metropolitan of Belgrade and Karlovci, and patriarch of Serbs.

Serbian immigrants came to the United States more for political than economic reasons and began arriving in large numbers around 1890. They worshipped at first in Russian churches, accepting the ministrations of Russian priests and the supervision of Russian bishops. The Serbian patriarchate of Yugoslavia approved the organization of the Diocese of the United States and Canada in 1921, and in 1926, with thirty-five Serbian churches making up the American Diocese, Archimandrite Mardary Uskokovich was consecrated by Patriarch Dimitriji of Serbia as the first bishop of the Serbian Orthodox Church in America.

Today the Serbian Eastern Orthodox Church has two dioceses in North America: the New Gracanica Metropolinate Diocese of America and Canada, based in Libertyville, Illinois; and the Diocese of Western America, based in Alhambra, California. The cathedral of the Serbian Church, built and opened in 1945, is located in New York City. The extended conflict in the Balkans during the 1990s brought great distress to Serbs living in North America. The Serbian Eastern Orthodox Church played an important role in conveying information to Serbs in the United States and Canada and in offering them spiritual and psychological support. It also sought to present a comprehensive picture of Serbian life and culture to the American public.

The Serbian Orthodox Church in North and South America is a full member of the Assembly of Canonical Orthodox Bishops in the United States and is in communion with the patriarch of Constantinople.

For more information: www.serborth.org

Office of External Affairs: 2311 M Street Northwest Suite 402, Washington, DC 20037

SYRIAC (SYRIAN) ORTHODOX CHURCH OF ANTIOCH (ARCHDIOCESES IN THE USA AND CANADA)

Founded: 50 CE; American Archdiocese est. 1957
Membership: est. 32,500 in 32 parishes (2012)

The Syrian Orthodox Church dates back to the apostolic age. It was in Antioch that the followers of Jesus were first called Christian, and tradition holds that Peter established the first patriarchate in Antioch. The Syrian Orthodox use the ancient liturgy of St. James of Jerusalem in worship. The Syriac Scripture is one of the oldest translations of the Bible and continues to be vital for Syrian Christianity. The Syrian Orthodox Church continues to have its patriarchal see in Damascus. The Syrian Orthodox use a number of ancient liturgies in worship, the principal being that of St. James. The official liturgical language remains classical Syriac.

Syriac Christianity was divided during the Nestorian controversy. The followers of Nestorius, who taught that there were two separate persons in the incarnate Christ, one divine and one human, were persecuted and found refuge in Persia. The Syrian Orthodox Church has always held to the one-nature position of St. Cyril of Alexandria and professes the faith of the first three ecumenical councils. When the Council of Chalcedon adopted a formula that seemed to endorse Nestorius's ideas, the Syrian Orthodox refused to comply with the patriarch of Constantinople. The Syrian Orthodox experienced persecution under the Byzantine Empire, but found a degree of toleration under Muslim rule until the Mongol invasions in the thirteenth century.

Syrians were few in number in the United States until the turn of the twentieth century. Syrian Orthodox silk weavers from Diyarbakir, Turkey, settled in New Jersey, a major area of the silk industry. Families from Harput, Turkey, were drawn to Massachusetts. The first priest, the Very Rev. Hanna Koorie, arrived in 1907; their first patriarchal vicar, Archbishop Mar Athanasius Y. Samuel, was appointed on May 13, 1952. On November 15, 1957, Patriarch Ignatius Yacoub III set his seal upon the document officially establishing the Archdiocese of the Syrian Orthodox Church in the United States and Canada. The next year, a cathedral in the name of St. Mark was consecrated in Hackensack, New Jersey. It was relocated in 1994 to a new complex in Teaneck, New Jersey.

From the 1960s through the 1980s, new Syrian Orthodox parishes were established throughout North America. Following the death of Archbishop Samuel in 1995, the Holy Synod of the Syrian Orthodox Church of Antioch divided the North American Archdiocese into three separate patriarchal vicariates: the Syrian Orthodox Archdiocese for the Eastern United States, the Syrian Orthodox Archdiocese of Los Angeles and Environs, and the Syrian Orthodox Archdiocese of Canada.

The Syrian Orthodox Church of Antioch is not a member of the Assembly of Canonical Orthodox Bishops of the United States and is not in communion with the patriarch of Constantinople. It is considered a non-Chalcedonian Orthodox church and an Oriental Orthodox church.

For more information: www.syrianorthodoxchurch.org

Headquarters: Archdiocese for Eastern United States: 55 West Midlands Avenue, Paramus, NJ 07652

UKRAINIAN ORTHODOX CHURCH OF THE USA

Founded: 1924
Membership: 50,000 in 118 parishes (2012)

Around the year 862, the first Orthodox Christian community was founded on the outskirts of Kyyiv (Kiev), during the reign of two princes, Askold and Dyr. Disciples of Saints Cyril and Methodius brought Slavonic liturgies and scriptures to Kiev, bringing both a new faith and a written language to the Slavic people there. Instrumental in making Orthodox Christianity known in Rus-Ukraine was the Kyyivian Princess Olha, baptized in 975, grandmother of St. Volodymyr (Vladimir) the Great. After considerable reflection and investigation, Volodymyr (baptismal name Basil) proclaimed Orthodox Christianity the official faith of his kingdom of Rus-Ukraine in 988. Thus the introduction of Christianity to Russia came through Ukraine.

In 1686 the Ukrainian church was forced to submit to the patriarchate of Moscow, but after the 1917 Bolshevik Revolution, the Ukrainian Orthodox Church sundered jurisdictional ties with Moscow and declared autocephaly (independence) in 1921. The June 5, 1990, Sobor (council) of the Ukrainian Autocephalous Orthodox Church in newly independent Ukraine established its own patriarchate and elected as its first patriarch Metropolitan Mstyslav, at that time Primate of the Ukrainian Orthodox Church of the USA.

The Ukrainian Orthodox Church of the USA was established in 1924, when its first bishop, Metropolitan Ioan (John) Teodorovych, arrived from the Ukraine. He served as leader of the church until his death in 1971. He was followed as metropolitan by Mstyslav, who served from 1971 until his death in 1993, at age ninety-five. In 1996 the church united with the former Ukrainian Orthodox Church of America.

The church's heaviest concentration is in the New York-New Jersey-Pennsylvania area. The church maintains St. Andrew Center, a Ukrainian cultural center, in South Bound Brook, New Jersey. The center is home to St. Andrew Memorial Church, a monument to Ukrainian Cossak Baroque architecture, and to St. Sophia Seminary.

The Ukrainian Orthodox Church of the USA is a full member of the Assembly of Canonical Orthodox Bishops of the United States and is in fellowship with the patriarch of Constantinople.

For more information: www.uocofusa.org

Headquarters: PO Box 495, South Bound Brook, NJ 08880

CATHOLIC CHURCHES

Christians in many different churches profess their faith in "the one, holy, catholic church" using the words of the Apostles' Creed. "Catholic" in this sense does not necessarily refer to a particular religious institution but to the idea of the universality of the church. The catholic church is the church that exists around the world and through the ages. Obviously, though, religious institutions will have differing understandings about the institutional expression of that catholicity. In this section are included those bodies that hold most dearly to a view of the church that is universal in time and space and united institutionally. Although for most of its cultural and political history, the United States has been dominated by Protestants, it is important to remember that Roman Catholicism came to the New World with Christopher Columbus. Today, the Roman Catholic Church is by far the largest religious organization in America. Though there are thousands of Protestant denominations, it is important to remember that most of the world's Christians are in the Roman Catholic Church. At the same time, it is important to know that the Roman Catholic Church is only one of several denominations that claim to be the true institutional, organizational embodiment of the Catholic Church.

The use of the adjective "catholic" (or "Catholic") for these church bodies, denominations, is somewhat accidental in that they all also claim, like the Eastern churches, to be "orthodox." Similarly, the Eastern churches, described in the immediately preceding section of this *Handbook,* all claim to be "catholic." So do some Protestant denominations. So, technically, both the churches of that first section here and the churches of this section could all be called "Orthodox Catholic" or "Catholic Orthodox." All place great emphasis on the institutional unity of the body of Christ across time and space and on the continuity of correct doctrine from ancient times to today.

The main differences between the denominations labeled "Orthodox" (Eastern or Oriental) and the denominations here labeled "Catholic" (Roman or non-Roman) have to do with geography, history, and worship. When the Roman Empire divided between East and West—over a period of time beginning with Constantine—the Eastern half centered around Constantinople (modern Istanbul), spoke mostly Greek, and was strongly influenced by Hellenistic, that is "Greekish," culture. The Western half centered around

Rome, spoke mostly Latin, and was influenced by Western European culture. The two halves of Christianity gradually drifted apart and then severed relations in 1054. (This traditional account of the separation does not even take into account the so-called Oriental Orthodox churches that separated from Eastern and Western churches over the Chalcedonian doctrine of the Person of Jesus Christ or were never part of the Christianity of the Roman Empire.)

"Catholic" Christianity has come to be the dominant label for those (mostly) Western churches that looked to the patriarch of Rome, the "pope," as not only the first among equals of all the patriarchs and bishops, but also as the supreme spiritual leader of Christendom. "Orthodox" Christianity has come to be the dominant label for those (mostly) Eastern churches that look to the patriarch of Constantinople as the first among equals among the ecumenical patriarchs of Christendom including the bishop of Rome. Orthodox Christians, however, consider themselves truly catholic and Catholic Christians consider themselves truly orthodox.

Alongside the Eastern Orthodox Church (or family of churches) and the Roman Catholic Church exist many smaller denominations not considered "canonical" by the patriarchs or "catholic" by the pope. Some of these smaller non-Roman catholic bodies broke away from the Roman Catholic Church over developments within it regarding the status of the pope, the bishop of Rome. For example, several catholic denominations broke away from the Catholic Church of Rome when it declared the pope infallible in 1870.

The paragraphs that follow here refer primarily to the Roman Catholic Church although not to the absolute exclusion of the separate, independent catholic bodies that do not regard the pope as infallible or supreme.

Catholic churches see themselves in unbroken continuity with the institutional expression of Christian faith in the West since the days of the apostles. They differ markedly from Restorationist bodies, for example, which view most of Western history as a decline and fall of the church and thus sought to restore the New Testament church. For Catholics, the Holy Spirit continued to work through historical development in order to bring the faith to its richest and fullest expression. In particular, the writings of the church fathers (e.g., Jerome [c. 345–c. 420] and Augustine [354–430]) instruct the faithful in how to understand the scripture and live a Christian life. It was during the patristic age (the time from the death of the apostles to the close of the eighth century) that much Catholic doctrine, polity, and devotion were established.

Catholic History. The history of the Catholic Church for a thousand years is basically the history of Christianity. There is not space in this volume to give a full account of that history, but it should be noted that during the first five centuries of Christianity there were numerous struggles over the nature of Christian doctrine and ecclesiastical authority. Gradually the lines of orthodoxy were established through the authority of creeds, especially the Nicene Creed, and the episcopacy (bishops, archbishops, and patriarchs).

During this process of development there were no fundamental divisions between Eastern and Western Christianity.

The East and the West did develop some distinctive liturgical and administrative practices, due in part to the greater sophistication of Byzantine (Eastern) culture. Most important, the Eastern bishops and theologians tended to define the church in terms of orthodox belief and practice, while in the West institutional allegiance became paramount, particularly during the rising social chaos of the early Middle Ages.

The church in the West gained secular authority and power when it emerged as the only body strong enough to provide stable government as Germanic ("barbarian") tribes migrated in large numbers into France and Italy. One of the most significant events in this period was the sack of Rome by the Vandals in 410 CE. Ravaged first by Goths, Vandals, and Franks, and then by Saxons, Danes, Alemanni, Lombards, and Burgundians, western Europe found its only steadying hand in the Roman church. The church in the West was seen as a unifying force in the chaos of society, and thus the word *catholic* ("universal") was increasingly applied to those who were loyal to the bishop of Rome.

The first mention of the term *catholic* was made by Ignatius of Antioch about 110–15 CE, but it was the theologian Augustine in the fifth century who provided the theological and philosophical structure that gave the papacy its justification and defense. In the early church the bishop of Rome was one of five patriarchs, and he had supreme authority over the church in the West. The general consensus in Western Christianity was that there should be a single ecclesiastical institution with a single head who served as Christ's representative in the church. The bishop of Rome was seen as the Vicar of Christ. To be catholic, in this sense, was to be under the authority of the Vicar of Christ who governed in Rome.

Until 1054 the bishop of Rome and the bishop of Constantinople served as the heads of the Western and Eastern churches, respectively, without one asserting absolute authority over the other, but in that year each bishop formally excommunicated the other. Relations between East and West were strained further when the Fourth Crusade conquered Constantinople instead of Jerusalem in 1204. They looted the city and forced the patriarch to submit to the pope. Eventually, the emperor and patriarch regained control, but the break between East and West was complete.

The Roman Catholic Church was the most significant institution in Western society for most of the Middle Ages. It preserved and spread Christianity during the days of barbarian invasion; preserved and spread classical education through monasteries, convents, cathedral schools, and universities; stabilized feudal society; promoted architectural and artistic achievements; and established the basis for the Western legal system. The great cathedrals of Europe are an enduring testimony to the beauty and grandeur of medieval Catholicism.

For more than three hundred years, the church launched military campaigns (called crusades) against Muslims in the Middle East. Schisms, heresies, and divisions began appearing in the late Middle Ages, and the church established Inquisitions to enforce orthodox teaching and church authority. New religious orders, most notably the Dominicans, Franciscans, and Templars were established to deal with heresy and the perceived threat of Islam. In 1415 the Council of Constance executed the theologian John Hus, a forerunner of reformer Martin Luther, igniting the Hussite revolution in Central Europe.

It was the Protestant Reformation, ignited by Martin Luther (1483–1546), that permanently splintered Western Christianity. Roman Catholic scholars acknowledge that there were corrupt individuals within the church and that reform was necessary. Indeed, reform was underway even before the Reformation. Erasmus (1469–1536), Thomas More (d. 1535), Savonarola (1452–98), and others wrote and preached against the corruption and worldliness of leaders and laypeople, but they tried to stay in the church.

Although the Catholic Church rejected most of the proposals of the Protestant reformers, the Reformation encouraged the Roman Church to reform and re-organize itself. Indeed, some historians, Catholic and Protestant alike, would date the founding of the modern Roman Catholic Church as a self-conscious and distinctive religious body to the great Council of Trent (1545–63) when many Catholic doctrines were officially defined for the first time and where the current ecclesiastical structure was codified. The Tridentine (or post–Council of Trent) church was in many ways a stronger and more effective institution than the Renaissance church. The newly established Society of Jesus (Jesuits) led the way in winning back areas lost to Protestantism and, along with the Franciscans, in courageously bringing Christianity to the recently discovered lands east and west of Europe. Thanks, in part, to the success of European colonialism, by 1700 the Catholic Church was established across the globe. For a brief time, it appeared that even China might become Christian.

Having reformed the papacy of many of the abuses that had fueled the Reformation, the Tridentine church increasingly looked to the papacy as the guarantor of Catholic unity and continuity. As the Enlightenment took hold in Europe in the eighteenth century and revolutions convulsed the European kingdoms in the nineteenth, Catholic bishops and theologians held up the Roman pontiff as the symbol of stability, authority, and order in church and society.

This led to the declaration of papal infallibility by the First Vatican Council in 1870, a move that inspired a number of Catholics, calling themselves Old Catholics,* to separate from the Roman Catholic Church. These churches, which seek to be true to the historic Catholic Church without endorsing papal supremacy, are discussed in this section of the *Handbook*. Also, within the nineteenth-century Anglican Church, the Oxford Movement stressed the idea that the Church of England was part of the Catholic rather than the Protestant tradition. This led to the creation a variety of small Anglo-Catholic bodies. Ecumenical dialogue between Anglicans and Catholics in the twentieth century brought the two bodies very close to reunion, but Catholics reject the ordination of women and gay and lesbian people in the Episcopal Church*.

Beliefs and Practices. The faith and doctrine of the Roman Catholic Church are founded upon what the First Vatican Council referred to as "that deposit of faith given to it by Christ and through his apostles, sustained by the Bible and by tradition." Thus, like other Catholic and Orthodox bodies, the church accepts the decisions of the first seven ecumenical councils; however, Roman Catholics view the later councils of the Western church, such as the Fourth Lateran Council (1215) and the Council of Trent as equally authoritative. According to Catholic teaching, these councils, down to the Second Vatican Council (1962–65), clarify and enrich without changing the "deposit of faith," and they become part of the apostolic tradition. The church also accepts the Apostles' Creed, the Nicene-Constantinople Creed, the Athanasian Creed, and the Creed of Pius IV, also called the Creedal Statement of the Council of Trent. These creeds set forth many doctrines common to most Christian bodies, such as the Trinity and the full humanity and divinity of Christ.

Like the Orthodox, Roman Catholics stress the sacraments more than most Protestants. The sacraments are a visible means of receiving God's grace and are thus holy. For Catholics there are seven sacraments:

1. Baptism, necessary for membership in the church, is administered to infants born to Catholic parents or to adult converts. Anointing with oil (the holy chrism) in the form of a cross follows baptism.

2. Confirmation, which is an adult profession of faith, is done with laying on of hands, ordinarily by a bishop, as a sign of the gift of the Holy Spirit. Today priests may confirm if necessary.

3. The Eucharist, or Holy Communion, is the central act of Catholic devotion. The laity may receive the Eucharist in the forms of bread and wine. This is not a mere sign or symbol for believers. The bread and wine are actually believed to become the body and blood of Christ (transubstantiation) so that the worshipper communes spiritually and physically with the Savior. Since the bread (or Host) is the body of Christ, it may be placed in a sacred vessel on the altar for veneration by the faithful.

4. Through the sacrament of reconciliation (formerly called penance), post-baptismal sins are forgiven.

5. Anointing of the sick is for the seriously ill, the injured, or the aged. It is particularly important for Catholics to receive penance and anointing at time of death, which is popularly called the Last Rites.

6. The sacraments of holy orders is for the ordination of deacons, priests, and bishops. Ordination grants a man the authority and power to

perform the sacraments. Women cannot be ordained to holy orders, but they may take vows and enter a religious order.

7. Marriage is a sacrament that "cannot be dissolved by any human power"; this rules out remarriage after divorce. However, improper marriages may be annulled under certain circumstances.

Members are required to attend Mass on Sundays and on obligatory holy days. They should also fast and abstain on certain appointed days, confess at least once a year, and receive the Holy Eucharist during the Easter season. In addition, laity are expected to contribute to the support of the church, and to strictly observe the marriage regulations of the church, which includes the prohibition of birth control.

The Roman Catholic liturgical calendar is more elaborate than that of Protestant churches, with days to remember and venerate hundreds of heroes of the faith, known as saints. Of particular importance in Roman Catholic devotion in the United States and around the world is Mary, the mother of Christ, who serves as an intercessor for the faithful. The importance of Mary in Catholic devotion increased over the centuries, and in 1954 the idea that she was conceived without original sin (the Immaculate Conception) was declared official Catholic dogma. Since then, some theologians have referred to her as a "Co-redemptrix" with Christ.

The central act of Catholic worship is the Mass. Its two principal parts are the liturgy of the word and the liturgy of the Eucharist. Until 1963 Latin was the only appropriate liturgical language, but now the entire Mass is recited in the vernacular by both priest and people. Many Catholics also participate in devotions such as benediction, the rosary (a cycle of prayers usually counted on a string of beads), stations of the cross (prayers occasioned by depictions of Christ's journey from Pilate's house to the tomb), and novenas (a period of nine days of public or private devotion). Pilgrimages to holy sites, especially places where people had visions of the Virgin Mary, remain an important part of Catholic devotion.

Religious Orders. At least since the fourth century, religious orders have been an integral part of Catholicism. *The Official Catholic Directory* lists over 130 religious orders for men and nearly 450 for women. These orders differ widely in their work. Some are contemplative, which means that the members remain in monasteries or cloistered convents and focus on prayer and study. Most monks and nuns live in active or mixed religious orders that engage in teaching, caring for the sick, missionary work, writing, or social work. Brothers and sisters are required to take vows of poverty, chastity, and obedience, but are not ordained. Ordination is a separate step, and many priests are also members of a religious order. Parishes in the United States are typically under the charge of a particular order, such as the Franciscans.

Originally monks or nuns were individuals who embraced an ascetic lifestyle of poverty and celibacy as a way to share in the witness of the martyrs who died for the faith. Voluntary asceticism was viewed as a way to "take up the cross" and follow Christ. Over time more organization and discipline were provided for those who chose to serve Christ instead of pursuing family or personal ambitions. In the sixth century, Benedict of Nursia established a monastery on his estate of Monte Cassino in Italy. His rule for the men there became the basis for all Western monasticism, male and female. Among the key features of his rule were the vow of obedience to the abbot (head of the monastery) in addition to vows of poverty and chastity; moderation of ascetic excess; and participation in physical labor in addition to prayer.

Through the centuries other religious orders were established, some in an attempt to reform perceived abuses in an older order, some in order to respond to some unmet need in the church and society. Among the most important of these orders were the Cistercians and the Carthusians, established in the twelfth century in protest against the luxury and laxity of many Benedictine houses. These orders stress austerity and generally impose silence on the monks.

With the rapid urbanization of Europe in the late Middle Ages, new orders were established to reach out to secular society. The Franciscans embraced a radical devotion to poverty and initially lived by begging. The Dominicans also stressed poverty, but they focused their efforts on preaching, especially in areas where heresy was strong. Known as friars (brothers), rather than monks, members of these orders quickly established a strong presence in the burgeoning universities of the Middle Ages. The Franciscans have an order for women (the Poor Claires) and what is called a tertiary order, for laypersons who continue to live in secular society. Altogether, the Franciscans are the largest Catholic order, and the followers of Francis have been particularly active in service to the poor and outcast.

Numerous orders were established during the Reformation in order to reform the Roman Catholic Church internally and to respond to the Protestant challenge externally. Chief among them was the Society of Jesus (Jesuits), founded by Ignatius Loyola (1491–1556). Worldwide, there are over eighteen thousand Jesuits. The Jesuits were pioneers in missions, especially in Asia, but their involvement in European politics led to their suppression in the late eighteenth century. The order was reorganized and reestablished in 1814, and it played a strong role in the promotion of Catholic education and theology. There are now 235 Catholic colleges and universities in the United States, including Notre Dame, Fordham, Georgetown, Boston College, St. Louis University, Marquette, Loyola, and Villanova, most of them closely connected with various religious orders.

Religious orders have provided an important focus of ministry for women in the Roman Catholic Church since the early days of the church. Some of the male orders have branches for women, but in general women have established their own institutions. There are the Carmelites who produced the great mystic Teresa of Avila (1515–82); the Ursulines, who embraced a mission of educating young women; and the Sisters of Mercy, founded by Mother Teresa of Calcutta (1910–97). In the United States, women religious have been the backbone of the extensive Roman Catholic parochial school system. In the 1990s there were some seven thousand parochial and private schools in this country with about two million students, including over thirteen hundred Roman Catholic high schools.

Women religious have also been vital in staffing Catholic hospitals and establishing countless charitable institutions. It is indicative of the work of Roman Catholic women that the first American officially to be declared a saint of the church was Elizabeth Seton (1774–1821), noted for her sacrificial role in alleviating social misery. The National Conference on Catholic Charities helps to coordinate charity and welfare work on state and national levels; work is also conducted by several religious orders whose members devote full time to the relief of the poor in homes or institutions, and many dioceses have bureaus of charity.

The Society of St. Vincent de Paul is perhaps the largest and most effective charitable organization. But there are many others (particularly women's orders, such as Little Sisters of the Poor, Sisters of Charity, Daughters of Charity of the Society of St. Vincent de Paul, and Sisters of Mercy) that are active among the poor in Catholic hospitals, orphanages, and homes for the aged. The church operates over fourteen hundred homes for the aged and about 150 orphanages. More than seventy-five million patients are treated annually in Catholic hospitals and health-care centers. One of every three beds in the nation's private hospitals is provided by the Catholic hospital system.

Besides religious orders and congregations, Catholics may join secular institutions whose members also observe poverty, chastity, and obedience but do not wear distinctive garb or live together in a community. Before receiving approval as secular institutes engaged in apostolic work, these groups may operate as approved "pious unions." Some of the prominent leaders of the American labor movement and other advocates for social justice were Catholic. Among them were Dorothy Day, Thomas Merton, and Daniel Berrigen. Catholic bishops have issued a number of important statements calling for great attention to social justice in America.

Catholicism in America. Missionaries came with Coronado and other early Spanish explorers to the southern and western regions of what would become the United States. The first permanent Catholic parish was established at Saint Augustine, Florida, in 1565, half a century before the first Protestant baptism in the Americas. The intrepid French explorers, voyageurs, and colonizers, such as Cartier, Jolliet, and Marquette, who live in North American lore, were Roman Catholics. They were generally accompanied by missionaries or were missionaries themselves. New France became a vicariate apostolic in 1658, with Bishop Laval at its head. The See of Quebec (1675) had spiritual jurisdiction over the vast French provinces in North America, reaching down the valley of the Mississippi to Louisiana.

In 1634, Roman Catholics from England founded Maryland in part as a refuge for Catholics during the turmoil of the English Civil War and Puritan Commonwealth. Catholic activity in the English colonies was restricted by law, even in Maryland, until after the American Revolution. In 1763, there were fewer than twenty-five thousand

Roman Catholics in a colonial population of two million, and they were under the jurisdiction of the vicar apostolic of London. Even so, among the signatures on the Articles of Confederation, the Declaration of Independence, and the Constitution are found those of three Catholics: Thomas Fitzsimmons (1741–1811), Charles Carroll (1737–1832), and Daniel Carroll (1730–96). Religious equality became law with the adoption of the Constitution in 1787.

The status of the Roman Catholic Church in the new nation was unclear until the Reverend John Carroll (1735–1815) of Baltimore, elder brother of Daniel Carroll, was named Superior, or prefect apostolic, of the church in the new United States. In 1800, he was the head of some one hundred and fifty thousand Roman Catholics. By 1890 that number had grown to over six million, primarily due to the flood of emigration from the Catholic countries of Europe.

Catholics faced a number of unique problems in the United States. There is only one Roman Catholic Church worldwide, with a single head, unlike most Protestant churches, which have separate national organizations. For example, while there is an Anglican communion worldwide, it is made up of largely independent Anglican churches in the various former British colonies. Episcopalians in the United States are not under the direct authority of the Archbishop of Canterbury the way Roman Catholic bishops are under the authority of the pope. Thus there has been tension in the Roman Catholic Church over the issue of Americanization: How much independence could the American bishops exert while still remaining obedient to Rome?

This was a particularly touchy problem following the First Vatican Council (1869–70), when the European bishops rejected a number of ideas, such as democratic government, that were at the core of American values. James Gibbons (1834–1921), the archbishop of Baltimore and primate of the Catholic Church in America, guided the church through these difficult issues and gained permission for Catholics in the United States to participate fully in American political and social life while remaining loyal to the Roman church. Ultimately, the Second Vatican Council (1962–65) approved of many proposals long advocated by American bishops.

Vatican II and Beyond. John XXIII (pope 1958–63) summoned all the bishops of the church to the twenty-first ecumenical council, which met at the Vatican in Rome. Following John XXIII's death, Pope Paul VI reconvened the council, which made the most radical changes to Catholic life in centuries. Vatican II and the papacy approved the use of the vernacular in the Mass, encouraged modern methods of biblical study and interpretation, promoted more active involvement of the laity in the life of the parish, placed the church on the side of the poor in Catholic countries, and allowed Roman Catholics to participate in ecumenical and interfaith dialogue. Such changes alienated some conservative Catholics, however, leading to the formation of organizations dedicated to preserving pre-Vatican II Catholicism, especially the Latin Mass.

Before Vatican II, Catholics had been forbidden to attend meetings of the World Council of Churches; now Catholic observers attend council sessions, and bishops of the church have entered into theological dialogue with several larger Protestant denominations. Since then, the church has been rebuilding bridges to the Orthodox churches and has even exonerated Martin Luther of heresy. John Paul II (pope 1979–2005), even made dramatic steps toward greater friendship with Judaism and Islam, praying in synagogues and mosques. John Paul II was the first pope from Poland, and he was fluent in several languages. He was one of the most widely traveled world leaders, having made official visits to 129 countries, often at great personal risk.

John Paul II was succeeded by Joseph Cardinal Ratzinger, head of the Sacred Congregation for the Doctrine of the Faith (formerly known as the Inquisition) who took the papal name Benedict XVI (2005–2013). As pope, he pulled back from the ecumenism of his predecessor and took a firm stance against women's ordination and birth control. Controversially, he also forbade Catholics from referring to Protestant churches as "churches," naming them "ecclesial communities" (parachurch organizations). Like John Paul II, Benedict spoke against the materialism of Western society and urged governments to give greater attention to the stewardship of God's creation.

Benedict XVI stunned the world by resigning from office and going into retirement, a rare event in Catholic history. Most popes, like John Paul II and his immediate predecessors, have died in office. The cardinals of the church elected an Argentinian Jesuit his successor; he took the papal name Francis (without a numeral because he is the first pope with that name). Pope Francis (2013–present) has signaled a new, special emphasis on "mercy" as the theme of his papacy. His style of leadership has been markedly different, less formal and imperial, from that of Benedict XVI.

In 1968, Pope Paul VI reaffirmed the official church position against any form of artificial birth control in the encyclical *Humanae Vitae*. Many theologians, priests, and laity protested this strict interpretation of sexuality, but the bishops of many industrialized nations, such as France, Canada, Belgium, Holland, Switzerland, Austria, and West Germany, interpreted the papal position in the light of freedom of the individual conscience.

Dissension has been a common feature in contemporary Catholic life in the United States, and many Catholics make their own judgments on birth control, abortion, the role of women in the church, and the official positions of the church on political and economic matters. The evidence of ecclesiastical misconduct on the part of bishops has encouraged further dissent in the church and has contributed to the decline in membership in the American church. Many of the newer Catholic denominations were formed in response to the growing conservatism of the Roman Catholic Church in the late twentieth century. Most of these new churches reject papal teaching on birth control, abortion, women's ordination, and homosexuality.

Another issue facing the church worldwide, including in the United States, is the effect of Protestant movements on Catholicism. The charismatic movement began making inroads in Catholic parishes in the 1970s, and now the number of "Spirit-filled" Catholics—that is, those who believe in and claim charismatic gifts, such as speaking in tongues, healing, interpretation, and prophecy—is well over three hundred thousand. Politically conservative but liturgically innovative, it is not clear how these "born again" Catholics will fit into the emerging church. Worldwide the Catholic Church has lost many members to Pentecostal churches, especially in Latin America.

SUGGESTIONS FOR FURTHER READING

Bokenkotter, Thomas S. *Concise History of the Catholic Church*. Rev. ed. New York: Image Books, 1990.

Chinnici, Joseph. *Living Stones: The History and Structure of Catholic Spiritual Life in the United States*. New York: MacMillan, 1989.

Dolan, Jay P. *In Search of an American Catholicism: A History of Religion and Culture in Tension*. New York: Oxford University Press, 2002.

Greeley, Andrew M. *The Catholic Myth: The Behavior and Beliefs of American Catholics*. New York: Charles Scribners' Sons, 1990.

Johnson, Kevin Orlin. *Why Do Catholics Do That? A Guide to the Teachings and Practices of the Catholic Church*. New York: Ballantine, 1995.

Mann, Arthur. *The One and the Many: Reflections on the American Identity*. Chicago, IL: University of Chicago Press, 1979.

Orsi, Robert A. *The Madonna of 115th Street: Faith and Community in Italian Harlem, 1880–1950*. New Haven, CT: Yale University Press, 1985.

Pruter, Karl. *A History of the Old Catholic Church*. Scottsdale, AZ: St. Willibrord's Press, 1973.

AMERICAN CATHOLIC CHURCH IN THE UNITED STATES

Founded: 1999
Membership: 5,500 in 14 parishes (2015)

The American Catholic Church in the United States (ACCUS) was founded in response to the growing conservatism in the Roman Catholic Church. It seeks to continue the reforms of the Second Vatican Council, and it welcomes those who have felt alienated in other churches. It does not exclude people from the sacraments because of marital status or sexual orientation. The church defines its ministry in terms of compassion rather than doctrine, and it offers support for persons facing difficult medical decisions. Priests are expected to have outside employment and receive no salary for administering the sacraments. There is also a zero tolerance policy for sexual abuse by clergy. The ACCUS has no connections to the Roman Catholic Church or the Old Catholic Churches but claims to be in apostolic succession. The liturgy is Catholic and the seven traditional sacraments are the basis of devotion. The founding bishop was Lawrence J. Harms who was succeeded by Archbishop William Johnson.

For more information: www.accus.us

Headquarters: 5595 Rivendell Place, Frederick, MD 21703-8673.

THE CATHOLIC CHURCH IN THE UNITED STATES (ROMAN CATHOLIC CHURCH)

Founded: ca. 60 CE (came to the United States in the sixteenth century)
Membership: 68 million in 18,199 parishes (2012)

The Roman Catholic Church is the largest single religious body in the United States and has the oldest continuous institutional existence. Nearly one in four Americans is a member of the Catholic Church, but over 30 percent of Americans were raised Catholic. Catholicism offers one of the most comprehensive and sophisticated theological systems of any religion. Moreover, the Catholic Church in the United States has played a very prominent role in the promotion of social justice, peace, religious toleration, and economic improvement. The church has had a profound impact on American society through its numerous educational and medical facilities. Many of the nation's most respected political figures were nurtured in the Catholic faith.

Officially, the Roman Catholic Church traces its beginning from the moment of Christ's selection of the apostle Peter as guardian of the keys of heaven and earth and chief of the apostles (Matt 16:18-19). Although the basic liturgy, doctrine, and organization of the Catholic Church are standard throughout the United States, there is a great deal of diversity on the local level. Much popular Catholic devotion focuses on the praying of the rosary and veneration of Mary, the mother of Jesus. Parishes offer a variety of groups for fostering greater devotion and personal piety.

Structure. The government of the Roman Catholic Church is hierarchical, but Vatican II, the twenty-first "ecumenical council," encouraged more lay participation in parishes. At the head of the structure stands the pope, who is also bishop of Rome and "Vicar of Christ on earth and the Visible Head of the Church." His authority is supreme in all matters of faith and discipline. Next is the College of Cardinals. Although laypeople once were appointed as cardinals, the office has been limited to priests since 1918. Many cardinals live in Rome, acting as advisers to the pope or as heads or members of the various congregations or councils that supervise the administration of the church. When a pope dies, cardinals elect the successor and hold authority in the interim. The Roman Curia is the official body of administrative offices through which the pope governs the church. It is composed of Roman congregations, tribunals, and pontifical councils and acts with the delegated authority of the pope.

In the United States an archbishop is in charge of an archdiocese and has precedence in that province. Bishops, who lead dioceses, are appointed by Rome, usually upon suggestions from the United States hierarchy. They are the ruling authorities in the dioceses, but appeals from their decisions may be taken to the apostolic delegate at Washington, DC.

The parish priest, responsible to the bishop, is assigned by the bishop or archbishop and holds authority to celebrate Mass and administer the sacraments with the help of such other priests as the parish may need. Priests are educated in theological seminaries, typically connected to Roman Catholic colleges and universities. The usual course of study covers a period of eight years—four years of philosophy and four years of theology. Those in religious orders also spend one or two years in a novitiate.

The clergy of the church also include deacons. Since the restoration of the Permanent Diaconate in 1967, more than eleven thousand people have completed the training course and been ordained deacons. Most of these deacons are married and over the age of thirty-five. They are empowered to preach, baptize, distribute Holy Communion, and officiate at weddings. Deacons typically support themselves in secular jobs and exercise their ministry during weekends and evenings.

Three ecclesiastical councils form an important part of the Roman Catholic system: (1) the general, or ecumenical, council is called by the pope or with his consent. It is composed of all the bishops, and its actions on matters of doctrine and discipline must be approved by the pope; (2) the plenary, or national, council is made up of the bishops of a given country; its acts, too, must be submitted to the Holy See; (3) provincial and diocesan councils make further promulgation and application of the decrees passed by the other councils and approved by the pope.

With the most centralized government in Christendom, the Holy See at Rome has representatives in many countries of the world. Roman Catholic churches have been established in over 230 countries, with a total membership of more than one billion. The majority of Italians, Spanish, Irish, Austrians, Poles, Latin Americans, Belgians, Hungarians, southern Germans, Portuguese, French, and Filipinos are baptized Roman Catholics. The Society for the Propagation of the Faith is the overall representative missionary body.

Almost every diocese publishes a weekly newspaper; more than four hundred Catholic newspapers and magazines are published in the United States and Canada. Some of the largest and most influential periodicals are *The National Catholic Reporter, Commonweal, America, Columbia, United States Catholic, St. Anthony Messenger, Catholic Digest, Catholic World, Ligourian, Catholic Twin Circle,* and *The National Catholic Register.*

Ethnic Parishes. One of the major issues that has faced the Roman Catholic Church in the United States is immigration. Catholics in Europe were united in their obedience to Rome, but they were organized on national lines. Spaniards had Spanish priests, Spanish bishops, and venerated Spanish saints. Likewise, the Catholic churches of Ireland,

Germany, France, Poland, and elsewhere had their own national character. There was often great tension between ethnic groups, and there was a correspondingly strong impulse for these ethnic identities to determine the structure of the Catholic Church in America. In other words, there were those who wanted to recreate the old national churches on American soil with separate hierarchies for each major ethnic group. There would have been many Catholic churches loyal to Rome, but separated from each other in the United States. This would have been similar to the Lutheran* pattern in America. James Cardinal Gibbons (1834–1921) in the late nineteenth century charted the course that led to a parochial system in which local parishes could be organized on ethnic lines, but the national church would be a single American church. Thus diversity and unity were preserved.

There is much that Catholics share in common; however, it is important to note the rich diversity of traditions within Catholicism in the United States, even in a single metropolitan area. When immigrants arrive in this country, they tend to group in neighborhoods in major cities and there re-create some familiar features of the Old World. Thus, although the basic elements of the Mass are the same in every Roman Catholic parish and the same high holy days are observed, at the local level there are many variations liturgically and in popular devotion. A sampling of a few of the major Catholic ethnic groups within the United States includes:

Irish. It is estimated that more than four million people fled Ireland for the United States during the nineteenth century, joining at least one hundred thousand more who arrived before the American Revolution. Irish emigration was connected with the subjugation of Ireland to the British Crown. Once Protestantism was firmly established in England, Catholicism became a mark of national resistance for the native Irish who clung tenaciously to their faith.

In the New World, Catholicism continued to be a bond among the immigrants and to the homeland. Countless Irish benevolent and mutual aid societies were established in the United States, often with a close connection to the church. Saint Patrick's Day became a major holiday in many northern cities and an expression of Irish pride. From the time of the first American bishop, John Carroll, to the present more dioceses and archdioceses have had prelates of Irish descent than of any other nationality. In many ways, the Irish have largely defined American Catholicism, and it was a bishop of Irish descent, James Gibbons, who established the pattern for Catholicism in America.

Italians. By 1908 more than two and half million persons had emigrated from Italy to the United States, settling mainly in the major cities of the Northeast, particularly New York City, and the upper Midwest. The Franciscans provided most of the pastoral leadership for Italian immigrants. Notable among them were Father Pamfilo da Magliano, founder of St. Bonaventure's College at Allegany, New York (1858), and Father Leo Paccillio, pastor of the first Italian parish in New York, St. Anthony's. The Franciscans were followed by the Jesuits, the Scalabrini Fathers, the Salesians, the Passionists, and the Augustinians. In some cases priests of other nationalities learned Italian in order to minister to the needs of the Italians in areas where no Italian priest was available. Italian Catholics continued to honor the patron saints of their native Italian towns, naming benevolent societies after them and holding parish festivals on the saints' days. Particularly important in this regard have been St. Anthony and St. Joseph.

Poles. Poland gradually disappeared as a political entity during the eighteenth century as Russia, Prussia, and Austria divided the territory among them. Partition, however, did not destroy Polish identity or patriotism. Particularly in western Poland, German efforts to assimilate the Poles into German Protestant culture served to heighten devotion to the Roman Catholic Church. There were Poles in the United States during colonial days, and some served prominently in the American Revolution; but the immigration of the Polish masses began in the 1850s. In 1851, Father Leopold Moczygemba (1824–91), a Franciscan, came to the United States and soon after induced nearly one hundred families from Upper Silesia to come to Panna Maria, Texas, where they built the first Polish church in the United States in 1855. Immigration, particularly from Polish Prussia, increased rapidly, primarily to Illinois, Michigan, and Pennsylvania. By 1890 there were some 130 Polish churches. Most of the schools were conducted by the Felician Sisters and the School Sisters of Notre Dame. The election of the first Polish pope, John Paul II, in 1978 was a great boon to Polish Catholics in the United States

Hispanic. Catholicism came to the New World primarily by way of Spain, whose monarchs were strong supporters of the Counter Reformation. The first universities in the Americas were founded in the Spanish colonies, and indigenous cultures blended with the religious practices of the conquering Spaniards to create a great variety of vibrant subcultures of the faith. Missionaries to the American Southwest made some progress in converting native peoples, and by 1800 beautiful adobe missions dotted the West.

For most of United States history, Mexicans have been the dominant Hispanic group, and in some cities it is common to see devotion to the Virgin of Guadalupe and the spectacular Day of the Dead festival, which is celebrated around the time of Halloween. Since World War II immigration has increased from other Latin American countries, making the Hispanic population the fastest growing portion of the Roman Catholic Church in the United States.

By 1970, a quarter of Catholics in the United States spoke Spanish, and in that year the first Mexican American Catholic bishop, Patricio F. Flores, was consecrated in San Antonio. During the 1970s, an organization of Hispanic priests called PADRES (Priests for Religious, Educational, and Social Rights) worked effectively to focus the church's attention to the special needs of the often-neglected but rapidly growing Spanish-speaking population. In large part due to a shortage of priests and economic distress, there has not been as great a tendency among Hispanic Catholics toward the creation of parishes along national lines as there was among Europeans in nineteenth century. Some parishes do primarily use Spanish, and many parochial schools teach in Spanish. But in general there has been a greater blending of immigrants from different Latin American countries and cultures than was the case with European immigrants in the nineteenth century.

Catholicism Today. The Roman Catholic Church remains a strong, vibrant, and growing religious body in the United States, but it also reflects the diversity and divisions in American society generally. By the end of the twentieth century, conservative Catholics often found they had more in common with conservative evangelicals, despite their differing theologies, than with more liberal Catholics. Catholics and evangelicals often joined forces to oppose abortion and LGBT rights. At the same time, progressive Catholics often find concord with liberal Protestants on social issues. The doctrinal unity of the Roman Catholic Church is found in the ancient creeds of Christianity and in the decrees of the ecumenical councils; it may be found in official summary form in the Catechism of the Catholic Church of 1992, which was promulgated by Pope John Paul II. It is published in book form in English by the United States Conference of Catholic Bishops and is readily available to read on the Internet at: http://ccc.usccb.org/flipbooks/catechism/index.html. In spite of this doctrinal unity, one can find tremendous diversity among Roman Catholics in the United States—perhaps more so than anywhere else in the world. One may observe a "charismatic mariachi mass" at a Catholic cathedral in Texas and a traditional Latin Mass at a Catholic church in Minnesota and an outdoors Mass among the homeless in an urban center in Colorado. Some US Catholic priests favor liberation theology; others favor neo-Pentecostalism. There is no accurate stereotype of all Catholics in the United States.

For more information: www.usccb.org

Headquarters: United States Conference of Catholic Bishops, 3211 Fourth Street, Washington, DC 20017

EASTERN RITE CATHOLIC, UNIATE CHURCHES

Founded: various dates
Membership: est. 500,000 (2000)

The Eastern Rite churches hold a special position within the Roman Catholic Church. Historically and liturgically they are closely related to the Eastern Orthodox churches, but each has chosen to come under the jurisdiction of the Roman Catholic Church while preserving its own distinctive language, rites, and canon law. Most of these churches, for instance, are permitted to have married clergy and have always served both the bread and the wine of the Eucharist to the laity.

There are five major families of Uniate churches: Alexandrian (Copts and Ethiopians); Antiochene (Maronites, Syrians, Malankarese); Armenian, Chaldean (Chaldean and Malabarese); and Byzantine (Hungarian, Yugoslav, Melkites, Ukrainian). The largest Eastern Rite church is the Ukrainian Catholic Church, which was formed when Ukrainian subjects of the king of Poland were united with Rome in 1596. This church was outlawed by the Soviet Union following World War II, but has resumed open activity since the collapse of the USSR. The Maronites of Lebanon established ties with Rome during the Crusades.

Each of the Eastern Rite churches is headed by its own patriarch who has jurisdiction over the bishops, the clergy, and the people of that rite. All of the patriarchs are members of the Congregation for the Oriental Churches, which governs the relations of the Vatican with the Eastern Rite Churches.

ECUMENICAL CATHOLIC CHURCHES IN THE UNITED STATES

Two Catholic denominations in the United States share the name "Ecumenical Catholic" and exist apart from the Roman Catholic Church in order to create "space" for Catholic Christians to worship and practice their faith in a more liberal or progressive atmosphere. Both exist somewhat in reaction to the perceived conservative reaction to Vatican II that set in during the papacy of John Paul II. Both claim apostolic succession and ordain women to the priesthood; both are also "welcoming and affirming" with regard to gay and lesbian people. Both also permit use of artificial birth control methods. Both trace their roots to the Old Catholic Church movement in Europe. (See Old Catholic Churches.)

THE ECUMENICAL CATHOLIC CHURCH+USA

Founded: 2003
Membership: est. 2000, members in 4 churches

The Ecumenical Catholic Church (ECC) is part of the Old Catholic movement that was founded in response to the increasingly conservative direction of the Roman Catholic Church in the nineteenth century. It claims to be "An Old Catholic Church in name, spirit, and polity." Like other Old Catholic churches it does not recognize the infallibility of the bishop of Rome, the pope. The ECC defines itself as Catholic in doctrine and liturgy, and it considers its bishops to be in apostolic succession from Peter. However, it also sees its mission as "a response to the messianic call of the Spirit to preach the Gospel of liberation and justice; to offer a refuge in Christ for those who suffer prejudice; to stand open to dialogue with others so called and, to conform our lives to the life and teachings of the Lord Jesus Christ." In specific it promotes the ordination of women, progressive views of sexuality and birth control, and gives the laity a greater say in the life of the parish than is common in the Roman Catholic Church. While it welcomes all kinds of people into membership, it does not perform same-sex marriages. About 85 percent of the current members were formerly Roman Catholic.

For more information: www.ecc-usa.org

Contact: Vilatte Institute, 1100 Whispering Pines Drive, Dardenne Prairie, MO 63368-6958

THE ECUMENICAL CATHOLIC COMMUNION

Founded 2003
Membership: est. 3000 members, in 40 churches

The Ecumenical Catholic Communion began about the same time as the Ecumenical Catholic Church and, to outsiders, they appear very similar in terms of traditions and ethos. The Ecumenical Catholic Communion also identifies as an Old Catholic Church and was also founded to provide a progressive ethos for Catholic Christians within a traditional liturgy led by priests in apostolic succession. The "ecumenical" refers to the fact that the church welcomes all Christians to the sacrament of the Eucharist. The church also ordains women, permits priests to marry, and sanctions use of artificial birth control. The church also approves of and performs same-sex marriages.

For more information: www.catholiccommunion.org

Contact: Ecumenical Catholic Communion, 483 East Lockwood Avenue Suite 3, Webster Grove, MO 63119

OLD CATHOLIC CHURCHES

Founded: 1871 (came to the United States in 1914)
Membership: statistics not available

Old Catholic churches in the United States are an outgrowth of the Old Catholic movement, centered in the See of Utrecht in the Netherlands. Conflicts between Dutch Catholics and the papacy date to the Jansenist controversy over grace and determinism in the eighteenth century, which resulted in a schism in the Roman Catholic Church in Holland. The schismatic Dutch body continued its existence into the next century, attracting new followers when Pope Pius IX (1846–78) affirmed the First Vatican Council's statement on papal infallibility in 1870.

A significant number of Swiss, German, and Austrian Roman Catholic priests also refused to accept the doctrine of papal infallibility and were excommunicated in 1871.

Ignatz von Döllinger (1799–1890) presided over a number of conferences attended by Catholics who could not accept the new dogma on papal authority and representatives of the Anglican and Lutheran churches in the mid-1870s. Old Catholic bishops were ordained by the bishops of Utrecht and were eventually welcomed into communion with the Anglican Church and several Orthodox bodies.

In 1889 the Declaration of Utrecht was issued as the doctrinal statement of Old Catholics. The declaration affirms the main lines of the Catholic tradition up to about the year 1000. Especially important for the Old Catholics are the first seven ecumenical councils (before the division between East and West) and most of the medieval liturgy. However, the declaration rejected more recent doctrines of the Roman Catholic Church,* especially papal infallibility, the Immaculate Conception of Mary, and compulsory celibacy of the priesthood. The church maintains that the five patriarchal sees of the ancient church remain the equal heads of the church. The Slavic branch of the Old Catholic Church has a separate history.

The Old Catholic movement in the United States first emerged with the work of Père Joseph René Vilatte (1854–1929) in Wisconsin near Green Bay, where several parishes were organized. A group of English-speaking Old Catholics was also gathered together by a former Roman Catholic monk, Augustine de Angelis (William Harding), who had organized a community of men devoted to the Religious Rule of St. Benedict at Waukegan, Illinois, around the turn of the century. The Old Catholic episcopacy in the United States was established in 1914 when the English Archbishop Arnold Harris Matthew (1852–1919) consecrated Bishop de Landas Berghes et de Rache (1873–1920), a prince of the house of Lorraine-Brapan. He was succeeded by Father Carmel Henry Carfora (1878–1958), an Italian Franciscan friar, who led the church until his death in 1958.

At that time, the North American Old Catholics split into several ecclesial bodies, not all recognized by Old Catholics in Europe. Perhaps as many as seventeen bodies have claimed to be Old Catholic in the United States, but the major bodies originating in the Utrecht movement are the Old Catholic Church of America, the Old Roman Catholic Church of North America, the North American Old Catholic Church, the North American Old Roman Catholic Church (Archdiocese of New York), and the Old Roman Catholic Church (English Rite). Most of the Old Catholic churches have fewer than ten parishes in the United States.

In the United States, the Old Catholics often represent a conservative form of Catholicism despite their early identification as "liberal." The sweeping liturgical and devotional changes of the Second Vatican Council led some conservative priests to join the Old Catholics in order to preserve the old traditions, such as prayers for the dead. Several conservative churches in the Anglican* tradition may be classified with the Old Catholic churches as well. Most of these bodies use the 1928 edition of *The Book of Common Prayer,* reject the ordination of women, and emphasize catholic ritual in worship. Most of these bodies would agree with the statement of purpose for the Holy Catholic Church

(Anglican Rite): "to perpetuate the Faith, Order, Worship and Witness of Western Catholicism as it existed in the Church of England from around 200 A.D., to the time of the Great Schism, and set forth by the 'ancient catholic bishops and doctors,' and especially as defined by the Seven Ecumenical Councils of the undivided Church."

Perhaps the main ecclesial expression of the Old Catholic Church in America is the Old Catholic Church in the United States, which considers itself the American independent affiliate of the Old Catholic Confederation that arose out of the Union of Utrecht. The contact information below is for it specifically.

For more information: www.occus.org

Contact: Old Catholic Church in the United States, Saint Willibrord Court, 180 Candy Road, Mohnton, PA 19540

POLISH NATIONAL CATHOLIC CHURCH OF AMERICA

Founded: 1897
Membership: More than 25,000 in 126 parishes (2016)

The Polish National Catholic Church (PNCC), along with a few smaller Slavic national churches in the United States, represents a different type of the Old Catholic movement as Eastern European immigrants sought to have parishes in their native tongue. The Polish body was formally organized at Scranton, Pennsylvania, on March 14, 1897, in protest over the lack of a Polish bishop and a desire to have more control over parish affairs. Some 250 families then began work on a new church, St. Stanislaus, and called a native Pole, Francis Hodur (1866–1953), to be their priest. A constitution for the new church was adopted by the Scranton parish in 1897, claiming the right to control all churches built and maintained by Poles and to administer such property through a committee chosen by each parish. This action was not accepted by authorities in Rome, and Hodur was subsequently excommunicated.

Other Polish parishes followed the Scranton example and began referring to themselves as "National Churches." Joining together, they held their first synod at Scranton in 1904, with almost 150 clerical and lay delegates representing parishes in Pennsylvania, Maryland, Massachusetts, and New Jersey. Hodur was consecrated a bishop in 1907 at Utrecht, Holland, by three bishops of the Old Catholic Church. Following the first synod, the vernacular, first Polish and then English, gradually replaced Latin as the liturgical language. A second synod at Scranton in 1909 officially adopted the church's present name. The PNCC adopted the "Confession of Faith," written by Bishop Hodur, at a general synod in Chicago in 1914.

There are five dioceses: Buffalo-Pittsburgh, Canadian, Central, Eastern, and Western. Polish and English are used in worship and in the educational programs of parish schools taught largely by pastors. Clergy have been allowed to marry since 1921, but only with the knowledge and permission of the bishops. Because of its opposition to the ordination of women, ties between the PNCC and the Old Catholic Church in Utrecht have been severed.

For more information: www.pncc.org
Headquarters: 1004 Pittston Avenue, Scranton, PA 18505

REFORMED CATHOLIC CHURCH

Founded: 1988
Membership: est. 57,000 in 100 parishes (2012)

The Reformed Catholic Church (RCC) is one of several bodies that separated from the Roman Catholic Church in the 1980s in order to promote greater openness to the modern world without denying traditional Catholic worship, spirituality, and sacramental theology. The church seeks to continue the reforming work of Pope John XXIII, whom it regards as a saint. Its constitution, ratified in 2006, describes the RCC as "an affiliation of autonomous member churches whose traditions and sacramental form of worship are Catholic, but who function fully independent of Rome." The church practices open Communion for all Christians regardless of marital status or sexual orientation. It allows the ordination of all people, regardless of sexual orientation or gender identity, and it leaves medical decisions up to individual conscience. Its liturgy is Catholic, but is influenced by Eastern Orthodoxy. It denies the infallibility of the bishop of Rome and is what traditionalist Roman Catholics would call "modernist" in theology and posture toward culture.

The church has close connections to the Old Catholic churches, but most of the clergy and members came from the Roman Catholic Church. It has two dioceses: The Diocese of St. George–Western United States; and the Diocese of St. John XXIII–Eastern United States; led respectively by Presiding Bishops Chris Carter and William Heller.

For more information: www.reformedcatholic.org
Headquarters: PO Box 28710, Columbus, OH 43228

SOCIETY OF SAINT PIUS X

Founded: 1969
Membership: est. 20,000, in 103 chapels

The Society of Pius X views itself as a society of priests within the Roman Catholic Church rather than a separate denomination, but that claim is not recognized by the Vatican. It was founded by Archbishop Marcel Lefebvre, a priest of the Holy Ghost Order who had been bishop of Dakar before returning to his native France in 1962 as bishop of Tulle. He was a vocal opponent of the modernization of the church effected at the Second Vatican Council, and in 1968 resigned as head of the Holy Ghost Order rather than implement the changes required by the Council. The following year he established a conservative seminary, the Society of Pius X, named for the first pope of the twentieth century to be canonized. Pius X was a key figure in resisting secularization and liberalism in France. Although initially supported by Vatican officials, the Society was officially suppressed in 1975. Lefebvre's defiant ordination of twelve traditionalist priests in the following year furthered the separation of the Society from the Vatican.

The major focus of the Society's work is promotion of the traditional Latin Mass and the decrees of the first Vatican Council through an aggressive grassroots campaign. It may seem ironic that a Society that proclaims the doctrine of papal infallibility could rebel against the Vatican and criticize the pope's words and actions, but in their view, the Second Vatican Council and its decrees corrupted the church and the papacy. Priests in the Society attempt (and sometimes succeed) to "liberate" parishes from the modern Mass and restore the pre-Vatican II liturgy. The Society has also founded many chapels around the country. Though stronger in France, Argentina, and Africa, the number of priests and seminarians is growing in the United States. There are about ninety priests in the Society in the United States. There are no membership statistics for the laity since the Society does not view itself as a separate church. The Society operates twenty-three primary schools, one college, four retreat centers, and a seminary. Its publishing house is Angelus Press. In 2008 Pope Benedict XVI welcomed four of the schismatic bishops back into the Catholic fold and gave priests permission to celebrate the Mass in Latin.

For more information: www.sspx.org

Headquarters: Regina Coeli House, 11485 North Farley Road, Platte City, MO 64079

EPISCOPAL AND ANGLICAN CHURCHES

The Episcopal Church has been one of the most influential churches in American history and has provided many national leaders, including presidents, Supreme Court justices, and generals. Episcopalians built numerous educational institutions, hospitals, homes for the elderly, and many of the most beautiful houses of worship in the country. The Episcopal Church and its offshoots trace their origins to the Church of England (the Anglican Church), which severed allegiance to the papacy during the Protestant Reformation. In doing so, however, the Church of England sought to maintain an unbroken historical continuity to the Christian church in England from the early fourth century.

The Anglican Church has often been viewed as a "middle way" between Roman Catholicism and Protestantism. Through the years, there has been tension in Anglican churches between those who favor a more Catholic stance and those who adopt more Protestant principles. The historical succession of bishops, or the episcopacy, is the visible sign of this long tradition of English Christianity. Bishops are recognized as important symbols of unity in the church. The other two orders of ministry are priests and deacons.

Though King Henry VIII first rejected papal supremacy in the 1530s, it was his successors, Edward VI and Elizabeth I, who made the Anglican Church clearly Protestant with the adoption of *The Book of Common Prayer* and the Thirty-Nine Articles of Religion. The so-called Edwardian Homilies, sermons preached by leading Anglican divines (priests, theologians) during the brief reign of Edward VI, have been traditionally viewed by Anglicans as having some special, normative authority for doctrine. In the 1600s Puritans agitated for a more Reformed* style of Christianity, but episcopacy and the prayer book were firmly established in the Anglican Church with the restoration of the monarchy after the English Civil War.

The Anglican theologian Richard Hooker (ca. 1554–1600) helped shape the Anglican approach to worship and theology. He is widely considered to have been the architect of the so-called Elizabethan Settlement that created within the Church of England, and Anglicanism generally, a somewhat uneasy combination of Protestant and Catholic elements. The church's sources of belief and practice are the Bible, the tradition of the church, and reason. Hooker fought against the Puritans, many of whom wanted to discard bishops in favor of a presbyterian or even congregational form of church polity. Hooker won within the Church of England and the worldwide Anglican communion, but many Puritans left them to establish new, "non-conforming," and dissenting denominations without bishops, a union between church and state, and a common prayer book. Hooker also defended apostolic succession, much to the Puritans' dismay. Bishops in Anglican churches, including the Episcopal Church in the United States, stand, like Catholic and Orthodox bishops, in apostolic succession. Aesthetic in orientation, Anglicanism incorporates theology into liturgy and makes use of the senses of sight and taste as well as those of hearing and speaking. This church is distinctive in leaving undefined the exact nature of the presence of Christ in the Eucharist, regarding it as a spiritual mystery. Although Hooker and other early Anglican leaders controversially kept some aspects of Catholic tradition and practice within Anglicanism, the theology of the Thirty-Nine Articles of Religion and the Edwardian Homilies are distinctly Protestant.

The Anglican Church came to America along with English colonization. Francis Fletcher planted a cross and read a prayer when Sir Francis Drake landed on the western coast of North America in 1578, and the first Anglican baptisms were conducted in Sir Walter Raleigh's colony on the Outer Banks of North Carolina. In several colonies, especially in the South, the Church of England was the established church, but many colonists were suspicious of the state church. The Society for the Propagation of the Gospel was established in England in 1701 to help support the poorly paid American clergy and spread the work of the church westward. With this increased support, the church grew in the colonial period. The College of William and Mary in Virginia was established in 1693.

The American Revolution almost destroyed the colonial Church of England since clergy had to choose whether to flee to England or Canada, remain as Loyalists in the face of persecution, or break their vows of allegiance. Many leaders of the American cause, including George Washington and Patrick Henry, were Anglicans, but in the popular mind, episcopacy was associated with the British Crown rather than with independence. At war's end the church in America had no bishop, no association of the churches, and not even the semblance of an establishment, but the clergy who remained in the new nation reorganized the church.

In 1783 a conference of the Anglican churches met at Annapolis, Maryland, and they formally adopted the name "Protestant Episcopal Church." Also in 1783, the clergy in Connecticut elected Samuel Seabury (1729–96) as their prospective bishop. He went to England to be consecrated but was denied by the English bishops. He then went to Scotland and obtained consecration there in 1784. Two other bishops-elect (from New York and Pennsylvania) were consecrated by the Archbishop of Canterbury in 1787 in recognition of the legitimacy of the American church. In 1789, the church constitution was adopted and *The Book of Common Prayer* was revised for American use, removing prayers for the British monarch.

The Anglican Church spread to all parts of the British Empire in the eighteenth and nineteenth centuries thanks to a vigorous mission program. There are about eighty-five million members of the Anglican Communion worldwide and forty-four national or regional churches. The episcopacy remains a glue that holds this diverse and active church together. The Archbishop of Canterbury functions as the titular head of the Anglican Communion, and the primates (highest ranking bishop of a national or regional church) meet regularly to discuss common mission and doctrine. After World War II, immigrants from former British colonies began moving to England and America in large numbers, bringing their forms of Anglicanism with them.

The Book of Common Prayer has been one of the glues uniting the Anglican Communion worldwide, the Episcopal Church in the United States, and other American Anglican churches. Two sacraments, baptism and the Eucharist, are recognized by Anglican churches as "certain sure witnesses and effectual agencies of God's love and grace." Baptism by any church in the name of the Trinity is recognized as valid. Without defining the holy mystery, the Episcopal Church believes in the real presence of Christ in the elements of the Eucharist. The church also recognizes a sacramental character in confirmation, penance, orders, matrimony, and the anointing of the sick.

So-called Anglo-Catholics in the church emphasize the church's roots in the Roman Catholic Church* and promote dialogue with the Catholic and Orthodox churches aimed at eventual reunion. They are sometimes referred to as "high church" because of their use of incense and other liturgical features associated with the High Mass. The "low church" perspective emphasizes the Anglican Church's roots in the Protestant Reformation. In the late nineteenth century, there was a desire for a greater sense of catholicity in the Episcopal Church. At the Lambeth Conference in Chicago in 1886, the bishops developed the Quadrilateral, which governs Anglican ecumenical discussion. The four key points of ecclesiology are: the Bible, the ancient ecumenical creeds, the sacraments of baptism and Eucharist, and the historic episcopacy. During the 1960s the Episcopal Church began to fragment theologically with some congregations embracing the charismatic movement and evangelical theology, and with others embracing very liberal theology and emphasizing progressive social justice as the main mission of the church.

During the first decades of the twenty-first century, Anglicanism worldwide has been racked with controversy over the United States' Episcopal Church's acceptance of openly gay and lesbian priests and bishops. Normally there can be only one united Anglican denomination per nation state or territory, but that tradition has been challenged as new breakaway groups of Anglicans have separated to protest what they regard as declension from biblical and traditional beliefs and practices. In 2016 the Anglican Communion suspended the Episcopal Church and temporarily recognized its breakaway group, the Anglican Church in North America, as its United States affiliate.

During the same time some US Episcopal and Anglican churches reached out to African Anglican bishops to come under their jurisdiction. In almost every case this was due to the Episcopal Church's perceived leniency with regard to openly gay and lesbian bishops and priests.

In 2008 a new organization called Global Anglican Future Conference (GAFCON) held its first meeting in Jerusalem with more than one thousand Anglican "witnesses" from around the world attending. Its clear purpose was to oppose perceived doctrinal and ethical changes within some Anglican churches. The catalyst for this new conference, which threatens to become an alternative to the Anglican Communion, is probably the consecration of gay and lesbian priests and bishops by some Anglican churches—especially the Episcopal Church in the United States. GAFCON held its second meeting in Nairobi, Kenya, in 2013. About thirteen hundred delegates attended representing thirty-eight nations and twenty-seven provinces of the Anglican Communion. A third meeting is scheduled for 2018 in Jerusalem.

SUGGESTIONS FOR FURTHER READING

Albright, Raymond W. *A History of the Protestant Episcopal Church.* New York: MacMillan, 1964.

Butler, Diana Hochstedt. *Standing against the Whirlwind: Evangelical Episcopalians in Nineteenth-Century America.* New York: Oxford University Press, 1995.

Caldwell, Sandra M., and Ronald J. Caldwell. *The History of the Episcopal Church in America, 1607–1991: A Bibliography.* New York: Garland Publishing, 1993.

Konolige, Kit. *The Power of Their Glory: America's Ruling Class, the Episcopalians.* New York: Wyden Books, 1978.

Prelinger, Catherine M. *Episcopal Women: Gender, Spirituality, and Commitment in an American Mainline Denomination.* New York: Oxford University Press, 1995.

Prichard, Robert W. *A History of the Episcopal Church.* Harrisburg, PA: Morehouse, 1991.

Woolverton, John Frederick. *Colonial Anglicanism in North America.* Detroit, MI: Wayne State University Press, 1984.

ANGLICAN CHURCH IN NORTH AMERICA

Founded: 2009
Membership: est. 112,504, in 983 churches (2016)

The Anglican Church in North America (ACNA) was officially formed in 2009, in the wake of the controversy surrounding the consecration of the Right Reverend Gene Robinson as bishop of the New Hampshire diocese of the Episcopal Church in 2003.

The ACNA objected to the consecration of an openly gay man to the episcopacy, especially when this was done against the wishes of the majority of primates in the Anglican Communion. The ACNA was a merger of many organizations that came out of that controversy, including the Anglican Mission in the Americas, the Convocation of Anglicans in North America, the American Anglican Council, and the Anglican Network in Canada. The Reformed Episcopal Church is also included as a founding member. Unlike the various Continuing Anglican Churches, the Anglican Church in North America is committed to remaining in the worldwide Anglican Communion, and some of the primates in the Anglican Communion, including a former archbishop of Canterbury, have supported the efforts of parishes and even dioceses to break with the Episcopal Church. There have been a number of court cases throughout the United States as parishes have attempted to leave the Episcopal Church while retaining possession of their buildings and other property. For the most part, the courts have recognized the legal claims of the Episcopal Church. In 2009 the Church of Nigeria became the first church in the Anglican Communion to formally recognize the ACNA and enter into full communion with the church. More important, the Church of Nigeria recognized the ACNA as its partner in North America rather than the Episcopal Church. The ACNA has also been recognized by the Church of Uganda, the Anglican Province of the Southern Cone, and the Church of the Province of Southeast Asia. As of 2016 the Anglican Church in North America is the recognized affiliate of the Anglican Communion in the United States while the Episcopal Church is on suspended status. Also in 2016 another North American Anglican group called PEARUSA (The North American Missionary District of Province de L'Eglise Anglicane Au Rwanda) joined the ACNA. Also, The Convocation of Anglicans in North America, a "continuing Anglican" communion, is now a "jurisdiction" within the ACNA.

According to the church's mission statement, it exists "to bring the good news of Jesus Christ, as expressed in the Anglican tradition, both to those who have never heard it, and to those in our Church who have been given a 'different gospel.' We are committed to missionary work and church planting in North America and throughout the world. We especially seek to support the spiritually vibrant but materially poor ministries of our fellow Anglicans in the Global South." Ordained persons can affiliate directly with the ACNA, but laity may do so only through parishes or dioceses. The church is seeking to be recognized as a national province of the Anglican Communion. Robert Duncan was installed as the first archbishop and primate of the ACNA in June 2009. He was succeeded in that role by Foley Beach in 2014. The church has parishes all over the United States and Canada, with large concentrations in Pennsylvania, Virginia, Texas, and Southern California.

For more information: www.anglicanchurch.net

Headquarters: 800 Maplewood Avenue, Ambridge, PA 15003

ANGLICAN PROVINCE OF AMERICA

Founded: 1998 with roots to 1968
Membership: est. 4,000, in 50 congregations

The Anglican Province of America (APA) was founded in 1998 but says its history stretches back to 1968 with the founding of the American Episcopal Church, which was a result of perceived liberalizing trends in the Episcopal Church in the United States. The APA is in communion with a number of other relatively conservative Anglican communions within the United States, including the Anglican Church of North America. The church is divided into three dioceses by regions of the United States: East, Middle America, and West. The presiding bishop is Walter Grundorf. The APA is a relatively traditionalist church that uses the 1928 American edition of the Anglican *Book of Common Prayer* and practices "closed Communion." The church has congregations in India, Ecuador, Haiti, and the Philippines. Like other "continuing Anglican" churches, ordination is restricted to heterosexual men. This denomination is mentioned here as a particular example of the many "continuing Anglican" groups that have emerged in the United States since 1977. (See Continuing Anglican Churches on the following page.)

For more information: www.anglicanprovince.org

Headquarters: 3348 West State Road 426, Oviedo, FL 32765

COMMUNION OF EVANGELICAL EPISCOPAL CHURCHES

Founded: 1997
Membership: Unknown*

The Communion of Evangelical Episcopal Churches (CEEC) grew out of the worldwide Convergence Movement inspired largely by the works of British theologian and missionary Lesslie Newbigin (1908–98) of the Church of South India in the 1940s. Newbigin proposed that the fullness of the body of Christ required a flowing together of several "streams" of Christianity: the Catholic emphases of "incarnation and creation"; the Protestant focus on "biblical proclamation and conversion"; and the Orthodox or Pentecostal experience of "the mystical and the Spirit." Newbigin's vision played a key role in the formation of the Church of South India out of five different churches that received apostolic succession through Anglican bishops in India. Thus, the Convergence Movement brings together liturgical and charismatic churches around the world, using the Lambeth Quadrilateral of Anglicanism as a guiding principle.

In the United States, Robert Webber (1933–2007), a professor at Wheaton College, encouraged evangelical leaders to take the early church seriously as a model for the modern church. He personally moved from a fundamentalist evangelical background into the

Anglican tradition and numerous Wheaton students followed him. A handful of participants in the Vineyard movement and other liturgically minded charismatics and evangelicals gathered in 1993 to discuss the "streams of Christianity" idea. This led to more serious discussion, and Bishop Michael Owen agreed to be the chief consecrator for the first two bishops of an American network of Convergence churches. Russell McClanahan and John Kivuva were so consecrated at a service in Virginia in 1995. In 1997 this new group of Anglican churches was incorporated as the Communion of Evangelical Episcopal Churches. The CEEC is in communion with the larger, worldwide Communion of Convergence Churches, now known as Christian Communion International, rather than with the Anglican Communion.

The CEEC is theologically conservative but not fundamentalist. Many regard it as an American alternative to the liberal-leaning Episcopal Church. It uses *The Book of Common Prayer* in worship and follows apostolic succession for leadership (bishops). It regards and advertises itself as a communion of Anglican churches in the historical and theological, but not organizational, continuity with the Church of England. Clearly, however, it has added to that the dimension of being charismatic and evangelical. The CEEC does ordain women but does not ordain openly gay or lesbian people.

For more information: www.theceec.org

Headquarters: 6620 Southpoint Drive, Suite 302, Jacksonville, FL 32216

*Attempts to obtain this information have been unsuccessful.

CONTINUING ANGLICAN CHURCHES

Founded: 1977
Membership: statistics not available, but est. over 100,000 in over 1,000 parishes

"Continuing Anglican Churches" or "Continuing Episcopal Churches" are not denominations but a category composed of several relatively small Anglican and Episcopal denominations that separated from the Episcopal Church over a perceived modernist drift in that denomination. Some Continuing churches would say they did not exactly "separate" from anyone but started up to provide a more traditionalist doctrine and form of worship than was previously available to Episcopal people in the United States. These churches have tended to "come and go" as they join with each other in various arrangements of mutual understanding, intercommunion, splits, and mergers.

Some observers date the origin of the Continuing Anglican movement in the United States to an international Congress of Concerned Churchmen comprised of nearly two thousand Anglican bishops, clergy, and laypeople. They met in 1977 in Saint Louis to voice their opposition to changes in the Episcopal Church, particularly the ordination of women and revisions to the prayer book. The Affirmation of Saint Louis, which affirms traditional teachings as unalterable, serves as a primary doctrinal statement for several small bodies that were formed in the wake of the Saint Louis meeting. They call themselves "continuing" Episcopal churches in opposition to the Episcopal Church, which they declared out of continuity with traditional Anglican teaching. The traditionalist churches promote the canon of scripture, the creeds and statements of the seven ecumenical councils of the early church, the 1928 edition of *The Book of Common Prayer*, the writings of the church fathers, and the historic succession of male bishops, priests, and deacons.

These churches often see themselves as being in communion with the Eastern Orthodox and Roman Catholic churches because of their common affirmation of the decrees of the ecumenical councils before the division of 1054. Despite their common affirmation of the historical episcopacy, the continuing churches have had difficulty remaining in communion with one another or with Eastern Orthodox or the Roman Catholic Church.

The Anglican Catholic Church was a direct result of the 1977 Saint Louis meeting. Its first constitution was adopted in 1978. The Province of Christ the King separated in 1979 and has about fifty parishes nationwide. The United Episcopal Church separated in 1980 and has about twenty parishes. The Anglican Rite Jurisdiction of the Americas was established in 1991 through a merger of the American Episcopal Church and a sizable portion of the Anglican Catholic Church. Also notable is the Evangelical Anglican Church of America, based in California, which draws upon the heritage of the eighteenth-century evangelists John Wesley and George Whitefield to promote both personal conversion and traditional Anglican ritual. Similar to that group is the Communion of Evangelical Episcopal Churches, which also considers itself a continuing Anglican church but with a strong influence from American evangelical leaders including charismatics, neo-Pentecostals, and "Third Wave" teachers and evangelists.

Many traditionalist Anglican bodies adopt much of the practice of Eastern Orthodoxy* or identify themselves as part of the Old Catholic movement.* When the Reverend James Parker Dees resigned from the priesthood of the Protestant Episcopal Church in 1963 to protest "its failure to proclaim firmly the biblical doctrine, and . . . its emphasis on the social gospel and pro-communist program," he founded the Anglican Orthodox Church. Dees was consecrated bishop by Bishop Wasyl Sawyna of the Holy Ukrainian Autocephalic Orthodox Church and Bishop Orlando J. Woodward of the Old Catholic succession. The church is headquartered in North Carolina, but is in communion with bodies in Africa and Asia. It emphasizes the doctrines of the virgin birth, the atoning sacrifice of the cross, the Trinity, the bodily resurrection of Jesus, the second coming, salvation by faith alone, and the divinity of Christ. A split led to the formation of the Episcopal Orthodox Christian Archdiocese of America, which came under the jurisdiction of the Anglican Rite Synod in the Americas in 1999. That body, in turn, is under the jurisdiction of the Philippine Independent Catholic Church. Along with other traditionalists groups around the world, they are part of the Orthodox Anglican Communion.

Likewise, the Anglican Rite Archdiocese of the Americas is a traditional Anglican body that uses the 1928 edition of *The Book of Common Prayer* and the Anglican Missal. It is in alliance with the Orthodox Church of Canada; therefore it claims membership in the "oldest denomination in the world." The church holds to the seven sacraments and the teachings of early Christianity and believes that other churches "diminish" the true faith through "social teachings" and political correctness. The church also identifies itself as "a safe harbor" from political and theological battles in other churches.

One particular denomination of "continuing Anglicans" has emerged during the second decade of the twenty-first century—in America—as the largest and most influential. It is the Anglican Church of North America mentioned earlier. The Anglican Province of America, also mentioned (with its own entry) earlier, is also considered a "continuing Anglican" church. The lists of continuing Anglican and Episcopal churches in North America constantly shifts; most scholars agree, however, that there are well over one thousand continuing Anglican or Episcopal churches in the United States.

One "umbrella" organization of Continuing Anglican Churches in America is the Federation of Anglican Churches in the Americas (FACA) founded in 2006. It includes six Anglican, Episcopal, or similar jurisdictions (denominations or sub-denominations, dioceses within other denominations), all of which are considered traditionalist compared with the Episcopal Church. All are creedal, liturgical, and sacramental; and all reject doctrinal and practical innovations introduced within the Episcopal Church that put it in tension with traditional interpretations of the Bible, some African and Asian Anglicans, and traditional Christian moral norms.

For more information: www.anglicansonline.org; www.anglicancatholic.org; www.anglicanprovince.org; www.anglicanpck.org; www.theceec.org; www.faca-us.org.

EPISCOPAL CHURCH

Founded: 1789
Membership: est. 2 million, in 6,794 parishes (2012)

The largest body to come out of the Church of England in the United States has been known as the Episcopal Church since 1967. Members of the Episcopal Church profess two of the ancient Christian creeds: the Apostles' Creed and the Nicene Creed. Thirty-five articles, derived from the Church of England's thirty-nine, are accepted as a general statement of doctrine, but adherence to them as a creed is not required.

At their ordination, clergy profess their belief in the scriptures and a willingness to conform to "the doctrine, discipline, and worship of the Episcopal Church." The church expects its members to be loyal to the "doctrine, discipline and worship of the one Holy

Catholic and Apostolic Church" in all the essentials, but permits great liberty in non-essentials. It allows for variation, individuality, independent thinking, and religious liberty. Some Episcopal churches are "high," with elaborate ritual and ceremony; others are described as "low," with a less stylized ceremony and more of an evangelistic emphasis. Liberals, conservatives, modernists, and evangelicals find common ground for worship in the 1979 edition of *The Book of Common Prayer*. Stained-glass windows, gleaming altars, vested choirs, and a glorious ritual give the worshipper a deep sense of the continuity of the Christian spirit and tradition.

The local congregation, or parish, elects its own minister (rector or priest), who is vested with pastoral oversight of the congregation by the bishop. Lay officers administer the temporal affairs and the property of the parish along with the priest or rector. Each parish, mission, and chapel is represented in the annual diocesan convention by its clergy and elected lay delegates. Each diocese is in turn represented in the triennial General Convention of the church by its bishop (or bishops), clergy, and lay deputies. Between sessions of the General Convention, the work of the church is carried on by the presiding bishop and an executive council. The church maintains national headquarters in New York City.

All of the US dioceses are self-supporting with the exception of the Church in Navajoland. The church participates actively with mission work in the Caribbean, South America, and Southeast Asia. The domestic missionary program has traditionally emphasized grants and ministry for urban mission, and ministry to African American, Hispanic, Native American, and Asian American congregations and organizations. In recent years, attention and funding have turned to evangelism and the incorporation of youth in planning and decision-making.

The church sponsors ten accredited seminaries in the United States. There are eight Episcopal colleges and one university in the United States and two colleges overseas. Over one thousand Episcopal schools and early childhood education programs are in operation. Each diocese sponsors social service and health organizations including homes for seniors, youth care, hospitals and hospice centers, and centers for the homeless and destitute. Sixteen religious orders are scattered across the United States; the church also recognizes eleven Christian communities.

When Presiding Bishop John Hines called a Special General Convention in 1969 to address the problems of racial segregation and urban decay, the church entered upon a path of engagement with modernity and American culture. Since then, the church has discussed and debated issues of liturgical reform, equal access to ordination, sexuality, and ecclesiastical authority. Black Episcopalians continue to lead the church in addressing institutional racism and its complicity in the larger problem of racism in America. Women, who had so long provided the energy in labor and fund-raising for the church's missionary work, adjured their "auxiliary" status. This process opened the door to a series of profound changes in the understanding of authority, the stewardship of resources, and the full participation of the faithful in the life of the church.

After much trial and debate, the General Convention adopted a new standard of *The Book of Common Prayer* in 1979. This was the first revision of the American prayer book since 1928, and it provides alternate rites that use more contemporary usage and idiom. A new hymnal, the first since 1940, was approved in 1982. Liturgical reform led directly to a participatory theology that was finally encoded in 1988 into the church's canons emphasizing "the development and affirmation of the ministry of all baptized persons in the Church and in the world," and the full and equal ministry of all the faithful.

Liturgical reform coincided with a vigorous pursuit of women's ordination. Ordination of women to the priesthood finally passed the General Convention in 1976, and in 1989 the Reverend Barbara C. Harris was ordained the Suffragan Bishop of Massachusetts and the first woman bishop in the historic succession. The inclusion of formerly marginalized groups into the circles of governance, program, and ordinary parish life, begun in 1969, continues. In 2003 the church chose to ordain an openly gay bishop, Gene Robinson, of the Diocese of New Hampshire. The ordination of gay and lesbian people and the blessing of same-sex unions promise to be difficult tests for the cohesion of the Episcopal Church, if not its essential unity. In 2009 six bishops requested permission to adapt the wedding ceremony in *The Book of Common Prayer* for use for same-sex couples getting married.

These changes in traditional Episcopal practice set off a firestorm of controversy that led to numerous schisms throughout the 1970s and into the twenty-first century. As mentioned in the previous entry about "Continuing Anglican Churches," the Episcopal Church has lost hundreds of parishes to newly formed traditionalist Anglican and Episcopal denominations. Especially African Anglican bishops have criticized the Episcopal Church and the Anglican Communion, of which they are members, for deviating from perceived traditional moral and theological norms. In 2016 the Anglican Communion voted to suspend the Episcopal Church and invite the Anglican Church of North America, a continuing Anglican denomination, temporarily to become the US affiliate in place of the Episcopal Church.

Through all of the controversy the Episcopal Church has reached out to other Protestant denominations in the United States to establish intercommunion and pulpit exchange in displays of ecumenical good will. In 2000 the Episcopal General Convention approved full formal communion with the Evangelical Lutheran Church in America, and in 2009 full communion with the Moravian Church was approved. Currently there is greater emphasis on domestic evangelism than in the past. In 2006 the church adopted the United Nations Millennium Development Goals as mission goals for the denomination.

For more information: www.episcopalchurch.org

Headquarters: 815 Second Avenue, New York, NY 10017

INTERNATIONAL COMMUNION OF THE CHARISMATIC EPISCOPAL CHURCH

Founded: 1992
Membership: 117 parishes (2009)

Founded by Randolph Adler, this communion seeks to combine Pentecostal or charismatic experience with liturgical worship. Worship is liturgical, but it includes expressions of charismatic gifts, such as speaking in tongues, prophecy, and divine healing through prayer. It is a fellowship of charismatic churches that maintain their identification with traditional Anglicanism. The church is not part of the Anglican Communion, although it has an episcopal structure and many parishes use the 1928 edition of *The Book of Common Prayer*. Tracing its origins to an expressed desire among various evangelicals in the 1970s for connection with "historical Christianity," the church endeavors to bring the rich sacramental and liturgical life of the early church to searching evangelicals and charismatics. It is part of the Convergence Movement inspired by the writings of Lesslie Newbigin and Robert Webber that attempts to bring together three streams of Christianity: charismatic, evangelical, and liturgical-sacramental.

The governance of the church is in the hands of bishops who are understood to be pastors of the church and who must be rectors in their own parishes. In 1996, the church named its first patriarch, Randolph Adler, who had been consecrated a bishop four years earlier. In 1997 all of the clergy of the denomination were ordained by bishops in the Brazilian Catholic Apostolic Church, which was established by Rt. Rev. Carlos Duarte in 1945. Bishop Duarte broke with the Roman Catholic Church because the Vatican had given passports to Nazi war criminals fleeing to Brazil.

The Charismatic Episcopal Church's doctrine was given explicit formulation in the San Clemente Declaration in 1999. Church teaching gives priority to worship and liturgical practice in community life. The church explicitly affirms the authority of the Bible, the first seven ecumenical councils, and the historic episcopacy. It administers the seven traditional sacraments of the Catholic Church. Stressing that it is not a splinter group but an intentional religious community drawing on a rich theological and liturgical heritage, the Communion intends to "provide a home for all Christians who seek a liturgical-sacramental, evangelical, charismatic church and a foundation for their lives and gifts of ministry." The Communion is an international body with more than seventeen hundred parishes worldwide. Its growth has been most dramatic in Africa and South America.

The church in the United States suffered a crisis in 2006 that led to the departure of seven bishops and nearly one-third of the congregants. The church's presiding officers addressed several concerns raised about the denomination, and in 2008 Craig W. Bates was chosen to succeed Adler as the patriarch.

For more information: www.iccec.org

Headquarters: 50 Thomas Place, Malverne, NY 11565

REFORMED EPISCOPAL CHURCH

Founded: 1873
Membership: est. 15,000, in 110 parishes (2009)

The Reformed Episcopal Church was organized in New York City by Bishop George D. Cummins (1822–76), eight clergy, and twenty laypersons who had been members of the Protestant Episcopal Church. This body emerged during the long Tractarian controversy in England and the United States, in which the issues of church ritual and ecclesiastical authority became prominent. Cummins was a leader of the low-church, evangelical party within the Protestant Episcopal Church. He protested what he perceived to be intolerance of other Protestant churches among those influenced by the Oxford Movement, the movement within the church of England that sought to restore pre-Reformation ideas and practices of the church.

In October 1873, Cummins participated in an ecumenical, evangelical Communion service held in Fifth Avenue Presbyterian Church in New York. In the face of public criticism from other bishops, and in the conviction that the ecumenical nature and mission of the Protestant Episcopal Church were being lost, Cummins withdrew to found the new denomination. In 1873 he drew up the Declaration of Principles, which are understood to be the evangelical response to the issues of the nineteenth-century controversies.

Doctrine and organization are similar to those of the parent church, with some notable exceptions. The church affirms that it is: creedal, sacramental, liturgical, and episcopal. Clergy are required to subscribe to the Church of England's Thirty-Nine Articles of Religion, as revised by the Protestant Episcopal Church in 1801. *The Book of Common Prayer* (BCP) has been revised in accordance with the English prayer book tradition, bringing it into conformity with the English 1662 BCP and the American 1928 BCP.

Parish and diocesan units prevail in the administration of the church. The triennial General Council is like the General Convention of the Episcopal Church; however, its bishops do not constitute a separate house. The church has seven dioceses in North America (four in the United States) and carries out oversees work in India, France, Brazil, Liberia, and Germany. There are seminaries in Blue Bell, Pennsylvania; Summerville, South Carolina; and Houston (The Woodlands), Texas. The denomination is one of the founding jurisdictions of the Anglican Church in North America. The Presiding Bishop is the Reverend Royal Grote.

For more information: www.rechurch.org
Headquarters: 4142 Dayflower Drive, Katy, TX 77449

LUTHERAN CHURCHES

In the early sixteenth century, a German theologian named Martin Luther (1483–1546) set out to reform the Roman Catholic Church of his day. Although he did not intend to create a new church, his followers were nicknamed "Lutherans." These Protestants, as they were called after a famous protest at the Diet of Speyer in 1529, affirmed the message of the Bible as the sole authority for church life and Christian belief and practice without rejecting the historical church. To this day, Lutheranism retains much of the tradition of the ancient and medieval church, including a sense of participation in the historic people of God and in the traditional liturgy, revised to accord with Protestant Biblicism. Lutherans are devoted to sound doctrine, systematically developed and expressed in thoughtful preaching. Luther's teachings on the supremacy of scripture over tradition, justification by faith, and on the universal priesthood of believers might be called the cornerstone of Protestantism. However, many Protestants believe neither Luther nor the main Lutheran denominations that began after him practiced these doctrines sufficiently radically. That belief gave rise to many other Protestant denominations and churches.

History. The story of Luther's rebellion against the Roman Catholic Church is well-known. His position, briefly, was that the papacy had no special divine rights in things spiritual. Scripture, not the priest or the church, has final authority over conscience. Luther held that the Bible is the clear, perfect, inspired, and authoritative word of God and guide for humankind. He also believed that the individual conscience is responsible to God alone; therefore all Christians should have access to God's word in the Bible. Luther's translation of the Bible in German remains a hallmark of German literature.

Luther argued that people are forgiven and absolved of their sins, not by good works or by a church rite but by turning from sin directly to God, with the help of the Holy Spirit. Drawing on the writings of the Apostle Paul, Luther declared that justification—reconciliation with God—is attained by grace alone through faith alone, not through good works or sacraments. Faith, for Lutherans, is not subscription to the dictates of the church, but "the heart's utter trust" in Christ. Luther called this theology "evangelical" because it was rooted in the gospel (in Greek *evangelion*) message of justification by faith through grace alone. Contrary to a common belief, however, Luther (and Lutherans) did not reject good works. Luther wrote an entire treatise explaining that good works are the natural result of justification, not its cause. Faith alone brings reconciliation with God to the individual and faith alone is possible only because of God's grace through Jesus Christ and his atoning death and the Holy Spirit's enablement.

In 1529 Luther wrote both his *Large Catechism* and his *Small Catechism*. A year later, Philip Melanchthon (1497–1560) authored the statement of faith known as the Augsburg Confession. The year 1537 brought the Schmalkald Articles of Faith, written by Luther, Melanchthon, and other German Reformers; in 1577, the Formula of Concord was drawn up. These documents, compiled in the *Book of Concord*, offer an explanation of Luther's theology and form the doctrinal basis of Lutheranism. Over the centuries, however, and especially since the Enlightenment and rise of modernity, Lutherans have fallen into disagreement about how strictly to adhere to these doctrinal documents and standards.

Most prominent in Germany, Lutheranism spread to Poland, Russia, Lithuania, Bohemia, Austria, Hungary, France, and Holland. It became the state church of Denmark, Norway, Sweden, Finland, Iceland, Estonia, and Latvia. Each national church developed its own governing structure and style of worship, but most Lutheran churches ascribe to the *Book of Concord* with varying degrees of strictness.

Luther himself never intended to break from the Catholic Church of Rome, but he was excommunicated by the pope due to his challenges to traditional Catholic doctrines and practices, many of which became official at the Council of Trent (1560s) in reaction to Protestant dissents. Luther and his closest faithful followers (many left the Lutheran movement to found, lead, and join other reforming groups) wanted to stay close to some aspects of Catholic and Orthodox teachings and practices. Luther believed, for example, that even Protestant churches should listen to and be guided by the "magistrates"—civil leaders of national and state governments. This led to a major split among early Protestants between the so-called magisterial and radical reformers. Luther and Calvin belonged to the first group; the Anabaptists (e.g., Mennonites) belonged to the second group because they wanted to restore the New Testament church ("radical" means going back to the roots) and cleanse Protestantism of all elements of Catholic tradition. Lutherans have generally held to a theory of "two kingdoms"—God's in and through the church and humans' in and through God-ordained governments. And they have generally believed Christians should submit to human government and cooperate with it so long as it does not violate Christian conscience. Many European Lutheran churches have been "state churches"—supported by governments. Radical reformers rejected that theory of "two kingdoms" opting instead to pit them against each other or at least separate them.

Lutherans in Europe after Luther tended to emphasize Luther's principle of "simul justus et peccator"—that a Christian is by faith both righteous and a sinner at the same time—and emphasize the objective sides of salvation and relationship with God. In salvation God declares the baptized (or converted) person righteous without imparting righteousness inwardly to him or her. This happens on account of faith—even in the case of a baptized infant. Some Lutherans in the late seventeenth and early eighteenth centuries called "pietists" began to emphasize a more subjective side to salvation and relationship with God. The pietists placed greater emphasis on conscious repentance, the need for personal decision of faith (for authentic Christianity), and a life of devotion in which feeling or emotions should play some role. A spiritual divide began to open up among European Lutherans over pietism and some European governments aligned with Lutheran churches that persecuted pietists when they formed "conventicles," small groups for Bible study and prayer, outside the auspices of the state churches. Many Lutheran immigrants to the New World were Lutheran pietists looking for freedom to believe and practice their "heart-centered" Christianity in their own ways. Many of them established new Lutheran denominations in the New World and many converted to more revivalist branches of Protestant Christianity once they were free of the limitations imposed by state churches and governments in Europe.

Lutherans in the United States. The first Lutheran worship service in America was a Christmas service held at Hudson Bay in 1619. The first European Lutherans to remain permanently in this country arrived at Manhattan Island from Holland in 1623. The first independent colony of Lutherans, New Sweden, was established at Fort Christiana along the Delaware River in 1638, now present-day Wilmington, Delaware. The great influx of Lutheran immigrants, however, went to Pennsylvania, where by the middle of the eighteenth century Lutherans numbered about thirty thousand, four-fifths of whom were German, the remainder Swedish.

The first churches were small and poor, often without pastors. The situation was relieved with the coming of Henry Melchior Muhlenberg (1711–87) from the University of Halle, the headquarters of the pietist movement. In 1748 he united the pastors and congregations in Pennsylvania, New Jersey, New York, and Maryland into what came to be called the Ministerium of Pennsylvania. Muhlenberg recognized the need for American Lutherans to govern themselves years before the American Revolution. Synods (roughly synonymous with "denomination" although some Lutheran denominations include more than one synod) were formed in New York in 1786, North Carolina in 1803, Maryland in 1820, and Ohio in 1836.

Each synod adjusted itself to its peculiar conditions of language, natural background, previous ecclesiastical relationship with Lutheran authorities abroad, and geographical location. The need for even further organization was evident from the ever-increasing flood of Lutherans from Europe, resulting in the formation of the General Synod in 1820. The General Synod extended its efforts to the west, and the Missouri Synod was formed in 1847. From 1850 until 1860, one million Germans arrived in the United States, the majority of them Lutheran. By 1870, Lutherans were the fourth-largest Protestant group in the country, with approximately four hundred thousand members.

The Civil War brought the first serious break in Lutheran ranks, with the organization of the United Synod of the South in 1863. Three years later a number of other synods, led by the Ministerium of Pennsylvania, withdrew from the General Synod to form the General Council. To increase the complexity, Lutheran immigrants continued to arrive in larger and larger numbers. These immigrants spoke different languages and came from nations where the church was organized in different ways. From 1870 until 1910, approximately 1.75 million Scandinavians arrived, bringing a slightly different form of Lutheranism than the older, now-established German congregations. Numerous small synods were organized.

At one time there were about 150 Lutheran bodies in the United States. Consolidation, unification, and federation in the twentieth century reduced that number to about a dozen. In 1988 three of the largest Lutheran denominations, the American Lutheran Church, the Lutheran Church in America, and the Association of Evangelical Lutheran Churches merged to form the Evangelical Lutheran Church in America. With each major merger, new separate churches were also formed in protest.

Groups of lay and ministerial delegates from major Lutheran churches in twenty-two countries formed a Lutheran World Federation in 1947 for the purpose of relief and rehabilitation on a global scale among Lutherans. Perhaps the most cooperative effort in the history of American Lutheranism is found in Lutheran World Relief, through which more than $300 million in cash and food (including United States government-donated commodities) has been distributed throughout the world.

Belief and Practices. In spite of their divisions, there has been unity among Lutherans based more on faith than on organization. All the churches represent a single type of Protestant Christianity, built on Luther's principle of justification by faith alone. Lutherans maintain that the Bible is the inspired word of God and the rule and standard of faith and practice. They confess their faith through the three general creeds of Christendom (Apostles', Nicene, and Athanasian), which they believe to be in accordance with the scriptures. They also believe that the Augsburg Confession is a correct exposition of the faith and doctrine of evangelical Lutheranism, although there is disagreement over which version is preferred. The two catechisms of Luther, the Schmalkald Articles, and the Formula of Concord are held by most Lutherans to be faithful interpretations of Lutheranism and of the Bible. However, especially the Evangelical Lutheran Church of America (ELCA) has increasingly permitted flexibility and leniency in interpretation of the Bible, the creeds, and the Lutheran confessions.

Baptism and the Lord's Supper are not merely signs or memorials, but are believed to be channels through which God bestows forgiving and empowering grace upon humankind when they are accompanied by faith. The real body and blood of Christ are believed to be present "in, with, and under" the bread and wine of the Lord's Supper and are received by the faithful sacramentally and supernaturally. Pastors baptize infant children of members, and baptized persons are believed to receive the gift of regeneration from the Holy Spirit. However, Lutherans, in distinction from Orthodox and Catholic believers, insist that faith is essential for grace to be conveyed sacramentally. The faith of parents and congregations can "stand in" (proxy faith) for an infant's until confirmation. Pietist Lutherans, however, have traditionally added an emphasis on a "personal decision of faith" and a strong devotional life for fully formed Christian existence. This theological difference has led to a distinction between "sacramental spirituality" among some Lutherans and "conversional spirituality" among others (although none reject sacraments as real means of grace).

Polity. The local congregation is usually administered between its annual meetings by a church council consisting of the pastor and a number of elected lay officers. Pastors are called by the voting members of the congregation. Congregations are united in synods composed of pastors and lay representatives elected by the congregations and have authority as granted by the synod constitution. Some Lutheran denominations have bishops; others do not. Where they do exist Lutheran bishops are considered administrative leaders as opposed to persons possessing special spiritual qualities or authority. Very few Lutherans emphasize apostolic succession although the ELCA, the largest Lutheran denomination in the United States, has agreed to submit to apostolic succession in its ecumenical agreement with the Episcopal Church for mutual recognition of ordinations and pulpit exchange. (ELCA pastors can pastor Episcopal congregations and Episcopal priests can pastor ELCA congregations.) Since the agreement all ELCA ordinations include an Episcopal bishop. Some Scandinavian Lutherans (e.g., the Church of Sweden) have always practiced apostolic succession.

Synods (conferences or districts) are united in a general body that may be national or even international and are called variously "church," "synod," or "conference." Some of these general bodies are legislative in nature, some consultative; they supervise the work in worship, education, publication, charity, and mission. Congregations have business meetings at least annually; synods, districts, and conferences hold yearly conventions; the general bodies meet annually or biennially.

During the late twentieth century and first decades of the twenty-first century many new Lutheran denominations have formed—most of them schisms from the ELCA over the latter's perceived theological latitudinarianism (lowering of enforcement of doctrinal standards) and openness to Lutheran congregations hosting same-sex weddings and having gay and lesbian people serve as pastors and congregational leaders. The spectrum of Lutheran denominational theological strictness versus pluralism runs the gamut—from fundamentalism to theological liberalism.

SUGGESTIONS FOR FURTHER READING

Cimino, Richard. *American Lutherans Today*. Grand Rapids, MI: Wm. B. Eerdmans, 2003.

Gritsch, Eric W. *Fortress Introduction to Lutheranism*. Minneapolis, MN: Augsburg-Fortress Press, 1994.

Groh, John E., and Robert H. Smith, eds. *The Lutheran Church in North America*. Saint Louis, MO: Concordia Press, 1979.

Huber, Donald L. *World Lutheranism: A Select Bibliography for English Readers*. Lanham, MD: Scarecrow Press, 2000.

Knudsen, Johannes. *The Formation of the Lutheran Church in America*. Philadelphia, PA: Fortress Press, 1958.

Neve, H. T., and B. A. Anderson, eds. *The Maturing of American Lutheranism*. Minneapolis, MN: Augsburg Press, 1968.

Schlink, Edmund. *Theology of the Lutheran Confessions*. Trans. Paul F. Keohneke and Herbert J. A. Bouman. Philadelphia, PA: Muhlenberg Press, 1961.

THE AMERICAN ASSOCIATION OF LUTHERAN CHURCHES

Founded: 1987
Membership: est. 16,000, in 70 congregations (2010)

The American Association of Lutheran Churches (AALC) was formed by laity and pastors of the former American Lutheran Church in America who did not wish to participate in that church's 1988 merger with the Lutheran Church in America and Association of Evangelical Lutheran Churches (see ELCA). The AALC holds to a high view of the divinely inspired, revealed, and inerrant word of God, joyfully submitting to this as the only infallible authority in all matters of faith and life. The emphasis has been on the primacy of reaching people through the ministries of evangelism and world missions through the local congregations. The AALC is generally considered a conservative, confessional Lutheran church body.

The congregations of the AALC are divided into five regions, mainly in the northern and western states. The primary decision-making body is the annual General Convention, to which each congregation has proportionate representation. The Joint Council, with three representatives from each Region, governs the church body the rest of the time. The AALC has entered into a special partnership with the larger Lutheran Church—Missouri Synod (LCMS) in which both denominations recognize each other as separate but also interdependent. The AALC seminary (American Lutheran Theological Seminary) holds seminary classes on the campuses of LCMS Concordia Seminaries in Saint Louis, Missouri, and Fort Wayne, Indiana.

For more information: www.taalc.org

Headquarters: TAALC, 921 East Dupont Road #920, Fort Wayne, IN 46825

APOSTOLIC LUTHERAN CHURCH OF AMERICA

Founded: 1872, 1928
Membership: est. 9,000, in 57 churches (2016)

Sometimes called the Laestadians for Lars Levi Laestadius (1800–61), a naturalist, a revivalist, and a minister of the state church of Sweden, this church originated with Finnish immigrants in and around Calumet, Michigan, in the middle years of the nineteenth century. The church was first incorporated in Michigan in 1928 under the name "Finnish Apostolic Lutheran Church of America."

Conservative in theology and revivalist in ethos, this church stresses the infallibility of scripture and the importance of an experience of conversion for justification by faith. Such an experience is required for voting membership in spiritual matters; supporting members may vote on temporal matters only. The church accepts the ecumenical creeds and puts strong emphasis on the confession of sins, absolution, and regeneration. Confession may be made to another Christian, but for some publicly known sins, a person "should confess them publicly before the congregation and receive absolution." Local congregations are quite free to govern themselves. The annual church convention elects an executive board, which elects officers for the denomination.

For more information: www.apostoliclutheran.org

Contact: *Christian Monthly* (magazine), PO Box 2996, Battle Ground, WA 98604

ASSOCIATION OF FREE LUTHERAN CONGREGATIONS

Founded: 1962
Membership: 41,174, in 273 churches (2013)

This association was formed by congregations of the Lutheran Free Church, which rejected the merger with the newly formed American Lutheran Church in 1962 (now part of the Evangelical Lutheran Church in America*). It has its roots in a revival movement that swept through Scandinavian Lutheran churches in the late nineteenth century. It is conservative theologically and maintains that the local congregation is subject to no authority but the word and Spirit of God. Doctrinal emphases include the infallibility and supreme authority of the Bible as the word of God, congregational polity, the spiritual unity of all true believers, evangelical outreach for the purpose of leading persons to an experience with and devotion to Christ, the Lordship of Christ in one's personal life, and conservatism on social issues.

The association elects a president and a coordinating committee that maintains a clergy roster and fosters cooperation between churches in ministry to youth, evangelism, parish education, and other matters. Association members also sponsor a theological seminary and a Bible school in Plymouth, Minnesota.

For more information: www.aflc.org

Headquarters: 3110 East Medicine Lake Boulevard, Plymouth, MN 55441

CHURCH OF THE LUTHERAN BRETHREN OF AMERICA

Founded: 1900
Membership: 26,695, in 105 churches (2006)

The Church of the Lutheran Brethren is an independent Lutheran body made up of autonomous congregations scattered across the United States and Canada. The synod was organized in 1900 to assist in Christian education and in home- and world-missions. The church maintains a firm commitment to the supreme authority of the scriptures. It accepts the basic Lutheran teachings and emphasizes the need for a personal faith in the Lord Jesus Christ that demonstrates itself in daily life. Membership in the local congregation is based on an individual's personal profession of faith. Worship services use traditional and contemporary music, lay participation, and biblical teaching and preaching that is evangelistic and personal in application. The congregations support a seminary, a Bible school, and a four-year secondary academy. These institutions, as well as the headquarters, are located in Fergus Falls, Minnesota. Mission projects are carried on in Chad, Cameroon, Japan, and Taiwan.

For more information: www.clba.org

Headquarters: 1020 West Alcott Avenue, PO Box 655, Fergus Falls, MN 56538

CHURCH OF THE LUTHERAN CONFESSION

Founded: 1960
Membership: 7,000, in 78 churches (2016)

This confessional church was organized by clergy and laypeople who had withdrawn from several synods of the Synodical Conference of North America over the issue of uniting with other synods. The Church of Lutheran Confession (CLC) holds firmly to the doctrine of verbal inspiration and inerrancy of the Bible, and it maintains that there can be no church union (even with other Lutherans) unless there is full agreement in doctrine. It holds without reservation to all the historic confessions of the Lutheran faith. Membership is concentrated in South Dakota, Minnesota, and Wisconsin. It also engages in mission work in India and Nigeria. A high school, a college, and a seminary in Eau Claire, Wisconsin, are supported by the church.

For more information: www.clclutheran.org

Headquarters: 501 Grover Road, Eau Claire, WI 54701

EVANGELICAL LUTHERAN CHURCH IN AMERICA

Founded: 1988
Membership: 4,181,219, in 9,846 churches (2012)

The Evangelical Lutheran Church in America (ELCA) is the youngest of the large US Lutheran church bodies, but it is also the oldest. The ELCA was constituted in 1987 and began operation in 1988 as a result of the union of the American Lutheran Church (ALC), Lutheran Church in America (LCA), and Association of Evangelical Lutheran Churches (AELC), but it traces its history through predecessor church bodies to the formation in 1748 of the first synod in North America, the Ministerium of Pennsylvania. The ELCA represents historical continuity for Lutherans from colonial days as well as the weaving together into one body all of the threads of Lutheran history in North America.

Two of the uniting churches that formed the ELCA were the result of mergers. The American Lutheran Church was formed in 1960, bringing together four churches of German, Norwegian, and Danish heritage. Subsequently, in 1962, the Lutheran Church in America was established in a four-way merger of German, Danish, Finnish, and Swedish heritage churches. Those mergers of the early 1960s marked a movement away from ethnic identity for American Lutheran church bodies. The American Evangelical Lutheran Church, in contrast, resulted from a break in 1976 from the Lutheran Church—Missouri Synod in a dispute over the authority and interpretation of scripture.

Efforts to form the ELCA formally began in 1982 when the three uniting churches elected a seventy-member commission to draft the constitution and other agreements. In August 1986, the conventions of the three churches approved the merger, and the ELCA's constituting assembly was held in May 1987. The Reverend Herbert W. Chilstrom was elected the first presiding bishop and the Reverend Lowell G. Almen, the first secretary. The ELCA's main office is in Chicago. Its congregations are grouped into sixty-five synods throughout the United States and the Caribbean region. Each synod is led by a bishop elected by voting members at a Synod Assembly to six-year, renewable terms.

The highest governing authority in the ELCA is the Churchwide Assembly, which includes six hundred lay voting members, equally divided by gender, and about four hundred clergy voting members. A thirty-seven-member Church Council, elected by the assembly, serves as the board of directors and interim legislative authority between assemblies. The presiding bishop is the ELCA's chief pastor and the executive officer of the church-wide organization. Both the presiding bishop and secretary are elected by the

Churchwide Assembly. Their terms of office are six years and incumbents are eligible for reelection. The treasurer is elected by the Church Council to six-year renewable terms. A lay vice president, who is elected to the volunteer position by the Churchwide Assembly, chairs the Church Council.

Units within the church-wide organization include: congregational ministries, rostered ministries, outreach, higher education and schools, church in society, and global mission. Ecumenical relations are coordinated through the presiding bishop's office and include ecumenical, inter-Lutheran, and inter-religious activities as well as administration of relationships with the Lutheran World Federation, World Council of Churches, and National Council of the Churches of Christ in the USA. The publishing unit, located in Minneapolis, is known as Augsburg Fortress. The pension board also is based in Minneapolis and provides pension and other benefit programs for clergy, other church workers, and congregations. The main periodical of the ELCA is *The Lutheran*, published monthly.

A formal relationship of full communion was established in 1997 between the ELCA and the Presbyterian Church (USA), Reformed Church in America, and the United Church of Christ. In 1999, relationships of full communion were formed with the Episcopal Church and with the Moravian Church. As a member of the Lutheran World Federation, the ELCA affirmed in 1999 the "Joint Declaration on the Doctrine of Justification" with the Roman Catholic Church.

The ELCA promotes the Lutheran theological and liturgical tradition while allowing greater freedom for laity and clergy to address contemporary social and intellectual concerns than most of the other Lutheran denominations. It also engages in extensive ministries to promote both greater social justice and mercy in the world.

During the last decades of the twentieth century and the first decades of the twenty-first century the ELCA experienced debate and division (churches leaving to form or join new Lutheran bodies) over topics related to human sexuality—same-sex marriage and ordination of persons who do not identify as heterosexual. The ELCA does not officially endorse such, but latitude is allowed on the congregational level. Like the Episcopal Church the ELCA holds within itself a wide variety of types of churches—from charismatic to ones focused primarily on social justice to congregations that are "welcoming and affirming" of LGBT persons.

The ELCA supports the world's largest Lutheran seminary—Luther Theological Seminary in Saint Paul, Minnesota. It also supports several other seminaries as well as numerous colleges in the United States.

For more information: www.elca.org

Headquarters: 8765 West Higgins Road, Chicago, IL 60631

EVANGELICAL LUTHERAN SYNOD

Founded: 1918
Membership: 19,291, in 124 churches (2012)

This synod traces its roots to the formation of a synod for Norwegian immigration in the middle of the nineteenth century. The Evangelical Lutheran Synod (ELS) was organized in 1918 by a minority group that declined to join the other Norwegian groups when they united in the Norwegian Lutheran Church (later, the Evangelical Lutheran Church) in 1917. The jurisdiction of the synod is entirely advisory. The officers and boards of the synod, however, direct work of common interest insofar as they do not interfere with congregational rights or prerogatives. The ELS is doctrinally conservative and confessional and is in fellowship with the Wisconsin Synod. It does not ordain women to ministry and holds to a traditional view regarding marriage as between one man and one woman. It maintains Bethany Lutheran College and Bethany Theological Seminary at Mankato, Minnesota.

For more information: www.els.org

Headquarters: 6 Browns Court, Mankato, MN 56001

LATVIAN EVANGELICAL LUTHERAN CHURCH IN AMERICA

Founded: 1957, 1975
Membership: 5,360, in 40 churches (2016)

This body grew out of the Federation of Latvian Evangelical Lutheran Churches and is part of the international network of Latvian Lutherans around the world as well as a member of the Lutheran World Federation. It considers itself a synod within the Evangelical Lutheran Church of Latvia Abroad, which includes congregations in many countries outside of Latvia but looks to the Evangelical Lutheran Church of Latvia. It has no US headquarters but has congregations in the United States.

The Latvian Evangelical Lutheran Church in America (LELCA) holds to the traditional doctrinal statements of Western Christianity (the Apostles', Nicene, and Athanasian creeds) and the statements of traditional Lutheranism (the Unaltered Augsburg Confession, the smaller and larger catechisms, and the *Book of Concord*). In addition to promoting Lutheran worship, spirituality, and theology, the LELCA preserves the customs and traditions of Latvian Protestantism. It is a member of the World Council of Churches and the Lutheran World Federation.

One difference between the LELCA and the Evangelical Lutheran Church in Latvia is over ordination of women. The "home church" in Latvia does not ordain women; the LELCA and many other Latvian Lutheran churches "abroad" do ordain women.

For more information: www.lelba.org

LUTHERAN CHURCH—MISSOURI SYNOD

Founded: 1847
Membership: 2.2 million, in 6,100 churches (2016)

This second-largest Lutheran denomination in the United States was founded in Missouri by German immigrants who left their homes in 1839. Many of these immigrants had rejected the planned merger of the Lutheran and Reformed churches in Prussia. They were led by a pastor named C. F. W. Walther, who served as the first president of the synod. From the beginning the synod has included churches outside of Missouri, but remained heavily German until the twentieth century. World War I accelerated the process of adopting English as the language of worship. The church has always been devoted to the maintenance of confessional Lutheranism, coupled with a strong sense of mission outreach. It stresses the authority of the classic Lutheran confessional statements and the inerrancy of scripture. The church insists on the "three *solas*": salvation by *grace alone* through *faith alone* based on *scripture alone*. The Lutheran Church—Missouri Synod (LCMS) was the first Christian denomination to urge its members to donate body organs, and it has called for a constitutional amendment to ban abortions. The church views homosexual behavior as sinful and does not endorse same-sex marriage. Nor does it ordain women to the ministry.

The LCMS stresses Christian education for members of all ages, and the synod operates ten universities and colleges as well as two theological seminaries in North America. In addition, its elementary and secondary school system is the largest of any Protestant denomination in the United States. The synod has long been considered a leader in the field of communications. It operates the world's oldest religious radio station, KFUO in Saint Louis, Missouri. Since 1930 it has produced the "Lutheran Hour," heard in more than forty different languages and forty countries. It also operates Concordia Publishing House, one of the largest religious publishers in the United States. Its *LifeLight* curriculum has been enormously popular. In addition, for many decades the church has given great attention to ministry to deaf and blind persons. Each month volunteers in many work centers distribute Braille magazines, large print publications, and CDs and DVDs of devotional and educational material.

Because of differences in doctrine and practice, the Missouri Synod was not a part of the 1988 merger that united three other Lutheran denominations. The LCMS, for example, does not have bishops or ordain women. However, it continues to cooperate with other Lutheran churches in a variety of ministries, particularly in areas of social work, such as world hunger relief and the resettlement of refugees. The church has over six thousand pastors plus numerous chaplains, educators, and other church professionals. It began sending out foreign missionaries in the 1890s. It now has active work in eighty-five countries on every inhabited continent. In the early 1990s the church declared the United

States to be a "world mission field," and it conducts intentional mission work among Latinos, African and Asian immigrants, Native Americans, Jews, and Arabic-speaking groups. The church's headquarters are in the International Center, in suburban Saint Louis. Directors for the church body are set by a triennial convention of pastors and laypeople, whose members represent the congregations of the synod. The church is divided into thirty-five administrative districts, which in turn are organized into six hundred circuits containing eight to twenty congregations. National assemblies take place every third year. Though the denomination participates in many ecumenical dialogs, it does not share in Communion with churches unless there is agreement in the confession of the gospel in all articles. In other words, it practices closed Communion toward all who do not share its beliefs about the Lord's Supper.

Although the LCMS remains strong, it has suffered occasional defections to the more liberal Evangelical Lutheran Church in America (ELCA). One of the denominations joining the ELCA at its founding was a breakaway group from the LCMS called the Association of Evangelical Lutheran Churches, which had about 250 formerly LCMS congregations. In 1988 it merged with two other Lutheran denominations to form the ELCA. The schism began with the LCMS firing of the president of one of its two seminaries over issues of modern biblical interpretation. Several students and faculty members of Concordia Theologial Seminary (LCMS) left to found a separate Lutheran seminary known as Seminex ("Seminary in Exile"). Eventually Seminex folded and most of the faculty and students moved on to ELCA seminaries.

The LCMS remains a stalwart defender of what it considers traditional Lutheran theology and practice with the *Book of Concord* functioning as its secondary authority after scripture itself. The denomination generally discourages belief in evolution, holding to a literal six-day creation. It also considers the office of the papacy of the Roman Catholic Church the antichrist of the New Testament book of Revelation. The LCMS discourages its ministers from participating in ecumenical services of worship.

For more information: www.lcms.org

Headquarters: 1333 South Kirkwood Road, Saint Louis, MO 63122-7295

LUTHERAN CONGREGATIONS IN MISSION FOR CHRIST

Founded: 2001
Membership: est. 300,000, in 734 churches (2016)

Lutheran Congregations in Mission for Christ (LCMC) began in 2001 with twenty-five Lutheran congregations leaving the Evangelical Lutheran Church in America (ELCA) over perceived doctrinal and ethical drifts in that denomination away from traditional Lutheran beliefs and practices. The LCMC has grown steadily since its origin. That growth has largely been fueled by conservative, evangelical Lutherans, many of them charismatic or leaning toward the charismatic movement, very dissatisfied with the ELCA's decision to permit individual congregations to make their own decisions regarding participation—including membership, marriage, and ordination—of people who identify as gay or lesbian. The LCMC also believes the ELCA's emphasis on social justice activism, although not wrong in and of itself, has largely replaced evangelism.

The LCMC says that "We believe, teach, and confess the gospel, recorded in the Holy Scriptures and confessed in the ecumenical creeds and Lutheran confessional writings, as the power of God to create and sustain the priesthood of all believers for God's mission in the world." It considers itself in communion with all Christians who agree.

The LCMC exists in thirteen distinct districts, some of which are geographical (including in West Africa) and some of which are devoted to special purposes. Each LCMC congregation is autonomous but must agree to abide by the statement of faith and ethical beliefs of the denomination.

The LCMC and its member congregations only recognize marriages that are between one man and one woman, and they only ordain heterosexual people. The LCMC permits individual congregations to ordain women and have women ministers including senior pastors.

The LCMC wants to walk a path between what its congregations consider the liberal theology and practice of the ELCA and the much more conservative theology and practice of the LCMS.

For more information: www.lcmc.net

Headquarters: 7000 North Sheldon Road, Canton, MI 48187

NORTH AMERICAN LUTHERAN CHURCH

Founded: 2010
Membership: 140,000, in 400 churches (2016)

The North American Lutheran Church (NALC) was constituted in Columbus, Ohio, out of a Lutheran renewal movement called Lutheran CORE (Coalition for Renewal). It began with seventeen churches and rapidly grew to four hundred. The denomination has four core values: Christ Centered, Mission Driven, Traditionally Grounded, and Congregationally Focused. Most of its churches either left the Evangelical Lutheran Church in America or are church plants. The church affirms traditional Lutheran doctrines including the inspiration and authority of scripture and justification by grace alone through faith alone. It also affirms the major creeds and Lutheran confessions including the Unaltered Augsburg Confession.

The denomination supports the North American Lutheran Seminary in Ambridge, Pennsylvania. It is led by a bishop and district superintendents ("deans") of twenty-seven regions. NALC seeks ecumenical relations of intercommunion and cooperation with like-minded churches including the LCMS and the Anglican Church of North America.

NALC holds to a traditional view of marriage and sexuality stating that "We teach and practice that sexual activity belongs exclusively within the biblical boundaries of a faithful marriage between one man and one woman." Both women and men can be ordained to the ministry as long as they are married or are celibate.

For more information: www.thenalc.org

Headquarters: 3500 Mill Run Drive, Hilliard, OH 43026

WISCONSIN EVANGELICAL LUTHERAN SYNOD

Founded: 1850
Membership: 385,558, in 1,287 congregations (2012)

Organized in Milwaukee as the German Evangelical Lutheran Synod of Wisconsin, this church merged with the Minnesota and Michigan synods in 1917 to become the Evangelical Lutheran Joint Synod of Wisconsin and Other States. Today it is known as the Wisconsin Evangelical Lutheran Synod (WELS). This synod subscribes to confessional Lutheranism and is committed without reservation to the inspiration and infallibility of Holy Scripture. It seeks fellowship with those who believe that full agreement in doctrine and practice is necessary for biblical fellowship.

Divided into twelve districts, it maintains it national headquarters in Milwaukee. Mission churches are supported in Malawi, Zambia, Cameroon, Nigeria, Albania, Bulgaria, Japan, Russia, Sweden, Norway, Finland, Hong Kong, Indonesia, Taiwan, Thailand, India, Brazil, Colombia, Dominican Republic, Mexico, Puerto Rico, and among Native Americans in Arizona, and well as 190 locations in North America and the West Indies. WELS has one of the largest Christian prison ministries in the United States, and distributes hundreds of thousands of Bibles to inmates and offers Bible correspondence courses to inmates.

For the education of its pastors, teachers, and staff ministers, WELS maintains a college in New Ulm, Minnesota, and a seminary at Mequon, Wisconsin, and two preparatory schools (in Watertown, Wisconsin, and Saginaw, Michigan). The church has one of the larger parochial school systems in the country. WELS is a member of the Confessional Evangelical Lutheran Conference, which includes twenty confessional church bodies throughout the world.

WELS is generally considered one of the most conservative Lutheran denominations in the United States. It affirms the infallibility of the Bible, ordains only heterosexual men, rejects non-heterosexual marriage, and practices closed Communion. It is not interested in ecumenical cooperation or unions with denominations of differing doctrines and practices.

For more information: www.wels.net

Headquarters: North16 West 23377 Stone Ridge Drive, Waukesha, WI 53188

REFORMED, PRESBYTERIAN, AND CONGREGATIONALIST CHURCHES

2009 marked the five-hundredth anniversary of the birth of John Calvin (1509–64), perhaps the most influential theologian in the Reformed tradition of Protestantism—at least for Reformed Christians in the United States. The anniversary year provided an opportunity for all branches of the Reformed faith to celebrate their rich heritage, and to mark the occasion the World Alliance of Reformed Churches and the Reformed Ecumenical Council uniting to form the World Communion of Reformed Churches (WCRC), which represents more than seventy-five million Christians in over two hundred countries. About 120 denominations around the world belong to the WCRC—including, ironically, the Remonstrant Brotherhood of the Netherlands (an Arminian denomination). Worldwide, "Reformed" is an extremely broad category. Historically, for example, Lutherans have tended to lump all non-Lutheran Protestants together as "Reformed." On the other hand, some Reformed Christians narrowly limit the label "Reformed" to a few churches that regard as especially authoritative, under scripture itself, the "three symbols of unity": the Heidelberg Confession of Faith, the Belgic Confession of Faith, and the Canons of Dort. So, "Reformed" is an essentially contested category—even among Christians who proudly wear that label. Still, and nevertheless, all agree that it is a family of Protestant Christians rooted in the Swiss Reformation that coincided with the German Lutheran Reformation.

The Reformed family of churches originated in the Swiss Reformation, especially in Zurich, under the city's chief pastor Ulrich Zwingli (1484–1531) and Geneva, where Calvin served as a pastor and teacher. Reformed churches are often called "Calvinist," because of Calvin's influence, but Reformed churches have often disagreed on how to apply his theology. Calvin viewed himself primarily as an interpreter of scripture, and he bequeathed a strong Biblicism to the Reformed tradition. Basic to Calvin's thought was God's sovereignty over the world and people's lives; humans are completely dependent upon God for their lives and salvation. The most controversial Calvinist proposition was "double predestination," which means that eternal salvation and damnation are predetermined by God. Calvin also taught that the natural world as well as human history work according to God's rational law and providential will.

Doctrine in many Reformed Churches is based primarily on the Belgic Confession (1561), the Heidelberg Catechism (1563), and the Canons of the Synod of Dort (1618). Presbyterian churches also use the Westminster Confession of Faith (1648). These confessions emphasize salvation through Christ and the primacy of God's power in human life. More cerebral and verbal than emotional and aesthetic, Reformed theology places particular value on understanding, learning, and doctrinal unity than most branches of Christianity. Reformed worship also tends to focus on biblical exposition and preaching rather than music and the sacraments.

The Reformed churches in Europe developed along national lines. Particularly strong were the Reformed churches in the Netherlands (Holland), Germany, England, Scotland, Hungary, Bohemia, and Poland. Presbyterian Churches are in the Reformed tradition, but the Scottish reformer John Knox (ca. 1513–72) played as great a role in their formation as John Calvin. Though they were often tolerated or even supported by local governments, the Reformed churches were officially outlawed throughout Europe until the Peace of Westphalia in 1648. Their theology and church structure were thus formed in the midst of persecution and a struggle for religious and political independence. It was the Reformed churches that rejected the idea of "divine right" for monarchs.

In England, the Reformed tradition was represented by the Puritans who sought to reform the Church of England along Calvinist lines. During the English Civil War, the Westminster Assembly (1643–48) met in an effort to resolve the struggle over the compulsory use of the Anglican *Book of Common Prayer* in all English parishes. That assembly produced a Larger and a Shorter Catechism; a directory for the public worship of God; a form of government; and the Westminster Confession of Faith, which became the doctrinal standard of Scottish, British, and American Presbyterianism.

The Reformed tradition was the most influential religious tradition in colonial America, and it has had a profound impact on American religion and culture. The separatist Puritans (Congregationalists) in New England were representatives of the Reformed tradition, as were the Scots-Irish Presbyterians who immigrated to the middle colonies and southward. Many of the institutions of higher education in colonial America were founded by Reformed churches (Harvard, Yale, Princeton, Dartmouth), and those schools produced some of America's best theologians, such as Jonathan Edwards (1703–58). Reformed thought and practice influenced American literature, law, education, and government during the formative period of the country.

Types of Reformed Churches. Many of the divisions among Reformed churches in the United States can be traced to different interpretations of Calvin's teaching and the authority of the basic doctrinal confessions. They can be traced also, and perhaps even more, to different forms of church government. Over time, many pastors and congregations in the Reformed tradition turned away from Calvin's strict teaching on predestination and adopted a more covenantal understanding of God's relationship to the world and to believers. Although all Reformed denominations reject bishops, they disagree about congregational autonomy versus accountability to each other in "presbyteries" and "synods." Congregationalists emphasize church autonomy; Presbyterians emphasize mutual accountability and connectionalism.

Because of their deep commitment to local authority, whether through congregations or presbyteries, Reformed churches developed along ethnic lines. Language, culture, and national heritage were closely connected to theological and liturgical concerns. Several Reformed denominations in the United States continue to reflect their European national origins.

As mentioned above, some divisions within the Reformed family of churches involve church order. All of the Reformed churches rejected episcopacy (rule by bishops) and attempted to follow the structure of the New Testament church, but there were disagreements over the details of that structure. Calvin promoted a presbyterial system in which a council of clergy (presbyters) exercised authority within a geographical region. Reformed and Presbyterian churches follow Calvin's approach. The governing body in the local church is called a consistory, session, or council depending on the denomination. Typically, it is made up of elders, deacons, and ministers, who undertake the administrative duties common to congregational life. Churches in a geographical area are then organized into a presbytery or classis that supervises congregations and clergy within its bounds. This body is generally composed of elder delegates from each congregation and the ministers in the area. The presbytery or classis is in turn under the authority of regional synods that supervise planning and programming. The highest legislative and judicial body of most Reformed and Presbyterian churches is a representative body called General Synod or General Assembly, which meets once a year,

In Congregationalism, the assembled body of believers on the local level has final authority. Local and national assemblies may provide programming and assist in cooperative ministries, but they have little direct power over congregations and pastors. The Puritans in colonial New England were generally Congregationalists while Presbyterians, also Reformed in their basic theology, tended to cluster in the middle colonies. Over time the two groups of Puritans began to recognize each other as equally Christian and Reformed and exchanged ministers. Jonathan Edwards, for example, although originally a Congregationalist, became Presbyterian to become president of the College of New Jersey (later renamed Princeton College).

Congregationalists in America. In 1609, John Robinson (1575–1625) fled persecution in England and settled at Leiden in the Netherlands. There he met William Ames (1576–1633), Congregationalism's first theologian, who was also a fugitive from the ecclesiastical courts of England. Robinson and his congregation enjoyed peace and freedom under the Dutch but wanted to remain English. A large company sailed for the American colonies in 1620 aboard the historic *Mayflower,* earning the name "Pilgrims." Between

1630 and 1640, twenty thousand more Puritans, mostly Congregationalists, arrived at Massachusetts Bay. There they established a "theocratic" government based on biblical law and Calvin's theology. Contrary to popular belief, it was not a stern and rigid regime of the saints, but it was strict and intolerant of religious dissent. When four Quakers, including a woman, were hanged on Boston Common in the 1660s, there was a public outcry in England. New England was forced to accept the Act of Toleration in 1689.

Congregationalists in New England were leaders in the American Revolution, in part because they rejected the "divine right of kings" and argued that the people can determine their own government under God's laws. During the next century Congregationalism played a major role in developing American institutional and religious life. In the field of education, Congregationalists founded Harvard in 1636, Yale in 1707, and Dartmouth in 1769. Dartmouth developed from Eleazer Wheelock's (1711–79) school for Native Americans.

The American Board of Commissioners for Foreign Missions, organized in 1810, was concerned at first with both home and foreign missionary work. It included representatives from Congregationalist, Presbyterian, Dutch Reformed, and Associate Reformed churches. Missionaries were sent to more than thirty foreign countries and American territories. In 1826, the American Home Missionary Society was founded, and in 1846 the American Missionary Association, which was active in the South before the Civil War, was founded.

Meanwhile, differences of opinion between theological liberals and conservatives developed during the nineteenth century. A famous sermon by the Unitarian William Ellery Channing (1780–1842) at Baltimore in 1819 made a division inevitable. In spite of the Unitarian separation, Congregationalism continued to grow until a national supervisory body became necessary. A council held at Boston in 1865 proved so effective that a regular system of councils was established.

Unity and cooperation across denominational lines have been outstanding characteristics of Congregationalism. Christian Endeavor, at one time the largest young people's organization in Protestantism, was founded in 1881 by a Congregationalist, Francis E. Clark (1851–1921). By 1885 it had become interdenominational.

Dutch and German Reformed Churches in America. The Reformed Church came to America along with the first Dutch colonists. As early as 1614, there was informal Reformed worship along the upper reaches of the Hudson River near modern Albany, New York. The Reformed were numerous enough to require the services of lay ministers, two of whom came from Holland in 1623 as "comforters of the sick." By 1628 the Dutch in New Amsterdam had a pastor of their own, Jonas Michaelius (b. 1577) who organized the first church in the middle colonies.

When the English took possession of New Amsterdam in 1664, perhaps eight thousand Dutch church people were holding services in their own language. It was difficult and expensive to send native-born ministerial candidates to Holland for education and ordination, so a college and seminary were established at New Brunswick, New Jersey. This institution later became New Brunswick Theological Seminary and Rutgers University. Michael Schlatter (1718–90) was sent to the middle colonies by the Reformed Synod of South and North Holland. He worked tirelessly to bring organization to the Reformed churches and improve the quality of the ministry.

A large majority of the clergy and laypeople of the Reformed Church supported the American Revolution. As the Dutch became Americanized, the English language gradually became accepted in churches, but not without a struggle. A second emigration from the Netherlands began in the middle of the nineteenth century, bringing entire congregations with their pastors. One group, led by Albertus van Raalte (1811–76), established a community called Holland in western Michigan. Van Raalte and his group became part of the Reformed Church in America in 1850.

German Reformed churches in America originated in the flood tide of German immigrants to Pennsylvania in the eighteenth century. More than half the Germans there in 1730 were Reformed, but the congregations often lacked ministers and employed school teachers to lead the services. Johann Philip Boehm (1683–1749), a schoolmaster, led worship services and in 1725 he assumed the pastoral office for German Reformed settlers in southeastern Pennsylvania. He worked closely with the Dutch Reformed minister Michael Schlatter in expanding and organizing Reformed congregations. Lutheran pietist leader Nicholas Ludwig von Zinzendorf tried to unite all German Protestants (Lutherans, Reformed, and sectarians) into a Church of God in the Spirit in the 1740s, but the effort failed.

The American synod declared its independence in 1793, taking the name German Reformed Church. In that year it reported 178 congregations and fifteen thousand communicants. The word *German* was dropped from the name in 1869, and thereafter the denomination was called the Reformed Church in the United States. Difficulties arose in the early years of the nineteenth century. Older Germans preferred the use of the German language, but members raised in the United States demanded English. Some churches withdrew to form a separate synod, but returned in 1837 when compromises were made. District synods of both German-speaking and English-speaking congregations were created, and two Hungarian classes from the Old Hungarian Reformed Church were added in 1924.

The Evangelical and Reformed Church was the product of a union of the Evangelical Synod of North America and the Reformed Church in the United States in 1934. Few difficulties were encountered in reconciling the doctrines of the two bodies. Both churches were German in ethnicity and Calvinistic in doctrine. The Evangelical and Reformed denomination eventually merged with the American Congregational Churches to form the United Church of Christ.*

Presbyterians in America. After Oliver Cromwell's death in 1658 and the ending of Puritan rule in England, English Presbyterians fled to North America with the

Congregationalists. When the British Crown attempted to establish episcopacy in Scotland in the 1660s, many Presbyterians left Scotland and settled in Northern Ireland. Economic difficulties and religious inequalities in Ireland drove many of these Scots-Irish to immigrate to the United States. From 1710 until 1750, between three and six thousand Scottish immigrants arrived annually, settling primarily in Pennsylvania and Virginia, from whence they migrated to the west and south.

The first American presbytery or association of local churches was founded in Philadelphia in 1706. In 1729 Presbyterians adopted the Westminster Confession of Faith, together with the Larger and the Shorter Catechism. The same synod denied civil magistrates any power over the church and banned the persecution of anyone for religious faith.

In the 1720s, William Tennent Sr. (1673–1746) organized a "log college" in a cabin at Neshaminy, Pennsylvania, to train Presbyterian ministers and evangelists. Eventually it became the College of New Jersey (later Princeton University), and it produced a stream of revivalistic Presbyterian preachers who played leading roles in the Great Awakening of the 1740s. Such preachers, especially Gilbert Tennent (1703–64), promoted an emotional "new birth" revivalism, which conflicted with the old creedal Calvinism.

The camp-meeting revival, which had its roots in Scotland, grew out of that Great Awakening enthusiasm; however, it split the denomination. Preachers on the "Old Side" opposed revivalism, while those of the "New Side" endorsed it, claiming that less attention should be paid to college training of ministers and more to recruiting regenerated common men. The two sides quarreled until they reunited in 1757.

The next year, in the first united synod, there were ninety-four ministers in the colonial Presbyterian Church, with two hundred congregations and about ten thousand members. One of the ablest of the new-side preachers was John Witherspoon (1723–94), president of Princeton, who was the only ordained person to sign the Declaration of Independence. The Scots-Irish accepted the Revolution with relish; their persecution in England and Northern Ireland had made them solid anti-British dissenters. Their old cry, "No bishop and no king," was heard back in England.

After the Revolution, Presbyterian and Congregational preachers and laypeople moving into the new western territory worked together. Ministers of the two groups preached in one another's pulpits, and members held the right of representation in both the congregational association and the presbytery. The plan worked well on the whole, absorbing the fruits of the national revivals and giving real impetus to missionary work at home and abroad. This co-operation with the Congregationalists, though, contributed to the split between "Old School" and "New School" Presbyterians over matters of discipline and the expenditure of missionary money. The General Assembly of 1837 expelled four New School synods, which promptly met in their own convention to form a new General Assembly.

More tragic was the division between the southern and northern Presbyterians over the issue of slavery. In 1846, the Old School assembly regarded slavery as no bar to Christian Communion, but in that same year, the New School condemned the practice strongly. By 1857, several southern New School synods had withdrawn to form the United Synod of the Presbyterian Church. The greater schism came in 1861, following the outbreak of the Civil War, when forty-seven southern presbyteries of the Old School formed the Presbyterian Church in the Confederate States of America. In 1867, following the war, they merged to form the Presbyterian Church in the United States (PCUS).

The Old School and New School bodies of the northern Presbyterian Church were united in 1870 on the basis of the Westminster Confession. Most of the Cumberland Presbyterian churches joined them in 1907; the Welsh Calvinist Methodists joined in 1920. In the decades from 1920 until 1950, an emphasis on theology was evident in a liberal-conservative struggle.

The twentieth century saw a plethora of divisions among Reformed Christians in the United States with new denominations appearing every few years. No branch of Reformed Protestantism was immune to it. The so-called Dutch Reformed churches split over many issues including participation in "secret societies" referring especially to Freemasonry. They also divided over details of God's sovereignty and whether world missions and evangelism usurps it. Presbyterians suffered numerous divisions over so-called modernism—accommodations to modern science and philosophy. Many conservative Presbyterians became fundamentalists while many openly embraced theological liberalism. Later in the twentieth century Presbyterians divided over ordination of women and women pastors and then, in the twenty-first century, over ordination of openly gay people. Congregationalists also suffered many divisions over so-called modernism, theological liberalism, and ordination of women and of gay people.

Identifying exactly what all the denominations here lumped together as "Reformed, Congregationalist, and Presbyterian" have in common is challenging, but no more so than identifying what unites Baptists—an extremely diverse family of churches in the United States and around the world. Perhaps the only two things uniting them are first, historical-theological roots in the Swiss Reformation of the 1520s and especially in Geneva, which Presbyterian founder John Knox called "the most perfect school of Christ since the days of the apostles"; and second, an emphasis on God's majesty and sovereignty. All could belong to the World Communion of Reformed Churches if they chose to but many do not.

Some rough generalizations may help identify what *most* of these churches have in common *compared with* Lutheranism with which they share a basically Protestant heritage of theology. Luther taught, and most Lutherans agree, that the two sacraments of baptism and the Lord's Supper convey saving grace—when faith is present. Luther believed and most Lutherans agree that baptism regenerates the person being baptized; they are born again by the Holy Spirit through the waters of baptism when faith is present. Luther believed and most Lutherans agree that in the Lord's Supper Christ's body and blood are truly present "in, with, and under" the elements of bread and wine. Most Reformed Christians, whether Dutch and German Reformed, Puritan, or Presbyterian, following Calvin, believe that baptism is the "new covenant" equivalent of "old covenant" circumcision—a ritual of inclusion in the people of God but not salvific—and that there is no "real presence" of the body of Christ in the Lord's Supper but only a "spiritual" presence of Christ. The meaning of "sacrament" differs considerably between the two Reformation traditions and that is what kept them apart from the very beginning.

Here, so far, emphasis has been on the Reformed heritage and tradition in three "streams": Dutch and German Reformed, Scottish-Irish Presbyterian, and New England Congregationalism. However, there are many Christians within the Anglican tradition who consider themselves theologically Reformed. Some of the most influential Anglican and Episcopal theologians have proudly professed their Reformed theological orientation. Other Reformed Christians, however, view that profession and identification with some degree of doubt due to Anglicans' belief in bishops in apostolic succession. Many non-Anglican Reformed Christians secretly hold the attitude that *if* Reformed Anglicans (and Episcopalians) were serious about being Reformed they would come out of Anglicanism and join a Reformed, Congregationalist, or Presbyterian denomination. In some locales in the United States, however, some Episcopalian and Anglican churches have closer fellowship with some Reformed congregations than with fellow Episcopalian and Anglican churches. One specific denomination, the Reformed Episcopal Church, exists to combine the two traditions. To both Anglicans and Reformed Christians, however, it is a kind of uneasy hybrid. That is a common American tradition—to search for and create hybrids of older traditions.

SUGGESTIONS FOR FURTHER READING

Bercovitch, Sacvan. *The Puritan Origins of the American Self.* New Haven, CT: Yale University Press, 1975.

Bozeman, Dwight. *To Live Ancient Lives: The Primitivisit Dimension in Puritanism.* Chapel Hill, NC: University of North Carolina Press, 1988.

Bratt, James D. *Dutch Calvinism in Modern America.* Grand Rapids, MI: Eerdmans, 1984.

Dunn, David, et. al. *A History of the Evangelical & Reformed Church.* Philadelphia, PA: Westminster, 1961.

Gunnemann, Louis H. *The Shaping of the United Church of Christ.* New York: United Church Press, 1977.

Hart, D. G., and Mark A. Noll, eds. *Dictionary of the Presbyterian and Reformed Tradition in America.* Downers Grove, IL: InterVarsity Press, 1999.

Horton, Douglas. *The United Church of Christ: Its Origins, Organization, and Role in the World Today.* New York: Thomas Nelson, 1962.

Hutchinson, William R. *Between the Times: The Travail of the Protestant Establishment in America, 1900–1960.* New York: Cambridge University Press, 1989.

Miller, Perry. *The New England Mind.* 2 vols. Boston, MA: Beacon Press, 1961.

Porterfield, Amanda. *Female Piety in Puritan New England: The Emergence of Religious Humanism.* New York: Oxford University Press, 1992.

Smylie, James H. *A Brief History of the Presbyterians.* Louisville, KY: Geneva Press, 1996.

Thompson, Ernest T. *Presbyterians in the South.* 3 vols. Richmond, VA: John Knox Press, 1963–73.

VandenBerge, Peter M., ed. *Historical Directory of the Reformed Church in America: 1628–1978.* Grand Rapids, MI: Eerdmans, 1978.

ASSOCIATE REFORMED PRESBYTERIAN CHURCH

Founded: 1782
Membership: 29,317, in 281 congregations (2016)

The Associate Reformed Presbyterian Church (ARPC) traces its origin to controversies in the national Presbyterian Church in Scotland in the eighteenth century, when a group of presbyters seceded from the national church in protest over a number of issues of polity and worship. The controversy over the "Seceders" and "Covenanters" was carried to Northern Ireland with the Scottish migration there. The Scots-Irish immigrants to North America established congregations along the lines followed in the British Isles, but in 1782 two of the seceding branches united to form the Associate Reformed Synod in Philadelphia.

Eight years later, the Associate Reformed Presbytery of the Carolinas and Georgia was formed in Abbeville County, South Carolina, followed in 1803 by the division of the entire church into four Synods and one General Synod. In 1822 the Synod of the South was granted separate status, and by the end of the nineteenth century was the sole remaining body of the Associate Reformed Presbyterian Church, as several mergers over the years had absorbed the rest of the denomination into the old United Presbyterian Church. There are now nine presbyteries in North America, primarily in the east.

The doctrinal standards of the Apostles' Creed and the Westminster Confession are followed. For some years the only music in this church was the singing of psalms. This was modified in 1946 to permit the use of hymns.

The ARPC is a conservative, evangelical denomination in the Reformed tradition. It affirms the inspiration and inerrancy of scripture and opposes ordination of women to position of ordained elder. It also affirms that marriage is only between one man and one woman and sexual acts outside of marriage are sinful.

The General Synod of the church meets annually to elect officers and conduct business. The chief officers are the Moderator (one-year term), who presides over the General Synod and is the spokesperson for the church during the year, and the Principal Clerk (four-year term), who establishes and maintains the official records for the General Synod. These and other officers serve as the Executive Board of the General Synod.

Associate Reformed Presbyterian Church foreign mission fields are located in Germany, Mexico, Pakistan, Turkey, Spain, Ukraine, Wales, and Scotland. *The ARP* is published monthly at Greenville, South Carolina, and is the official publication of the denomination. Erskine College and Erskine Theological Seminary are in Due West, South Carolina. The church supports an assembly ground, Bonclarken, at Flat Rock, North Carolina, and three retirement centers.

For more information: www.arpchurch.org

Headquarters: One Cleveland Street Suite 110, Greenville, SC 29601

CHRISTIAN REFORMED CHURCH IN NORTH AMERICA

Founded: 1857
Membership: 237,830, in 1088 congregations (2015)

This Reformed group originated with Dutch immigrants in Michigan in 1847 during the great wave of Dutch immigration to the Midwest in the mid-nineteenth century. It was affiliated with the Reformed Church in America from 1850 until 1857, when it found itself in disagreement on matters of doctrine and discipline—including whether Reformed Christians should belong to secretive "fraternal organizations" such as the Freemasons. A conference held at Holland, Michigan, effected the separation of the True Holland Reformed Church, which, after a series of name changes, became the present Christian Reformed Church in North America. Emigration from Holland brought several other groups into the new organization, rapidly increasing its membership.

The Christian Reformed Church (CRC) today is largely English-speaking, although the Dutch, Spanish, French, Navajo, Zuni, Korean, Chinese, and Vietnamese languages are used in some of the churches. Conservative theologically, the CRC holds to the three historic Reformed statements as the basis of union: the Belgic Confession (1561), the Canons of Dort (1618), and the Heidelberg Catechism (1563). Organization bears the usual Reformed characteristics. There are forty-seven "classes" (thirty-five in the United States, twelve in Canada) that meet every four months (in some cases every six months) but no intermediate or regional synods between the classes.

A general synod made up of two clergy and two elders from each classis meet annually. The general synod makes decisions regarding theological, liturgical, and ethical matters. It also oversees the ministries shared by CRC churches generally. To this end, the synod has created eight boards and agencies to oversee its ministries, including general church administration, radio and TV ministries, Calvin Theological Seminary, Calvin College, home missions, world relief, publications, and world missions.

Christian Reformed Home Missions provides guidance and financial assistance to some two hundred new and established churches that maintain ministries in many North American communities, including among Navajos, Zunis, African Americans, Asian Americans, Hispanic Americans, and on many university campuses. Almost three hundred foreign missionaries are stationed in Latin America, the Caribbean, Africa, Eastern Europe, and Asia. The Christian Reformed World Relief Committee carries on a relief program serving in twenty-seven countries.

The "Back to God Hour" radio program, broadcast from a chain of stations in the United States and abroad, reaches Europe, Africa, and Asia as well as South America; a television ministry also broadcasts in the United States and Canada. The church sponsors a publishing house in Grand Rapids that provides literature for the church and its agencies, as well as educational material for many other churches.

The CRC has long been an especially productive American denomination in terms of Christian scholarship. Several evangelical Christian liberal arts colleges are associated with it, but its Calvin College and Calvin Theological Seminary in Grand Rapids, Michigan, are centers of evangelical Christian philosophy and theology. It is often regarded as the more evangelical-leaning, but not fundamentalist, counterpart to the older Reformed Church in America (formerly known as the Dutch Reformed Church) from which it split. During the latter decades of the twentieth century the CRC suffered controversies over whether women should be ordained as clergy. The official decision was to permit each "class" (group of congregations) to decide the matter for itself. This led to several defections from the CRC and the founding of new, smaller Reformed denominations.

For more information: www.crcna.org

Headquarters: 2850 Kalamazoo Avenue Southeast, Grand Rapids, MI 49560

CONSERVATIVE CONGREGATIONAL CHRISTIAN CONFERENCE

Founded: 1948
Membership: 42,756, in 316 churches (2016)

The origins of this group go back to 1935 and the work of H. B. Sandine, a pastor in Hancock, Minnesota. He was convinced that the Congregational Christian churches had departed from the beliefs, policy, and practices of historic Congregationalism. He carried on an educational effort through mimeographed documents until 1939, when his efforts were consummated in a monthly publication. A Conservative Congregational Christian Fellowship was organized at Chicago in 1945. The ongoing process of merger among Congregational bodies precipitated the Fellowship's reorganization into the Conservative Congregational Christian Conference in 1948.

The Conference's statement of faith is conservative and evangelical. It includes belief in: the infallibility and authority of the scriptures; the Trinity; the deity, virgin birth, sinlessness, atoning death, resurrection, ascension, and promised return of Jesus Christ; regeneration by the Holy Spirit; the resurrection of both the saved and the lost; and the spiritual unity of all believers in Christ. Local churches are completely autonomous. An annual meeting of clergy and lay representatives from member churches elects a board of directors and a set of officers for the Conference. Work is largely in the areas of missions, church planting, and Christian education, carried on through recognized evangelical home and foreign mission agencies, Bible institutions, colleges, seminaries, and Sunday school publishing houses. The conference is especially active in the fields of church extension, pastoral placement, and regional activities.

For more information: www.ccccusa.com

Headquarters: 8941 Thirty-third Street North, Lake Elmo, MN 55042

CUMBERLAND PRESBYTERIAN CHURCH

Founded: 1810
Membership: 70,810, in 685 congregations (2016)

This church was a product of the great revival known as the Second Great Awakening that swept across the United States between around 1800 to 1840. On February 4, 1810, in Dickson County, Tennessee, three Presbyterian ministers, Finis Ewing (1773–1841), Samuel King (1775–1842), and Samuel McAdow (1760–1844), constituted a new presbytery. They objected to the doctrine of predestination in the Westminster Confession of Faith and insisted that educational standards for ordination of the clergy be more flexible in view of the extraordinary circumstances that then existed on the American frontier. The General Assembly of the church was organized in 1829.

A confession of faith was formulated in 1814, drawing on the Westminster Confession, but affirming key points made by the founders of the church: (1) there are no eternal reprobates (persons predestined by God to hell); (2) Christ died for all humankind, not for the elect alone; (3) there is no infant damnation; and (4) the Spirit of God operates in the world coextensively with Christ's atonement, so "as to leave all men inexcusable." This confession was revised in 1883 and again in 1984. The 1984 document expresses a clear recognition of God's action in the salvation of human beings, noting that repentance is a necessary condition of salvation but not a sufficient one, as God's grace is the fundamental element.

An attempted union with the Presbyterian Church (USA) in 1906 was only partially successful. A considerable segment of the Cumberland Presbyterian membership, to whom the terms of merger were unsatisfactory, perpetuated the church as a separate denomination. Congregations are located for the most part in southern and border states. The church sponsors missionaries in Colombia, Japan, Hong Kong, and Liberia in West Africa. It supports Bethel College in McKenzie, Tennessee; Memphis Theological Seminary; and a children's home in Denton, Texas.

Generally speaking, the Cumberland Presbyterian Church is considered moderately evangelical but not fundamentalist and broadly Reformed in theology (but not strictly Calvinistic). The denomination has many racially integrated churches.

For more information: www.cumberland.org

Headquarters: 8207 Traditional Place, Cordova, TN 38016

CUMBERLAND PRESBYTERIAN CHURCH IN AMERICA

Founded: 1874
Membership: 15,142 (1996), in 107 congregations (2010)

This church developed after the Civil War, when African American pastors and lay members of the Cumberland Presbyterian Church sought to establish their own organization. It has been estimated that some twenty thousand African Americans were associated with the parent church at the time. Led by Moses T. Weir, a former slave, black ministers formed the Synod of Colored Cumberland Presbyterians in 1869. In 1874 the first General Assembly of the Colored Cumberland Presbyterian Church was held. The parent church offered some financial support in the early years of the denomination and has continued to work with the African American body on various issues, including theological formulations.

The Colored Cumberland Presbyterian Church eventually became known as the Second Cumberland Presbyterian Church and, late in the twentieth century, as the Cumberland Presbyterian Church in America. The church's doctrinal position is similar to that of the Cumberland Presbyterian Church. Members of the two bodies worked together on the 1984 Confession of Faith. This document gives contemporary expression to the historic Presbyterian witness, with particular emphasis on God's saving grace. In 2012 the two denominations formed a joint task force to explore possible union.

The Cumberland Presbyterian Church in America now has four synods, primarily in the Midwest and the South. The church's ministers are trained at the Cumberland Presbyterian Church College in McKenzie, Tennessee, and at its seminary in Memphis.

Serious conversation continues concerning unification with the Cumberland Presbyterian Church.

For more information: www.cpcaga.org

Headquarters: 226 Church Street, Huntsville, AL 35801

ECO: A COVENANT ORDER OF EVANGELICAL PRESBYTERIANS

Founded: 2012

Membership: est. 100,000, in 300 congregations (2016)

ECO was officially organized as a new Presbyterian denomination at a meeting of approximately twenty-two hundred delegates in Florida in 2012. This was the result of several previous meetings among evangelical Presbyterians including one in Minneapolis in 2011 that formed The Fellowship of Presbyterians, a precursor to ECO. Most of the founding members of ECO were ministers and laypeople of the more liberal, "mainline" Presbyterian Church (USA). The word *ECO* is not an acronym; it stands for the denomination's concern to strengthen the ecosystems of congregations.

ECO affirms the authority of the Bible and Christ-centered theology and ministry. It also affirms the ordination of women and permits women to serve equally with men in all forms of ministry including elder. (In the Presbyterian system "ruling elders" are normally laypeople selected by the congregation and "teaching elders" are the pastors.)

ECO is one of the newest denominations in the United States and is still developing (2016). It has 502 pastors and continues to grow as people and congregations leave the Presbyterian Church (USA) over its progressive theological and social views including especially the welcoming and affirming stance toward LGBT persons of many Presbyterian Church (USA) congregations.

The denomination has fourteen presbyteries (regions of congregations). It is presbyterial (representative) in its form of church government. Theologically ECO affirms the traditional doctrinal standards of the Reformed tradition in its Presbyterian expression. *The Book of Confessions* of the historic Presbyterian tradition including the ecumenical creeds of Christianity and the Reformed confessions of faith, including the Westminster Confession and Catechism, is affirmed as its doctrinal "treasure." However, it seeks to give contemporary expression to these Reformed confessions and the doctrines they contain. In other words, it is broadly Calvinistic in theology without placing especially strong emphasis on doctrines such as predestination.

For more information: www.eco-pres.org

Headquarters: 5638 Hollister Avenue, Suite 200, Goleta, CA 93117

EVANGELICAL ASSOCIATION OF REFORMED AND CONGREGATIONAL CHURCHES

Founded: 1998
Membership: statistics unavailable; about 75 churches

The Evangelical Association is made up primarily of congregations that left the United Church of Christ because of disagreements over theological and social issues. The church grew rapidly after 2005 when the UCC allowed same-gender marriage ceremonies and ordination of persons regardless of sexual orientation. The Evangelical Association holds to basic Reformed (Calvinist) teachings, and explicitly rejects abortion, extra-marital sexual relations, and same-gender sexual relations. The denominational is Congregationalist in ecclesiology, and member churches are permitted to be in more than one association. The national organization is minimal. The denomination was founded in New Braunfels, Texas, but is strongest in North Carolina.

The Evangelical Association permits ordination of women and women pastors of local congregations; it views that as a matter of congregational autonomy (each congregation decides for itself whether to ordain women and whether to have women pastors). It embraces a basically conservative and evangelical theology without fundamentalism. Its ethos is empowerment of local congregations for ministry and mission. There is no hierarchy within the denomination. Member churches do not ordain openly gay people or call them to minister.

For more information: www.evangelicalassociation.net
Headquarters: 9051 Watson Road #241, Saint Louis, MO 63126

EVANGELICAL PRESBYTERIAN CHURCH

Founded: 1981
Membership: est. 150,000, in 575 congregations (2016)

The Evangelical Presbyterian Church (EPC) grew out of a series of meetings of conservative Presbyterian pastors and church elders held in Saint Louis, Missouri, in 1980–81. They wished to form a church informed by scripture and the historic confessions of the Christian faith and committed to evangelism. The EPC is a conservative denomination composed of eight presbyteries in the United States, with churches in twenty-nine states. It identifies itself as "Reformed in doctrine, presbyterian in polity, and evangelical in spirit." The EPC places high priority on church-planting in the United States and world missions. About eighty world outreach missionaries serve the church's mission at home and abroad. High priority is also placed on developing its women's ministries and youth ministries.

The Westminster Confession and its catechisms are the church's doctrinal standards. Unlike other conservative Presbyterian bodies, it includes chapter 34, "Of the Holy Spirit," and chapter 35, "Of the Love of God and Missions" in the Confession. The historic motto "In essentials, unity; in nonessentials, liberty; in all things, charity" expresses the irenic spirit of the EPC. To the broader world, the General Assembly bears witness on particular issues through position papers.

The EPC has experienced significant growth in the first decades of the twenty-first century as some Presbyterian Church (USA) congregations have sought a more theologically and socially conservative denomination with which to affiliate. While the EPC rejects same-sex marriage within the church and is not "welcoming and affirming" with regard to gay and lesbian people, it does affirm the possible pastoral leadership of women including women's ordination. It positions itself somewhere between the more liberal-leaning Presbyterian Church (USA) and the more conservative Presbyterian Church in America*, which does not affirm the ordination or pastoral leadership of women. The EPC also, unlike most Presbyterian denominations, is friendly toward charismatics.

For more information: www.epc.org

Headquarters: 17197 North Laurel Park Drive, Suite 567, Livonia, MI 48152-7912

KOREAN AMERICAN PRESBYTERIAN CHURCH

Founded: 1976
Membership: 55,000, in about 300 churches (2010)

The Korean American Presbyterian Church (KAPC) was established to serve Korean immigrants in North America. It is affiliated with the Presbyterian Church of Korea, one of the largest Christian churches in Korea. The first Korean Presbyterian pastor was Sun Sang-Ryun, who founded a congregation in 1884. An American physician named Horace Newton Allen (1858–1932) was sent to East Asia by the Presbyterian Board of Foreign Missions in 1883 and the next year arrived in Korea as part of the American Legation. In addition to founding medical centers, Allen helped change Korean policy toward Christian missions. By the end of the century, he was serving as the United States counsel in Seoul. Presbyterian missionary John Ross completed his translation of the Bible into Korean in 1887. Several Korean Presbyterian leaders participated in the March First Movement, which declared independence from Japanese control in 1919. The movement failed, and the church suffered persecution. Korean theologians used native Korean concepts, such as *han* (unjust suffering) to interpret Christian doctrine. Theologians like Kim Young-Sam created *Minjung* theology, which focuses on the image of God in all people, especially the poor and oppressed. Until 1950, most Protestants in Korea lived in the north, but the Korean War and subsequent division of the country caused many to flee to the south. The South Korean government promoted Christianity as part of its anti-communist, pro-American policy, but some Christian leaders used *Minjung* theology to protest the militarism of the government. During the 1980s millions of Koreans converted to Christianity, in part because of the church's support of democracy and human rights.

During that same period, many Koreans immigrated to the United States, and the KAPC was formed to minister to them. The church is theologically conservative. In addition to the Westminster Confession and the Larger and Shorter Catechisms, pastors ascribe to a creed that emphasizes biblical inerrancy, the absoluteness of God, the sin of Adam and Eve, and the necessity of faith. Works and obedience to the law of God result from saving faith. The Presbyterian Church (USA) and the KPCA ratified a covenant relationship in 2009.

For more information: www.kapc.org

Headquarters: 309 State Street, Hackensack, NJ 07601

NATIONAL ASSOCIATION OF CONGREGATIONAL CHRISTIAN CHURCHES

Founded: 1955
Membership: est. 63,392, in 432 churches (2012)

This association was organized in order to "preserve historical Congregational forms of freedom and fellowship (the Congregational Way)." It is the largest of Congregational bodies that did not participate when the General Council of Congregational Churches and the Evangelical and Reformed Church merged to form the United Church of Christ* in 1957. The National Association brings local churches together for counsel, inspiration, and fellowship, but preserves the independence and autonomy of the local churches. It describes its mission as encouraging and assisting local churches "in their development of vibrant and effective witnesses to Christ in congregational ways."

There is no binding ecclesiastical authority and no required creed or program. Members are "bound together not by uniformity of belief but by the acceptance of a covenant purpose to be 'the people of God.'" The association leaves to each church any decision to participate in social and political questions and action. A moderator presides over an annual meeting of representatives of all the member churches; an executive committee of twelve acts for the association between meetings. There is widespread missionary work in the United States and around the world in the Philippines, Mexico, Bulgaria, Kenya, Nigeria, Ghana, India, and Honduras.

For more information: www.naccc.org

Headquarters: 8473 Howell Avenue, PO Box 288, Oak Creek, WI 53154

NETHERLANDS REFORMED CONGREGATIONS IN NORTH AMERICA

Founded: 1907
Membership: about 10,146, in 27 congregations (2012)

The Netherlands Reformed Congregations in North America broke away from the Christian Reformed Church over doctrinal differences. This body stresses the classic doctrines of the Reformed tradition as expressed in the Belgic Confession of Faith (1561), the Heidelberg Catechism (1563), and the Canons of Dort (1618). The church stresses "experiential Calvinism," which means that feelings are as important as intellectual assent in matters of faith. It also stresses the need for regeneration or rebirth through personal faith. The church has a formal liturgy based on Dutch models, and it remains closely connected to conservative Reformed churches in the Netherlands. It supports several home and foreign missions, especially in Bolivia, and twelve schools. A seminary was established in Grand Rapids, Michigan, in 1996.

A smaller, breakaway denomination known as the Heritage Reformed Congregations is very similar to the Netherlands Reformed Congregations in North America and the two groups cooperate on some endeavors. Yet another small and similar denomination that also cooperates with them is the Free Reformed Churches of North America.

For more information: www.netherlandsreformed.org

Contact: Netherlands Reformed Book and Publishing, 1233 Leffingwell Northeast, Grand Rapids, MI 49505

ORTHODOX PRESBYTERIAN CHURCH

Founded: 1936
Membership: 31,200, in 278 congregations (2015)

This church originated in protest against what were believed to be modernistic beliefs and practices in the Presbyterian Church in the USA. The dissenters, led by Princeton professor J. Gresham Machen (1881–1937), were suspended from the Presbyterian Church in the USA and organized the Presbyterian Church of America. However, an injunction was brought against the use of that name by the parent body, and in 1938 the name was changed to Orthodox Presbyterian Church.

Machen was a notable leader in the early fundamentalist movement in the United States. He was a highly educated New Testament scholar and theologian who wrote, among other books, *Christianity and Liberalism* (1923) in which he argued that liberal Protestantism is not Christian due to perceived radical differences from historic, creedal, orthodox Christian doctrines. Machen helped found Westminster Theological Seminary in Philadelphia as a rival seminary to Princeton where he had earlier taught.

Orthodox Presbyterians lay strong emphasis on the infallibility and inerrancy of the Bible. They believe that the writers of the books of the Bible were "so guided by [God] that their original manuscripts were without error in fact or doctrine." Fundamental doctrines include original sin; the virgin birth, the deity, and substitutionary atonement of Christ; his resurrection and ascension; his role as judge at the end of the world and the consummation of the kingdom; the sovereignty of God; and salvation through the sacrifice and power of Christ for those "the Father purposes to save." Salvation is "not because of good works [but] in order to do good works." The Westminster Confession and the Larger and the Shorter Catechisms are accepted as subordinate doctrinal standards or creedal statements.

The Orthodox Presbyterian Church has published *Trinity Hymnal*, probably the only hymnal designed as a worship supplement to the Westminster Confession of Faith. The denomination has churches in almost every state. Ordained elders must be heterosexual men. It has 535 ordained ministers (2015).

For more information: www.opc.org

Headquarters: 607 North Easton Road, Building E, Box P, Willow Grove, PA 19090

PRESBYTERIAN CHURCH IN AMERICA

Founded: 1973
Membership: 370,332, in 1,861 congregations (2015)

The Presbyterian Church in America (PCA) was formed in 1973 when delegates from 260 conservative congregations that had withdrawn from the southern Presbyterian Church in the United States (PCUS) convened a general assembly. These congregations opposed the PCUS's ecumenical involvements in the National Council of the Churches of Christ, the World Council of Churches, and the Consultation on Church Union. They also opposed the impending merger with the more liberal United Presbyterian Church in the United States of America. The PCA also rejected (and rejects) the ordination of women at a time when the older PCUS was placing strong emphasis on women's ordination. At first known as the National Presbyterian Church, the present name was adopted in 1974.

The Westminster Confession of Faith is the PCA's primary doctrinal standard. The church teaches that the Holy Spirit guided the writers of the scriptures so that the writings are free of error of fact, doctrine, and judgment. They also emphasize the doctrines of total human depravity, unconditional election (of individuals to salvation), Christ's death for the elect only, irresistible grace, and the perseverance of the saints. This is commonly called "five points of Calvinism." The church takes a conservative stance on many social issues, especially related to homosexuality and abortion, and it sponsors dozens of military chaplains.

The PCA maintains the historic polity of Presbyterian governance: rule by presbyters (or elders) and the graded courts, the session governing the local church; the presbytery for regional matters; and the general assembly at the national level. It makes a distinction between the two classes of elders: teaching elders (ministers) and ruling elders (laymen).

In 1982, the Reformed Presbyterian Church, Evangelical Synod (RPCES), joined the PCA, bringing with it Covenant College on Lookout Mountain, Georgia, and Covenant Theological Seminary in Saint Louis, Missouri. The PCA headquarters is in Atlanta, where work by three program committees is coordinated: Mission to the World, Mission to North America, and Christian Education and Publications. The denomination has congregations in nearly every state, and has grown rapidly in recent years. It also has an extensive mission to the world, with over five hundred full-time missionaries and thousands of short-term missionaries.

One of the best-known and most-influential PCA ministers is New York pastor and best-selling author Tim Keller who is widely recognized even outside the PCA for his contemporary defenses of orthodox, evangelical Christianity and his modern ministry to urban dwellers in Manhattan. The PCA has resisted internal attempts by ultra-conservative pastors and laypeople to establish as doctrine so-called young earth creationism.

For more information: www.pcanet.org

Headquarters: 1700 North Brown Road, Suite 105, Lawrenceville, GA 30043

PRESBYTERIAN CHURCH (USA)

Founded: 1983
Membership: 1,775,917 (2015), in 10,560 congregations (2012)

Following formal separation that began during the Civil War and lasted for 122 years, the two largest American Presbyterian churches (PCUS and UPCUSA) were reunited on June 10, 1983, to form the Presbyterian Church (USA) [PCUSA]. Over the next fifteen years, great effort was expended to work out the administrative details of combining the two denominations and their numerous presbyteries and ministry groups.

The southern denomination had been established as the PCUS at the time of the Civil War, and its church government developed parallel to that of the northern churches. Offices were gradually centralized in Atlanta under the General Assembly Mission Board; mission work was always undertaken on a worldwide scale, a special source of pride to southern Presbyterians.

The northern body (PCUSA) merged with the United Presbyterian Church of North America (UPCNA) in 1958. The UPCNA had been formed exactly a century earlier by a merger of the Associate Presbyterian Church with the Associate Reformed Presbyterian

Church. Their doctrines, traditions, and institutions were preserved in the new church's presbyterial style of government by local sessions, presbyteries, synods, and general assembly.

The Westminster Confession (1647) had been the basic doctrinal statement of American Presbyterians since colonial times, but with the merger of the two northern denominations in 1958 it was noted that the Westminster Confession was more than three hundred years old. In 1967, the first new major Presbyterian doctrinal statement since 1647 was ratified by the General Assembly. The confession is Christ-centered and avoids what many saw as the confusing terminology of the Westminster Confession. Instead it stressed the concepts of love, sin, eternal life, and the work of reconciliation in God, Christ, and the church.

Some felt that the new document watered down the Westminster Confession, but most United Presbyterians accepted the document as reflecting true Presbyterianism and as offering a wide theological basis on which all Presbyterians could stand together. With the acceptance of the new confession, the PCUSA has a *Book of Confessions* with nine creeds and confessions of faith: the Nicene Creed, the Apostles' Creed, the Scots Confession of 1560, the Heidelberg Confession of 1563, the Westminster Confession of 1647, the Larger Catechism of 1647, the Shorter Catechism of 1647, the 1934 Theological Declaration of Barmen, and the Confession of 1967. This *Book of Confessions* was adopted by the PCUSA with the reunification of 1983.

The PCUSA follows typical Presbyterian polity. The yearly General Assembly is the final authority, but it cannot amend the church's constitution without ratification from the presbyteries. There are two officers of the General Assembly: a stated clerk (the chief executive officer of the church) is elected for a four-year term and may be reelected; a moderator is chosen each year to preside over the meetings and often speaks for the church during the year.

In 1988 the national headquarters of the new denomination was dedicated in Louisville, Kentucky. The national organization was restructured in the 1990s, and the church struggles with declining membership. The church has operated two publishing companies, now united in Louisville as Westminster John Knox Press. The church has a long and rich history of education and theological inquiry. There are sixty-eight Presbyterian-related colleges, eleven seminaries, and six secondary schools in the United States. The PCUSA has a strong history of social justice ministries and advocacy for disadvantaged groups. In recent years, the denomination has experienced conflict over the issue of extending ordination to people who do not identify as heterosexuals and blessing same-sex marriage; its perceived leniency and progressivism on these practices has led to the departure of many PCUSA congregations and the formation of new, more conservative Presbyterian denominations.

For more information: www.pcusa.org

Headquarters: 100 Witherspoon Street, Louisville, KY 40202

PROTESTANT REFORMED CHURCHES IN AMERICA

Founded: 1926
Membership: 8,478, in 32 congregations (2016)

In 1924, three consistories and the pastors of the Classes Grand Rapids East and Grand Rapids West of the Christian Reformed Church in North America were deposed from that denomination as the result of a disagreement over the doctrines of universal grace and evangelism. Christian Reformed pastor-theologian Herman Hoeksema (1886–1965) was foremost among those who taught that grace for the elect alone is an essential aspect of Reformed faith. Those who objected to the doctrine and were forced out of the church formally organized as the Protestant Reformed Churches in America (PRCA) in 1926.

The distinctive doctrine of the PRCA is sometimes called "hyper-Calvinism" by critics. Defenders of the doctrine (who reject that appellation) believe it is simply the logical extension of Calvinism's belief in unconditional election and irresistible grace. The controversial doctrine, rejected by the Christian Reformed Church and most Reformed churches, but held by the PRCA, is that the gospel's offer of salvation to the unsaved is for the elect and should not be made indiscriminately to all people as if anyone can be saved. The Christian Reformed Church and most other Reformed churches believe the offer of salvation through the gospel proclamation to all people, including the non-elect, is a "well-meant offer."

The PRCA holds to the three basic Reformed confessions (the Heidelberg Catechism of 1563, the Belgic Confession of 1561, and the Canons of Dort of 1618) as the basis of their belief in the infallible word of God. Their form of church government is presbyterian. There are two classes, organized geographically; a general synod meets annually in June. Membership is found mainly in the upper Midwest. The church maintains a theological seminary at Grand Rapids, Michigan.

For more information: www.prca.org
Headquarters: 4949 Ivanrest Avenue, Grandville, MI 49418

REFORMED CHURCH IN AMERICA

Founded: 1792
Membership: 246,024, in 886 congregations (2012)

The Reformed Church in America (RCA) was established in North America in 1628, when the Dutch Reformed Church established its first congregation in New Amsterdam. By the time the English took possession in 1664, Dutch Reformed congregations had been organized in several boroughs. Gradually the churches became Americanized, severing ties with the Netherlands and adopting the English language. In order to provide an educated pastorate, the church established Queen's College (now Rutgers University) and New Brunswick Theological Seminary in New Jersey.

The Reformed Church remained largely an eastern church until the mid-1800s, when a second wave of Dutch immigrants came to the New World. One group, led by Albertus van Raalte, established a community called Holland in western Michigan. Another was established in Iowa. Beginning in the 1920s the church spread westward. A substantial number of Reformed churches organized or revitalized in recent decades have been African American, Asian American, and Hispanic. The Reformed Church has been a mission-minded denomination from the beginning. RCA personnel were among the first Christian missionaries in Arabia, China, Japan, and India. The church continues to support more than one hundred missionaries on five continents.

The church holds to the traditional Reformed doctrinal statements, especially the Belgic Confession (1561), the Heidelberg Catechism (1563), and the Canons of Dort (1618); but it interprets them more flexibly than do many Reformed groups. The church also affirms the Apostles' Creed, the Athanasian Creed, and the Nicene Creed. A contemporary statement of faith, "Our Song of Hope," was approved in 1978. The church emphasizes the need to be obedient to the will of God, which includes active engagement in social justice. The RCA ordains women to pastoral ministry and, like most so-called mainline Protestant denominations, struggles with issues of ordaining people who do not identify as heterosexual and of same-sex marriage. Its general position is what many would describe as "welcoming but not affirming."

The church follows typical Reformed polity (presbyterian). The highest representative body is the General Synod, which meets once a year. The services and ministries of the denomination are overseen by a representative body called the General Council. Today the greatest numerical strength is in New York, Michigan, New Jersey, Iowa, Illinois, and California. Throughout the later part of the twentieth century the best-known RCA congregation was the now-defunct Crystal Cathedral in Garden Grove, California, pastored by Robert H. Schuller. In 1998, the church entered into full communion with the Evangelical Lutheran Church in America, the Presbyterian Church (USA), and the United Church of Christ. In 2007 it established full communion with the Christian Reformed Church in North America as well.

For more information: www.rca.org

Headquarters: 475 Riverside Drive, 18th Floor, New York, NY 10115

REFORMED CHURCH IN THE UNITED STATES

Founded: 1986 with roots to 1934
Membership: 3,720, in 50 congregations (2016)

The Reformed Church in the United States (RCUS) is one of the more conservative Reformed denominations in the United States. It began as a breakaway from the Evangelical and Reformed Church, which was created in 1934 by an amalgamation of previously existing German-based Reformed and Lutheran denominations. The Eureka classis decided not to join the new united denomination due to the Lutheran influence and its perceived "Americanization." In 1986 the Eureka classis dissolved to form the RCUS.

The RCUS holds firmly to the classical, orthodox creeds of Christianity (Nicene and Athanasian); and to the historic Reformed "symbols of unity" (confessions): the Heidelberg Confession and Catechism, the Belgic Confession, and the Canons of Dort. It affirms the inerrancy of scripture, denies women's leadership in church decision-making, and embraces a literal interpretation of Genesis but not of Revelation. It claims to be non-fundamentalist because it does not believe in the premillennial return of Christ and does not condemn consumption of alcoholic beverages. It is not revivalistic.

For more information: www.rcus.org

Headquarters: 407 West Main Street, Grass Valley, CA 95945

REFORMED PRESBYTERIAN CHURCH
OF NORTH AMERICA

Founded: 1809
Membership: 7,035, in 88 congregations (2016)

The Reformed Presbyterian Church of North America (RPCNA) traces its roots to the Covenanter Presbyterians of Scotland in the eighteenth century who resisted the British monarch's attempts to impose Anglican religious beliefs and practices on them. A synod of Scottish Presbyterian immigrants to the United States was constituted at Philadelphia in 1809, only to split into Old Light and New Light groups divided by the revivalism of the Second Great Awakening in 1833. Another dispute concerned citizenship and the right of church members to vote or participate in public affairs. However, restriction was finally removed in 1964, and members are free to participate in civil government and to vote on issues and for political candidates committed to Christian principles of civil government. The church places special emphasis on the inerrancy of scripture, the sovereignty of God, and the Lordship of Christ over every area of human life. Church government is thoroughly presbyterian, except that there is no general assembly. Members use only the Psalms in their worship services; no instrumental music is permitted. Members cannot join secret societies. Home missionaries work in seven states; foreign missionaries are stationed in Japan, Cyprus, and Taiwan. Geneva College is located at Beaver Falls, Pennsylvania, and the Reformed Presbyterian Theological Seminary is in Pittsburgh.

For more information: www.reformedpresbyterian.org

Headquarters: 7408 Penn Avenue, Pittsburgh, PA 15208

UNITED CHURCH OF CHRIST

Founded: 1957, with roots to the colonial period
Membership: 914,871, in 5,032 congregations (2015)

The United Church of Christ (UCC) traces its origins to the Congregationalists of New England but it also represents one of the most significant products of the ecumenical movement. In 1957 two major American denominations united to constitute the United Church of Christ: the Congregational Christian Churches and the Evangelical and Reformed Church in the United States. These two denominations were themselves results of earlier mergers. Within the new denomination, local congregations for the most continued to observe the liturgy and theological positions they had before the merger. In essence, the UCC remains a federation of two denominations with related but distinct identities.

On July 8, 1959, at Oberlin, Ohio, representatives of the Congregational Christian Churches and the Evangelical and Reformed Church, upon merging into the United Church of Christ, adopted a statement, understood as a "testimony rather than a test of faith." It affirms belief in God the creator who "in Jesus Christ, the man of Nazareth, our crucified and risen Lord . . . has come to us and shared our common lot, conquering sin and death and reconciling the world to himself." The statement also identifies the church as a "covenant faithful people of all ages, tongues, and races," which is called to "the service of men." Although this statement was not intended to set forth doctrinal positions or to stand as a substitute for the historic creeds, confessions, and covenants of the churches involved, it served as a witness to the faith, charity, and understanding of the merging groups.

The UCC represents a union of two forms of church government: Congregationalism and presbyterianism. The church establishes Congregationalism as the rule for the local congregation and presbyterianism as the basis of organization of the member churches' connectional life. The constitution is explicit: "The autonomy of the local church is inherent and modifiable only by its own action. Nothing . . . shall destroy or limit the right of each local church to continue to operate in the way customary to it."

Local churches in a geographical area are grouped into an association, which assists needy churches; receives new churches into the denomination; licenses, ordains, and installs clergy; adopts its own constitution, bylaws, and rules of procedure; and is made up of the ordained ministers and elected lay delegates of the area. Associations are grouped into conferences, again by geographical area, with the exception of the Calvin Synod, which consists of churches from the Hungarian Reformed tradition. A conference acts on requests and references from the local churches, associations, general synod, and other bodies. Its main function is to coordinate the work and witness of its local churches and associations; to render counsel and advisory service; and to establish conference offices, centers, institutions, and other agencies.

The General Synod is the highest representative body. It meets biennially and is composed of conference delegates and voting members of boards of directors of the Covenanted Ministries of the church. An Executive Council is elected by the General Synod to act for the synod between its meetings. It recommends salaries for officers of the church as part of a national budget, has responsibility for the church's publications, and appoints committees not otherwise provided. It also submits to the General Synod "any recommendation it may deem useful" for the work of the church. General church offices are located in Cleveland, Ohio, as is the church's publishing arm, Pilgrim Press.

Since 1985, the UCC has enjoyed an ecumenical partnership with the Christian Church (Disciples of Christ). Both denominations are active in the Consultation on Church Union; and they join in common witness through Global Ministries, which operates teaching and service ministries throughout the world. Twenty-nine colleges and universities are related to the UCC, six of which are historically African American. The UCC makes social justice a high priority in its Christian witness.

The UCC is one of the most progressive (critics would say "liberal") Protestant denominations in the world. While it officially adheres to orthodox Christian doctrinal standards it permits wide latitude in doctrinal and ethical opinions among its ministers and members. The UCC has shed most of the traditional Calvinism of its Puritan roots in New England Congregationalism and German Reformed Protestantism. The denomination permits ordination of openly gay and lesbian persons to ministry as well as performance of same-sex marriage ceremonies in its churches. It was among the first major American "mainline" Protestant denominations to place emphasis on the full and equal ministry of women. The denomination's progressivism has led to the loss of many members and congregations to more conservative Reformed and Congregational denominations.

For more information: www.ucc.org

Headquarters: 700 Prospect Avenue, Cleveland, OH 44115

UNITED REFORMED CHURCHES IN NORTH AMERICA

Founded: 1996
Membership: est. 22,500, in est. 105 congregations

The United Reformed Churches in North America (URCNA) is one of the youngest Reformed denominations in the United States. It was founded by a group of disaffected

Christian Reformed Church (CRC) pastors and members who believed that denomination was straying from historical, conservative Reformed beliefs and practices. One specific issue was the CRC's permission of ordination of women. Another was the teaching of theistic evolution at the CRC's colleges. The United Reformed Church holds very firmly to the historic, orthodox creeds of Christianity including especially the Nicene Creed and to the three "symbols of unity" of Reformed theology: the Heidelberg Confession and Catechism, the Belgic Confession, and the Canons of Dort. The denomination only allows heterosexual men to serve as elders (ordained pastors or lay leaders of congregations). It does not permit the performance of same-sex weddings in its churches.

The URCNA supports missions in many countries around the world including Ecuador and the Philippines. It does not have its own seminary but recognizes Westminster Theological Seminary (Escondido, California) as one institution for training its ministers.

For more information: www.urcna.org

Headquarters: 227 First Avenue Southeast, Sioux Center, IA 51250

MENNONITE AND ANABAPTIST CHURCHES

Dating from the 1520s in Central Europe, these Protestants take their name from Menno Simons (ca. 1496–1561), an early Dutch leader of the "Radical Reformation." These reformers rejected the "magisterial Reformation" of Martin Luther and John Calvin whom they believed compromised Jesus's teachings. The first Anabaptist congregation of historical record was organized at Zurich, Switzerland, in 1525 by Protestant reformer Ulrich Zwingli's own followers who strongly disagreed with him about several issues including especially infant baptism. They denied the scriptural validity of infant baptism and hence were labeled Anabaptist, or "rebaptizers." They also disagreed with the pace of reformation in Zurich wanting it to go more quickly and further in departing from Catholic beliefs and practices. Zwingli, chief pastor of the city, allowed the city council to set the pace. The Anabaptists wanted greater separation between church and state. On January 21, 1525, Conrad Grebel (1496–1526) baptized George Blaurock (1491–1529), who then baptized others. In 1527 a group of radical reformers in Germany signed the Schleitheim Confession, which called for separation of church and state and restoration of the simplicity of the New Testament church. They were, then, the original "restorationists" and many other Protestant denominations in the United States would be influenced by their strong desire to restore the New Testament church stripped of centuries of accumulated traditions. These radical reformers denied that they were rebaptizing anyone because they did not believe infant baptism is real baptism at all. They argued that Protestant reformers such as Luther and Zwingli were falling into contradiction with themselves by insisting on salvation by faith alone and continuing to baptize infants because infants cannot have faith. They placed a great emphasis on personal decision to become a Christian and voluntary church membership. They set themselves firmly against "Christendom"—the union or even cooperation between church and state begun by Roman Emperor Constantine.

There were many kinds of religious radicals during the Reformation who were treated as outsiders, heretics, and outlaws by Catholics and Protestants alike. Many of the early Anabaptist leaders were executed, often in gruesome fashion. Their primary concerns were not with proper theology, the sacraments, or liturgy. Rather, they believed themselves called to exemplify godly living based on the Sermon on the Mount (Matt 5:1–7:29). Until recently, most of those quietly dedicated Christians frowned on involvement in secular activity, refusing to take oaths, bear arms, vote, or hold public office. They are a "called-out" (from the state, from conventional society) fellowship of believers. Always emphasizing the local congregation, some groups insist on living in "intentional communities."

Menno Simons, a former Roman Catholic priest who was baptized by an Anabaptist preacher in Holland, organized so many congregations that his name became identified by many with the Anabaptist movement. Simons was a strict pacifist, and his writings continue to influence the Mennonites and other Anabaptists. Mennonite beliefs are based on a confession of faith signed at Dordrecht, Holland, in 1632. In eighteen articles, the following doctrines were laid down: faith in God as creator; humanity's fall and restoration at the coming of Christ; Christ as the Son of God, who redeemed humankind on the cross; obedience to Christ's law in the gospel; the necessity of repentance and conversion for salvation; baptism as a public testimony of faith; the Lord's Supper as an expression of common union and fellowship; matrimony only among the "spiritually kindred"; obedience to and respect for civil government, except in the use of armed force; exclusion from the church and social ostracism of those who sin willfully; and future reward for the faithful and punishment for the wicked.

Their pacifism and rejection of the state religion brought severe persecution, and the number of Anabaptist martyrs might have been much greater had it not been for the haven offered by Quaker William Penn (1644–1718) in the American colonies. Several families settled in Germantown near Philadelphia in 1683, and eventually a Mennonite congregation was established there. Mennonite immigrants from Germany and Switzerland spread over Pennsylvania, Ohio, Virginia, Indiana, Illinois, and into the far-western United States and Canada; these were later joined by others from Russia, Prussia, and Poland. Other groups of Anabaptists mirrored Mennonites but with slight differences of belief and practice. Many of them also settled in the American colonies to find freedom from persecution in Europe by both Catholics and magisterial Protestants.

The Lord's Supper is served twice a year in almost all Mennonite congregations; in most, baptism is by pouring ("effusion") and only follows a personal and preferably public profession of faith. Most also observe foot-washing as an ordinance in connection with the Lord's Supper, after which they salute one another with the "kiss of peace." Mennonites and most Anabaptists baptize only on confession of faith, refuse to take oaths before magistrates, oppose secret societies, and strictly follow the teachings of the New Testament. They have a strong intra-church program of mutual aid and provide worldwide relief through the Mennonite Central Committee.

The local congregation is more or less autonomous and authoritative, although in some instances appeals are taken to district or state conferences. The officers of the church are bishops (often called elders), ministers, and deacons (almoners). Many ministers are self-supporting, working in secular employment when not occupied with the work of the church. Other officers are appointed for Sunday school, young people's work, and other duties.

The Amish are the most conservative branch of the Anabaptist movement. Jacob Amman (ca. 1656–1730), a Swiss Anabaptist bishop, insisted on strict adherence to the confession of faith, especially in the matter of shunning excommunicated members. This literalism brought about a separation in Switzerland in 1693. Early Amish immigrants to the United States concentrated in Pennsylvania and spread into Ohio, Indiana, Illinois, Nebraska, and other western states and into Canada.

Many Amish, distinguished by their severely plain clothing, are found in the Conservative Amish Church and Old Order Amish Church. They are still the literalists of the movement, clinging tenaciously to the Pennsylvania Dutch language and seventeenth-century culture of their Swiss-German forebears. Most Amish oppose the use of automobiles, telephones, and higher education and are recognized as extremely efficient farmers. On the other hand, some Amish groups are less strict in rejecting modern technology. The Beachy Amish, for example, drive cars and use cell phones.

Over the centuries since the movement's beginnings Anabaptists have divided into numerous groups over degrees of separation from modern society and culture, degrees of involvement with government entities, interpretations of pacifism, and even, in some cases, styles of clothing. Anabaptists in the United States run the gamut from extremely conservative Amish, best known to most people through numerous cable television programs about them (some of which are entirely fictional and do not faithfully represent the group), to more modern Mennonites and Brethren groups who are often barely distinguishable from (for example) mainstream Baptists—except for the Anabaptists' emphasis on pacifism.

What do all the groups here categorized as Mennonites and (other) Anabaptists have in common besides a common history rooted in the Radical Reformation? All reject infant baptism and emphasize voluntary church membership. All believe full Christian existence, even salvation, begins with a conscious decision of repentance and faith made public in believer baptism, which is not sacramental but symbolic (an act of commitment). They are all "peace churches" that reject deadly violence by Christians while often admitting that the state must practice it for the safety of citizens. All emphasize separation of church and state and believe churches and worship should be simple, unadorned, stripped of all that accumulated through post-New Testament traditions. They emphasize the New Testament and even the Sermon on the Mount as a kind of "canon within the canon" of scripture and stress "discipleship" following the example of Christ and the earliest apostles. While they have doctrines, highly systematized theologies are not their interest. They are very concerned with community, including accountability, within and among their churches. Many of them make church decisions by consensus rather than hierarchical authority. Some have leaders they call "bishops," but they do not embrace apostolic succession (except as a succession of true New Testament teaching and practice). Many people wonder about the relationship between Anabaptists and Baptists. One influential Baptist theologian coined the term "baptist"—with a small *b*—to cover both traditions and others with similar beliefs and practices (especially voluntary church membership and strong emphasis on separation of church and state). One interpretation of Baptist history connects the beginnings of the Baptist movement with Mennonites in the Netherlands; some scholars even go so far as to merge Baptist history into Anabaptist history, blending the two movements together as really one historically and theologically. However, the early Baptists were strongly influenced by English Puritans as well, which was not the case with Mennonites and other Anabaptists. Few Baptists groups have been pacifists.

The Young Center for Anabaptist and Pietist Studies is part of Elizabethtown College, a Church of the Brethren institution in Pennsylvania. It provides wonderful resources for the study of Anabaptist (and pietist) culture, religion, and history.

SUGGESTIONS FOR FURTHER READING

Dyck, Cornelius J. *An Introduction to Mennonite History*. Scottdale, PA: Herald Press, 1993.

Hostetler, Beulah Stauffer. *American Mennonites and Protestant Movements: A Community Paradigm*. Scottdale, PA: Herald Press, 1987.

Hostetler, John A. *Amish Society*. 4th ed. Baltimore, MD: Johns Hopkins University Press, 1993.

Hostetler, John A. *Hutterite Society*. Baltimore, MD: Johns Hopkins University Press, 1974.

Kraybill, Donald B., and Mark A. Olshan. *The Amish Struggle with Modernity*. Hanover, NH: University Press of New England, 1994.

MacMaster, Richard K. *Land, Piety, Peoplehood: The Establishment of Mennonite Communities in America 1683–1790*. Scottdale, PA: Herald Press, 1990.

Williams, George Huntson. *The Radical Reformation*. Philadelphia, PA: Westminster, 1962.

AMISH CHURCHES

Founded: 1720s
Membership: est. over 200,000, in over 1,000 congregations (2012)

Amish Christians are very conservative Anabaptists who tend to reject modernity, including the industrial revolution, as "worldly." Americans have become more familiar with them in the early twenty-first century due to numerous books ("Amish Romances"), movies (e.g., *Witness*), and television programs about them. However, some of these non-Amish portrayals of the Amish amount to little more than stereotypes and caricatures. The Amish are very diverse, even when they are geographically close together. In one Pennsylvania county, for example, one can find several distinct groups of Amish who do not have Christian fellowship with each other due to different beliefs and practices. Most Amish do not drive automobiles, but some will ride in them and even fly in airplanes. Most Amish reject modern "conveniences" and attempt to live as much like they did before the Industrial Revolution as possible. Often the men wear beards and distinct clothing while the women wear very modest clothing and do not cut their hair. There are some more "progressive" Amish groups such as the Beachy Amish who drive automobiles and use cell phones.

The Amish tradition of Anabaptism began in Europe with the ministry of Jacob Ammann in 1693 who led a schism among the Swiss Brethren, the main body of Swiss and Alsatian Anabaptists. One issue was the practice of church discipline or "shunning"—how it should be practiced and toward whom and why. This has remained a matter of controversy among the Amish most of whom practice shunning to some degree. Once a child raised among them reaches a certain age (usually sixteen or eighteen) he or she is faced with the decision of being baptized by pouring and then coming under the discipline of the church. Should they reject that, they are usually shunned—at least from participation in the churches.

The Amish are like Mennonites, but have different roots in European Anabaptism. Many who leave Amish communities and churches, however, join Mennonite congregations due to their similar beliefs in nonresistance and "plain living." Traditionally, all Anabaptists discourage conspicuous consumption including expensive clothing, jewelry, and so on.

It is extremely difficult even to estimate the number of Amish churches and members in the United States as there is no central headquarters. A few Amish groups such as the Wisler and Wenger Amish or Old Order Mennonite churches have established websites and published statistics. The vast majority of Amish, however, live on farms, gather with like-minded Amish "folks" for worship in homes (rarely if ever church buildings) led by men called bishops or elders, and eschew accommodations to modern culture. One point of controversy among Amish is whether young male members should register for the Selective Service or not. Like other Anabaptists, Amish are pacifists and do not participate in war or believe even in violent self-defense.

Some observers who study the Amish distinguish between "Old Order" and "New Order" Amish with the difference lying in degrees of accommodation to modern American culture and degrees of and reasons for shunning. Old Order Amish are the most conservative while the New Order Amish are slightly more progressive. There is no definite line between them, however, and most Amish would reject such a distinction's validity.

Two of the better-known Amish denominetworks are the Wisler Amish and the Wenger Amish or Mennonites. Most Amish choose no particular name for their networks and organizations; occasionally they are given names by outsiders that gradually become accepted by the Amish such as the Schwartzentruber Amish. Both the Wisler and the Wenger groups are relatively small but are becoming better known because of their openness to being studied. There is no Amish-supported website (other than for commercial purposes such as selling handmade furniture) or headquarters.

BEACHY AMISH MENNONITE CHURCHES

Founded: 1927
Membership: est. 13,000, in 201 churches (2012) (Statistics include Canada)

These churches are made up mostly of Amish Mennonites who separated from the more conservative Old Order Amish over a period of years, beginning in 1927. They were led by Bishop Moses M. Beachy, and they are now found principally in Pennsylvania and Ohio. They believe in the Trinity and that the Bible is the infallible word by which all people will be judged. To some degree, they resemble the Old Order Amish in garb and general attitude, but their discipline is somewhat milder. Individuals confess their sins to elders before taking Communion, and they practice foot-washing. The focus is on humility and service rather than individual achievement. These Mennonites worship in church buildings, have Sunday schools, and are active in supporting missionary work. The Beachy Amish are not opposed to automobiles, electricity, or other modern conveniences, but television and movies are forbidden. Nearly all of the churches sponsor Christian day schools. The denomination does not have a national headquarters, but it does have a publishing arm and runs educational ministries. The Mission Interests Committee sponsors homes for the aged and handicapped as well as missions in the United States and Europe.

For more information: www.beachyam.org
Contact: 3015 Partridge Road, Partridge, KS 67566

CHURCH COMMUNITIES INTERNATIONAL

Founded: 1920, came to United States in 1954
Membership: est. 1,775 members, in 13 congregations (2009)

Though small in terms of actual membership, the Church Communities International represent one of the newer manifestations of the Anabaptist communal witness. Originally called the Bruderhof, the movement began in Germany following the economic and social devastation of the First World War. Founded by Eberhard Arnold (1883–1935), a theologian and writer, the movement spread to England in the 1930s. As World War II heated up, the British government was suspicious of a community with German nationals in it, and in 1941 the Bruderhof chose to relocate to the jungles of Paraguay. In the 1960s, the group moved to the United States and gained national attention in North America during the 1960s. There are several communities in the United States, Australia, England, and Germany where men, women, and children live in common. They share their property, work and worship together, and in all things seek unity. Several thousand people are associated with the movement without being members.

Theologically the Church Communities International affirm the Apostles' Creed but place their emphasis on the expectation of God's kingdom coming to this earth. They hold that followers of Jesus are empowered by the Spirit to live now in accordance with God's rule and reign as expressed in the Sermon on the Mount (Matt 5:1–7:29). The mission of the Church Communities International is to witness to the good news that in Christ it is possible to live a new life and to share this life together with others in brotherhood, community, and justice: "We acknowledge God's working in all who strive for justice and peace, no matter their religion or creed. All the same, we take Christ's commands seriously."

Because of Jesus's teachings, the Church Communities International affirm the sanctity of every life; thus they oppose every form of violence and killing, including abortion, capital punishment, war, and physician-assisted suicide. They also believe in the sanctity of marriage (between one man and one woman) and the sanctity of sex (sexual intimacy within marriage only). They do not proselytize but instead seek to work together with others, whatever their belief and wherever possible, in the spirit of Christian unity and common concern. In 2007 the Bruderhof Foundation was established to promote charitable work and the name of the church was changed to Church Communities International.

For more information: www.bruderhof.com

Contact: Woodcrest, 2032 Route 213, Rifton, NY 12471

CHURCH OF GOD IN CHRIST, MENNONITE

Founded: 1859
Membership: 15,066, in 154 churches (2015)

This church grew out of the preaching and labors of John Holeman (1832–1900), a member of the Mennonite Church in Ohio, who became convinced that many Mennonites had moved from the doctrines and practices of their Anabaptist forebears. He preached ardently on the necessity of the new birth, Holy Ghost baptism, more adequate training of children in the fundamentals of the faith, disciplining of unfaithful members, avoidance of apostates, and condemnation of worldly-minded churches. He separated from the Mennonite Church and in 1859 began to hold meetings with a small group of followers.

The Church of God in Christ, Mennonite, not to be confused with the Pentecostal Church of God in Christ, holds that the same confession of faith must be believed and practiced by all churches, "from the time of the apostles to the end of the world," and that the Bible, as the inspired, infallible word of God, must govern all doctrine and teaching. It accepts the Eighteen Articles of Faith drawn up at Dordrecht, Holland, in 1632. Women are required to cover their heads and men to wear beards. Non-involvement in the military and in secular government is enforced. The church teaches nonconformity to the "world" (contemporary culture) in dress, bodily adornment, sports, and amusements.

Most congregations in the church maintain a Christian school for the education of their children. Around the world members are found in Belize, Brazil, Burkina Faso, Canada, Dominican Republic, Ethiopia, Ghana, Guatemala, Haiti, India, Jamaica, Kenya, Latvia, Malawi, Mexico, Mozambique, Nicaragua, Nigeria, the Philippines, Romania, Uganda, Ukraine, and Zimbabwe. In the United States, Kansas is the state of heaviest concentration.

For more information: www.cogicm.org

Contact: Information and Gospel Publishers, CGIC, Mennonite, PO Box 230, Moundridge, KS 67107

CONSERVATIVE MENNONITE CONFERENCE

Founded: 1910
Membership: 12,474, in 108 churches (2016)

The Conservative Mennonite Conference (CMC) is an affiliation of autonomous congregations within the Mennonite tradition that was formed in 1910 in a meeting of concerned Amish Mennonite church leaders who were reluctant to adopt the Old Order Amish Mennonite conservatism toward cultural expressions but who were also more conservative than the prevailing Mennonite approach to culture of that time. The present name of the association was adopted in 1954.

The CMC subscribes to the Conservative Mennonite Statement of Practice (2007) and the Conservative Mennonite Statement of Theology (1991). These documents affirm the full humanity and full divinity of Jesus Christ, the full inspiration and inerrancy of the scriptures, believers' baptism, and nonviolence. Members are expected to refrain from gambling, alcohol, tobacco, immodest attire, swearing oaths, and premarital and extramarital sexual activity.

The highest decision-making body is the semi-annual Minister's Business Meeting, which elects an executive board and a general secretary to oversee the day-to-day operations of the conference. Internationally affiliated church bodies are found in Costa Rica,

Nicaragua, Ecuador, Haiti, India, Germany, and Kenya. Rosedale Bible College in Irwin, Ohio, offers an associate's degree in various Christian studies.

For more information: www.cmcrosedale.org

Headquarters: 9910 Rosedale-Milford Center Road, Irwin, OH 43029

EVANA (EVANGELICAL ANABAPTISTS)

Founded: 2015
Membership: unknown in est. 75 congregations

EVANA is one of the newest and youngest Anabaptist-Mennonite groups in the United States. It was born out of a meeting of 170 concerned evangelical Mennonites in 2015. They were dissatisfied with the direction of the Mennonite Church USA with regard to perceived accommodations to secular culture. EVANA's founders did not want to be overly reactionary by becoming like the Amish, withdrawing from secular culture, but sought instead to revive what they believed to be the evangelical ethos of traditional Mennonite faith and practice. EVANA is a non-exclusive network of evangelical Anabaptist congregations and ministries still (2016) in the process of being created. Many of its churches and members are also members of the Mennonite Church USA.

EVANA's basic statement of belief is the 1995 Confession of Faith in a Mennonite Perspective, which affirms biblical inspiration and authority, basic Christian orthodoxy (deity and humanity of Christ, God as Trinity), and traditional Anabaptist practices such as believer baptism, foot-washing, peace witness, and so on. The denominetwork affirms traditional heterosexual, monogamous marriage without singling out homosexuality as a special category of sin.

For more information: www.evananetwork.org

Headquarters: 104 South Main Street, Goshen, IN 46526

FELLOWSHIP OF EVANGELICAL CHURCHES

Founded: 1865
Attendance: est. 9,000, in 65 churches (2012)

Formerly known as the Defenseless Mennonite Church, the Fellowship of Evangelical Churches was founded as a result of a spiritual awakening among the Amish in Indiana under the leadership of Henry Egly, who stressed the need for repentance and regeneration before baptism. Egly's practice of rebaptizing Amish who experienced conversion led to conflict within the Amish community, leading to the formation of the Fellowship of

Evangelical Churches. It continues to emphasize regeneration ("born again" experience), separation from and nonconformity to culture, and nonresistance (pacifism).

The Fellowship of Evangelical Churches program today is largely one of missions and church-extension evangelism. A children's home in Flanagan, Illinois, and a camp near Kalamazoo, Michigan, are maintained. The name Evangelical Mennonite Church was adopted in 1949; however, representatives voted on August 2, 2003, to change the name to the Fellowship of Evangelical Churches because of the changing constituency of the church. In so doing, the Fellowship of Evangelical Churches (FEC) affirmed its core values anchored in evangelical theology and Anabaptist identity, and its mission to help the local church accomplish the Great Commandment and the Great Commission.

For more information: www.fecministries.org

Headquarters: 1420 Kerrway Court, Fort Wayne, IN 46805

HUTTERIAN BRETHREN

Founded: ca. 1530 (came to the United States in 1870s)
Membership: est. 40,000, in est. 400 colonies in North America (2016)

This is one of the few American Anabaptist groups to stem directly from the Radical Reformation movement without being connected to the Mennonites. Like others in the Radical Reformation, the Hutterian Brethren, a network of independent, religious, intentional communities, reject infant baptism and insist on separation of church and state. The New Testament, particularly the Sermon on the Mount (Matt 5:1–7:29), is taken as the literal authority for true Christians; therefore, they embraced nonviolence. They got their name from their founder Jacob Hutter, a sixteenth-century Tyrolean Anabaptist who advocated communal ownership of property. The communities he and his followers founded thrived in the under-populated areas of Central Europe, particularly Moravia, but always lived under the threat of persecution. Hutter himself was martyred in Austria in 1536. Over time, Hutterites migrated to Russia, where the need for hard-working and peaceful farmers was evident. As persecution there increased in the nineteenth century, many Hutterites left Russia for Canada and the United States.

Most Hutterites are of German or Swiss ancestry and use the German language in their homes and churches. Aside from the idea of common property, they are quite similar to the Old Order Amish. They seek to express their Bible-centered faith in brotherly love and aim at the recovery of New Testament spirit and fellowship. They feel this requires nonconformity to the world; accordingly, they practice nonresistance, refuse to participate in politics, and dress in traditional, modest attire. Choral singing plays a major role in Hutterite worship and daily life. They maintain their own schools, in which the Bible is paramount. There are different branches of Hutterites in America, including the

Schmiedeleut, Lehrerleut, and Dariusleu. Hutterites are not opposed to modern technologies that contribute to the welfare of the entire colony, such as farm equipment and computers.

There is no central headquarters of all Hutterites. Each colony or community is led by men called bishops or elders. There is no separation within colonies or communities between religion and culture; colonies or communities tend to keep to themselves except when shopping in towns nearby. They are recognizable to non-Hutterites who live near them and are often confused with Amish because of their distinctive forms of hair, dress, and language. And yet they often drive trucks and cars. The colonies or communities thrive mostly on agriculture and furniture-making and are mostly found in the upper Midwest (e.g., North and South Dakota) and in central Canada. In some Hutterite colonies or communities children are raised communally after early childhood. Hutterites only marry among themselves, which has led to some perceptions by outsiders of marriages between people too closely related. Some Hutterites have made attempts to draw outsiders into their colonies or communities, but they are not especially known for evangelism or proselytizing.

For more information: www.hutterites.org

MENNONITE CHURCH USA

Founded: 2001 with roots to 1525
Membership: 104,684, in 920 churches (2009)

This is the major American Mennonite body and was brought to Germantown, Pennsylvania, in 1683 by Dutch and German immigrants. In 2001 this church merged with the General Conference Mennonite Church (founded in 1860). In 1995, General Conference Mennonites and members of the Mennonite Church adopted a new "Confession of Faith in a Mennonite Perspective." The confession is the most recent in a series of historical Anabaptist faith statements, beginning with the Schleitheim Articles, written in 1527. The new confession of faith includes twenty-four articles that interpret Mennonite beliefs about God, Jesus Christ, the Holy Spirit, scripture, creation, sin, salvation, the church, Christian life and mission, peace and justice, and the reign of God.

The Mennonite Confession of Faith of 1995 is similar to an older Mennonite confession adopted in 1963, which sought to set forth the major doctrines of scripture as understood in the Anabaptist-Mennonite tradition. The confession stresses faith in Christ, the saved status of children, the importance of proclaiming God's word and "making disciples," baptism of believers, absolute love, nonresistance rather than retaliation as one's personal response to injustice and maltreatment, and the church as a non-hierarchical community. Because of their insistence on freedom from the traditional Mennonite regulations on attire, this group has been regarded as "liberal in conduct" by some other Mennonites, but it still represents the Radical Reformation in its ethos. The denomination's General Assembly meets every two years. It brings together representatives from all area conferences and from many congregations throughout North America. Discussion is open to all; however, only elected delegates (women and men, ordained and lay) may vote. Church-wide program boards are in charge of mission, congregational ministries, education, publishing, and mutual aid work; all are under the supervision of the church's general board. Home missions stress evangelism, and missions are found in Asia, Africa, Europe, and Central and South America. The church sponsors hospitals, retirement homes, and child-welfare services. Membership is strongest in Pennsylvania and the Midwest states. Associated Mennonite Biblical Seminary in Elkhart, Indiana, trains Mennonite Church pastors, missionaries, pastoral counselors, peace workers, and lay leaders. All leadership roles are open to women.

The Mennonite Church USA is a leading partner in the worldwide Mennonite Central Committee (MCC) that works especially in underdeveloped countries for community development. The MCC, supported by the Mennonite Church, is also deeply involved in peace-making efforts in many places of violent conflict in the world.

For more information: www.mennoniteusa.org

Headquarters: 3145 Benham Avenue, Suite 1, Elkhart, IN 46517

MISSIONARY CHURCH

Founded: 1969
Membership: 38,206 (2012), in est. 500 churches (2016)

The Missionary Church is made up of two groups that merged in 1969, the Missionary Church Association and the United Missionary Church. Both former denominations had a Mennonite heritage and came into existence through the holiness revivals of the late 1800s. In a sense, then, the Missionary Church is a blend of two Protestant traditions—Anabaptist and Holiness. The Missionary Church is conservative and evangelical in theology and practice. Local churches are free to manage their own affairs, but recognize and adhere to the authority of a general conference made up of clergy, missionaries, and laity, held biennially.

Working under the general conference is a general board that oversees a variety of agencies and missions activities. The president, vice president, and secretary are elected for terms of four years. The international ministry of the Missionary Church is done under the name of World Partners USA. Primary activities include evangelism, discipleship, church planting, Bible translation, theological education, leadership development and community development. The church is affiliated with one educational institution in the United States: Bethel College in Mishawaka, Indiana.

While the Missionary Church is rooted in Anabaptism via its Mennonite background, some observers (including former members raised in the denomination) say it is not as committed to traditional Anabaptist or Holiness theology and practice (e.g., pacifism and entire sanctification) as earlier. Like many American evangelical denominations, its historical, theological, and ethical particularities may not be as strongly emphasized as it comes under the influence of the wider American evangelical community.

The Missionary Church asserts that, in spite of civil government's decisions, within itself, only heterosexual sex within committed, monogamous marriage is without sin.

For more information: www.mcusa.org

Headquarters: 3811 Vanguard Drive, Fort Wayne, IN 46809

US MENNONITE BRETHREN CHURCHES OR MENNONITE BRETHREN, US CONFERENCE

Founded: 1878
Membership: est. 35,818 adherents, in 200 congregations (2016)

Mennonites in eighteenth-century Prussia found it difficult to avoid compulsory military service during the reign of Frederick the Great. Many of them accepted the offer of Czarina Catherine the Great to migrate to Russia where they established their own rural colonies in Ukraine. These were agricultural communities where Mennonites could live as the "quiet of the land." In the mid-nineteenth century, a Lutheran Pietist preacher named Eduard Wuest was the catalyst for a major revival among the German-speaking Mennonites in Russia. There was conflict between the more traditional Mennonites and those who sought greater attention to prayer and Bible study. These Pietist Mennonites retained many features common to Anabaptists, but they wanted a more emotional form of spirituality and greater attention to church discipline. Eventually, the Mennonites in Ukraine split over the issues of revivalism and home communion, and in 1860 eighteen people signed a "letter of separation" that became the charter for the Mennonite Brethren. The charter emphasized the need for experiential religion and personal holiness. A few years later, the Russian government began to insist that Mennonites enlist in the military. Thousands of Mennonites immigrated to North America, including hundreds of Mennonite Brethren. The first organizational meeting of the Brethren in the United States was held in 1878 in Nebraska. It was called for the purpose of supporting missions.

A General Conference of Mennonite Brethren Churches was formed in 1954, uniting Canadian and American Mennonite Brethren. The Krimmer Mennonite Brethren merged with this church in 1960, and the General Conference Mennonites continued to work closely with other Mennonites in mission. A 1982 study of members indicated a waning in the peace witness of the Mennonite Brethren, but a strong commitment to evangelism. In recent years the church has become more ethnically diverse and has a special district focused on Latino congregations in the Southwest. In 2000 the General Conference was disbanded and separate United States and Canadian conferences were organized. The church has five regional districts and is strongest in the western states, but has a presence in North Carolina and Texas as well. The church operates a theological seminary with campuses in Fresno, California; Langley, British Columbia; and Winnipeg, Manitoba. The seminary offers several masters degrees. The church also operates two colleges, one in Kansas (Tabor College) and the other in Fresno (Fresno Pacific University). The denomination has a national office, but congregations retain a great deal of autonomy.

One distinctive of the Mennonite Brethren is believer baptism by full immersion. (Most Anabaptists baptize believers by pouring.) The Mennonite Brethren denomination fits more closely into the broader American evangelical tradition and community than some other Mennonite and Anabaptist groups possibly because of its pietistic and revivalistic roots and ethos. It is conservative doctrinally and ethically while maintaining its emphasis on peace, simple living, and the priesthood of every believer.

For more information: www.usmb.org

Headquarters: 1701 Signal Ridge Drive, Suite 140, Edmond, OK 73013

RELIGIOUS SOCIETY OF FRIENDS (QUAKERS)

Dating from the 1650s in England, the Friends, popularly known as Quakers, often referred to collectively as the Religious Society of Friends, is an unconventional but esteemed Protestant movement. They believe in an "Inner Light," which is the spiritual nerve center that God has placed in every person. Since Friends believe that all people have the Inner Light, they typically deny the validity of clergy, liturgy, and sacraments. Friends believe that the practice of inward listening and obedience to God results in lives that begin to reflect the character of Jesus. From this arise the Friends' testimonies to peace, simplicity, equality, moral purity, and integrity. The fact that every person has this inward spiritual endowment has prompted Friends to stand for the equality of all people and thus to oppose slavery and to be exceptionally service-minded.

Despite their small numbers, Friends have had a deep and lasting influence on Western society. Contributions in both religious and humanitarian spheres have won them universal respect and admiration, and their loyalty to their quiet faith offers a challenge and inspiration to all churches. Friends take seriously the prophetic vision of the world at peace, and cooperate with the historic peace churches such as Anabaptists in the context of the wider ecumenical movement. In the United States, seven colleges and three seminaries reflect Friends' long-standing emphasis on the importance of education.

History. The Friends movement began with the vision of George Fox (1624–91), a seeker after spiritual truth and peace during the turmoil of the English Civil War and its aftermath. After failing to find satisfactory truth or peace in the churches of his time, Fox discovered what he sought in a direct personal relationship with Christ: "When all my hopes in [churches] were gone . . . I heard a voice which said, 'That is the Inner Voice, or Inner Light,' based upon the description of John 1:9: 'the true Light, which lighteth every man that cometh into the world'" (KJV). This voice, Fox maintained, is available to all and has nothing to do with the ceremonies, rituals, or creeds over which Christians have fought. Every heart is God's altar and shrine.

Fox and his early followers not only refused to attend the state church, they also insisted on freedom of speech, assembly, and worship. They would not take oaths in court and would not go to war. They condemned slavery and abuse of prisoners and the mentally ill. The names they adopted—Children of Truth, Children of Light, and Friends of Truth—aroused ridicule and fierce opposition. When Fox, hauled into court, advised one judge to "tremble at the Word of the Lord," the judge called him "a quaker," thus coining a term that became a name for the movement. Fox spent six years in jail. From 1650 until 1689, more than three thousand suffered for conscience's sake, and three hundred to four hundred died in prison. In spite of persecution, the group grew, and the Religious Society of Friends was founded in 1652. When Fox died in 1691, Quakers numbered fifty thousand.

Friends soon brought their message to the American colonies. Ann Austin (d. 1665) and Mary Fisher (ca. 1623–98) arrived in Massachusetts from Barbados in 1656. They were promptly accused of being witches and were deported. Eventually, four Friends were hanged in Boston, but the passage of the Act of Toleration of 1689 ended most persecution. William Penn (1644–1718) was granted the colony of Pennsylvania by the British Crown, and made it a refuge for his fellow Quakers. Penn's "Holy Experiment" allowed complete religious toleration in the colony of Pennsylvania, removing the government from the business of religion. This was a milestone on the path to full religious freedom in the American Constitution.

As persecution waned and Friends settled down to business and farming in the eighteenth century, many grew prosperous. Meetings and community life became well organized, and it was a time of creativity as well as mystical inwardness. Closely knit family life was emphasized. Quaker philanthropy increased and became widely admired. Their ideas on prison reform began to take effect, and their schools increased in number and attendance. The Quakers lost control of the Pennsylvania legislature in 1756 over the issue of taxation to pay for a war against the Shawnee and the Delaware peoples.

Quaker leaders, now looking within rather than without, began to enforce such strict discipline upon their members that they became, in fact, a "peculiar people." Members were disowned or dismissed for even minor infractions; thousands were cut off for "marrying out of Meeting." Pleasure, music, and art were taboo; sobriety, punctuality, and honesty were demanded in all matters; dress was plain; and speech was biblical. They were "different" and dour; they gained few new converts and lost many old members during this period. A number of separate groups were formed as a result: the Hicksites in 1827, the Wilburites in 1845, and the Primitives in 1861.

Influenced by revival movements of the nineteenth century, most Friends in the United States abandoned the quietism of an earlier generation and many engaged with other Christians in evangelism and the world missionary movement. Independently, various "orthodox" yearly meetings—a name for Quaker denominations—started missions in Mexico, Cuba, Jamaica, and Palestine that combined emphases on evangelism, education, and economic development. In 1887, these yearly meetings gathered to issue a Declaration of Faith, which reacted against two trends in American Quakerism. They opposed, on the left, a mysticism that seemed to disconnect the "inner Light" from the cross of Christ;

and, on the right, they opposed use of outward rituals to celebrate baptism and Communion. Friends traditionally view baptism and Communion as purely inward and spiritual. **Service and Peace Work.** Even during the quietistic phase of Quaker life, Friends continued to work for peace, public education, temperance, democracy, and the abolition of slavery. In 1688 the Friends of Germantown, Pennsylvania, announced that slavery violated the Golden Rule. It took nearly a century for Quakers to rid their own society of slavery. The writings of Friends John Woolman (1720–72) and John Greenleaf Whittier (1807–92) helped to further the abolition movement in American society.

During World War I, Friends from all branches of society were at work in the American Friends Service Committee (AFSC) in relief and reconstruction efforts abroad. The AFSC remains today one of the most effective of such agencies in the world. The AFSC and its British counterpart were jointly awarded the Nobel Peace Prize in 1947. Friends who enter military service are no longer disowned from membership, but many leave the society and join a church that does not profess pacifism. Conversely, pacifists brought up in other traditions often join the Friends in young adulthood. Peace conferences have had a prominent place in Friends' ministries.

Worship and Polity. The Inner Light is the heart of Quaker theology and practice. Friends believe that grace, the power from God to help humankind pursue good and resist evil, is universal among all people. They seek not holiness but "perfection"—a higher, more spiritual standard of life for both society and the individual—and they believe that truth is unfolding and continuing. They value the Bible but many prefer to rely on fresh individual guidance from the Spirit of God, who produced the Bible, rather than follow only what has been revealed to others.

Worship and business in the societies are conducted in monthly, quarterly, and yearly meetings. The monthly meeting is the basic unit, made up of one or more meetings (groups) in a neighborhood. It convenes each week for worship and once a month for business. It keeps records of membership, births, deaths, and marriages; appoints committees; considers queries on spiritual welfare; and transacts all business. Monthly meetings join four times a year in a quarterly meeting to stimulate spiritual life and decide on any business that should be brought to the attention of the yearly meeting. The yearly meeting corresponds to a diocese in an episcopal system. In Friends' business meetings at every level, there often is frank inquiry into members' conduct of business and treatment of others.

Group decisions await the "sense of the meeting." Lacking unity of opinion, the meeting may have a "quiet time" until unity is found, or it may postpone consideration of the matter or refer it to a committee for study. Minority opinion is not outvoted, but convinced. Every man, woman, and child is free to speak in any meeting; delegates are appointed at quarterly and yearly meetings to ensure adequate representation, but enjoy no unusual position or prerogatives. Church officers, elders, and ministers are chosen for recognized ability in spiritual leadership, but they too stand on equal footing with the rest of the membership. A few full-time workers are paid a modest salary, and "recorded" ministers who serve as pastors in meetings that have programmed worship also receive salaries.

Worship may be either programmed or unprogrammed, but the two are not always distinct. The former more nearly resembles an ordinary Protestant service, although there are no outward sacraments. While Friends believe in spiritual Communion, partaking of the elements is thought unnecessary. In unprogrammed meetings there is no choir, collection, singing, or pulpit; the service is devoted to quiet meditation, prayer, and communion with God. Any vocal contributions are prompted by the Spirit.

Friends World Committee for Consultation (FWCC), organized at Swarthmore, Pennsylvania, following the Second World Conference of Friends in 1937, functions as an agent, or clearinghouse, for interchange of Quaker aspirations and experiences through regional, national, and international inter-visitation, person-to-person consultations, conferences, correspondence, and a variety of publications. The FWCC maintains a world office in London, England, and, as a nongovernmental organization (NGO), helps to operate a program at UN headquarters to forward world peace and human unity. Something of a world community has been set up in the Wider Quaker Fellowship, in which non-Friends in sympathy with the spirit and program of Quakerism may participate in the work without coming into full membership.

Quakers have often been featured characters in Hollywood movies and in television programs—similarly to the Amish (although they are very different). To outsiders especially they seem "peculiar," a term early Friends embraced because it meant to stand out as different from the ordinary. Until the late nineteenth and early twentieth centuries many Quakers spoke in what some people would call the "King James English," using "thee" and "thou" instead of "you." That's because "thee" and "thou" were terms of familiarity and equality, not hierarchy and class difference.

The main differences among Friends in the early twenty-first century have to do with theology and worship. So-called evangelical Friends hold Sunday morning worship services not very different from many evangelical Protestant churches. These Friends meetings are known as "programmed." However, unlike other evangelical Protestants, they do not baptize in water or celebrate the Lord's Supper. Most of them also have a quiet time during the worship service during which any Friend may speak as the Spirit leads. More traditional Quakers worship without structure or leadership, sitting in silent contemplation until and unless the Spirit moves one to speak to the group. These meetings are known as "unprogrammed." Some Friends are theologically liberal and some are more conservative. Liberal Friends are barely distinguishable from Unitarians in terms of their ethos—doctrinal belief is considered a matter of individual discernment and conscience. Evangelical Friends are barely distinguishable from moderate Baptists or Mennonites in terms of expecting members to read and believe the Bible and hold to basic Christian orthodoxy.

There are many independent Quaker meetings that do not belong to any of the three major "yearly meetings" described here. Most of these are found in the Midwest and are descended from a form of Quakerism known as "conservative Friends"—maintaining an older version of Friends existence lacking modern accommodations including denominational associations. There is no way of counting them as they do not have any headquarters or information centers to which they belong. (A drive through the back roads of Iowa, for example, will reveal some of these.) These conservative Friends congregations may form voluntary and informal fraternal associations with others in their vicinity, but they lack affiliation with any "annual meeting" (denomination).

SUGGESTIONS FOR FURTHER READING

Bacon, Margaret Hope. *Mothers of Feminism*. San Francisco, CA: HarperSanFrancisco, 1986.

Barbour, Hugh, and J. William Frost. *The Quakers*. New York: Greenwood Press, 1980.

Brock, Peter. *Pioneers of a Peaceable Kingdom: The Quaker Peace Testimony from the Colonial Era to the First World War*. Princeton, NJ: Princeton University Press, 1972.

Hall, Francis. *Friends in the Americas*. Philadelphia, PA: Friends World Committee, 1976.

Hamm, Thomas D. *The Transformation of American Quakerism: Orthodox Friends: 1800–1907*. Bloomington: University of Indiana Press, 1988.

Stoneburner, Carol and John, eds. *The Influence of Quaker Women on American History*. Lewiston/Queenston, NY: The Edwin Mellen Press, 1986.

Weeks, Stephen B. *Southern Quakers and Slavery*. Baltimore, MD: Johns Hopkins University Press, 1986.

EVANGELICAL FRIENDS CHURCH, INTERNATIONAL

Founded: 1989
Attendance: 34,565, in 306 meetings or congregations (2012)

This is the newest and one of the largest organizations of Friends annual meetings in the United States. It grew out of the Evangelical Friends Alliance, which was formed in 1965 to encourage evangelical emphases and denominational unity. The Evangelical Friends represent one part of the general evangelical renewal that profoundly shaped American Christianity in the latter part of the twentieth century.

The Evangelical Friends (EFI) is organized into six regions of the United States, with commissions devoted to missions, education, youth ministry, and communication. Worship is programmed and includes scripture readings, congregational singing, and a sermon by the pastor. The theology is generally conservative, and Evangelical Friends cooperates with other evangelical bodies. Of primary concern is the Great Commission (Matt 28:19) to make disciples of all nations. Worldwide, EFI has nearly eleven hundred churches with over one hundred fifty thousand regular attendees.

Evangelical Friends supports several colleges including George Fox University in Oregon and Friends University in Kansas. The denomination belongs to the National Association of Evangelicals. A few of their congregations have begun to celebrate the Lord's Supper as a memorial meal and not as a sacrament.

One of the best-known and most influential of the Evangelical Friends is Quaker theologian and spiritual director Richard Foster, founder of the ecumenical Renovaré Movement and author of numerous books about Christian spirituality including especially *Celebration of Discipline: The Path to Spiritual Growth*.

While maintaining its traditional Quaker emphasis on peace and inwardness, the Evangelical Friends Church has moved ever closer to American evangelicalism, which has embraced Foster and his interpretation of Quaker spirituality within a broader evangelical framework.

For more information: www.friendschurchsw.org

Headquarters: PO Box 2079, Yorba Linda, CA 92885

FRIENDS GENERAL CONFERENCE

Founded: 1900
Membership: est. 35,000, in est. 650 meetings (2016)

Friends General Conference is an association of fourteen yearly meetings and regional associations and ten monthly meetings of Friends (Quakers) in the United States and Canada. It is less a denomination than a service organization that provides resources for yearly and monthly meetings. Most of these meetings are "unprogrammed," meaning that worshippers meet in silence, expecting that one or more Friends may be moved by the Spirit to speak. No pastors are employed; the responsibilities handled by pastors in other denominations are shared among the members of the meeting. This group of Friends emphasizes the Quaker belief that faith is based on direct experience of God and that God is found in every individual through the "Inner Light." Some liberal-leaning Quakers interpret the Inner Light as a universal presence of God while some more conservative-leaning Quakers interpret it as the image of God that can be activated by the Holy Spirit in a special way.

Friends General Conference serves the members of affiliated meetings by preparing and distributing educational and spiritual materials, providing opportunities for Friends to share experiences and strengthen the Quaker community, and helping monthly and yearly meetings to nurture and support the spiritual and community life of Friends in North America. It is best known for the annual "Gathering of Friends," which attracts between fifteen hundred and two thousand Quakers from all over North America. Friends

General Conference offices are in Philadelphia, Pennsylvania. The Conference publishes various books and religious education materials and a newsletter.

Friends General Conference views itself and its meetings as more "liberal" theologically and socially than Evangelical Friends. Its focus tends to be on social reform through peace and justice advocacy more than evangelism or spiritual formation through Bible reading and prayer.

For more information: www.fgcquaker.org

Headquarters: 1216 Arch Street #2B, Philadelphia, PA 19107

FRIENDS UNITED MEETING

Founded: 1902
Membership: 36,302, in 600 meetings (2012)

Friends United Meeting was formed in 1902 as the umbrella for Friends mission activities and the communications arm for a broadly Christian understanding of the Quaker movement. Friends United Meeting is an international association of twenty-six yearly meetings (regional bodies of Quaker meetings) the purpose of which is "to energize and equip Friends through the power of the Holy Spirit to gather people into fellowships where Jesus Christ is known, loved and obeyed as Teacher and Lord." Friends United Meeting includes Friends meetings with both pastor-led services and those that practice traditional unprogrammed silent waiting on God.

The international work of Friends United Meeting includes medical, educational, and children services in Kenya, Palestine, and the Caribbean as well as pastoral leadership training through the Friends Theological College in Kaimosi, Kenya. There are more Friends of this group in East Africa than in the United States.

The US headquarters in Richmond, Indiana, houses departments of Global Ministries and Communications, which includes a bookstore, press, denominational magazine, and Internet outreach. Also located there is the historic Quaker-related Earlham College.

For more information: www.fum.org

Headquarters: 101 Quaker Hill Drive, Richmond, IN 47374

BRETHREN AND PIETIST CHURCHES

An international religious revival began in Germany in the late 1600s with the preaching and writings of Philipp Jakob Spener (1635–1705), an influential Lutheran pastor and theologian. Spener decried the barren intellectualism, theological factionalism, and general ineffectiveness of the Protestant churches of his day. He called for a new type of Reformation that would complete the promise of Luther's Reformation. Luther had reformed the church doctrinally and liturgically; Spener wanted to reform it morally and spiritually. He called for pastors to find ways to make the doctrine of the priesthood of all believers effective in the hearts and souls of the people. His pietist manifesto was entitled *Pia Desideria*, which means "pious desires." It stirred up a spiritual awakening among European Protestants and also created controversy among them.

Spener proposed that pastors form small groups of believers known as "collegia pietatis" (later "conventicles") to meet for study, prayer, and mutual encouragement. The staples of modern church life, such as Sunday school, youth fellowship, and women's circle meetings, grew out of this idea. Also, Spener urged pastors to leave polemics aside and concentrate on edifying preaching that could transform individuals from sinners to laborers for God. The focus of Spener and the whole pietist movement was not doctrine but inward transformation through experience of God. This "religion of the heart" spread throughout Protestant Germany and profoundly influenced John Wesley's (1703–91) early Methodist movement. When pietism, as it was called in Germany, came to the United States in the 1740s, it helped to fuel the First Great Awakening.

The Pietist (from here on capitalized for referring to the movement) awakening began among Lutherans in Germany but quickly spread to Lutherans in other countries—especially in Scandinavia—and sparked a Protestant movement of world missions and social activism. Spener's successor as leader of the movement was August Francke (1663–1727) who founded the Halle Institutes in Halle, Germany, which became the informal headquarters of Pietism in Europe. Francke emphasized the necessity of a "struggle of repentance" for authentic Christian conversion. All Pietists emphasized a Christian life of devotion, prayer, Bible reading, and witness. The Pietist movement was the true beginning of what later came to be known as "evangelical Protestant Christianity." It spread from central Europe to Great Britain and North America, and to India and Central America.

However, Spener, Franke, and other early Pietists were harshly criticized by more traditional Protestant leaders for allegedly undermining the objectivity of justification by grace through faith alone and returning to "mysticism"—something associated with Catholicism. While the earliest Pietists held firmly to the crucial "*solas*" of Luther's theology they also wanted to take the principle of the priesthood of the believer further and emphasize the possibility, even normativity, of an unmediated relationship between the Christian and God. Many leaders of the state churches accused Pietists of "sectarianism," "enthusiasm" (fanaticism), and anti-clericalism (if not downright heresy).

Besides Spener and Franke, and closely associated with them in the beginning of the movement, was German nobleman Count Nicholas Ludwig von Zinzendorf who allowed a group of Hussite Protestants from Moravia to settle on his estate in Saxony. Eventually he became their bishop and spiritual leader. They formed a sub-denomination of Lutherans known as Unitas Fratrum (Unity of the Brethren)—a name later picked up and used by other Pietist groups rooted in Hussite Moravian Protestantism. Their community was called "Herrnhut" or "The Lord's Watch" and so some called them "Herrnhuters." This group tended toward a more emotional form of worship; they were the "charismatics" of their time. Even some other Pietists were wary of their passion. Zinzendorf was one of the most influential religious leaders of the eighteenth century, traveling around Europe, Great Britain, and North America attempting to unite all Protestants into one denomination he called the Congregation of God in the Spirit. Instead, Pietists tended to divide into numerous subgroups distinguished by different views of the sacraments and degrees of emphasis on inward experience of God. The two main branches of Pietism were "churchly" and "independent" with the former maintaining church forms, institutions, and sacraments, and the latter emphasizing mystical experiences and esoteric knowledge.

In the 1750s Philip Otterbein (1726–1813), a German Reformed pastor of Pietist leanings, began his career as an evangelist in Pennsylvania and Maryland. His activities led to the formation of the United Brethren Church, later called the Evangelical United Brethren (EUB). This body was one of the groups that eventually formed The United Methodist Church in 1968. Although there are only a few, relatively small denominations in the United States that emerged out of German Pietism, American Christianity in all its varieties has been influenced by this spiritual movement.

Many Pietist bodies use the name "Brethren" in various forms. (It should be noted, however, that the label "Brethren" is also used by some non-Pietist groups such as the Plymouth Brethren.) For them, the church is primarily a company of brothers and sisters in Christ joined together by the Holy Spirit for mutual edification. The inner spiritual life, piety, is cultivated in prayer and study of scripture and through association with fellow believers. For most Brethren, the local church is central, but they are often bound in close-knit national communities. The church claims their primary loyalty and is understood more as a community of people who love God and one another than as part of an organization or a body that formulates doctrine.

Brethren do not emphasize rigid doctrinal standards; rather, the Spirit of God within each person, which binds them together in love, takes precedence for them. Some place emphasis on prophecy and direct inspiration from the Holy Spirit. They usually live a simple, unadorned life. In their early decades in Europe and the United States, most Brethren were separatists from the state and conventional churches. While not manifesting a judgmental attitude, they devoted themselves to a moral purity that set them apart from other Christians as well as from general society.

Many Pietist groups took the New Testament literally and endeavored to put its teachings into practice, even in the minute details of their daily living. At the heart of their religious ritual was the love feast, or agape, and the serving of the Lord's Supper, preceded by a ceremony of foot-washing. They saluted one another with a kiss of peace, dressed in simple clothing, covered women's heads at services, anointed their sick with oil for healing and consecration, refrained from worldly amusements, and refused to take oaths, go to war, or engage in lawsuits. Those Pietist groups that were not Brethren tended to be more embracing of the secular world.

Many of the Brethren churches stem from the work of Alexander Mack Sr. (1679–1735), in Schwarzenau in Wittgenstein, Germany. After his experience of conversion, Mack was convinced of the need for those who had experienced regeneration to form separate communities modeled on the early church's practice of sharing goods in common. Exiled from the Palatinate for preaching separatism, Mack gathered a company of fellow refugees and in 1708 took the bold, and at that time illegal, step of rebaptizing adult believers. Eventually persecution in Germany led these German Baptist Brethren to emigrate to the United States.

They were known for years simply as German Baptist Brethren, but that title has largely disappeared, except in the case of the Old German Baptist Brethren, who were also known as *Dunkers*. The terms *Brethren* and *Dunker* have been the cause of much confusion. *Dunker* is a direct derivation of the German *tunken*, "to dip or immerse," and is identified with the peculiar method of immersion employed by this group of churches in which the new believer is immersed three times, face forward, in the name of the Father, the Son, and the Holy Ghost.

Several communal societies in American history were established by Pietist groups. Such communes were an intense expression of the Pietist ideal of brotherhood and sisterhood, and in many cases were inspired by the vision of the New Jerusalem in the book of Revelation. Among the most important were Ephrata Cloister and Bethlehem in Pennsylvania, Salem in North Carolina, and Amana in New York (and later Iowa). Amana survived as a commune until 1932. At that time the organization was divided between the Amana Business Society and the Amana Church Society. The latter continues as a small denomination in Iowa that does not have an ordained ministry.

Pietism also had a large influence on Scandinavian Lutherans and led many of them to separate from the Lutheran state churches. Some of them maintained a Lutheran identity and theology as they immigrated to the New World to find religious freedom. In the Scandinavian countries they were persecuted for meeting outside the structures of the state churches for Bible study and prayer. Other Scandinavian Pietists left Lutheranism and founded new forms of Protestantism or became Baptists under the influence of Baptist missionaries.

What do all the denominations described in this section have in common? Primarily Pietist roots. In other words, while they may celebrate sacraments and ordinances they do not believe in "sacramental spirituality" over inward "conversional piety." All believe (or once believed) in the necessity of an individual experience of new birth, conversion, and regeneration for justification, reconciliation with God. All trace their spiritual-theological ancestry back to the European Pietism that began with Spener.

SUGGESTIONS FOR FURTHER READING

Atwood, Craig D. *Community of the Cross: Moravian Piety in Colonial Bethlehem.* Philadelphia: Pennsylvania University Press, 2004.

Bach, Jeff. *Voices of the Turtledove: The Sacred World of Ephrata.* University Park: Pennsylvania State University Press, 2003.

Brown, Dale. *Understanding Pietism.* Grand Rapids, MI: Wm. B. Eerdmans, 1978,

Durnbaugh, Donald F., ed. *The Brethren Encyclopedia.* 3 vols. Philadelphia, PA: Brethren Press, 1983–84.

Durnbaugh, Donald F. *The Church of the Brethren Past and Present.* Elgin, IL: Brethren Press, 1971.

Hoestetler, John A. *Hutterite Society.* Baltimore, MD: Johns Hopkins University Press, 1974.

Longenecker, Steve. *Piety and Tolerance: Pennsylvania German Religion, 1700–1850.* Metuchen, NJ: Scarecrow Press, 1994.

Olson, Roger E., and Christian T. Collins Winn. *Reclaiming Pietism: Retrieving an Evangelical Tradition.* Grand Rapids, MI: Eerdmans, 2015.

Stoeffler, Ernst, ed. *Continental Pietism and Early American Christianity.* Grand Rapids, MI: Eerdmans, 1976.

Wittlinger, Carlton O. *Quest for Piety and Obedience: The Story of the Brethren in Christ.* Nappanee, IN: Evangel Press, 1978.

BRETHREN CHURCH (ASHLAND)

Founded: 1882
Membership: 13,260 in 113 congregations (2010)

In 1882 the Church of the Brethren voted to expel a member for advocating Sunday schools, missions, a paid clergy, congregational polity, and more freedom in dress and worship. The supporters of such changes withdrew and formed the Progressive Convention of the Tunker Church in Ashland, Ohio. The following year it was officially organized as the Brethren Church. Most Brethren churches are still found in Ohio, Pennsylvania, and Indiana. The church has historic, relational, and functional ties to both a university and a seminary located in Ashland, Ohio (both of which are named "Ashland").

Theologically, the Brethren Church tries to seek a balance between the Calvinist and Arminian perspectives on salvation; however, for the Brethren, style of life is more important than doctrine. The believing community of faith leads believers into the path proposed in the Sermon on the Mount. Nonetheless, the church suffered a schism during the fundamentalist or modernist controversy that gripped American Christianity in the 1920s and 1930s. The more conservative ministers formed the Fellowship of Grace Brethren Church*.

The Brethren Church has two ministry councils that provide oversight for ministries in the United States and internationally. There is an Executive Board with responsibility for governance on behalf of the churches. The church collaborates with other churches and agencies for the purpose of church health, missional outreach at home and abroad, and relief activities worldwide.

Like many other Brethren denominations the Brethren Church includes a countercultural ethos moderately similar to some Anabaptist groups. It seeks to nurture an "alternative" Christian lifestyle not conformed to the consumerism and violence of much contemporary society. The Brethren Church is moderately evangelical in theology and practice, placing emphasis on conversion and baptizing believers only by immersion. The Church does not support ordination or marriage of gay or lesbian people. It does ordain women to the ministry.

For more information: www.brethrenchurch.org

Headquarters: 524 College Avenue, Ashland, Ohio 44805

BRETHREN IN CHRIST CHURCH

Founded: 1863
Membership: 22,920 in 211 congregations (2015)

This church began as a result of a spiritual awakening that took place in Lancaster, Pennsylvania, in the 1760s, inspired by the preaching of Philip Otterbein (1726–1813) and Martin Boehm (1725–1812). The group that gathered along the Susquehanna River was called simply the River Brethren until the Civil War. Primarily of Mennonite* descent, the River Brethren separated from the Mennonites over the issue of triple immersion in baptism (which the River Brethren espoused). The River Brethren were pacifists, and with the outbreak of the Civil War and the institution of a national military draft, it became necessary for the Brethren to obtain legal recognition as an established religious organization in order to protect the objectors. A council meeting in Lancaster

County, Pennsylvania, in 1863 adopted the name Brethren in Christ Church, but the group was not legally incorporated until 1904. In addition to typical Protestant doctrines, the Brethren in Christ insist on temperance and modesty of apparel. Many Brethren wear "plain dress" similar to that worn by the Amish*. The Brethren in Christ remains a "peace church," but members are not excluded from membership if they serve in the military.

While the government of this church is largely in the hands of the local congregations, there are eight regional conferences and a general conference, which is the ultimate authoritative body. Its publishing arm, Evangel Publishing House, is in Nappanee, Indiana. The church has two institutions of learning: Messiah College at Grantham, Pennsylvania, and Niagara Christian College at Fort Erie, Ontario. Missionaries are at work in Africa, India, Japan, London, Colombia, Nicaragua, Venezuela, and Cuba and are engaged in Mennonite Central Committee work around the world.

The Brethren in Christ Church recognizes three "streams" that together equally make up its ethos: Anabaptist, Pietist, and Holiness. This hybrid character constitutes its distinctiveness. It is an evangelical denomination that struggles somewhat to maintain its distinctive character as it experiences the "pull" toward a kind of generic American evangelicalism. The denomination only ordains heterosexual men and women. It does not sanction same-sex marriage.

For more information: www.bic-church.org

Headquarters: 481 Grantham Road, Mechanicsburg, PA 17055

CHURCH OF THE BRETHREN

Founded: 1708
Membership: 114,465 in 967 churches (2014)

The Church of the Brethren, the largest of the Brethren churches, was formed in 1708 in Schwarzenau, Germany, with the ministry of Alexander Mack. The early Brethren were influenced by the Anabaptists as well as by Pietism, and they covenanted to be a people shaped by personal faith in Christ, prayer, and study of scripture. They stressed daily discipleship and service to neighbors. Severe persecution and economic conditions prompted virtually the entire movement to migrate to North America between 1719 and 1729. Commonly known as German Baptist Brethren, or even Dunkers or Dunkards, in its bicentennial year, 1908, the group adopted "Church of the Brethren" as its official name. "Brethren" was seen as a New Testament term that conveyed the kinship and warmth of Jesus's early followers.

The Brethren emphasize right living more than right doctrine, and their current website invites those who are "fed up with doctrine and still hungry" to try the Brethren way, which includes "open-minded consideration of Jesus, the scriptures, and our own hearts." True to Pietist principles, the Brethren develop their understanding through community discussion and study, using Jesus's own teaching as a guide for modern living.

Although non-creedal, the Church of the Brethren has held firmly to basic tenets of the Free Church, or Believers Church, tradition. Among the most distinctive Brethren practices are the baptism of confessing believers by threefold immersion and the anointing of the ill for spiritual and bodily health. The Last Supper is observed with a service of footwashing that symbolizes servanthood, a fellowship meal that symbolizes family, and the commemorative Eucharist that symbolizes Saviorhood.

Brethren have long held an official peace witness, expressed often in conscientious objection to military service. During World War II, Civilian Public Health camps were maintained for religious objectors who performed work in the national interest. During and after the war, many of the programs were continued under the alternative service provisions of Selective Service, and voluntary service abroad, a forerunner of the Peace Corps, was introduced. Also growing out of the peace concern was a worldwide program of relief, reconstruction, and welfare, conducted by the Brethren Service Commission and later by the World Ministries Commission, as a service of love to those suffering from war, natural disasters, or social disadvantage. Since 1948, Brethren Volunteer Service has enlisted nearly five thousand men and women for one or two years of social service at home and abroad. Work with migrant laborers, inner-city dwellers, prison inmates, refugees, and victims of abuse exemplify the types of activity undertaken. Increasingly, older volunteers have enrolled in the program, quite often after they have reached retirement age.

Numerous projects initiated by the group have become full-scale ecumenical enterprises. Among them are the Heifer Project International, Christian Youth Exchange, Christian Rural Overseas Program (CROP), Sales Exchange for Refugee Rehabilitation Vocation (SERRV; handcraft sales for Third World producers), and International Voluntary Service. Other pioneering ventures were agricultural exchanges begun with Poland in the 1950s and with China in the 1980s and ecumenical exchanges with the Russian Orthodox Church in the 1960s.

In polity, the Brethren combine both congregational and presbyterian practices, with final authority vested in an Annual Conference of elected delegates. The General Board of elected and ex officio members is the administrative arm of the church. Congregations are organized into twenty-three districts in thirty-six states, usually with one or more full-time executives in each district. The heaviest concentration of churches is in Pennsylvania, Virginia, Maryland, Ohio, Indiana, and Illinois.

The Brethren are related to six accredited liberal arts colleges: Bridgewater College in Virginia; Elizabethtown and Juniata colleges in Pennsylvania; University of LaVerne in California; Manchester College in Indiana; and McPherson College in Kansas. The church sponsors one graduate school, Bethany Theological Seminary, in Richmond, Indiana. General offices are in Elgin, Illinois, also the home of Brethren Press, which produces the monthly publication *Messenger* and various books and curriculum resources.

For more information: www.brethren.org

Headquarters: 1451 Dundee Avenue, Elgin, IL 60120

CHURCH OF THE UNITED BRETHREN IN CHRIST

Founded: 1800, with roots to 1767
Membership: 18,259 in 178 congregations (2012)

This group had its origins in the Pennsylvania awakening led by Philip Otterbein (1726–1813) and Martin Boehm (1725–1812) in the 1760s. In 1800 the ministers of the Brethren officially adopted the name United Brethren in Christ and elected Otterbein and Boehm as the first bishops. In 1815 they adopted a confession of faith based on one that Otterbein had written in 1789. The United Brethren took a strong stand against slave holding in the 1820s; thus they did not spread in the South, but did make the western United States a mission area. In 1841 a constitution was adopted. When the constitution was changed in 1889, some members viewed the changes as unconstitutional and separated from the main body. The main body of United Brethren (Evangelical United Brethren) eventually merged with the Methodist Episcopal Church to form the United Methodist Church, leaving the name "United Brethren" to the smaller group.

United Brethren in Christ Church is a conservative evangelical denomination that believes in the inspiration and authority of scripture; the Trinity; and the deity, humanity, and atonement of Christ. Observance of "scriptural living" is required of all members, who are forbidden use of alcoholic beverages and membership in secret societies. Believer baptism and the Lord's Supper are observed as ordinances. Local, annual, and general conferences are held. The highest governing body, the General Conference, meets quadrennially. General church offices are located in Huntington, Indiana; the majority of local churches are found in Pennsylvania, Ohio, northern Indiana, and Michigan. Both men and women are eligible for the ministry and are ordained only once as elders. Missionary societies administer evangelism and church aid in the United States and in Costa Rica, El Salvador, Honduras, Hong Kong, India, Jamaica, Macau, Mexico, Myanmar, Nicaragua, Sierra Leone, and Thailand. Worldwide membership numbers over thirty-six thousand. The United Brethren Church maintains a college and a graduate school of Christian ministries at Huntington, Indiana, with secondary schools in Sierra Leone.

For more information: www.ub.org
Headquarters: 302 Lake Street, Huntington, IN 46750

EVANGELICAL CONGREGATIONAL CHURCH

Founded: 1894 and 1928, with roots to 1800
Membership: 13,750 in 124 congregations (2014)

This denomination traces its origin to the work of Jacob Albright (1759–1808), a Pietist and Methodist evangelist among the Germans of Pennsylvania in the early 1800s. Albright helped to organize the Evangelical Association that later became the Evangelical Church, which eventually merged with the United Brethren Church to form the Evangelical United Brethren Church. That body eventually merged with the Methodist Episcopal Church to form the United Methodist Church. A division within the church in 1891 was healed by a merger in 1922, but some congregations in the Ohio River valley region objected and continued their separate existence. They chose the name Evangelical Congregational Church in 1928. This church, like its parent Evangelical Church, is "Methodist in polity, Arminian in doctrine." It is a conservative but not fundamentalist evangelical denomination. Emphasis is on the inspiration and integrity of the Bible and "fellowship of all followers of Christ." The church lists its Core Values as "Passion for Christ, Compassion for the Lost, Servant Leadership, Healthy Ministries, and Unity in the Body of Christ."

Each congregation owns its property, determines its membership, manages its affairs, and chooses its ecclesiastical affiliation. There is a National Conference that supervises conference ministers. The stationing committee, composed of the bishop and conference ministers assigns pastors to churches. The Global Ministries Commission supervises the missionary programs. Church headquarters, the Evangelical Theological Seminary, and the New Dawn Christian Community Services are located at Myerstown, Pennsylvania.

For more information: www.eccenter.com

Headquarters: 100 West Park Avenue, Myerstown, PA 17067

EVANGELICAL COVENANT CHURCH

Founded: 1885
Membership: 231,273 adherents in 839 congregations (2015)

The Evangelical Covenant Church is not a Brethren church but grew out of Pietism in Sweden. It traces its roots from the Protestant Reformation through the biblical instruction of the Lutheran state church of Sweden to the great spiritual awakenings of the nineteenth century. The Covenant Church was founded by Swedish immigrants in the Midwest and adheres to the affirmations of the Reformation regarding the Holy Scriptures as the only perfect rule for faith, doctrine, and conduct. It has traditionally valued the historic confessions of the Christian church, particularly the Apostles' Creed, but emphasizes the sovereignty of the word of God over all creedal interpretations.

The Covenant Church's evangelical emphasis includes the necessity of the new birth, the ministry of the Holy Spirit, and the reality of freedom in Christ. It values the New Testament emphasis on personal faith in Jesus Christ as Savior and Lord and the church as a fellowship of believers that recognizes but transcends theological differences. Baptism and the Lord's Supper are seen as divinely ordained sacraments. The denomination has traditionally practiced both infant baptism and believer baptism (leaving the decision whether to have an infant baptized to the parents).

The local church is administered by a board elected by the membership; its ministers, ordained by the denomination, are called, generally with the aid and guidance of the denominational Department of the Ordered Ministry and the conference superintendent. Each of the ten regional conferences elects its own superintendent. The highest authority is vested in an annual meeting composed of ministers and laypeople elected by the constituent churches. An administrative board, elected by the annual meeting, implements its decisions. The Covenant Church sponsors churches in Burkina Faso, Cameroon, Central African Republic, Central Asia, Colombia, the Czech Republic, the Democratic Republic of Congo, Ecuador, Equitorial Guinea, France, Germany, Japan, Laos, Mexico, Spain, Taiwan, and Thailand. Educational institutions include North Park University and North Park Theological Seminary in Chicago, Illinois. The church maintains fifteen retirement communities and nursing homes in seven states, two hospitals, three homes for adults with developmental disabilities, a children's home, a ministry for victims of domestic violence, and several camps and conference centers across North America.

The "Covenant Church" is a moderately evangelical denomination with a strong Pietist ethos. It has experienced much growth through shedding its Scandinavian flavor and sponsoring experimental church plants including very small "emerging churches" and at least one mega-church in Oklahoma. The denomination ordains only heterosexual men and women. It resists performing gay weddings (although conversations about full inclusion of LGBT people are ongoing within the denomination).

For more information: www.covchurch.org

Headquarters: 8303 West Higgins Road, Chicago, IL 60631

EVANGELICAL FREE CHURCH OF AMERICA

Founded: 1950, with roots to nineteenth century
Membership: est. 357,186 in 1,470 congregations (2012)

The Evangelical Free Church (EFCA) traces its origin to the Pietist revivals in Scandanavia in the late nineteenth century. Immigration brought members of various "free" churches to the United States. A number of Swedish-speaking evangelical congregations, centered in Iowa, formed a fellowship of "free" congregations to be known as the Swedish Evangelical Free Mission in 1884. In that same year, two Norwegian-Danish groups began fellowshipping, one on the East coast and one on the West. In 1912, these merged to form the Norwegian-Danish Evangelical Free Church Association. In 1950 the Swedish denomination merged with the other Scandinavian bodies to form the present Evangelical Free Church, with headquarters in Minneapolis, Minnesotta.

Doctrinally, the church endorses a variation on the popular Pietist statement: "In essentials, unity. In non-essentials, liberty. In all things, charity [love]." In 1950 the merged denominations adopted a twelve-point doctrinal statement, which is now incorporated into the constitution of most local congregations. The constitution stresses faithfulness to evangelical beliefs while avoiding disputes over minor matters. Affirming both the rational and the relational dimensions of Christian faith, the church maintains that sound Christian doctrine must be coupled with dynamic Christian experience, facilitating a ministry of love and reconciliation. It includes belief in the premillennial return of Jesus and biblical inerrancy.

Local congregations are autonomous, but the church maintains administrative offices in Minneapolis, Minnesota. The president works with various boards and leadership teams to guide the several ministries of the denomination. Some six hundred missionaries serve stations in over forty countries around the world. The church sponsors Trinity International University, which includes Trinity Evangelical Divinity School (TEDS), with the main campus located in Deerfield, Illinois; other campuses of the university are maintained in Chicago, Illinois; Miami, Florida; and Santa Ana, California.

The Evangelical Free Church has become one of America's foremost "centrist" evangelical denominations without particular ties to any one Reformation tradition. Traditionally it avoided favoring either Calvinism or Arminianism, but under the strong influence of theologians at its seminary, TEDS, the denomination has been leaning slightly more toward the former theology. This represents a change of ethos as, in the past, the EFCA leaned more toward Holiness theology and a revivalist ethos. Both streams still exist within it. A recent EFCA survey of ministers showed them about evenly divided between Calvinists and Arminians.

The EFCA is a conservative evangelical denomination with regard to doctrine and ethics; it does not sanction the ordination of women or non-heterosexual men to serve as lead pastors in congregations nor does it sanction performance of same-sex weddings. It claims to be "welcoming but not affirming" with regard to gay and lesbian people. Women called by God can obtain a license for Christian ministry from the EFCA for service on church staffs.

For more information: www.efca.org

Headquarters: 901 East Seventy-Eighth Street, Minneapolis, MN 55420

FELLOWSHIP OF GRACE BRETHREN CHURCHES

Founded: 1939
Membership: 30,371 in 260 congregations (2012)

This body was part of the Brethren Church (Ashland) that separated from the main Church of the Brethren in the early 1880s. During the fundamentalist or modernist controversy of the 1920s and 1930s that church divided further. In 1939 the Ashland group and the Grace group went their separate ways. In 1969, the Grace group adopted its own statement of faith that expressed the church's beliefs, which include the primacy of the Bible; the Trinity; the church as made up of believers; the Christian life as a way of righteousness; the ordinances of baptism and the threefold Communion service (including foot-washing and the love feast); the reality of Satan; the second coming of Jesus; and the future life. The group was separately incorporated in 1987 as the Fellowship of Grace Brethren Churches and a new constitution was adopted in 1997.

Grace Brethren churches are grouped geographically into districts, which hold annual conferences. The entire church holds an annual conference, often held at Winona Lake, Indiana, where the group's headquarters is located. This conference, made up of delegates from Fellowship churches, elects a board of directors, known as the Fellowship Council, and general church officers. The church supports both international and North American missionary and relief efforts, and it maintains Grace College and Seminary in Winona Lake.

The Fellowship of Grace Brethren Churches, unlike most Brethren churches, embraces dispensationalism—an interpretation of the Bible popularized by British Plymouth Brethren leader and theologian John Nelson Darby and by the Scofield Reference Bible. Dispensationalism was and is especially popular among fundamentalists. It includes the idea of a distinction between Israel and the church in God's plan for salvation in which, after a "secret rapture" of gentile Christians, God will restore his relationship with the Jews who will come to accept Jesus Christ as their Messiah. This is one form of the eschatology known as "premillennialism" and was popularized by theologian-novelist Tim LaHaye in a series of books popularly known as the Left Behind series.

For more information: www.charisfellowship.us

Headquarters: PO Box 386, Winona Lake, IN 46590

MORAVIAN CHURCH

Founded: 1722 with roots to 1467 (came to the US in 1735)
Membership: 31,264 in 163 congregations (2010)

The Moravian Church is one of the few pre-Reformation Protestant churches. Its roots go back to John Hus (ca. 1372–1415), a Czech reformer who was burned at the stake by Catholics at the Council of Constance in 1415. A young man named Brother Gregory grew dissatisfied with the lifestyle and worship of the major Hussite church, and in 1457–58 he organized a community dedicated to living according to the Sermon on the Mount and the example of the early church. They called their pacifist, communitarian body *Jednota Bratrska,* "the Unity of the Brethren." At times they used the Latin form, *Unitas Fratrum,* which remains the official name of the church. In 1467 the group established an independent episcopacy and clergy.

Persecution under the Hapsburgs almost exterminated the church, but in 1722 refugees settled on the estate of Count Nicholas Ludwig von Zinzendorf (1700–60), one of the leaders of German Pietism, in Saxony. There they built the town of Herrnhut, a highly structured religious community that would be the model for similar communities in the

United States. Under the direction of Zinzendorf, a Lutheran who became the Moravians' bishop, the Moravians carried out an extensive mission enterprise, beginning with work among the slaves on Saint Thomas in the Virgin Islands. In the 1730s the Moravians became the first church to ordain women of African descent as pastors and evangelists. The Moravian evangelist David Zeisberger (1721–1808) had great success among the native tribes of the northern United States, but that effort was virtually destroyed by the massacre of Moravian Indians at Gnaddenhutten, Ohio, in 1782 by an American militia.

The Moravians attempted to establish a settlement in Georgia in the 1730s, but the only lasting result of that work was the conversion of John Wesley (1703–91) to "heart religion." Permanent work was established in Pennsylvania and North Carolina. In the nineteenth century, the church supported work among German and Scandanavian immigrants in the upper Midwest. Recent growth in the United States comes mainly from immigration from Central America and the Caribbean, where the Moravians have long had a strong presence.

The major doctrinal statement of the church is *The Ground of the Unity*, which emphasizes the love of God manifested in the life and death of Jesus, the teachings of Christ, the inner testimony of the Spirit, ecumenism, and Christian conduct in everyday affairs, including the pursuit of social justice. There has not been a schism in the church since 1495. In addition to infant baptism and Holy Communion, the Moravians observe the practice of the love feast, a simple meal taken communally. In the United States, Moravians are most famous for the Easter Sunrise Service and Christmas Eve love feast and candle service.

There is only one Moravian Church worldwide, but it is divided into twenty governing units, called provinces. The provinces in North America are the Northern (including Canada), Southern, and Alaskan provinces. The highest administrative body in each is the provincial synod, which meets every four years to direct missionary, educational, and publishing work and to elect a Provincial Elders' Conference, which functions between synod meetings. Bishops, elected by provincial and general synods, are the spiritual, not the administrative, leaders of the church. There are several female bishops in the church, and until recently the head of the Unity was Angelina Swart of South Africa.

Missionary work has always been a primary concern. There are nearly eight hundred thousand Moravians worldwide, more than half in Tanzania and South Africa. Always committed to education, the church founded Moravian College and Theological Seminary in Bethlehem, Pennsylvania, and Salem College in Winston-Salem, North Carolina. The church is also known for its distinctive musical heritage.

The theology of the Moravian Church is basically Lutheran Pietism, but the denomination has its own distinctive ethos and customs described above. At the heart of the denomination is the motto "In essentials unity, in non-essentials liberty, in all things charity [love]"—a motto the Moravians loaned to other Brethren groups. In recent decades the Moravian Church in America has lost much of its original Pietist and evangelical fervor and become more ecumenical if not liberal theologically. Some within the denomination are actively trying to revive its Pietist heritage and ethos.

It should be noted that the Moravians are not the only heirs of the pre-Reformation reforming work of John Hus. Scattered throughout Texas are many independent "Czech Brethren" congregations founded by Czechoslovakian immigrants who brought the original Unitas Fratrum (Bohemian Brethren or "Hussite") faith with them. These have no relationship with the Moravian Church and also have no headquarters or organizational structure. They refer to their network of churches simply as Czech Brethren or "The Unity of the Brethren."

For more information: www.moravian.org

Headquarters: 101 Center Street, PO Box 1245, Bethlehem, PA 18016-1245

OLD GERMAN BAPTIST BRETHREN CHURCH

Reorganized: 1881; divided in 2009
Membership: est. 6,800 in 56 congregations (before the divide) (2005)

While the Brethren Church left the Church of the Brethren because the latter body seemed too conservative in the early 1880s, the Old German Baptist Brethren left because they considered the Church of the Brethren not conservative enough. The dissenters stood for the old order and traditions. The salient point in their opposition lay in their suspicion of Sunday schools, salaried ministers, missions, higher education, and church societies. The basic objections still hold but with certain modifications. Children are not enrolled in Sunday schools, but are encouraged to attend the regular services of the church and to join the church by baptism during their teens; however, the decision is left entirely to the individual. Many congregations list a majority of members between fifteen and fifty years of age. The church today is not completely opposed even to higher education; most of the youth enter high school and some take training in college or professional schools.

The church stands for a literal interpretation of the scriptures in regard to the Lord's Supper and practices closed Communion, which excludes all but its own members. While it advocates compliance with the ordinary demands of government, it opposes cooperation in war. Any member who enters into military service will fall under the judgment of the church. Non-cooperation in political and secret societies is required; dress is plain, and all amusements deemed worldly are frowned upon. The group has no salaried ministers and enforces complete abstinence from alcoholic beverages; the members refuse to take oaths or engage in lawsuits, the sick are anointed with oil, the heads of the sisters are veiled, and wedding ceremonies are not performed for previously divorced persons while their former spouses are living.

The Old German Baptist Brethren Church split in 2009 resulting in a new denomination (or denominetwork) known as the Old German Baptist Brethren Church New Conference Fellowship. After the schism the original group was left with about forty-six congregations and 3,981 members. Statistics for the New Conference Fellowship were not available at the time of this writing. The cause of the schism is unclear. In 2016 the New Conference Fellowship adopted a detailed "We Believe" doctrinal statement that includes belief in the inerrancy of the Bible and the literal interpretation of creation of the universe in six days of twenty-four hours each.

SCHWENKFELDER CHURCH

Founded: 1782, with roots to 1519
Membership: est. 2,300 in 5 congregations (2008)

This church predates the Pietist movement, but shares so many Pietist features that it is included in this section as a "forerunner" of the movement. Though small in size, it represents such a unique branch of the Protestant Reformation that it merits inclusion in this *Handbook*. The church is named for Caspar Schwenckfeld von Ossig (1489–1561), a Silesian nobleman who experienced a spiritual awakening in 1518. Disappointed in his hope to help reform the Roman Catholic Church from within, he played a leading role in the Reformation. He broke with Martin Luther over the issue of the Lord's Supper, insisting that the bread remains bread, and he insisted on complete separation of church and state. Espousing a "Reformation of the Middle Way," Schwenckfeld and his followers emphasized the supremacy of the Spirit over literalistic interpretations of scripture. Many scholars believe Schwenckfeld indirectly influenced George Fox, the founder of the Friends (Quakers). By the end of the sixteenth century, the movement numbered several thousand, but the group was persecuted by other religious bodies and remained small and rather dispersed.

Schwenkfelders arrived in Philadelphia in six migrations between 1731 and 1737. Unable to find land for common purchase, the immigrants spread out and settled in the region between Philadelphia and Allentown, Pennsylvania. The Society of Schwenkfelders was formed in 1782, and the Schwenkfelder Church was incorporated in 1909. Although descendants of the original settlers live in all regions of the United States, the remaining Schwenkfelder churches are found within a fifty-mile radius of Philadelphia. All theology, the members hold, should be constructed from the Bible, but scripture is considered dead without the "indwelling Word." They believe that Christ's divinity was progressive, his human nature becoming more and more divine without "losing its identity." Faith, regeneration, and subsequent spiritual growth change human nature, but justification by faith must not obscure the positive regeneration imparted by Christ; thus the theology is Christocentric.

The Schwenkfelders have contributed much to Pennsylvania and American social and political life with several congressmen and senators coming from among its ranks. They tend to be highly educated and affluent even if little known outside a small region of their home state.

For more information: www.schwenkfelder.com
Headquarters: 105 Seminary Street, Pennsburg, PA 18073

BAPTISTS

The Baptists comprise one of the largest and most diverse groupings of Christians in the United States. Baptists are strongly congregational in polity: each local congregation is independent. However, Baptist churches are commonly grouped into larger associations for purposes of fellowship. National conventions have been established to carry on educational and missionary work and to administer pension plans for ministers. For the purposes of this *Handbook*, these national conventions are considered denominations.

Most state and regional conventions meet annually with delegates or "messengers" from all affiliated Baptist churches in a given area. These conventions receive reports, make recommendations, and help to raise national mission budgets; but they have no authority to enforce their decisions. However, they do sometimes expel a Baptist congregation from the convention in which case it can simply join another Baptist convention or conference. Baptists have traditionally insisted on freedom of thought and expression in pulpit and pew. They have insisted, too, on the absolute autonomy of the local congregation; each church arranges its own worship, "calls" its own pastors, and examines and baptizes its own members. There is no age requirement for membership, but the candidate is usually of an age to understand and accept the teachings of Christ. Candidates for the ministry are licensed by local churches and are ordained upon recommendation of a group of sister churches. Practices vary between groups of Baptists; some have formed more "connectional" associations and conventions while others have maintained absolute congregational autonomy and even separatism.

Doctrine and Polity. Despite their emphasis on independence and individualism, Baptists are bound together by an amazingly strong "rope of sand" in allegiance to certain principles and doctrines based generally on the competency of each individual in matters of faith. Baptists generally agree on the following principles of faith: the inspiration and trustworthiness of the Bible as the sole rule of faith and life; the lordship of Jesus Christ; the inherent freedom of persons to approach God for themselves; the granting of salvation through repentance and faith and contact with the Holy Spirit; two ordinances (rather than sacraments), the Lord's Supper and the baptism of believers by immersion; the independence of the local church; the church as a voluntary group of regenerated believers who are baptized upon confession of faith; and separation of church and state. Most Baptist churches have paid clergy, but they also believe any regenerated and baptized believer can preach and perform the ordinances. Clergy are called and ordained as trained leaders and teachers, not as possessors of special spiritual qualities or powers.

These overall doctrines have never been written into any official Baptist creed for all the churches, but they have been incorporated into several important confessions of faith. The Baptist churches of London wrote a Confession in the year 1689 that was enlarged by the Philadelphia Association in 1742. The New Hampshire State Baptist Convention drew up another confession in 1832. The Philadelphia Confession is strongly Calvinist, the New Hampshire Confession only moderately so. General (non-Calvinist) Baptists have written their own statements of faith including the Orthodox Creed of 1678. From the very beginnings of the Baptist tradition they have been divided between "Particular" and "General." Particular Baptists believe in Calvinism, including God's predestination of individuals to salvation (or not). General Baptists believe in free will and reject predestination of individuals to salvation (Arminianism).

Baptists in the United States. The Baptist movement in the United States grew out of English Puritanism and Anabaptism in the early seventeenth century. Convinced that Puritanism needed further reform, Separatists (Congregationalists) began to teach that only self-professed believers were eligible for membership in the church. That is, the church is properly made up of only regenerated people and is a voluntary association of true believers. Fleeing persecution under James I, some of the English Separatists settled in the Netherlands, where they encountered the Mennonites.* Many of the Mennonites' principles agreed with their own convictions, including the beliefs that the Bible is the sole authority for faith and practice; that church and state should be completely separated; and that church discipline should be rigidly enforced in business, family, and personal affairs. Before long the congregation of John Smyth (ca. 1570–1612) accepted another bedrock Mennonite principle and adopted the practice of "believer baptism"—that is, baptism only of persons old enough to make a voluntary profession of faith. Smyth rebaptized himself and his followers in 1609. Smyth's people eventually moved back across the channel and established a Baptist church in London.

In 1631, Roger Williams (ca. 1603–83) came to America and soon became the first great champion of freedom for faith and conscience in North America. Williams was a Separatist minister when he arrived. Preaching against the authority of the Puritan magistrates, Williams was forced to leave the Massachusetts Bay colony, and he established the town of Providence in Rhode Island. There he organized the first Baptist church in America. John Clarke (1609–76) established another Baptist church at Newport around the same time. Many scholars date the Providence church to 1638, and the Newport church to 1644.

The Baptist movement grew rapidly during the First Great Awakening of the 1740s, but a dispute soon arose among Baptists over the question of conversion. The Old Lights, or Regulars, distrusted the emotionalism of revivals, while the New Lights insisted on an experience of rebirth as a condition for membership in their churches. Despite internal disagreements Baptists continued to agitate for religious freedom in the new land and played a significant role in the adoption of the First Amendment to the United States Constitution.

Landmark Baptists. Many Baptists in America hold to the belief that the Baptist Church has existed since the days of John the Baptist in the first century CE. Of particular interest in this regard are the Landmark Baptists. The name originated with the writings of James Madison Pendleton (1811–91) and James Robinson Graves (1820–93) in Kentucky and Tennessee in the latter part of the nineteenth century. The four distinguishing tenets of Landmarkism are the following:

1. The church is always local and visible. While members of Protestant churches may be saved, they are not members of true churches.

2. The commission was given to the church; consequently, all matters covered by it must be administered under church authority. Clergy of other denominations are not accepted in Landmark Baptist pulpits.

3. Baptism, to be valid, must be administered by the authority of a New Testament (Baptist) church. Baptisms administered by any other authority are not accepted.

4. There is a direct historic succession of Baptist churches from New Testament times. Baptist churches have existed in practice, though not in name, in every century.

These principles are held primarily by the churches of the American Baptist Association and Baptist Missionary Association, though an estimated 1.5 million members of different Baptist churches hold to the Landmark position and doctrine, the largest concentration being in the South and the Southwest. More than fifteen Bible institutes and seminaries are supported by these churches.

Black Baptists. Baptist preachers were particularly effective in converting African Americans to Christianity before emancipation. The great majority of African Americans in pre-Civil War days were either Baptist or Methodist. In 1793 there were nearly seventy-five thousand Baptists in the United States, one-fourth of them black. When the Battle of Bull Run was fought in 1861, there were one hundred fifty thousand black Baptists, most of them slaves.

The church was one place where slaves and free, black and white, had social interaction, but slaves usually had to sit in the galleries of white churches. White Baptist preachers, sometimes assisted by black helpers, moved from one plantation to another, holding services more or less regularly. Occasionally a black preacher was emancipated so he could

work full-time among blacks. The first black Baptist church was organized at Silver Bluff, across the Savannah River, near Augusta, Georgia, in 1773. Other churches followed in Petersburg, Virginia, 1776; Richmond, Virginia, 1780; Williamsburg, Virginia, 1785; Savannah, Georgia, 1785; and Lexington, Kentucky, 1790.

The slave rebellion led by Nat Turner in 1831 appears to have been fueled by Christian rhetoric of freedom and divine justice. Whites were so frightened by the rebellion that laws were passed in most Southern states making it illegal to teach blacks to read. The book that the masters feared was the Bible, with its message of liberation of the oppressed. The story of the exodus inspired hope in the enslaved population that God would send a new Moses to free his people. The story of Jesus, who was flogged like a slave, also inspired hope for those suffering under the bondsman's lash. Jesus was more than the Lamb of God who takes away the sin of the world; he was a suffering servant who shared the burdens of those who suffer.

Almost everywhere slave meetings were monitored by owners, lest unrest be fomented, but slaves continued to conduct their own meetings hidden from sight and sound of the masters in "the invisible institution." Slaves developed a distinctive type of gospel music, called "spirituals," and sang about freedom, justice, and salvation. Evangelism and justice have always gone hand in hand in black theology. After the Civil War, Baptist congregations divided along racial lines, and countless black Baptist congregations emerged throughout the South. Thus it is not uncommon to see two churches named "First Baptist," one white and the other black, in southern towns. Aided by the Freedman's Aid Society and various Baptist organizations, nearly one million black Baptists were worshipping in their own churches by 1880.

Emancipation did not lead to the promised land for African Americans, but the church helped blacks endure decades of segregation. Large numbers of African Americans moved to northern cities in the late nineteenth and early twentieth centuries, and they took their faith with them. The black church served as an anchor for many people living in growing metropolises, and national conventions were organized to coordinate Baptist ministries.

Baptist Missions. Strongly evangelical in theology, the Baptists were early participants in foreign missions, following the lead of English Baptist William Carey (1761–1834) who went to India in 1793. In 1814, Baptists in the United States organized their own General Missionary Convention of the Baptist Denomination in the United States of America for Foreign Missions. This convention, representing a national Baptist fellowship, marked the first real denominational consciousness. It was followed eventually by other organizations that welded them firmly together: general Baptist conventions; a general tract society, later called the American Baptist Publication Society; various missionary societies for work at home and abroad; an education society; and the Baptist Young People's Union.

These organizations were on a national scale, but divided over the issue of slavery. In 1845, there was a dispute over whether a missionary could own slaves. Many Baptists had come to the conclusion that owning another human being was inconsistent with Christian faith. In response, Southerners defended slavery on biblical grounds. When a compromise could not be reached, they formed their own Southern Baptist Convention (SBC). The SBC took a literal view of the Bible, especially passages that defended slavery, and insisted that the church focus on evangelism and personal morality rather than social justice issues. The Northern Baptist Convention was not officially organized until 1907 and is now called the American Baptist Churches in the USA.

Some of the divisions caused by slavery and the Civil War have healed. The Baptist Joint Committee on Public Affairs, supported by the American Baptist Churches in the USA, some Southern Baptist churches, and some other Baptist bodies, is housed in Washington, DC. This committee serves mainly to spread Baptist convictions on public morals and to safeguard the principle of separation of church and state. The Baptist World Alliance, organized in 1905, now includes more than forty million Baptists. It meets every five years to discuss common themes and problems and is purely an advisory body.

The twentieth century brought new conflicts in the Baptist family, which resulted in the formation of new denominations. First was the fundamentalist-modernist controversy in the 1920s. Baptist theology respects the right of individuals to read and interpret the Bible on their own, but the methods of modern biblical criticism disturbed many Baptist preachers. Baptists divided over how literally one should read the Bible. Since World War II, Baptists have argued over the church's role in society. Should the church encourage the expansion of civil rights to all people or should the church insist on traditional gender roles? In 2008 a new initiative called the New Baptist Covenant was launched by prominent Baptists, most notably former president Jimmy Carter, who teaches Sunday school in a Baptist church in Plains, Georgia. The New Baptist Covenant is an attempt to reunite all Baptist churches in a common expression of faith focused on the redeeming work of Christ and God's plan for justice in the world.

The most divisive issues among Baptists in the United States have to do with the Bible and God's sovereignty. Both are old issues in new forms; Baptists have always struggled among themselves over these divisive issues. Fundamentalist Baptists insist on the "inerrancy" of the Bible, that every statement in the Bible is factually correct "in the original autographs." Some fundamentalist Baptists also insist on use of the King James Version of the Bible (the "Authorized Version"). Other, non-fundamentalist Baptists confess belief in the inspiration and even infallibility of the Bible but acknowledge its cultural conditioning and interpret much of it, such as Genesis and Revelation, non-literally. This difference about the nature of the Bible and its interpretation has led to numerous schisms among Baptists. Some fundamentalist Baptists practice "biblical separation," which means refusal of Christian fellowship with even other Baptists who do not believe in or interpret the Bible as they do.

Baptists have always disagreed among themselves about the nature of God's sovereignty; some are Calvinists ("Reformed Baptists") and some are Arminians ("Free Will

Baptists"). Some Baptist groups have agreed to permit disagreement over this set of doctrines within their conventions and congregations. Others have formed distinct denominations that exclude either Calvinists or Arminians from their ranks.

Some scholars estimate there are about thirty-five million Baptists in the United States, making them the second largest Christian group (after Catholics) and the largest group of Protestants. They are, however, divided among themselves into numerous denominations and subdenominations as well as absolutely independent and separate congregations ("unaffiliated Baptists"). Some of these have dropped the word *Baptist* from their names while remaining Baptist in beliefs and practices (e.g., requiring believer baptism by immersion for church membership). All over the United States one sees independent Baptist churches using many different names that are not affiliated with any organized group. Some network together with like-minded Baptist congregations in local or regional associations but have no headquarters, hierarchy, or even a website.

*Note: Some Baptist groups are included in this *Handbook*'s section "Fundamentalist and Bible Churches." That is not because they are any less Baptist than ones included here but because they are at least as well known for being fundamentalist as for being Baptist. The introduction to that section will explain this matter in more detail.

SUGGESTIONS FOR FURTHER READING

Ammerman, Nancy T. *Baptist Battles: Social Change and Religious Conflict in the Southern Baptist Convention*. New Brunswick, NJ: Rutgers University Press, 1990.

Balmer, Randall. *Mine Eyes Have Seen the Glory: A Journey into the Evangelical Subculture of America*. New York: Oxford University Press, 1989.

Brackney, William H. *The Baptists*. New York: Greenwood Press, 1988.

Dayton, Donald W., and Robert K. Johnston, eds. *The Variety of American Evangelicalism*. Downer's Grove, IL: InterVarsity Press, 1991.

Fitts, Leroy. *A History of Black Baptists*. Nashville, TN: Broadman Press, 1985.

Lincoln, C. Eric, and Lawrence H. Mamiya. *The Black Church in the African American Experience*. Durham, NC: Duke University Press, 1990.

Gardner, Robert. *Baptists of Early America: A Statistical History, 1639–1790*. Atlanta, GA: Georgia Baptist Historical Society, 1983.

Hill, Samuel S., ed. *Encyclopedia of Religion in the South*. Macon, GA: Mercer University Press, 1984.

Hill, Samuel and Robert G. Torbet. *Baptists: North and South*. Valley Forge, PA: Judson Press, 1964.

Leonard, Bill J., ed. *Dictionary of Baptists in America*. Downers Grove, IL: InterVarsity Press, 1994.

Leonard, Bill J. *God's Last and Only Hope: The Fragmentation of the Southern Baptist Convention*. Grand Rapids, MI: Eerdmans, 1990.

MacBeth, Leon. *The Baptist Heritage*. Nashville, TN: Broadman Press, 1987.

Matthews, Donald G. *Religion in the Old South*. Chicago, IL: University of Chicago Press, 1977.

McLoughlin, William G. *Soul Liberty: The Baptists' Struggle in New England, 1630–1833*. Hanover, NH: University Press of New England, 1991.

Pelt, O. D., and R. L. Smith. *The Story of the National Baptists*. New York: Vantage Press, 1960.

Sernett, Milton C., ed. *Afro-American Religious History: A Documentary Witness*. Durham, NC: Duke University Press, 1985.

Wardin, Albert W. *Baptists Around the World: A Comprehensive Handbook*. Nashville, TN: Broadman and Holman Publishers, 1995.

ALLIANCE OF BAPTIST CHURCHES

Founded: 1987
Membership: est. 35,000 in 142 churches (2016)

The Alliance of Baptists is a confederation of Baptist congregations and individuals that separated from the Southern Baptist Convention* during the conservative-moderate conflict of the 1980s. The Alliance stresses the historic Baptist principles of individual and congregational autonomy, particularly in regard to biblical interpretation and missions. The Alliance churches encourage the use of modern methods of biblical study, theological education, and free inquiry into the history of Christianity. Most important, the Alliance has dedicated itself to social and economic justice and equity. Women are encouraged to seek ordination and assume leadership roles in the Alliance and in congregations. Leadership of the Alliance is composed of three elected officers who serve no more than two years and a thirty-four-member Board of Directors. The annual meeting of the Alliance is held each spring and reviews all decisions of the Board. There are nine standing committees that supervise such areas as women in ministry and interfaith dialogue.

The Alliance of Baptists is widely considered the most progressive (to critics "liberal") of Baptist denominetworks—possibly alongside of, if not more progressive than, the American Baptist Churches, USA. The two share a common ethos described above. They place strong emphasis on "soul competency," which means the right of every Christian, especially every Baptist, to interpret the Bible for himself or herself, under the guidance of the Holy Spirit, without ecclesiastical or creedal interference.

Since 2004 the Alliance has supported same-sex marriages and the ordination of gay and lesbian people; some openly gay and lesbian people pastor Alliance churches. The Alliance has a working relationship with the United Church of Christ, which is often considered the most progressive (or liberal) Protestant denomination in the United States. People friendly to the Alliance, many of them exiles from the Southern Baptist Convention, applaud its progressive stances as continuing the civil rights movement beyond racial equality to full equality of women with men and LGBT people with straight people—including within the churches.

For more information: www.allianceofbaptists.org

Headquarters: 3939 LaVista Road Suite E-122, Atlanta, GA 30084

AMERICAN BAPTIST ASSOCIATION

Founded: 1905
Membership: 203,374 adherents in 1,368 congregations (2010)

Organized in 1905 as the Baptist General Association, this group adopted its present name, American Baptist Association (ABA), in 1924. Teaching that the Great Commission of Christ (Matt 28:18-20) was given only to a local congregation, members believe that the local church is the only unit authorized to administer the ordinances (baptism and Communion) and that the congregation is an independent and autonomous body responsible only to Christ. Because of their belief that no universal church or ecclesiastical authority is higher than a local congregation, members of the American Baptist Association claim that those Baptists organized in conventions are not faithful to Bible mission methods. The ABA holds to historic Baptist Landmarkism as described in the introduction to this section of the *Handbook* about Baptists. (It would be a mistake to confuse this group of Baptists with the similarly named American Baptist Churches, USA, which is very different.)

Maintaining that their own way is the true New Testament form, they hold themselves separate from all other religious groups. They strongly protest the trend of many Baptist groups to identify themselves with Protestantism, since they believe that their faith preceded the Protestant Reformation, and indeed has a continued succession from Christ and the apostles. They do not accept as valid baptisms performed in other Baptist churches, and they serve Communion only to members of the local congregation.

The Association's doctrine is strictly fundamentalist* and includes the verbal inspiration of the Bible, the Triune God, the virgin birth and deity of Christ, the suffering and death of Christ as substitutionary, and the bodily resurrection of Christ and all his saints. The second coming of Jesus, physical and personal, is to be the crowning event of the gospel age and will be premillennial. There is eternal punishment for the wicked; salvation is solely by grace through faith, not by law or works. There must be absolute separation of church and state and absolute religious freedom. Members denounce abortion on demand, homosexuality, and premarital sex as being contrary to biblical teachings. The ABA does not condone ordination of women to the gospel ministry.

Government of both the local congregation and the annual meeting of the association is congregational in nature. Missionary work is conducted on county, state, interstate, and international levels, the program originating in the local church; and missionaries are supported by the cooperating churches. Educational work is pursued through the Sunday schools, home schooling, numerous Bible colleges (some of which also contain seminaries), and correspondence courses. The greatest strength of this group is found in the South, Southeast, Southwest, and West, but much new work has begun in recent years in the East and the North.

A comprehensive publishing program includes fourteen monthly and semimonthly periodicals, Sunday school literature designed to cover the entire Bible in a ten-year period, and literature for young people and vacation Bible schools. National and state youth camps are held annually, as are pastors' and missionaries' conferences on regional and national levels.

For more information: www.abaptist.org

Offices: 4605 N. State Line, Texarkana, TX 75503

AMERICAN BAPTIST CHURCHES IN THE USA

Founded: 1814 or 1845
Membership: 1,240,000 members in 5,402 churches (2015)

This body, American Baptist Churches in the USA (ABCUSA), has had several changes in name over the decades. It traces its origins to May 1814, when representatives from various Baptist associations and churches met in Philadelphia to organize the General Missionary Convention of the Baptist Denomination in the United States of America for Foreign Missions. This body quickly became known as the Triennial Convention. The American Baptist Publication Society and the American Baptist Home Mission Society were established in 1824 and 1832 respectively. By 1841, sectional and theological differences centered around the issue of slavery began to erode the unity of the foreign mission board. In 1845, one year after the final meeting of the Triennial Convention, the northern and southern groups met and reorganized separately. The northern group became the American Baptist Missionary Union and the southern group became the Southern Baptist Convention.

Separate appeals for funds to support these competing societies created confusion and dissatisfaction, leading eventually to the formation of the Northern Baptist Convention in 1907. This convention was actually a corporation with restricted powers in conducting religious work, receiving and expending money, and affiliating itself with other bodies. The Convention reorganized in 1950, changing its name to the American Baptist Convention. In 1972 the convention adopted its third and present name and restructured to strengthen the representational principle and to integrate more fully the national program bodies into the larger organization. A larger (two-hundred-member) general board composed of election-district representatives and at-large representatives makes up the policymaking body. A general council of chief executives and staff of national program boards, chief executives of regions, and other American Baptist bodies serves to coordinate the corporate affairs of the denomination under the leadership of the general secretary.

The denomination is at work in and supports many children's homes and special services, numerous retirement homes and communities, hospitals and nursing homes, several theological seminaries, and several senior colleges and universities. Judson Press is its publishing arm. The Board of National Ministries has workers in thirty-six states. This board supports Bacone College for Native Americans in Oklahoma and carries on special ministries among Native Americans and Asians in the United States. The Board of International Ministries currently supports missionaries in six countries in Asia (Hong Kong, India, Japan, the Philippines, Singapore, and Thailand), two countries in Africa (South Africa and Zaire), and seven countries in Latin America and the Caribbean (Bolivia, Costa Rica, the Dominican Republic, El Salvador, Haiti, Mexico, and Nicaragua).

In matters of faith, American Baptist Churches hold to typical Baptist doctrines described above. They have historically taken a stand on such controversial issues as abolition, temperance, racial and social justice, and the equality of women. They have traditionally been a denomination with diversity of race, ethnicity, culture, class, and theology. The ordinances of baptism and the Lord's Supper are considered aids more than necessities for salvation. Generally it may be said that Baptists represented in the American Baptist Churches in the USA are less conservative in thought and theology than those in the Southern Baptist Convention. American Baptists are represented in the National Council of the Churches of Christ in the USA and the World Council of Churches; Southern Baptists are represented in neither. American Baptists have made gestures toward union with General Baptists, Southern Baptists, the National Baptist Convention, Seventh-Day Baptists, Disciples of Christ, Church of the Brethren, and the Alliance of Baptists and have welcomed Free Will Baptists into full fellowship.

Like many historic so-called mainline Protestant denominations, American Baptists struggle with the issues symbolized by the phrase "welcoming and affirming" of LGBT people. In 2005, however, the denomination did declare homosexual behavior incompatible with the Bible. It then also declared that marriage is between one man and one woman. Still and nevertheless, some ABCUSA churches have formed a network of "welcoming and affirming" congregations within the ABCUSA. Critics say a permissiveness toward such churches and ministers is one reason for the denomination's declining membership. Supporters point to the autonomy of the local church and oppose any denominational opposition to full inclusion of people. As of this writing, the matter is left by the national board in the hands of ABCUSA regions for each to decide whether to expel congregations and ministers for ordaining gay and lesbian people and blessing same-sex marriages. The ABCUSA has long recognized the full and equal ministry of women including ordination and women as lead pastors of congregations.

For more information: www.abc-usa.org

Headquarters: PO Box 851, Valley Forge, PA 19482-0851

ASSOCIATION OF REFORMED BAPTIST CHURCHES OF AMERICA

Founded: 1997
Membership: est. 7,000 members; 59 churches (2016)

This association, the Association of Reformed Baptist Churches of America (ARBCA), held its first annual General Assembly, in Mesa, Arizona, on March 11, 1997. The pastors and elders from twenty-four Reformed (Calvinist) Baptist churches in fourteen states were present. Reformed Baptists have their origin in the Particular Baptists of the seventeenth century and have been heavily influenced by the nineteenth-century Baptist theologian and popular preacher Charles Haddon Spurgeon (1834–92). During the mid-twentieth century the works of another Baptist theologian and writer, A. W. Pink, were the catalyst for the resurgence of "five-point Calvinism" that gave rise to the modern Reformed Baptists. In the early twenty-first century Baptist theologian and pastor John Piper has re-energized Calvinism among Baptists in the United States.

Member churches subscribe to the Second London Baptist Confession of Faith of 1689, and agree with the doctrines of the Synod and Canons of Dort (1618–19) and the Westminster Confession of Faith (1646), except in the areas of church government and infant baptism. They profess belief in total human depravity, unconditional election, limited and definite atonement, irresistible (or effectual and invincible) grace, and the final perseverance of all true saints. The Reformed Baptists believe that the Bible presents a Baptist understanding of covenant theology (in contrast to a Presbyterian view). The church rejects dispensationalism, which is taught in some Baptist churches. The denomi-network gives prominence in worship to preaching but believes that prophecy ceased with the apostles.

As with many Baptist groups, the ARBCA churches resist any idea of denominational control over the member churches. Each member church is fully self-governing, yet voluntarily is accountable to sister churches through the Association. The ARBCA has no mission board per se but uses the services of the related Reformed Baptist Mission Services. Member churches also assist one another in sending evangelists to accomplish the call of missions at home and abroad. The association operates the Institute of Reformed Baptist Studies in Escondido, California, in cooperation with Westminster Theological Seminary.

The ARBCA is theologically conservative and almost certainly rejects ordination of gay people and same-sex marriage as not sanctioned by God. Only men are ordained to the gospel ministry by related churches and serve as lead pastors.

For more information: www.arbca.com

Headquarters: 401 East Louther Street Suite 303, PO Box 289, Carlisle, PA 17013

BAPTIST GENERAL CONVENTION OF TEXAS

Founded: 1848
Membership: 2,440,815 adherents in 5,318 churches (2016)

Baptists came to Texas in the 1830s when it was still part of Mexico. Baptist churches grew rapidly during the days of the Republic, and the Baptist State Convention was formed in 1848 in Anderson, Texas. Because of the size of the state and theological diversity among the Baptists, other conventions, such as the Baptist General Association were formed in various regions of the state. In 1886 the Baptist State Convention and Baptist General Association merged and adopted the name Baptist General Convention of Texas (BGCT.) In 1933 the fundamentalist preacher J. Frank Norris separated from the BGCT and formed the Premillennial Missionary Baptist Fellowship, but that did not end the controversy between modernism and fundamentalism in Texas Baptist circles. The BGCT was part of the Southern Baptist Convention (SBC) until the SBC adopted a new Baptist Faith and Message (BFM) statement in 2000. The BGCT rejected the new statement and reaffirmed the 1963 Baptist Faith and Message as its standard. A key difference is whether the Bible is to be interpreted through Jesus Christ, something affirmed by the 1963 statement but dropped in the SBC's 2000 version. The 1963 BFM stresses what it calls Baptist Distinctives: "the soul's competency before God, the priesthood of each believer and all believers, the autonomy of the local church, and a free church in a free state." Part of the controversy was over the ordination of women, which the 2000 BFM statement condemned. In 2007 the BGCT elected its first female president. The church gives special attention to spiritual formation, servant leadership, and being inclusive of all people. The Convention operates Baptist Way Press, which publishes a variety of educational and devotional materials. The primary focus of the Convention is on evangelism and church planting, but it also has an active disaster response ministry. Over one thousand congregations are primarily Spanish speaking. The church is part of the Baptist World Alliance. It does not interfere with BGCT congregations that ordain women and have women pastors, but it does discourage ordination of gay and lesbian people and same-sex marriage. A few BGCT congregations have been encouraged to leave the denomination when they became overtly "welcoming and affirming."

The BGCT includes many "moderate Baptist" congregations and it embraces a broadly evangelical and relatively conservative Protestant theology and ethos. It views itself as continuing the mission-driven spirit of the Southern Baptist Convention especially as it was before the late twentieth-century "takeover" by SBC conservatives. In response to the BGCT's implicit declaration of independence from the SBC over issues related to congregational autonomy the SBC formed its own rival Texas Baptist convention called Southern Baptists of Texas (SBT). Texas has been the major battleground between conservatives and moderates. For the most part, liberal Protestants view both the SBC (including the SBT) and the BGCT as theologically conservative; the main difference between them has to do with denominational control over seminaries, agencies, and individual congregations. Moderates claim the SBC treats the 2000 BFM as a creed, which, they argue, is contrary to Baptist principles.

The BGCT has a special relationship with several Texas Baptist universities and two seminaries—including Baylor University and its George W. Truett Theological Seminary. The BGCT has affiliated congregations in several states surrounding Texas.

For more information: www.bgtc.org and www.texasbaptists.org
Headquarters: 7557 Rambler Road Suite 1200, Dallas, TX 75231

CONSERVATIVE BAPTIST ASSOCIATION OF AMERICA (CBAMERICA)

Founded 1947
Membership: est. 200,000 in 1,100 congregations (2016)

The Conservative Baptist Association (CBA) is described as a "voluntary fellowship of sovereign, autonomous, independent, Bible-believing Baptist churches." The founders of this association of churches were active in the Fundamentalist Fellowship* that was started within the Northern Baptist Convention in 1920 (see American Baptist Churches). Doctrinal disagreement, which grew out of different views of the reliability and credibility of the scriptures, was aggravated by the "inclusive policy" by which both theologically liberal and conservative missionaries were sent to foreign and home fields.

The Conservative Baptist Foreign Mission Board (now CBInternational) was founded in 1943 for the purpose of sending only Bible-believing missionaries to the mission field. In 1947 the Conservative Baptist Association of America (now CBAmerica) was formed. Churches were free to belong to both this new association and the Northern Baptist

Convention. The Conservative Baptist Home Mission Society (now Mission to the Americas) and the Conservative Baptist Theological Seminary (now Denver Seminary) were begun by the leaders of this new church association. Western Seminary of Portland, Oregon, is also affiliated with the CBA.

The ministry of CBAmerica through regional offices and the national office includes providing resources and counsel in the areas of Christian education, church planting, women's ministry, pastoral placement, and church administration. Administering one benevolent fund for pastors, leaders, and their families and another for churches in crisis are responsibilities of the Association. Endorsing and administrating military chaplains, plus hospital, prison, and law enforcement chaplains is a major focus of ministry.

The name *Conservative* was chosen to indicate the desire to conserve the basic doctrines of historic, biblical Christianity. These include the infallibility of the scriptures; God as Father, perfect in holiness, infinite in wisdom, measureless in power; Christ as the eternal and only begotten Son of God—his sinlessness, virgin birth, atonement, bodily resurrection, ascension, and return to earth; the Holy Spirit as coming forth from God to convince the world of sin, of righteousness, and of judgment; the sinfulness of all people and the possibility of their regeneration, sanctification, and comfort through Christ and the Holy Spirit; the church as the living body of Christ, with Christ as the head; the local church as free from interference from any ecclesiastical or political authority; the responsibility of every human being to God alone; that human betterment is a direct result of the gospel; and the ordinances of believer's baptism by immersion and the Lord's supper.

CBAmerica is a moderately conservative, evangelical denomination not generally considered fundamentalist as it permits latitude and diversity of opinion about many matters of biblical interpretation and doctrine where fundamentalists traditionally do not. However, it does not encourage ordination of women to gospel ministry or women as lead pastors of congregations. Nor does it encourage ordination of gay men or same-sex marriage within its own ranks. Neither of these are controversial issues with which the CBA struggles.

For more information: www.cbamerica.org

Headquarters: 3686 Stagecoach Road Suite F, Longmont, CO 80504-5660

CONVERGE WORLDWIDE
(BAPTIST GENERAL CONFERENCE)

Founded: 1852
Membership: est. 260,000 in 1,289 churches (2016)

The history of what is now known as the Converge Worldwide (formerly the Baptist General Conference) began at Rock Island, Illinois, in 1852. Gustaf Palmquist, a middle-aged schoolteacher and lay preacher, had arrived from Sweden the previous year to become the spiritual leader of a group of Swedish immigrants who had been influenced by the Pietist movement within the (Lutheran) state church of Sweden. At Galesburg, Illinois, he came in contact with Baptists, and early in 1852 he was baptized and ordained a Baptist minister. Visiting the Swedish people at Rock Island, Palmquist won his first converts to the Baptist faith and baptized three in the Mississippi River on August 18, 1852. There were sixty-five churches when the national conference of the Swedish Baptist General Conference of America was organized in 1879.

For several decades the American Baptist Home Mission Society and the American Baptist Publication Society of the American (then Northern) Baptist Convention* aided the new work among the Swedish immigrants, but gradually the church became self-supporting. A theological seminary was founded in Chicago in 1871, and the first denominational paper was launched the same year. From 1888 until 1944, foreign missionary activities were channeled through the American Baptist Foreign Mission Society. The Swedish Conference set up its own foreign-mission board in 1944 and today has many regular and dozens of short-term missionaries in India, Japan, the Philippines, Ethiopia, Mexico, Argentina, Brazil, the Ivory Coast, Cameroon, France, Belize, Cambodia, the Caribbean, Central Asia, the Muslim world, Senegal, Singapore, Thailand, Ukraine, and Uruguay.

Following World War I, with its intensified nationalistic conflicts, the transition from Swedish- to English-language church services was greatly accelerated and was practically completed in three decades. In 1945, Swedish was dropped from the name of the conference. With the language barrier removed, the growth of the conference has been rapid and far-reaching. Less than half of the pastors are of Swedish descent, and a large number of churches contain few members of that descent.

Converge Worldwide, or BGC, partners with Bethel College and Seminary in Saint Paul, Minnesota, a four-year college and a three-year theological school, with campuses in Saint Paul, San Diego, Philadelphia, New York City, and Washington, DC. Also affiliated with the church are three children's homes; seven homes for the aged; and *Converge Point*, the official denominational publication. Harvest Publications offers Bibles, books, and Sunday school materials. Basically, the church's doctrine is theologically conservative, with unqualified acceptance of the word of God, and holds the usual Baptist tenets. It is a strong fellowship of churches, insistent upon the major beliefs of conservative Christianity but with respect for individual differences on minor points. The Pietist motto, "In essentials unity, in non-essentials liberty, in all things charity [love]," has governed and guided this non-fundamentalist, evangelical Baptist fellowship for its entire existence.

The Baptist General Conference changed its name to Converge Worldwide in 2008 as a result of its interest in focusing on church planting and becoming a mission-driven fellowship of churches. It did not intend to shed its Baptist identity even though some critics of the name-change interpreted the move that way. Some observers believe that the "Southern Baptist battles" of the last decades of the twentieth century gave the word *Baptist* such a negative connotation for many Americans that the BGC felt it would be to its mission-driven advantage to drop the word from its name. Many of its affiliated congregations had already done so. There is no evidence, however, of the denomination or individual churches becoming anything other than Baptist in theology and practice except that some congregations have adopted an elder-led model of church leadership, which is traditionally more presbyterian than Congregationalist (the traditional Baptist pattern of church organization). Converge still requires believer baptism, preferably by full immersion, for church membership. The denomination does not interfere with congregations that ordain women or have women pastors (although very few do), but it actively discourages a "welcoming and affirming" stance with regard to LGBT people.

Two very influential Converge pastors are Leith Anderson, a pioneer in the Church Growth Movement and executive leader of the National Association of Evangelicals (NAE), and John Piper, retired pastor of Bethlehem Baptist Church (a Converge congregation) in Minneapolis and author of numerous books of Calvinist theology. Both Anderson and Piper have exercised broad and deep influence on the wider evangelical world especially in North America but also (through their writings) outside it.

For more information: www.converge.org

Headquarters: 2002 South Arlington Heights Road, Arlington Heights, IL 60005

COOPERATIVE BAPTIST FELLOWSHIP

Founded: 1991
Membership: est. 1,000,000 in 1,800 churches (2016)

The Cooperative Baptist Fellowship (CBF) was formed during the years of struggle within the Southern Baptist Convention (SBC) between conservatives and moderates. Some of the moderates disapproved of the conservatives' tactics in gaining control of the SBC and believed that the Convention itself was in danger of violating some traditional Baptist principles such as "soul competency" and congregational autonomy. In 1991, the new CBF was formed as an alternative body to the SBC, although congregations are free to hold dual affiliation. In many cases, however, the SBC does not permit such.

The mission of the Cooperative Baptist Fellowship focuses on ministry rather than theology, as indicated by their mission statement adopted in 2000: "We are a fellowship of Baptist Christians and churches who share a passion for the Great Commission of Jesus Christ and a commitment to Baptist principles of faith and practice. Our mission is to serve Baptist Christians and churches as they discover and fulfill their God-given mission."

The CBF focuses its work on global missions among the world's most neglected (the impoverished, homeless, victims of HIV and AIDS, and other marginalized peoples) and the least evangelized. It also fosters advocacy of historic Baptist values, such as local church autonomy, the priesthood of all believers, and religious liberty. The CBF has partnerships with fifteen seminaries and theological schools and has helped found new schools of theology in historical Baptist colleges in the South.

The CBF is one of three major groups of Baptist churches breaking away from the Southern Baptist Convention due to the SBC's perceived fundamentalist leanings. The other two are the Baptist General Convention of Texas (some of whose churches are also aligned with the CBF) and the Alliance of Baptist Churches. The Baptist General Association of Virginia is possibly a fourth Baptist group in this category.

Unlike the Alliance of Baptist Churches, the CBF has not taken a definite position for or against ordination of gay or lesbian people or same-sex marriages, leaving that decision in the hands of member congregations. It does, however, encourage the full equality of women and men including ordination and women as lead pastors.

For more information: www.cbf.net

Headquarters: 160 Clairemont Avenue, Decatur, GA 30030

FULL GOSPEL BAPTIST CHURCH FELLOWSHIP INTERNATIONAL

Founded: 1994
Membership: Membership unknown in est. 2,500 congregations (2016)

The Full Gospel Baptist Church Fellowship International (FGBCFI) is one of the newest denominations in the United States. It emerged out of the National Baptist Convention, USA and many of its related churches are dually aligned with that historic African American denomination. The term "full gospel" has been used primarily for self-description by Pentecostals for over a century; it points to belief in the infilling of the Holy Spirit, often accompanied by the spiritual gift of speaking in tongues, as something every converted Christian should experience. It also points to the typical Pentecostal belief that all of the gifts of the Holy Spirit mentioned by the Apostle Paul in 1 Corinthians 12, including prophecy and healing, are for Christians of every age including the present one. So, there is a sense in which the FGBCFI is both Baptist and Pentecostal; it is included in this Baptist category of the *Handbook* because of its Baptist roots. There is still much overlap between it and its "parent" denomination (the National Baptist Convention, USA). Also, its statement of faith does not emphasize a "second blessing" after conversion or speaking in tongues as an "initial, physical evidence" of the infilling of the Holy Spirit (as is the case with most classical Pentecostal groups).

The FGBCFI began with the desire by some African American Baptists to experience the infilling of the Holy Spirit accompanied by manifestations of supernatural gifts of the Holy Spirit. In other words, they wanted to be free to be both Baptist and Pentecostal in some sense. Some use the term "Bapticostal." The founders also wanted women to be ordained as pastors of churches and to have an episcopal form of church government led by bishops. The latter feature is one major reason some Baptists do not consider them truly Baptist (as most Baptist churches and denominations have always held strongly to congregational church polity or government).

The FGBCFI touts its distinctive "transformational platform" with the acronym "S.H.I.F.T.," which stands for Sustainability, Holiness, Innovation, Family, and Transcendence. The denomination has eight regions led by bishops accountable to several "presiding bishops." At the same time, however, the FGBCFI affirms "congregational autonomy" but "with the added value of the Episcopacy as a covering."

For more information: www.fullgospelbaptist.org

Headquarters: 1691 Phoenix Boulevard Suite 370, Atlanta, GA 30349

GENERAL ASSOCIATION OF GENERAL BAPTISTS

Founded: 1823, organized as denomination 1870
Membership: 95,000 in 816 churches (2016)

The General Association of General Baptists (GAGB) marks its beginning with the founding of Liberty Baptist Church by Benoni Stinson (ca. 1798–1870) in 1823 in the Howell neighborhood of Evansville, Indiana. Stinson proclaimed the principle from Hebrews 2:9 that Jesus Christ "by the grace of God should taste death for every man." This theological understanding of general or universal atonement, which Stinson emphasized in the churches he helped start, can be traced back to the early 1600s when it was embraced by John Smyth and Thomas Helwys, founders of the first Baptist congregations in Europe. Those who adhered to this principle were labeled General Baptists, and Roger Williams is considered to be the first General Baptist minister in the American colonies. For all practical purposes, "General Baptist" is synonymous with "Free Will Baptist" in terms of theology; both point to an Arminian as opposed to a Calvinist approach to salvation. (Early Calvinist Baptists were called "Particular Baptists" due to their belief that Christ died only for particular people, the elect.)

Stinson's work spread to Kentucky, Illinois, Missouri, and Tennessee. Shortly after his death, these scattered associations of churches organized into a national denomination in 1870 called the General Association of General Baptists. Today, churches in this denomination reach from California to Florida and into New York City, though the bulk are in the "buckle" of the so-called Bible Belt: Illinois, Indiana, Missouri, Kentucky, Tennessee, and Arkansas. Mission work is active in China, Guam, Saipan, Jamaica, India, Honduras, the Philippines, and Mexico.

The General Baptist confession of faith is basically Arminian: Christ died for all; failure to achieve salvation lies completely with the individual; humankind is depraved and fallen and unable to save itself; conversion and regeneration are necessary for salvation; salvation comes by repentance and faith in Christ; Christians who persevere to the end are saved; the wicked are punished eternally; and the dead, both the just and the unjust, will be raised at the judgment. The Lord's Supper and believer baptism by immersion are the only authorized ordinances, but some General Baptist churches also practice foot-washing.

Their polity is similar to that found in most Baptist groups, but a peculiar feature of the General Baptist church lies in the use of a presbytery into which the ordained members of local associations are grouped. They examine candidates for the ministry and for the diaconate. Ministers and deacons are responsible to this presbytery, which exists only on the local level. So the GAGB is a mixture of congregational and presbyterian church polity.

The denomination maintains a liberal arts university in Oakland City, Indiana. Chapman Seminary for theological study is located on the campus. A publishing house, Stinson Press, is operated at Poplar Bluff, Missouri, where the monthly newspaper is issued. Also in Poplar Bluff are the denomination's Women's Ministries office and General Baptist Investment Fund office. The denomination has several facilities for the elderly and operates an adoption center in Oakland City.

The GAGB is a theologically conservative but not fundamentalist Baptist denomination; it does not take a definite stand regarding ordination of women although only a few women serve as pastors. That decision is left to the regional associations. The denomination condemns sex outside of monogamous, heterosexual marriage as sin and therefore does not permit the ordination of non-celibate single persons or allow them to serve as pastors.

For more information: www.generalbaptist.com

Headquarters: 100 Stinson Drive, Poplar Bluff, MO 63901

NATIONAL ASSOCIATION OF FREE WILL BAPTISTS

Founded: 1935
Membership: 185,798 in 2,369 churches (2012)

The rise of Free Will Baptists can be traced to the influence of Arminian-minded Baptists who migrated to the American Colonies from England. Unlike strict Calvinists, Arminians believe that Christ died for all people and each individual has the grace-enabled freedom to choose salvation. In other words, they reject the idea of divine predestination of individuals and preach that humans have free will in matters of faith.

The southern line, or Palmer movement, began in 1727 when Paul Palmer (d. 1750) established a church at Chowan, North Carolina. The northern line, or Randall movement, began with a congregation organized by Benjamin Randall in 1780 in New Durham, New Hampshire. Both groups taught the doctrines of free grace, free salvation, and free will. There were gestures toward uniting the northern and southern groups until the outbreak of the Civil War.

The northern body extended more rapidly into the West and the Southwest, and in 1910 this line of Free Will Baptists merged with the Northern Baptist Convention, taking along over 850 of its churches, all of its denominational property, and several colleges. In 1916 representatives of the 250 remnant churches from the Randall movement organized the Cooperative General Association of Free Will Baptists. By 1921 the southern churches had organized into new associations and conferences, and finally into a General Conference. The division continued until 1935, when the two groups merged into the National Association of Free Will Baptists (NAFWB) at Nashville, Tennessee.

Doctrinally, the church holds that Christ gave himself as a ransom for all, not just for the elect; that God calls all persons to repentance; and that "whosoever will" may be saved. Baptism is of believers only by immersion. Free Will Baptists practice open Communion and foot-washing. Government is strictly congregational. There are two Bible colleges and two liberal arts colleges. The church's greatest strength is in the South.

The NAFWB is doctrinally conservative and evangelical without being fundamentalist. It does not affirm same-sex marriage or ordain non-heterosexual people to the gospel ministry. The NAFWB does not officially oppose ordination of women or women pastors but says the "trend" has recently been in the "opposite direction" (away from women's ordination and women pastors).

For more information: www.nafwb.org

Headquarters: PO Box 5002, Antioch, TN 37011-5002

NATIONAL BAPTIST CONVENTION OF AMERICA, INC.

Founded: 1895

Membership: statistics not available, but est. 246,044 in 575 churches (2010)

"National Baptist" has been the name of some aspect of organized African American Baptist life since at least 1886. By 1876 all of the southern states except Florida had a state missionary convention, but smaller bodies had existed since the 1830s in the Midwest; organized missionary efforts date back to that same period in the North. The first black Baptist group, the Providence Baptist Association of Ohio, was formed in 1836, and the first attempt at national organization occurred in 1880 with the creation of the Foreign Mission

Baptist Convention at Montgomery, Alabama. In 1886, the American National Baptist Convention was organized at Saint Louis, and in 1893 the Baptist National Educational Convention was begun in the District of Columbia. All three conventions merged into the National Baptist Convention of America (NBCA) in 1895 at Atlanta. For the next twenty years a single National Baptist body functioned through a variety of activities, the publication of Sunday school material being a major one. It sponsored foreign mission enterprises, especially to African and Caribbean countries; and it founded some colleges and provided support for others, several of them the result of dedication to providing education for the emancipated people on the part of Northern Baptist and other churches.

In 1915 a division arose over the adoption of a charter and the ownership of the National Baptist Publishing Board. The group that rejected the charter continued to function as the National Baptist Convention of America. The group that accepted the charter became known as the National Baptist Convention, USA, Inc.* The former is frequently referred to as "the unincorporated" (although it did eventually incorporate in 1986) and the latter as "the incorporated," but both trace their beginnings to the Foreign Mission Baptist Convention. In 1988, the NBCA broke its ties to the Board. Churches that wished to continue a relationship with the publishing house formed the National Missionary Baptist Convention.

The NBCA adopted a mission statement in 1991 that focuses on education, evangelism, benevolence, stewardship, publication, social and economic justice, and commitment to religious liberty and Baptist doctrine. Much of the denominational activity revolves around the annual meeting in September, which is followed by additional meetings in February and June. The June convention meeting lasts four days and focuses on instruction from an approved curriculum with qualified teachers.

The NBCA has its greatest strength in Mississippi, Texas, and Louisiana, with large numbers of members also in Florida and California. The church holds an annual convention, and officers are elected each year.

The doctrines and practices of the NBCA are typically Baptist and the denomination historically has been deeply involved in the civil rights movement and other progressive social endeavors on behalf of the oppressed.

For more information: www.nbcainc.com

Headquarters: 777 S. R. L. Thornton Freeway, Suite 210, Dallas, TX 75203

NATIONAL BAPTIST CONVENTION, USA, INC.

Founded: 1895
Membership: statistics not available but est. 5,000,000 in 10,000 churches
(2012)

The largest body of African American Baptists in the United States shared a common history with the National Baptist Convention of America* denomination throughout the formative years of the two groups. Its formal origins date from 1895, with many roots and predecessors stretching back to the period around 1840. Until the disagreement that arose over control of the publishing house of the denomination in 1915, there was a single National Baptist body. With the division the National Baptist Convention of America took control of the publishing house, and the National Baptist Convention of the USA assumed control of foreign missions.

In 1990 the Baptist World Center was opened in Nashville, Tennessee, where the Sunday School Publishing Board is also located. Nashville is also the home of American Baptist College, which was opened in 1924 with the assistance of the Southern Baptist Convention. The school is now entirely under the authority of the National Convention. The convention meets annually, and a Board of Directors directs the convention's business between its annual sessions.

The church has had several strong presidents such as Joseph H. Jackson who served 1953–82. Jackson promoted the theory and practice of racial uplift in the tradition of Booker T. Washington (1856–1915). "From protest to production" was Jackson's motto. He led the body to steer clear of political and social involvements on any large scale. That policy placed this group mostly outside the civil rights movement of the period 1954–72, in which many black Baptist pastors and lay leaders worked for racial justice. Martin Luther King Jr.'s family had a long history with the National Baptist Convention, USA, but Jackson's reluctance fully to support King's tactics, such as civil disobedience, led to King leaving the denomination. As a result, another National Baptist schism occurred, out of which the Progressive National Baptist Convention* was formed in 1961. Since that period, however, the National Baptist Convention has shifted its practice and has been active in civil rights causes and voter registration drives. It does not oppose ordination of women or women pastors although that decision is left to individual congregations. The denomination does oppose same-sex marriage but has no official position with regard to ordination of gay or lesbian people to the ministry. It says, however, that very few of its churches would favor it.

This denomination, too, has been active in missionary, educational, and publication ministries. Recently it has established a ministerial pension plan. It has shown a particularly high degree of commitment to the support of colleges and seminaries, among them Morehouse School of Religion in Atlanta, Georgia, and Virginia Seminary in Lynchburg. The educational institutions are typically supported by Baptist churches and individuals rather than being affiliated officially with the Convention. The body supports missionary stations in the Bahamas, Jamaica, Panama, and Africa.

For more information: www.nationalbaptist.com

Headquarters: 1700 Baptist World Center Drive, Nashville, TN 37207

NATIONAL MISSIONARY BAPTIST CONVENTION OF AMERICA

Founded: 1988
Membership; statistics not kept, but claims 2,500,000 members (2012) in
1,283 congregations (2010)

The National Missionary Baptist Convention of America (NMBCA) began with the departure of several congregations from the National Baptist Convention of America in 1988. The issue was control of the several agencies including the National Baptist Publishing Board. Most of the membership of the NMBCA came with the departure of many NBCA congregations in California and Texas. This is one of the newest primarily African American Baptist denominations and it does not seem to have any doctrinal differences or differences of practice from the other main African American Baptist denominations. The denomination's vision statement is: "To edify our member churches, the nation, and the world through the wise use of our spiritual gifts, intellectual ability, and financial resources for the glory of God."

For more information: www.nmbca.com

Headquarters: 6925 Wofford Drive, Dallas, TX 75227

NATIONAL PRIMITIVE BAPTIST CONVENTION, USA

Founded: 1907
Membership: est. 53,630, in 547 churches (2000)

The black population of the South, throughout the years of slavery and civil war, generally worshipped with the white population in their various churches. The members attended white Primitive Baptist* churches until the time of emancipation, when their white co-worshippers helped them establish their own churches by granting letters of fellowship and character, ordaining deacons and ministers, and assisting in other ways.

The doctrine and polity are similar to that of other Primitive Baptists, though initially the members were opposed to all forms of church organization. There are local associations and a national convention, organized in 1907. Each congregation is independent, receiving and controlling its membership. Since 1900 this group has been establishing aid societies, conventions, and Sunday schools, over the opposition of some older and more traditional members. As with other Primitive Baptists, they call their pastors "elders," and they practice foot-washing as an ordinance alongside Holy Communion.

The National Primitive Baptist Convention, USA is doctrinally Calvinist, something relatively rare among African American Protestants. Yet the denomination differs from Caucasian Primitive Baptists by being more progressive socially and politically. The link "Daily Direction" at the denomination's website leads to an online publication called UrbanFaith—a cutting edge news and opinion magazine written primarily by and for postmodern black Christians. This primarily black network of churches emphasizes the autonomy of local congregations together with accountability through a national convention.

For more information: www.npbcconvention.org

Headquarters: PO Box 17727, Tallahassee, FL 32522

NORTH AMERICAN BAPTIST CONFERENCE

Founded: 1865
Membership: 65,000 in 410 churches (2014)

As a consequence of American Baptist evangelism among German immigrants in the 1840s, German Baptist congregations were organized and joined the local Baptist associations. In 1851 German pastors met to discuss common concerns. Subsequently a German hymnal was compiled and printed and a periodical for the churches was established. A German Baptist pastors' conference occurred annually. As settlement expanded westward a second regional conference was organized. A general conference of pastors and church delegates was called in 1865, which organized itself as a triennial General Conference to coordinate and promote local mission and church life, facilitate fellowship, and promote pastoral education.

Ministerial education began in 1858 when Rochester Theological Seminary inaugurated a German department for pastoral instruction in German. Over time that department became a self-standing German Baptist seminary associated with Colgate-Rochester Divinity School. In 1949 it relocated to Sioux Falls, South Dakota, then closer to the demographic center of the conference. The seminary was named North American Baptist Seminary and changed its name to Sioux Falls Seminary.

German Baptists were steadily assimilated into the United States and Canada so that foreign missions, the seminary, and church planting became the unifying force rather than ethnicity or language. In the 1940s the German Baptist General Conference of North America changed its name to the North American Baptist Conference (NABC). The churches are now as ethnically diverse as their neighborhoods.

A General Council, composed of representatives elected from twenty-one associations, acts for the Conference between its triennial sessions. The denomination supports six homes for the aged, two seminaries, and ministries in Japan, Brazil, Cameroon and Nigeria, the Philippines, and Russia.

The NABC is a centrist evangelical Baptist denomination with a generally conservative theology. It does not endorse women as senior or lead pastors and also does not endorse same-sex marriage or ordination of practicing homosexuals.

For more information: www.nabconference.org

Headquarters: 1219 Pleasant Grove Boulevard, Roseville, CA 95678

OLD REGULAR BAPTISTS

Founded: 1825, 1892
Membership: est. 15,218 in 326 churches (1995)

Old Regular Baptists trace their roots to the Second Great Awakening in eastern Kentucky in the early nineteenth century. Eight churches united to form the New Salem Association in 1825 and in 1892 they adopted the name Old Regular to distinguish themselves from the strictly Calvinist Primitive Baptists and the Arminian Free Will Baptists. They allow some diversity of belief on the issue of predestination, but emphasize the need for individuals to experience conversion, usually through a period of a struggle of repentance ("travail"). Baptisms are performed in running water, and foot-washing is an ordinance along with Holy Communion. They follow a strict patriarchal moral and social code based on New Testament teachings about men and women. Women have no formal voice in the church, but they do join in "shouting" during services. Women are forbidden to wear men's clothing, especially pants. Men are expected to own a home if they are married and to be master of the house. Formal education is not expected of ministers. There are seventeen regional associations and an annual convention, which includes extended preaching. The churches are located primarily in the Appalachian Mountains of Kentucky, but some may be found in other states. Old Regular Baptists are particularly known for their distinctive "lined-out" style of hymnody that preserves early American musical practices. Some call these churches "shouting Baptists" as calling out expressions of praise and agreement (with what is being preached) from the congregation is common.

This is far from an organized denomination. In fact, Old Regular Baptists are divided into "sub-denominations" by sociologists who study them. There is no central headquarters, hierarchy, or educational institution that binds them together. The only things that unite them are a common history, a common theology, and a common set of practices. Somehow Old Regular Baptists know each other (possibly partly through "circular letters") and network among themselves. They are encouraged to visit other Old Regular Baptist churches than their own, but once yearly Communion is closed to non-Old

Regular Baptists. Worship is extremely informal, unplanned, and preaching is extemporaneous by "elders."

For more information: www.oldregularbaptist.com

Headquarters: none

ORIGINAL FREE WILL BAPTIST CONVENTION

Founded: 1961, with roots to 1912
Membership: est. 30,000 in est. 250 churches (2010)

This body shares much in common with other Free Will Baptists and it traces its history back to the work of evangelist Paul Palmer (d. 1750) in the 1720s in North Carolina. In the early twentieth century, Free Will Baptists in North Carolina organized a state convention and in 1935 joined the National Association of Free Will Baptists. However, the North Carolina churches followed a slightly different ecclesiology than the other Free Will Baptist congregations. In particular, they believed that the annual conference should have greater authority to discipline local congregations. They also established their own liberal arts school, the University of Mount Olive (established 1920), rather than send students to the Association's Bible college in Nashville. The North Carolina group also wanted to establish a separate publishing house to produce Sunday school curricula. In 1961, most of the North Carolina Free Will Baptists formed a separate denomination with headquarters in Ayden, North Carolina (now moved to Mount Olive). In addition to the college and press, the Convention sponsors a Children's Home and supports missions in Bulgaria, India, Mexico, Nepal, and the Philippines.

The Convention is a conservative, evangelical Baptist denomination. Its governing statement of faith is the 1976 Revision of the Statement of Faith and Discipline for the Original Free Will Baptists. It is quite detailed and reflects the orthodoxy of the General Baptists of England in the 1600s. It affirms foot-washing as an ordinance alongside baptism by immersion only (of converted believers only) and the Lord's Supper. It assumes that ministers will be men (the pronoun "he" is the only one used of ministers). It affirms the infallibility of scripture. It is Arminian, not Calvinist, in affirming free will, universal atonement, and the possibility of apostasy (loss of salvation). It does not require belief in a millenial reign of Christ on earth ("premillennialism"). Churches are said to be independent but accountable to the convention. At the Convention's 2016 meeting the delegates passed a resolution stating that marriage is between one man and one woman; the resolution also rejected "gay-bashing" and expressed compassion for gay and lesbian persons.

For more information: www.ofwb.org

Headquarters: 201 West James Street, Mount Olive, NC 27576

PRIMITIVE BAPTISTS

Founded: 1827
Membership: est. 50,000 in 1,600 churches (2000)

Primitive Baptists have the reputation of being the strictest and most exclusive of all Baptist churches. (The word *primitive* in their name points to their belief that they are the "original" Baptists.) They have held to the Baptist belief of the autonomy of the local congregation to an unusual degree. In fact, they have never been organized as a denomination and have no administrative body of any kind beyond the local church and local association of churches (which has no authority). The movement originated in a nineteenth-century protest against money-based mission and benevolent societies. The Primitive Baptists maintained that there were no missionary societies in the days of the apostles and none are directed by the scripture; therefore, there should be none now. Spearheading this protest against new measures, in 1827 the Kehukee Association in North Carolina condemned all money-based and centralized societies as being contrary to Christ's teachings. Within a decade, several other Baptist associations across the country made similar statements and withdrew from other Baptist associations of churches.

The various associations adopted the custom of printing in their annual minutes their articles of faith, constitutions, and rules of order. These statements were examined by the other associations, and, if they were approved, there was fellowship and an exchange of messengers and correspondence. Any association not so approved was dropped from the fellowship. Calvinism runs strongly through the Primitive Baptist doctrine. In general, the members believe that through Adam's fall, all humankind became sinners; human nature is completely corrupt, and humans cannot by their own efforts regain favor with God; God elected God's own people in Christ before the world began, and none of these saints will be finally lost; Christ will come a second time to raise the dead, judge all people, punish the wicked forever, and reward the righteous forever; and the Old and New Testaments are verbally inspired and infallible. The authorized ordinances are the Lord's Supper, baptism of believers by immersion, and foot-washing.

Pastors are to be called by God, come under the laying on of hands, and be in fellowship with the local church of which they are members in order to administer the two ordinances. No theological training is demanded of ministers. In spite of their opposition to missionary societies, Primitive Baptist preachers travel widely and serve without salary, except when hearers wish to contribute to their support. The movement is concentrated in the South.

Primitive Baptist worship includes a cappela singing (unaccompanied by any musical instruments) and extemporaneous preaching. It is generally unprogrammed. Communion, the Lord's Supper, is closed to non-members. There is no discussion among Primitive Baptists about ordination of women or women leaders; that is out of the question.

Similarly, there is no question of affirming same-sex marriage or ordination of gay people. Marriage is simply assumed to be between one man and one woman for life with divorce considered sin.

There are three traditional Primitive Baptist groups. The largest is the Old-Line Primitive Baptists (about forty-seven thousand members) who teach that Christians are responsible for the salvation given by God. The Predestinarian Primitive Baptists or Absoluters stress God's predestination of all things, not just salvation. The Universalist Primitive Baptists (No-Hellers) believe that God predestines all people to salvation. The latter two groups are small and declining, with only about two thousand members between them.

For more information: www.oldschoolbaptist.org

Headquarters: none

PROGRESSIVE NATIONAL BAPTIST CONVENTION, INC.

Founded: 1961
Membership: est. 1,010,000 in 1,500 churches (2012)

This group of Baptists, Progressive National Baptist Convention, Inc. (PNBC), came into being in 1961, after several years of tension and discussion, breaking away from the National Baptist Convention, USA, Inc. In that year, Martin Luther King Jr. (1929–68) nominated Gardner C. Taylor as president of the convention against longtime president Joseph Jackson, who was opposed to the protest movement of King. The National Baptist Convention, USA followed a policy of disengagement from the civil rights movement and other social justice struggles during the revolutionary years following the 1954 Supreme Court decision concerning desegregation of public facilities.

Following the defeat of Taylor, who called for unity within the National Baptist Convention, USA, the Reverend L. Venchael Booth, chairman of the Volunteer Committee for the Formation of a New National Baptist Convention, issued a call for a meeting at his church in Cincinnati, Ohio. One of the central objectives of the new convention was support for the "freedom fighters" in the civil rights movement. The first president was Dr. T. M. Chambers, who served until 1967, at which point Gardner Taylor was elected to that office.

Once the convention was established, it became a focal point of the civil rights movement, and many leaders of that movement assumed significant positions in the new convention. In addition to King and Gardner, this included the famous preachers Ralph David Abernathy (1926–90) and Benjamin Mays (1895–1984). From its inception, the Progressive body has taken a highly active role in civil rights, social justice, and political causes. It also took a strong stand against apartheid in South Africa. Recently it has focused on the HIV and AIDS crisis in Africa and the United States.

The Progressive National Baptists are organized into four national regions. Eight departments include women, laymen, young adult women, young adult men, ushers, youth, moderator's council, and Christian education. From its beginning, the convention has been ecumenical in spirit, seeking to work harmoniously with other Christian denominations. The PNBC permits member churches to ordain women and have women pastors; it also leaves the decisions regarding same-sex marriage and ministry by gay and lesbian persons to local congregations.

For more information: www.pnbc.org

Headquarters: 601 Fiftieth Street, Northeast, Washington, DC 20019

PROGRESSIVE PRIMITIVE BAPTISTS

Founded: 1909
Membership: 95 churches (2016)

A group of churches, found mainly in the Southeast of the United States, emerged out of the Primitive Baptists in the first decade of the twentieth century and established its own identity using the term *Progressive* to designate the fact that, unlike other Primitive Baptists, they use musical instruments in worship and support extra-congregational Christian activities such as youth camps and missionary organizations. They were given the name Progressive Primitive Baptists, a name they embrace for their network of Calvinist Baptist congregations that are in other ways like traditional Primitive Baptists.

The Progressive Primitive Baptists have their own Statement of Faith, which is very Calvinistic (unconditional predestination of individuals to salvation) and based on the 1689 London Baptist Confession of the Particular Baptists; their own magazine, the *Banner Herald*; their own foundation for support of retired ministers; and their own associational meetings. In spite of the word *progressive* in their name, they remain conservative in matters of doctrine, ethics, and polity. They practice foot-washing as well as baptism of believers only by immersion only and the Lord's Supper.

For more information: www.progressivepb.org

Headquarters: none

SEPARATE BAPTISTS IN CHRIST

Founded: ca. 1877 and 1912, with roots to the colonial period
Membership: est. 8,000 in 100 churches (2012)

The Separate Baptists emerged during the First Great Awakening in the mid-eighteenth century. By the end of the century most Separate Baptist churches had merged with

Regular Baptists.* Some churches rejected the merger of Separate and Regular Baptists in Kentucky in 1803 and in 1806 formed their own association. Other local associations followed, and the first General Association was formed in 1877. It dissolved but was re-established in 1912. By 1991 there were seven regional associations within the General Association, but then a split occurred over the issue of the millennium after Christ's return.

Along with many other conservative Baptist groups, Separate Baptists do not claim to be Protestants: "We have never protested against what we hold to be the faith once delivered to the saints." Though officially non-creedal, Separate Baptists do have a statement of faith called "Articles of Doctrine for All Associations," which includes affirmation of the King James Version of the Bible as well as the infallibility of the scriptures and the Trinity; regeneration, justification, and sanctification through faith in Christ; and the appearance of Christ on judgment day to deal with the just and the unjust. The distinctive doctrines of Calvinism do not appear. The doctrinal statement rejects premillennialism—belief in a literal reign of Christ on earth after his visible return. These churches observe foot-washing as well as baptism of believers by immersion only, and the Lord's Supper as ordinances.

The General Association of Separate Baptists has incorporated a mission program called Separate Baptist Missions, Inc. Through this program, support is given to various mission fields and efforts, both in the United States and abroad.

For more information: www.separatebaptist.org

Headquarters: 905 South Main Street, Edinburgh, IN 46124

SEVENTH DAY BAPTIST GENERAL CONFERENCE

Founded: 1802, with roots to 1671
Membership: est. 5,000 in 110 churches (2016)

Differing from other groups of Baptists in its adherence to the seventh day (Saturday) as the Sabbath, the Seventh Day Baptists first appeared as a separate religious body in North America in the Colonial period. Stephen and Ann Mumford came from England in 1664 and entered into a covenant relationship with those who withdrew from John Clarke's (1609–76) Baptist Church in order to observe the Sabbath. In 1671, they officially organized a congregation. Other churches were organized in Philadelphia and New Jersey. Other than the Sabbath observance, their beliefs are similar to other Baptists.

Local churches enjoy complete independence, although all support the united benevolence of the denominational budget. The highest administrative body is the General Conference, which meets annually and delegates interim responsibilities to its president, executive secretary, and general council. The denomination participates in the ecumenical movement at local, regional, national, and world levels. The Seventh Day Baptist conferences include those in Australia, Brazil, England, Germany, Guyana, India, Jamaica,

Malawi, Mexico, Myanmar, the Netherlands, New Zealand, Nigeria, the Philippines, Poland, and South Africa, as well as in the United States and Canada.

The Seventh Day Baptist General Conference is an evangelical denomination that affirms the inspiration and authority of the Bible and traditional, orthodox Protestant doctrines. Its statement of faith, however, is not as detailed as those of many Baptist groups. It is somewhat progressive among Baptists in permitting the ordination of women and, at the time of this writing, has a woman president of the Conference. On the other hand, the Conference takes a traditional stance with regard to marriage, which it affirms as solely between one man and one woman.

Many people wrongly assume that Seventh Day Baptists are somehow related to the Seventh Day Adventist denomination; they are not. Some claim, in fact, that the Seventh Day Baptists constitute the oldest continuously existing Baptist organization in the United States. If anything, the Seventh Day Adventist group was influenced by the Seventh Day Baptists in taking up "sabbatarianism"—worship and rest on the seventh day of the week.

The Seventh Day Baptists have no college, university, or seminary of their own. Their pastors attend approved seminaries often of other Baptist denominations.

For more information: www.seventhdaybaptist.org

Headquarters: PO Box 1678, Janesville, WI 53547-1678

SOUTHERN BAPTIST CONVENTION

Founded: 1845
Membership: 16,136,044 in 45,727 churches (2012)

The largest Protestant denomination in the United States is the Southern Baptist Convention (SBC), whose membership, as its name suggests, is most numerous in the South. In recent years, however, the SBC has been expanding in all regions of the country. The name *Southern* has, therefore, become something of a misnomer.

The SBC came into being during the years leading up to the Civil War. Although there were significant disagreements between Baptists in the two regions over the question of centralized organization (the South favored one organization to control the various cooperative ministries), it was the issue of slavery that led directly to the formation of a separate Southern Baptist Convention. Specifically, the issue was whether slaveholders could be accepted as foreign missionaries. The mission board, located in Boston, refused to send slaveholders into the fields, and in May 1845, the Southern Baptist Convention (SBC) was organized in order to establish boards for foreign and home missions.

Along with the rest of the South, the Southern Baptist churches suffered great losses during the war. Homes, schools, churches, the livelihood of citizens, and indeed, the very pattern of southern society were destroyed, with devastating effect on religious bodies.

An anti-missionary movement further decimated Baptist ranks. Membership continued to decline when former slaves withdrew to form their own societies and conventions. The recovery of the Southern Baptist Convention was impressive, however. By 1890, there were over one million members, predominantly white.

On June 20, 1995, the SBC adopted a resolution to renounce its racist origins and to apologize for its founders' defense of slavery. In its apology to African Americans, the resolution declared that members of the church must "unwaveringly denounce racism, in all its forms, as deplorable sin" and repent of "racism of which we have been guilty whether consciously or unconsciously." As of 2000, nearly two thousand SBC congregations were predominantly African American.

In 1997 the SBC was reorganized. Twelve denominational agencies work with thirty-nine state conventions and two fellowships. The North American Mission Board operates throughout the United States and its territories, with nearly five thousand missionaries active in the field. The International Mission Board sponsors more than four thousand missionaries in over 120 nations and operates over three hundred medical facilities. Life-Way Christian Resources (formerly the Sunday School Board) is the world's largest publisher of religious materials. It provides the literature for some thirty-seven thousand SBC churches. The SBC maintains six theological seminaries.

The SBC grew rapidly in the last quarter of the twentieth century, but growth has slowed dramatically in this century. The church grew more factional as conservatives exerted control over the seminaries, agencies, and boards that belong to the Convention. Conservatives distinguish their position as a commitment to biblical inerrancy. Others in the convention take their stand on what may be termed the infallibility of biblical authority and a commitment to the traditional Baptist principle of local church autonomy.

In the late 1990s, controversy arose over the issue of women's ordination. At the SBC annual convention in June 2000, delegates voted to amend the "Baptist Faith and Message" confession of faith first formulated in the 1920s and then amended in 1963. The SBC stipulated that "while both men and women are gifted and called for ministry, the office of pastor is limited to men as qualified by Scripture." The 2000 gathering also put the convention on record as supporting the death penalty in cases of murder and treason.

The tensions within the SBC and between the SBC and other Baptist groups increased in 2004 when the SBC voted to withdraw from the Baptist World Alliance. The SBC accused the Alliance of promoting the idea of women preachers, liberal theology, and anti-American attitudes. During the 1990s and first part of the twenty-first century over one thousand SBC congregations formed two new Baptist denominations labeled *moderate*. One is the Alliance of Baptists and the other is the Cooperative Baptist Fellowship. Also two state SBC conventions, Texas and Virginia, began to operate separately from the SBC (although their members are still counted by the SBC).

Moderates within the SBC and who left it are considered "liberals" by many SBC leaders and pastors, whereas the conservatives who took control of the denomination are considered "fundamentalists" by those who call themselves moderates. Some moderates claim that the SBC continues to count them among their claimed 16 million members even though they would probably not be permitted to vote at the SBC annual convention or hold office in the SBC. No one knows by how many that number would be reduced if the SBC stopped claiming moderates as members, but it would almost certainly be millions.

It goes almost without saying that the SBC does not condone same-sex marriages within its ranks or permit member congregations to ordain gay men or call them as pastors.

For more information: www.sbc.net

Headquarters: 901 Commerce Street, Nashville, TN 37203

TRANSFORMATION MINISTRIES

Founded: 2006
Membership: est. 55,000 in 170 churches (2016)

Transformation Ministries is one of the newest Baptist "denominetworks" in the United States. It began in 2006 with the departure of many of the American Baptist churches of the Southwest from the American Baptist Churches, USA (ABCUSA). According to the separating churches the ABCUSA was wrong to permit member congregations to ordain gay and lesbian people and recognize same-sex marriages as blessed by God.

Transformation Ministries is a "collaboration" of independent churches in fellowship for mission. It is evangelical but not fundamentalist. It permits ordination of women and women pastors. It considers the practice of homosexuality incompatible with biblical teaching.

The denomination is aggressive in church planting and welcoming new churches. It plans to plant at least ten new churches each year and hopes to increase its membership (churches) by 50 percent in five years (from 2016).

For more information: www.transmin.org

Headquarters: 970 South Village Oaks Drive, Suite 101, Covina, CA 91724

UNITED AMERICAN FREE WILL BAPTISTS

Founded: 1901, with roots to early nineteenth century
Membership: Unknown in 35 churches (1995)

This African American denomination was organized as a separate institution in 1901, but its roots lie in the Free Will Baptist tradition of the eighteenth century. Robert Taft was the first African American to be ordained as a minister in the church (1827). Freed slaves formed the first African American Free Will Baptist congregations in North Carolina in 1867 and the first convention was held in 1870. Unlike other Free Will Baptists, the United American Free Will Baptists (UAFWB) does limit local church autonomy. Quarterly, Annual, and General Conferences exercise authority over local churches and may exclude congregations from membership. The church's statement of faith is an interesting variation on the Apostles' Creed that clarifies the church's own doctrine: "We believe in the Holy Ghost, the Free Will Baptist Church, the Communion of Saints, the forgiveness of sins, the resurrection of the body, and eternal life for all true believers who persevere in holiness to the end." Although many members moved north in the twentieth century, the church remains strongest in the South.

For more information: www.uafreewillbaptconf.org

Headquarters: 110 West Seventh Street, Lakeland, Florida 33805

METHODIST CHURCHES

Some scholars have called the nineteenth century in the United States "the Methodist century" because of the enormous influence of Methodism. Hundreds of American denominations, service organizations, and educational institutions have their roots in the Methodist movement. Until it was eclipsed by the Catholic Church, the Methodist Church was the largest religious organization in the United States, and it still has the greatest geographical scope in the United States of any religious body, being represented in virtually every county of the nation. Methodist hymnody is heard in Protestant and Catholic congregations throughout the English-speaking world.

Beginning as part of the Pietist movement within the Church of England in the 1730s, Methodism expanded greatly during the eighteenth century under the leadership of the Wesley brothers, John (1703–91) and Charles (1707–88), who preached and wrote hymns on the need for a personal experience of salvation and change of life. Methodism has been more concerned with ministry to the poor and disadvantaged than many other forms of Protestantism, and Methodists often express their faith more in compassion for the suffering than in creedal statements. In a variety of ways, the witness of the Spirit among Methodists has been an impelling force for worship, love of neighbor, personal piety, and evangelization. On the other hand, American Methodism has been racked by controversies and divisions, schisms, and accusations. The Civil War divided Methodism in the United States between North and South, a division that was later for the most part healed. The early twentieth century liberal-fundamentalist controversy created breakaway denominations from the Methodist Episcopal Church, the main American Methodist denomination rooted in John Wesley's own appointment of bishops for his American Methodist churches. To a large extent both the Holiness* and Pentecostal* movements sprang out of Methodism and left the main body of Methodists behind. Conservative and more liberal Methodists continue to struggle over ordination of openly gay and lesbian elders and deacons into the twenty-first century. The United Methodist Church, successor to the old Methodist Episcopal Church, has declined from a peak of about fourteen million members to fewer than eight million in the second decade of the twenty-first century.

History. The origins of Methodism can be traced to a small group of serious-minded students and fellows at Oxford University who were dubbed *Methodists* because of their strict regimen of prayer, fasting, Bible reading, and charitable works inspired by William Law's (1686–1761) *A Serious Call to a Devout and Holy Life*. Among the members of the group were the Wesleys and the future evangelist George Whitefield (1714–70), all three of whom would be ordained in the Church of England. After John and Charles Wesley left Oxford, they traveled to the American colonies, arriving in Georgia in 1735. It was an unsuccessful and unhappy two years for John, but while aboard ship, he met a group of Moravians* and was deeply impressed by their piety and humble Christian way of life. After his return to London, he went to the meeting of a Moravian religious society in Aldersgate Street. There he felt his heart "strangely warmed" as the meaning of the Luther's doctrine of "justification by faith" sank into his soul.

The Wesleys gradually separated from the Moravians (whom they never formally joined) and followed George Whitefield's example of preaching for conversion and holiness of life. When the Church of England closed its pulpits to them, they took to the open air and sought audiences among the large and often-ignored working class of the new Industrial Revolution. Converts came thick and fast, and they were soon organized into "societies." Between 1739 and 1744 the organizational elements of Methodism were instituted: a circuit system and itinerant ministry, class meetings and class leaders, lay preachers, and annual conferences. As early as 1739 John Wesley drew up a set of general rules that are still held by modern Methodists as an ideal delineation of biblical rules of conduct.

Methodism was primarily a lay movement, and John Wesley did his best to keep it within the Church of England. An evangelical party influenced by Methodism grew within that church that included such luminaries as hymn writer Isaac Watts (1674–1748) and the social reformer and abolitionist William Wilberforce (1759–1833). But it became evident that a separate Methodist organization was needed to deal with the large numbers recruited from among the unchurched. *A Deed of Declaration* in 1784 gave legal status to the yearly Methodist conference. Eventually the Church of England formally excommunicated the Methodists much to Wesley's dismay and even denial. What was intended to be a spiritual renewal movement for reformation within the Church of England became an independent denomination.

Methodists in the United States. By 1769, New York Methodists had built Wesley Chapel, now known as John Street Methodist Church. Captain Thomas Webb (ca. 1726–96) established societies in Philadelphia. Devereux Jarratt (1733–1801), an Anglican minister, led a revival in Virginia that won thousands. Wesley sent Francis Asbury (1745–1816) and Thomas Rankin (1738–1810) to supervise work of Methodism in America. Rankin presided over the first conference in the colonies, called at Philadelphia in 1773. Since Wesley's pro-British attitude aroused resentment in the colonies, it is surprising that the work of Asbury prospered during the Revolution. By the end of the war, membership had grown to fourteen thousand, and there were nearly eighty preachers. It was now an American church, free of both England and the Church of England. Wesley accepted the inevitable and ordained ministers for the colonies. The Christmas Conference, held at Baltimore in December 1784, organized the Methodist Episcopal Church and elected Thomas Coke (1747–1814) as one of its first superintendents (later called bishops). *The Sunday Service* (an abridgment of *The Book of Common Prayer*) and Articles of Religion were adopted as written by John Wesley with the addition of an article that the Methodists should vow allegiance to the United States government.

Under Asbury's energetic direction, Methodism was adapted to the American rural setting. Circuit riders, preachers on horseback who traveled the expanding frontier, went to mountain cabins, prairie churches, schoolhouses, and camp meetings, preaching the need for conversion and regeneration. The Methodist Book Concern was established in 1789, putting into the saddlebags of the circuit riders religious literature that followed the march of the American empire south and west. The revivalistic flavor of the camp meeting, born among the Presbyterians, was adopted by the Methodists. By the end of the Second Great Awakening in the early nineteenth century there were over one million Methodists in the United States.

Methodist evangelists had great success working with slaves and free blacks in the United States. Initially the church opposed slavery, but eventually evangelists tolerated the practice in order to be allowed to preach to enslaved persons. Hundreds of thousands of African Americans converted before 1861. Only the Baptists had more black members. The Methodist Church adopted the Moravian* practice of using converted slaves as lay preachers and evangelists who worked under the authority of ordained whites. In the northern cities, freed blacks were sometimes ordained as pastors. Between 1813 and 1917, large groups of African Americans formed independent churches: the African Methodist Episcopal Church, the Union Church of Africans, and the African Methodist Episcopal Zion Church.

The issue of slavery led to a devastating split between southern and northern Methodists in 1844. Bishop J. O. Andrew (1794–1871), a Georgian, owned slaves through inheritance, and his wife also was a slaveholder. The General Conference of 1844 requested that the bishop desist from the exercise of his office while he remained a slaveholder. Incensed, the southern delegates rebelled. A provisional plan of separation was formulated, and the Southerners organized their own church.

The split was not healed until 1939, when the Methodist Episcopal Church; the Methodist Episcopal Church, South; and the Methodist Protestant Church were reunited at Kansas City, Missouri, to form The Methodist Church. The uniting conference of that year adopted a new constitution in three sections: an abridgment of the Articles of Religion drawn up by John Wesley; the General Rules, covering the conduct of church members and the duties of church officials; and the Articles of Organization and Government, outlining the organization and conduct of conferences and local churches.

Another Methodist body with a distinct history was the Evangelical United Brethren Church, which had arisen from a series of mergers of two groups: United Brethren in Christ and the Evangelical Church. The Evangelical Church, originally Evangelical Association, began as a result of the labors of Jacob Albright (1759–1808) among the German people of Pennsylvania. Preaching first as a Lutheran Pietist and then as a Methodist exhorter, Albright was made a bishop at the first annual conference of the Evangelical Association in 1807. The name "Evangelical Church" was adopted in 1922.

Another group, Church of the United Brethren in Christ, developed in a parallel manner through the preaching of the Pietists Philip William Otterbein (1726–1813) and Martin Boehm (1725–1812) among the Germans in Pennsylvania, Maryland, and Virginia. They were elected bishops at a conference in September 1800. That conference created the Church of the United Brethren in Christ, which also was strongly Methodist in polity, doctrine, and practice. Each group had a *Discipline* modeled on that of the Methodists. The Church of the United Brethren in Christ and the Evangelical Church were merged into the Evangelical United Brethren Church (EUB) at Johnstown, Pennsylvania, in 1946.

In April of 1968, the Methodist Church merged with the EUB to form the United Methodist Church, which is generally believed to be the second largest distinct denomination (after the Southern Baptist Convention) in the United States. However, some groups of Methodists and EUB declined to join the union and formed their own separate denominations not part of the United Methodist Church. Most of them are conservative in doctrine and evangelical in ethos. The United Methodist Church has tended to embrace doctrinal pluralism and an emphasis on social reform although there are strong elements of evangelicalism within it.

Beliefs and Practices. Methodists have traditionally stressed the foundational beliefs of Protestantism: the authority of scripture over tradition, the doctrines of the deity of Christ and the Trinity, original sin (but not total depravity) and the need of conversion and repentance for salvation, justification by grace alone through faith alone, the atoning death of Christ, and the miracles of the virgin birth and resurrection. What has set Methodists of all kinds (in the United States) apart from some other Protestant denominations is their emphasis on sanctification alongside justification and their belief in freedom of the will. In terms of salvation, Methodists are Arminian, stressing the grace-enabled freedom of humans to choose salvation and a denial of the Calvinist doctrines of unconditional election and irresistible grace. In terms of sanctification they believe in the possibility of "Christian perfection" through the Holy Spirit, which means only a perfection of "heart," meaning motives. The Wesleys believed it possible for a Christian "heart" to be "perfected in love"—a condition called "entire sanctification"—in life before death. Lutheran and Reformed Protestants deny that condition before death and resurrection. Two sacraments, baptism and Communion, are observed by Methodists. Most Methodists baptize either infants by sprinkling or mature believers upon confession of faith—by either sprinkling or immersion. Especially in the twenty-first century Methodist parents are given the option for their children. Infant baptism as a sacrament of "prevenient grace" is the norm in most United Methodist churches.

The deepest divisions among Methodists have been along two "fault lines." First is the fault line of revivalism. Methodism was born in the fires of revivalism during the first Great Awakening in Britain and America and given great impetus in the United States during the Second Great Awakening. Those revival fires died down in the so-called mainline Methodist churches in the latter half of the nineteenth century as Methodism became an established middle class religious movement. However, some Methodists have always attempted to fan the flames of revival back to life—much to the dismay of more staid and formal Methodists who often look to the Episcopal Church for guidance.

The second fault line is accommodation to modern thought. Many Methodist universities and seminaries in the United States have adopted degrees of higher criticism of the Bible and liberal theologies. That has given rise to a conservative reaction with several "evangelical" movements within Methodism either breaking away from the "mainline" Methodist churches to establish conservative, evangelical Methodist denominations or staying within them to agitate for a more conservative approach to the Bible and theology.

"Methodism" here, as a category, includes not only the United Methodist Church but also other denominations whose roots lie in the ministry of John Wesley and his Methodist movement. These other Methodist denominations may have sprung up much later, but their historical-theological identity is closer to that of original Methodism than to any other tradition. Many such denominations deserve their own, separate category called "Holiness Churches." That will be explained in the introduction to that section of this *Handbook*. Most of the denominations identify as Methodist or began as a break-off from the so-called mainline Methodist Church (now the United Methodist Church) under one of its names.

Suggestions for Further Reading

Bucke, Emory S., ed. *History of American Methodism*. Nashville, TN: Abingdon Press, 1964.

Campbell, James T. *Songs of Zion: The African Methodist Episcopal Church in the United States and South Africa*. New York: Oxford University Press, 1995.

Heitzenrater, Richard P. *Wesley and the People Called Methodists*. 2nd ed. Nashville, TN: Abingdon, 2013.

Langford, Thomas A., ed. *Doctrine and Theology in The United Methodist Church*. Nashville, TN: Kingswood Books, 1991.

Lincoln, C. Eric, and Lawrence H. Mamiya. *The Black Church in the African American Experience*. Durham, NC: Duke University Press, 1990.

Marty, Martin E. *Protestantism in the United States: Righteous Empire.* 2nd ed. New York: Scribner; London: Collier Macmillan, 1986.

Matthews, Donald G. *Slavery and Methodism: A Chapter in American Morality, 1780–1845.* Princeton, NJ: Princeton University Press, 1965.

McEllhenney, John G. *United Methodism in America.* Nashville, TN: Abingdon Press, 1992.

McKinley, Edward H. *Marching to Glory: The History of the Salvation Army in the United States, 1880–1992.* Rev. ed. Grand Rapids, MI: Wm B. Eerdmans, 1995.

Richardson, Harry V. *Dark Salvation: The Story of Methodism as It Developed among Blacks in America.* Garden City, NY: Anchor Press, 1976.

Richey, Russell E. *Methodism in the American Forest.* New York: Oxford University Press, 2015.

Richey, Russell E., Kenneth E. Rowe, Jean Miller Schmidt. *American Methodism: A Compact History.* Nashville, TN: Abingdon Press, 2012.

-----------------. *The Methodist Experience in America Volume I: A History.* Nashville, TN: Abingdon Press, 2010.

-----------------. *The Methodist Experience in America Volume II: Sourcebook.* Nashville, TN: Abingdon Press, 2000.

Smith, Timothy L. *Revivalism and Social Reform.* Baltimore, MD: Johns Hopkins Press, 1980.

Walls, William J. *The African Methodist Episcopal Zion Church: Reality of the Black Church.* Charlotte, NC: AME Zion Publishing House, 1974.

AFRICAN METHODIST EPISCOPAL CHURCH

Founded: 1814
Membership: 2,500,000 in 7,000 congregations (2014)

The African Methodist Episcopal Church (AME) is one of the oldest and largest Methodist bodies in the world. It was founded by Richard Allen (1760–1831), a former slave from Delaware who had bought his freedom. Allen had been converted to Christianity while still a slave, and he began preaching to freed African Americans in Philadelphia up to five times a day. He regularly attended St. George's Methodist Church, where African Americans were welcomed but segregated from whites. In 1787 Absalom Jones (1746–1818), who later became the first African American Episcopal priest, was kneeling in prayer when white trustees physically removed him to the back of the church. When the congregational leadership supported this discrimination, Allen and Jones led the black members out of the congregation. In 1793, Allen established the Bethel Church for Negro Methodists in Philadelphia.

Although Francis Asbury dedicated the chapel in Philadelphia and ordained Richard Allen as its minister, Bethel Church was a center of controversy within the Methodist system. The whites in the denomination tried to keep Allen and his congregation from controlling their own property, but in 1816 the Pennsylvania Supreme Court ruled in favor of Allen, setting an important legal precedent for black persons in the United States. It was during the course of this struggle that the Bethel Congregation and five other predominantly black Methodist churches left the Methodist Church and formed the AME in 1814. Allen was consecrated by Asbury as the first bishop in 1816.

Around the same time, the AME Zion church separated from the Methodist Church in New York. Bishop Allen held strongly to the connectional system of the Methodists and tried to bring the new Zion Church* under his umbrella after 1816, but the members of Zion preferred to create their own denomination. In the years preceding the Civil War, the AME Church was largely confined to the Northern states, but following the war its membership increased rapidly in the South. Today it is found all across the nation.

The church affirms traditional Methodist doctrine, but the worship style tends to be more exuberant than that found in predominantly white churches. The church is strongly evangelistic and has active social justice ministries. There are twenty-one bishops (including the first woman bishop, who was elected in 2000), twelve general officers, and eighteen connectional officers in thirteen districts; a General Conference is held quadrennially. Foreign missions are supported in South Africa; West Africa; India; London, England; the Caribbean; and South America. The church supports six colleges and two theological schools. Journalism has been a central part of the church's work from its early years; the AME Book Concern dates to 1816, and the weekly *Christian Reader* has been published since 1848.

The AME Church ordains women and has a woman bishop. It does not ordain openly gay clergy or permit openly gay people to serve as pastors or officers of the denomination.

For more information: www.ame-church.com

Headquarters: 500 Eighth Avenue South, Nashville, TN 37203

AFRICAN METHODIST EPISCOPAL ZION CHURCH

Founded: 1821
Membership: 301,005 in 1,657 churches (2010)

This church (AME Zion) dates from 1796, when it was organized by a group of people protesting racial discrimination in the John Street Methodist Church in New York City. Their first church, named Zion, was built in 1800, and that word was later made part of the denominational name. The first annual conference was held in 1821, with nineteen preachers from six black Methodist churches in New Haven, Connecticut; Philadelphia, Pennsylvania; and Newark, New Jersey. James Varick (ca. 1750–1827), who had led the

John Street dissension, was elected the first bishop. The present name was approved in 1848. The word *Zion* was included to distinguish this church from the AME Church* founded in Philadelphia. The church spread quickly over the Northern states, and by 1880 there were fifteen annual conferences in the South. Departments of missions, education, and publications were created in 1892. AME Zion ministers were often spokesmen for African Americans in the decades following emancipation, and Bishop Alexander Walters helped found the National Association for the Advancement of Colored People (NAACP) in 1909. The church has always emphasized the importance of education, especially when educational opportunities were denied to black people. In addition to an extensive Sunday school network supervised by the Christian Education Department, the church founded several institutions of learning. Livingstone College, in Salisbury, North Carolina, the largest educational institution of the church, was established in 1879. The church also operates two junior colleges in the United States and one in Liberia. Hood Theological Seminary in North Carolina is its primary theological institution.

The church is heavily involved in evangelism and missions, and has a particularly strong presence in Liberia and Ghana in Africa. AME Zion missionaries were among the first Protestant missions to Africa. In the twentieth century, some of the church's bishops were involved in the Pan African Congress of Marcus Garvey. The church has twelve episcopal districts in the United States and is governed by a board of bishops. It is traditionally Methodist in doctrine and practice, emphasizing sanctification (holiness of life) alongside conversion and justification (forgiveness of sins).

In 2012 the AME Zion Church entered into full communion (mutual recognition of memberships and ministries) with several other Methodist denominations including the United Methodist Church. According to some sources, the AME Zion Church was the first predominantly black Protestant denomination to ordain women to the ministry (1891).

For more information: www.amez.org

Headquarters: 3225 Sugar Creek Road, Charlotte, NC 28269

CHRISTIAN METHODIST EPISCOPAL CHURCH

Founded: 1870
Membership: est. 290,601 in 1,462 churches (2010)

This body (CME Church) was established in 1870, in an amicable agreement between white and black members of the Methodist Episcopal Church, South. At the time of emancipation there were at least two hundred twenty-five thousand slave members of the Southern church, but following the Civil War, all but eighty thousand joined one of the two independent black bodies, the African Methodist Episcopal Church or the African Methodist Episcopal Zion Church. When the General Conference of the Methodist

Episcopal Church, South, met at New Orleans in 1866, a commission from the black membership asked to separate into a church of its own. The request was granted, and the Colored Methodist Episcopal Church was organized in Jackson, Tennessee. In 1954 the name was changed to Christian Methodist Episcopal Church.

The doctrine of the CME Church is typically Methodist as is its polity. There are ten episcopal districts, each supervised by a presiding bishop, who together form the College of Bishops. Ten departments oversee the national work, each chaired by a bishop assigned by the College of Bishops. The general secretaries of the various departments are elected every four years by the General Conference, and the president of the Women's Missionary Council is elected every four years by the quadrennial assembly of the Missionary Council. The church issues two periodicals and supports five colleges, a theological seminary, a hospital, and several low-rent and senior-citizen housing complexes. In the latter decades of the twentieth century, the church encouraged economic growth for African Americans as part of its ministry.

In 2012 the CME Church entered into a communion agreement with several other Methodist bodies including the United Methodist Church. The result of the agreement is recognition of each other's ministers and sacraments. The CME Church ordains women and has women bishops. In 2010 the denomination amended its Social Creed to reject recognition and performance of same-sex marriages; it defined marriage as between one man and one woman. The denomination does not ordain openly gay or lesbian people to the ministry or permit them to serve as elders (pastors). On most other social issues the CME Church is progressive including racial equality and alleviation of poverty in society. It is doctrinally conservative in the Wesleyan-Methodist tradition.

For more information: www.thecmechurch.org

Headquarters: 4466 Elvis Presley Boulevard, Memphis, TN 38116

CONGREGATIONAL METHODIST CHURCH

Founded: 1852
Membership: 15,518 in 151 churches (2015)

This church (CMC) was established in Georgia in protest against certain features of the episcopacy and itinerancy of the Methodist Episcopal Church, South. In the late 1880s more than half of this body in turn withdrew to join the Congregational Church. The church grew in the twentieth century and sent out its first missionary in 1947. In 1972 the headquarters moved to its current location in Florence, Mississippi. It continues to be located primarily in the South. Theologically, the CMC is close to both the fundamentalist and Holiness traditions. It affirms the inerrancy of the Bible, the premillennial return of Christ, and the possibility of entire sanctification of believers.

In contrast to most Methodist denominations, local pastors are called by the local churches; annual conferences grant licenses, ordain ministers, and review local reports. Annual and general conferences are recognized as church courts, empowered to rule on violations of church law and to coordinate, plan, and promote general church activities. Thus, the CMC is a hybrid of congregational, presybterian, and episcopal forms of church government (but without bishops). There is a missionary program among the Navajo in New Mexico and Mexico. The church founded Wesley College, which was accredited in 1976 and is located near the denominational headquarters in Florence, Mississippi.

The CMC does not ordain women or non-heterosexual men and does not perform or recognize same-sex marriages. As a denomination it seeks to revive and preserve the original revival spirit of John Wesley and early Methodism within an American context and in other contexts through missions.

For more information: www.cm-church.org

Headquarters: PO Box 9, Florence, MS 39073

EVANGELICAL CHURCH OF NORTH AMERICA

Founded: 1968
Membership: est. 15,000 in 128 congregations (2012)

When the Methodist Church merged with the Evangelical United Brethren to form the United Methodist Church* in 1968, a number of churches in the Brethren body withdrew to form the Evangelical Church of North America. The new church was organized at Portland, Oregon, and eventually came to include congregations across the country. In 1969 union occurred with the Holiness Methodist Church. From 1982 to 1990 the Northwest Canada Conference was part of the Evangelical Church. In 1990 the Northwest Canada Conference united with the Missionary Church of Canada to form The Evangelical Missionary Church of Canada. The major mission fields are Bolivia, Brazil, and Navajo churches in New Mexico with cooperative ministries with national churches in Japan, Germany, Eastern Europe, and Russia.

The doctrinal position of the Evangelical Church is Wesleyan-Arminian. In polity the local church owns its own property while the clergy are assigned by the conference superintendent. Conference superintendents oversee each annual conference (six); the general administration is carried on by annual conference sessions and program committees. Every four years, a general conference is held, at which the general superintendent is elected and oversees the denomination.

The Evangelical Church is conservative and evangelical in doctrine and practice. It has entered into a covenant agreement to share ministries with the Evangelical Methodist Church. Talks toward a full merger are ongoing. At one time the Evangelical Church provided the main support for Western Evangelical Seminary, but that has been absorbed into George Fox University of Newburg, Oregon, and is now that university's graduate school of theology. The Evangelical Church continues its affiliation with the seminary but is no longer its main denominational supporter.

For more information: www.theevangelicalchurch.com

Headquarters: 15 Eighty-Second Drive, Suite 140, Gladstone, OR 97027

EVANGELICAL METHODIST CHURCH

Founded: 1946
Membership: est. 7,348 in 108 churches (2016)

The Evangelical Methodist Church (EMC) is "fundamental in doctrine, evangelistic in program, and congregational in government." The denomination was formed just after World War II in Memphis, Tennessee, as a protest against the perceived liberalism of the Methodist Church. The founders sought to preserve and apply the spirit and revivalistic fervor of "primitive Methodism" to the needs of modern American society. They oppose the "substituting of social, educational, or other varieties of cultural salvation for the gospel message." The denomination rejected the "autocracy" of bishops, and local churches own and control their own property and select their own pastors. Over the years, the denomination absorbed some smaller conservative Methodist churches, but there were also divisions within the church over the issue of entire sanctification. In 2008 the superintendent of the church proposed a plan for restructuring that would have provided a more typically Methodist structure. It was defeated.

The EMC affirms the inerrancy of the Bible and the premillennial return of Jesus Christ. It is one of the most theologically and socially conservative of the many Methodist denominations in the United States.

For more information: www.emchurch.org

Headquarters: 6838 South Gray Road, Indianapolis, IN 46237

SOUTHERN METHODIST CHURCH

Founded: 1940
Membership: est. 6,000 in 101 churches (2012)

The Southern Methodist Church (SMC) was formed by Southern Methodists who opposed the merger of the Methodist Episcopal Church, South with the northern Methodist Episcopal Church in 1939 on grounds of the "alarming infidelity and apostasy found therein." There are no bishops, but there are the usual Methodist Annual and General Conferences; a president is elected every four years from the elders of the clergy. Laypeople and clergy have equal voice and voting privileges in the conferences. Local churches own and control their own property and buildings and call their own pastors, who must be approved by their Annual Conferences. There is one college, Southern Methodist College, and a publishing house, Foundry Press, both located in Orangeburg, South Carolina.

The SCM is doctrinally and ethically conservative in the traditional Wesleyan-Arminian manner but also affirms the inerrancy of the verbally inspired Bible and the premillennial return of Jesus Christ.

For more information: www.thesmc.org

Headquarters: 541 Broughton Street, Orangeburg, SC 29115

UNITED METHODIST CHURCH

Founded: 1968, with roots to 1784
Membership: 7,679,850 in 33,583 churches (2012)

The United Methodist Church (UMC) is one of the largest religious bodies in the United States and has a major impact on American culture. In many ways, it is the quintessential American denomination, but it has been steadily losing members over the past three decades, which is symptomatic of changes in American religiosity generally.

Two mergers of major importance produced the United Methodist Church. The first merger was the reuniting of three separated Methodist groups in 1939 when the Methodist Episcopal Church; the Methodist Episcopal Church, South; and the Methodist Protestant Church were joined under a new name, the Methodist Church. This merger helped heal some of the wounds of the Civil War.

In 1968, the Methodist Church merged with the Evangelical United Brethren (EUB), a product of the German Pietist movement with Methodist leanings, to form the United Methodist Church. Both the Methodist and the EUB churches, across the years, had been deeply conscious of their common historical and spiritual heritage. Their doctrines were similar. Both were episcopal in government and traced their origins to John Wesley. They had similar books of discipline. Their preachers often exchanged pulpits and congregations, worked together, and shared the same buildings. The only major difference was that of language: German among the Brethren, English among the Methodists, but in time this barrier began to mean less and less. Conversations concerning a merger began as early as 1803; but the long-considered merger was not consummated until the two churches became the United Methodist Church at Dallas, Texas, on April 23, 1968.

There was some dissent at Dallas; fifty-one congregations and nearly eighty ministers of the Evangelical United Brethren withdrew from the Pacific Northwest Conference to establish the Evangelical Church of North America; eighteen EUB congregations in Montana left to establish the Evangelical Church of North America in Montana. However, roughly seven hundred fifty thousand Brethren accepted the union, and their strength gave the new United Methodist Church a membership of nearly eleven million at its inception. In this union no significant changes were made in either doctrine or polity. The Confession of Faith of the Evangelical United Brethren Church, adopted in 1962, was placed beside the Methodist Articles of Religion. Similar systems of bishops and conferences were in use in both denominations, and the format is still maintained.

Above the several regional Annual Conferences are fewer Jurisdictional Conferences, established for geographical convenience in administrative matters. These meet quadrennially, at times determined by the Council of Bishops, to elect new bishops and to name the members of the larger boards and commissions. Outside the continental United States, central conferences correspond to jurisdictional conferences; they meet quadrennially and, when authorized to do so, may elect their own bishops. All bishops are elected for life (except in some overseas conferences, where the term is four years), and a Council of Bishops meets at least once a year "for the general oversight and promotion of the temporal and spiritual affairs of the entire church." The General Conference consists of one thousand delegates, half laity and half clergy, elected on a proportional basis by the Annual Conferences. The Judicial Council determines the constitutionality of any act of the General Conference that may be appealed, and it hears and determines any appeal from a bishop's decision on a question of law, in any district or annual, central, or jurisdictional conference. The UMC is broadly episcopal in church government; bishops appoint local pastors and congregations are accountable to their conferences led by bishops. They hold their property "in trust" for the denomination and cannot take it with them if they leave the UMC.

In social ministries and education, the church operates or supports 225 retirement homes and long-term care facilities, seventy hospital and health-care facilities, fifty child-care facilities, thirty ministries for persons with disabilities, eight two-year colleges, eighty-two four-year colleges, ten universities, and thirteen theological schools. United Methodists give more than $3.5 billion annually for clergy support and benevolences, local church building and debt retirement, and operating expenses. The church also gives considerable financial support to the National Council of the Churches of Christ in the USA. The World Methodist Council was organized in 1881. Headquartered at Lake Junaluska, North Carolina, the council is designed to draw the whole Wesleyan movement closer together in fellowship and devotion to the Wesleyan heritage.

The 1972 General Conference broadened the basis of doctrine in the church in the first restatement since the eighteenth century. The classic documents of the merging Methodist and Evangelical United Brethren churches were maintained, but the doctrinal door was left open to theological change and revision. A revised statement was adopted in 1988: "In theological reflection, the resources of tradition, experience, and reason are integral to our study of Scripture without displacing Scripture's primacy for faith and practice." Unofficially, the UMC is theologically pluralistic while officially adhering to the traditional ecumenical creeds of Christendom and the Methodist Articles of Religion found in the *Book of Discipline*.

Unusual among churches, The United Methodist Church has adopted a Social Creed that stresses human rights and ecological concerns. Since the 1972 General Conference the United Methodist Social Principles have stated that "the practice of homosexuality is incompatible with Christian teaching." In 1982 the *Book of Discipline* was amended to state that no "self-avowed practicing homosexuals" can be ordained as clergy or be given a pastoral appointment. This position remains controversial in the church with significant segments calling for greater openness to the full equality of gay and lesbian people in ministry. The UMC has been a leader among American denominations in promoting racial and sexual equality in church and society. The UMC ordains women and has women bishops.

For more information: www.umc.org

Headquarters: PO Box 320, Nashville, TN 37202-0320

HOLINESS CHURCHES

The Holiness movement grew out of American and British Methodism beginning in the mid-nineteenth century. Early Methodist ministry in the United States focused primarily on conversion and church extension, at times neglecting John Wesley's emphasis on sanctification and perfection. As Methodism became more established in the nineteenth century, there was renewed interest in the doctrine of perfection. One of the key figures in this revival of Holiness teaching and experience was the traveling evangelist and writer Phoebe Palmer (1807–74), who experienced sanctification by the Holy Spirit in 1837 as a "second work of grace" after conversion. She worked tirelessly to bring others to a similar experience of holiness.

Most Holiness denominations arose out of the nineteenth century Holiness movement spawned by Palmer and other evangelists and teachers who were Methodists but thought that the movement had lost its "first love" and become spiritually "cold." They interpret Wesley's doctrine of sanctification as a definite experience rather than a process. Some call it a "second blessing" after the first blessing of conversion and consider it available to every truly converted Christian. While they could not point back to Wesley himself for this interpretation of sanctification and Christian perfection, they could point to Wesley's designated theologian of Methodism John Fletcher (1729–84) who seems to have taught this idea of sanctification even before Palmer and other nineteenth-century Holiness revivalists.

The Holiness movement deeply affected many Methodist congregations, which became centers for it. Many of them eventually broke away from Methodism and joined newly established Holiness denominations that specialized in sanctification as an experience after conversion of being "filled with the Holy Spirit" and instantaneously "perfected in love." Around the same time, the second half of the nineteenth century, many Holiness groups adopted belief in divine healing through faith. The only thing lacking to make this movement Pentecostal—in the twentieth-century sense—was speaking in tongues. When that phenomenon began to break out in certain Holiness meetings such as at Azusa Street in Los Angeles in 1906 the Pentecostal* movement was born. Some Holiness individuals and groups joined it and others did not. The largest Holiness denomination, the Church of the Nazarene, originally called itself the Pentecostal Church of the Nazarene but dropped the word *Pentecostal* when it decided to reject speaking in tongues. Some Holiness individuals and groups such as influential "deeper life" evangelist A. B. Simpson (1843–1919), founder of the Christian and Missionary Alliance* denomination, took a middle position and coined the phrase "Seek not; forbid not" about speaking in tongues. Pentecostals, most of whom began within the Holiness movement, insisted that speaking in tongues is the "initial, physical evidence" of the infilling of the Holy Spirit. Some Pentecostal groups remained Holiness in terms of belief in sanctification but added a third experience they call "Spirit baptism" with the evidence of speaking in tongues. Other Pentecostals rejected entire sanctification.

Toward the end of the nineteenth century, the Holiness movement had spread throughout the country, becoming a source of controversy in many Methodist churches. Congregations divided; many Holiness-minded preachers left the Methodist Church in order to work independently; and a wide variety of small, often "store-front," churches sprang up in virtually every US community. Over time, many of these independent congregations formed denominations. For the first century of the movement Holiness teaching generally rejected various forms of popular entertainment, such as dancing, movies, popular music, makeup, fashionable clothing, gambling, drinking, and smoking. In many ways, the Holiness movement represented a countercultural movement in the United States, but its adherents continued to live and work in the midst of the wider society. Some were known for emotional "camp meetings" often held in the summer under tents or wooden, open-sided "tabernacles." Emotional manifestations such as "shouting" and "running" were not unusual especially at these revival meetings.

What do all the groups categorized together here as "Holiness" have in common? They share common roots in the nineteenth-century Holiness movement or in similar movements in Europe. They emphasize sanctification as more than mere "discipleship" and believe Christians' wills need to be transformed by the power of the Holy Spirit "poured out" in a Pentecost-like experience (but without speaking in tongues). They believe in a "higher" or "deeper" Christian life beyond justification and even being "born again" (although they do believe those happen at conversion). They stress Christian separation from "worldliness" and a Christian life of sacrifice of "worldly pleasures." Most believe in divine healing of sickness provided for by the atoning death of Christ—not as something guaranteed but as something made possible through prayer (but they do not reject modern medicine). They are often confused with Pentecostals and fundamentalists and have some features in common with those movements, but they should be recognized as a distinct "brand" of Protestant Christianity. At one time there was a flourishing umbrella organization called the American Holiness Association that promoted cooperation and mutual recognition among Holiness denominations and ministries, but that has expired. In the twenty-first century most Holiness denominations and churches have dropped the word *Holiness* and some have changed their doctrine to expunge belief in "eradication" of original sin in an instantaneous experience of entire sanctification. To some extent Holiness denominations and educational institutions have blended in with the wider evangelical movement in a kind of evangelical "genericizing" in which historical-theological distinctives are downplayed if not entirely dropped. On the other hand, some Holiness groups continue to promote their distinctive doctrines and experiences. Many Holiness denominations are also Pentecostal; they will be included in the Pentecostal category here. The same thing could be said the other way: many Pentecostal denominations are also Holiness (e.g., the Pentecostal Holiness Church); they will be included in the Pentecostal category. The distinguishing feature is the phenomena of speaking in tongues and prophecy—two "gifts of the Holy Spirit" mentioned in the New Testament that most Holiness churches do not practice whereas most Pentecostals do.

SUGGESTIONS FOR FURTHER READING

Dieter, Melvin Easterday. *The Holiness Revival of the Nineteenth Century*. Metuchen, NJ: Scarecrow Press, 1996.

Dupree, Sherry Sherrod. *African-American Pentecostal Holiness Tradition: An Annotated Bibliography*. New York: Garland Publishing, 1995.

Jones, Charles Edwin. *Perfectionist Persuasion: The Holiness Movement and American Methodism, 1867–1936*. Metuchen, NJ: Scarecrow Press, 1974.

Kostlevy, William C., and Gari-Ann Patzwald. *Historical Dictionary of the Holiness Movement*. Lanham, MD: Rowman & Littlefield, 2001.

Niebuhr, H. Richard. *The Social Sources of Denominationalism*. New York: Meridian Books, 1957.

Sanders, Cheryl J. *Saints in Exile: The Holiness-Pentecostal Experience in African American Religion and Culture*. New York: Oxford University Press, 1996.

Smith, Timothy L. *Called unto Holiness: The Story of the Nazarenes; The Formative Years*. Kansas City, MO: Nazarene Publishing House, 1962.

Stanley, Susan C. *Holy Boldness: Women Preachers' Autobiography and the Sanctified Self*. Knoxville, TN: University of Tennessee Press, 2002.

Synan, Vinson. *The Holiness-Pentecostal Movement in the United States*. Grand Rapids, MI: Eerdmans, 1971.

APOSTOLIC CHRISTIAN CHURCHES OF AMERICA

Founded: 1830s (came to the United States in 1847)
Membership: 11,245 in 88 churches (2016)

The Apostolic Christian Churches of America (ACCA) is the only American Holiness group that originated in continental Europe. It began in Switzerland when S.

H. Froehlich had a dramatic conversion experience that he felt marked the New Testament pattern of Christian experience. Froehlich's church first took the name Evangelical Baptist, but adopted the *Apostolic* title as it embraced the doctrine of holiness as entire sanctification. Froehlich himself came to the United States in the 1850s and ministered to Swiss and German immigrants in the Midwest. By that time, another Swiss pastor, named Benedict Weyeneth, already had organized the first congregation in the United States in upstate New York. The theology of the church reflects some of the concerns of German Pietism.

The church consists of members who have been "reborn" and baptized by full immersion upon public confession of faith, and who strive for full sanctification along with "friends of the truth" who sincerely and earnestly strive to attain adoption by God in Christ. Members are noted for a life of simplicity, separation from worldliness, and obedience to the Bible, which is embraced as the infallible word of God. Members may serve in the military, but they cannot bear arms since that would violate the commandment to love one's enemies. Though they strive to be good citizens, they do not swear oaths. There are no educational institutions for clergy, and they are not paid. A very close-knit fellowship and strong sense of community exist throughout the denomination, evidenced in the observance of the kiss of peace.

Traditionally ACCA worship services are marked by separation between men and women with the sexes, including married couples, seated on opposite sides of the sanctuary. Worship is informal and led by male elders with extemporaneous prayers and a sermon. Members greet one another with a chaste "holy kiss" as in the New Testament churches. All scripture readings are from the Authorized King James Version of the Bible. The ACCA considers marriage as always and only between one man and one woman. Women do not lead. The denomination is untouched by controversy over gay marriage or ordination. It is somewhat separatistic, viewing contemporary cultural trends and controversies as alien to itself.

A smaller, related body is called the Apostolic Christian Church (Nazarean).

For more information: www.apostolicchristian.org

Headquarters: 10699 Steiner Road, Rittman, OH 44270

THE BIBLE METHODIST CONNECTION OF CHURCHES

Founded: 1968
Membership: 3,500 members in 72 churches (2016)

The Bible Methodist Connection of Churches is a Protestant, Arminian, Methodist, Wesleyan-Holiness denomination organized in 1968 by churches that withdrew from the Wesleyan Methodist denomination when it merged with the Pilgrim Holiness Church.

The denomination is conservative in doctrine and practice with a strong emphasis on entire sanctification as a second definite work of grace after conversion.

The denomination is led by a General Conference but each congregation is autonomous; by design there is no centralized form of government. There are three regional conferences that operate three family camps, three youth camps and one Christian school. The denomination has strong ties to God's Bible School and College in Cincinnati, Ohio, and to Hobe Sound Bible College in Florida as their primary ministry-training schools.

The denomination has ordained women and had women pastors. It is a decision left by the denomination to its regional conferences. It believes that the only legitimate marriage is between one man and one woman and that homosexual behavior is sin. No practicing homosexual person can be ordained as a minister or missionary or teach or hold office in the denomination.

For more information: www.biblemethodist.org

Headquarters: none

THE CHRISTIAN AND MISSIONARY ALLIANCE

Founded: 1887
Membership: 428,721 in 1,978 churches (2007)

A. B. Simpson (1843–1919), a Presbyterian minister in New York City, left that church in 1882 to carry on independent evangelistic work. He became a renowned figure in the late-nineteenth-century American healing and "deeper spiritual life" movement. He authored numerous hymns and devotional books. Simpson's ministry led to the formation of two societies: the Christian Alliance, for home missions work; and the Evangelical Missionary Alliance, for work abroad. These merged in 1897, forming The Christian and Missionary Alliance (CMA). When the Assemblies of God was founded, about one-tenth of that constituency resulted from the departure of people from the Christian and Missionary Alliance. The difference was over speaking in tongues. Simpson's motto about that spiritual gift was "Seek not; forbid not." Pentecostals within the CMA wanted to recognize speaking in tongues as the necessary sign of the infilling of the Holy Spirit subsequent to conversion. Simpson and the majority of the CMA resisted that doctrine. The CMA remained a confederation of independent churches for over seventy-five years, but it formalized its status as a denomination with binding bylaws and a constitution in 1974.

Strongly evangelical, the CMA believes in the inspiration and inerrancy of the Bible, the atoning work of Christ, the reality of supernatural religious experiences, entire sanctification, and the premillennial return of Jesus Christ. It stresses the centrality of Christ as Savior, sanctifier, healer, and coming king (Simpson's "fourfold gospel," which strongly influenced early Pentecostalism also). True to its original purpose, the CMA sponsors foreign missions work in eighty-one countries in Latin America, Africa, Asia, the Pacific Islands, the Middle East, and Europe. There are over one thousand Alliance missionaries and some fifteen thousand national pastors and workers ministering to nearly two million persons. Ethnic groups within the alliance include Cambodian, Dega, Haitian, Hmong, Jewish, Korean, Laotian, Native American, Hispanic, and Vietnamese. Each member church or group is engaged in some way in missionary and evangelistic activities. An overall conference of delegates, the General Council, meets annually. The CMA in Canada became autonomous in 1980 but continues to support missions jointly with the US Alliance.

Through Simpson and other founders, the CMA was deeply influenced by the Keswick Movement that began in England and spread to the United States and across Europe and eventually around the world. The Keswick Movement was in some ways the late-nineteenth-century equivalent of the later charismatic movement in that it was trans-denominational and emphasized spiritual renewal of individuals and churches through a deeper, more profound experience of Christ through the Holy Spirit. Many Keswick teachers emphasized the possibility of total or entire "consecration" of life through dying to self. Many scholars have viewed the Keswick message and experience as a non-Wesleyan type of "Christian perfectionism" and belief in entire sanctification. The CMA came to embrace this message and experience although later, through influences of American fundamentalism and broad evangelicalism, the CMA downplayed this aspect of its history, doctrine, and spiritual life.

The CMA Statement of Faith reflects a conservative evangelical ethos and includes belief in the premillennial return of Christ, and the challenge for Christians to be "sanctified wholly" beginning with a second definite experience of the infilling of the Holy Spirit after conversion. It does not mention speaking in tongues. The Statement affirms the possibility of divine healing of the body through anointing with oil and prayer for the sick.

Women have played a very important role in the CMA's ministry and especially in its world missions and evangelism programs. However, in 1981 the CMA produced and promulgated a statement about women's ministry that denied women eldership, which is restricted to men. Only elders can serve as pastors of local congregations. This decision came as a shock to some CMA people because of the strong roles women played in the CMA's missionary and evangelism endeavors for almost a century.

The CMA does not recognize marriages between persons of the same sex and does not ordain gay people or allow them to serve in leadership positions.

For more information: www.cmalliance.org

Headquarters: 8595 Explorer Drive, Colorado Springs, CO 80929

CHURCH OF CHRIST (HOLINESS) USA

Founded: 1894
Membership: 12,960 in 139 churches (2012)

Church of Christ (Holiness) founder C. P. Jones was a nineteenth-century Baptist preacher in Alabama and Mississippi seeking a new church and faith that would make him "one of wisdom's true sons . . . like Abraham, a friend of God." He founded this church denomination in 1894. The body retained its non-Pentecostal Holiness emphasis when other early black churches such as the Church of God in Christ moved into Pentecostalism. The Church of Christ (Holiness) seeks to spread the gospel around the world, to reclaim those who have fallen away from the faith, to encourage believers to experience entire sanctification, and to support divine healing. The church has a strong eschatological focus as well.

Doctrinally, the church emphasizes original sin, the Holy Spirit as an indispensable gift to every believer, and Christ's atonement and second coming. There are two sacraments: baptism and the Lord's Supper. Foot-washing and divine healing are employed as aids to the growth of spiritual life. The church does not reject speaking in tongues, but does not consider it a special "sign gift" of reception of the Holy Spirit. The church has bishops who speak for it, but its government is representative, with final authority vested in a biennial convention made up of elders, clergy, and local lay leaders. There are eight US dioceses, each under a bishop's charge. Missionary work is conducted in the United States and in Liberia and Nigeria.

For more information: www.cochusa.org
Headquarters: PO Box 3135, Jackson, MS 39207

CHURCH OF GOD (ANDERSON, INDIANA)

Founded: 1881
Membership: 233,049 in 2,069 churches (2016)

The Church of God with general headquarters in Anderson, Indiana, grew out of the nineteenth-century American Holiness Movement, but both Anabaptist and Pietistic emphases also influenced it. Daniel S. Warner (1842–95) and several associates rejected denominational hierarchies and formal creeds. They understood unity as being a natural outgrowth of personal holiness, and holiness to be the basis of biblical unity. The Church of God's generally accepted doctrines include the divine inspiration of the scriptures; forgiveness of sin through the atonement of Christ and repentance of the believer; the experience of holiness; the personal (amillennial) return of Christ; the kingdom of God as the reign and rule of God in the human heart; resurrection of the dead; and a final judgment in which the righteous are rewarded and the wicked punished. Baptism by immersion is viewed as a witness to the new believer's regeneration by Christ and inclusion in the family of God. The Lord's Supper reminds participants of the grace experienced in the life of the believer. Foot-washing is practiced in acknowledgement and acceptance of the servant ministry of Christians to each other and to the world. These New Testament practices are understood as divine ordinances of the church.

Local churches are responsible for their own way of functioning. As a result, one finds a wide variety of organizational structures among congregations. Ministers and lay leaders meet in voluntary state and regional assemblies for inspiration and instruction as well as to conduct business. The General Assembly meets in connection with the annual international convention held in Anderson. In 1996 and 1997 the assembly initiated a restructuring of the church's work in the United States. The result was the formation of Church of God Ministries, Inc. The church's ministries emphasize outreach, congregational ministry, and service to pastors and others. Warner Press serves as the church's publisher of curriculum and other materials. There is no formal membership in the Church of God (Anderson), but persons are assumed to be members on the basis of conversion and holiness of life. Congregations are found mainly in the Midwest and Pacific Coast regions. It supports Anderson University and its School of Theology along with Mid-American Christian University, Warner University, and Warner Pacific College. It carries on work in ninety countries, involving nearly one million worshippers.

This denomination should not be confused with others also using the name Church of God. The Church of God (Anderson, Indiana) is entirely distinct from the Church of God (Cleveland, Tennessee), which is both Pentecostal and Holiness. Each uses the name of its headquarters city to distinguish itself from the other (and from other Churches of God). This church does not consider itself a denomination; it traditionally claims to be simply "the church of God" to which all true Christians belong in some sense. However, over the decades of its history that emphasis has tended to drop away and virtually all its adherents now recognize it as a denomination. Membership is de facto upon long-time association with a congregation.

The Church of God (Anderson, Indiana) is known for its multicultural emphasis and racial integration; many of its urban congregations are multi-racial. One of its best-known "products" is the musical team of Bill and Gloria Gaither who have written numerous evangelical Christian songs and hymns and produced and sold millions of records, CDs, and DVDs of inspirational music. (The Gaithers have also belonged to the Church of the Nazarene, which is close to the Church of God in terms of doctrine and practice.)

The Church of God (Anderson, Indiana) has from its very beginning ordained women to the gospel ministry and has many women pastors. It does not, however, perform same-sex marriages or ordain openly gay or lesbian people to the gospel ministry.

For more information: www.chog.org

Headquarters: PO Box 2420, Anderson, IN 46018-2420

CHURCH OF GOD (HOLINESS)

Founded: 1883
Membership: est. 8,000 in approx. 140 churches (2000)

The Church of God (Holiness) is an association of autonomous congregations that was founded by former Methodists* who were active in the Southwest Holiness Association. They believe that entire sanctification is a biblical doctrine and experience. They describe this as a second definite work of God's grace in the heart and life of the believer subsequent to regeneration, at which time the believer is cleansed of the sin nature and is completely submitted to the "controlling hand" of the Holy Spirit.

The church today is concentrated in Missouri and Kansas, and has a rapidly expanding work among Hispanics in the United States and Mexico. The Home Missions Department also works with Haitian immigrants in New York City and sponsors a Navajo mission in the Southwest. World missions are concentrated in Ghana, Liberia, Nigeria, India, Myanmar, Nepal, the Caribbean basin, Ukraine, Bolivia, and Colombia. In addition to Kansas City College and Bible School, the church operates The Herald and Banner Press, which produces Sunday school literature for all ages, devotional books, and a periodical. A General Convention is held annually. The denomination supports Kansas Christian College in Overland Park, Kansas.

The Church of God (Holiness) is doctrinally evangelical and socially conservative.

For more information: www.cogh.net

Contact: Kansas Christian College, 7401 Metcalf, Overland Park, KS 66204

CHURCH OF THE NAZARENE

Founded: 1908
Membership: 905,936 (adherents) in 5,085 churches (2015)

The Church of the Nazarene is one of the largest and most influential of the Holiness bodies, and it is one that has self-consciously held to its Wesleyan roots. It is now an international body that includes over two million people. The church resulted from the merger of three independent Holiness groups in the United States. In 1907, an eastern Holiness body, the Association of Pentecostal Churches of America, joined with a California body, the Church of the Nazarene. Then in 1908, this body merged with a Southern group known as the Holiness Church of Christ. The current name was adopted in 1919. While many were involved in the founding of the church, perhaps the principal figure was Phineas F. Bresee (1838–1915), who became its first general superintendent.

The church's theological background is Wesleyan-Arminian. Four of the first five general superintendents of the Church of the Nazarene, including Bresee, were former

Methodist ministers, and the church's *Manual* is similar to the Methodist *Book of Discipline*. The doctrine of the church is built around the justification and the sanctification of believers by faith. This includes a believer's entire sanctification as a second work of grace, subsequent to regeneration. All clergy, both men and women, and local church officials must profess this experience of entire sanctification. Other doctrines include belief in the plenary inspiration of the scriptures; the atonement of Christ for the whole human race (i.e., Arminianism); the justification, regeneration, and adoption of all penitent believers in Christ; the second coming of Christ; the resurrection of the dead; and the final judgment.

Members believe in divine healing but never to the exclusion of medical agencies. Nazarenes discourage use of tobacco and alcoholic beverages. Two sacraments, baptism by sprinkling, pouring, or (most often) immersion and Communion are accepted as "instituted by Christ." Baptism of young children is allowed, but believer's baptism predominates.

The General Assembly, the highest body of the church, elects six general superintendents whose terms last until the next General Assembly, and the General Board, consisting of an equal number of lay and clergy members. The General Board meets annually and oversees four administrative departments of the church: World Mission, USA/Canada, Sunday School & Discipleship Ministries, and the International Board of Education.

Structurally, the Church of the Nazarene exists at the local, district, and general level, which is international in scope. All districts are represented at the General Assembly on the same basis (based on district membership), and there are currently 466 districts worldwide, of which only seventy-five are in the United States. The year 1998 was the last year in which Americans and Canadians together made up 50 percent of the church membership. Today Americans make up only 26 percent. The denomination's worldwide membership is now at 2.44 million. The books, periodicals, and curricula of the church are produced at the Nazarene Publishing House in Kansas City (also known as Beacon Hill Press). The denomination's main seminary is Nazarene Theological Seminary in Kansas City, Missouri. It has many affiliated colleges and universities in the United States and around the world.

The Church of the Nazarene is doctrinally evangelical and conservative but ordains women to the ministry and has women evangelists and pastors. It affirms that homosexual practice is sinful and that true marriage is always only between one man and one woman. It does not ordain openly gay people or permit them to serve as pastors or other denominational ministers or leaders. On the other hand, the denomination affirms the dignity of all persons regardless of sexual orientation.

For more information: www.nazarene.org

Headquarters: 17001 Prairie Star Parkway, Lenexa, KS 66220

CHURCHES OF CHRIST IN CHRISTIAN UNION

Founded: 1909
Membership: 12,00 in 225 churches (2016)

This church, Churches of Christ in Christian Union (CCCU), began when five ministers and several laypersons withdrew from Christian Union churches in 1909. The Christian Union had been founded in 1864 in Ohio "to promote fellowship among God's people, to put forth every effort to proclaim God's saving grace to the lost . . . and to declare the whole counsel of God for the edification of believers." Some of the clergy in the Christian Union felt that key doctrines were being neglected, and so the Churches of Christ in Christian Union was organized "to allow a complete freedom in the preaching of full salvation as stated doctrinally by John Wesley." The first council was held that year at Jeffersonville, Ohio. The Reformed Methodist Church merged with the Churches of Christ in Christian Union in September 1952.

Churches in this body are generally evangelistic in faith and work; camp meetings, revivals, and soul-winning campaigns are held regularly throughout the denomination. Worship follows simple forms, with little prescribed ritual. Emphasis is placed "on the blessing of God rather than on the ingenuity of man." A general council meets every two years at Circleville, Ohio, the body's headquarters. Ohio Christian University, formerly called Circleville Bible College, established in 1948, trains clergy and lay workers.

The CCCU denomination is a unique blend of Restorationism (from its roots in the Christian Union) and the Holiness movement. It affirms the trans-denominational unity of all true Christian believers, the possibility of entire sanctification in an experience of Holy Spirit baptism after conversion, and the premillennial return of Jesus Christ to establish his kingdom on earth. It is doctrinally evangelical and socially conservative with regard to sexuality.

For more information: www.cccuhq.org
Headquarters: 1553 Lancaster Pike, Circleville, OH 43113

FREE METHODIST CHURCH OF NORTH AMERICA

Founded: 1860
Membership: 110,000 adherents in 900 congregations (2016)

The Free Methodist Church (FMC) was formed as part of the abolitionist movement prior to the Civil War. Its founder was the Reverend B. T. Roberts (1823–93) who objected to "new school" Methodism, which he and his associates believed compromised the Wesleyan standards of the church. They called for a return to stricter doctrine and lifestyle in the Methodist Church, which included the abolition of slavery, abolishing the practice

– 212 –

of pew rentals, opposition to secret societies, and more freedom in worship. They were "read out" of their churches and organized the Free Methodist Church in Pekin, New York, in 1860.

Doctrinally, the Free Methodists stress the virgin birth and the deity of Jesus, and his vicarious atonement and resurrection. No one may be received into membership without undergoing confession and forgiveness of sin (conversion), and the experience of entire sanctification is sought in all members. However, the FMC baptizes both infants and mature believers; the decision whether to baptize infants is left to the parents.

The church is connectional, in a basic Methodist pattern, with a board of bishops who supervise the basic geographic areas of the church; a General Conference that meets every four years; Annual Conferences; and districts, in a basic Methodist pattern. The publishing arm of the church is Light and Life Communications. The church operates several colleges, universities, and seminaries including Seattle Pacific University and Seminary. Social services include a health care foundation, pregnancy and adoption services, retirement and nursing facilities for the elderly, day-care centers for children, homeless shelters, drug and alcohol abuse recovery ministries, a boarding high school, and many services for the poor and disenfranchised.

The FMC is a world fellowship, consisting of fourteen General Conferences (Brazil, Burundi, Canada, Congo, Democratic Republic of Congo, Dominican Republic, Egypt, Japan, Mozambique, Philippines, Rwanda, South Africa, Zimbabwe, and the United States) with a common constitution. Free Methodist churches are found in eighty countries, and the membership (adherents) outside the United States is over one million.

The FMC was one of the first Protestant denominations to ordain women and have women pastors of churches. Founder Roberts was a well-known progressive with regard to social issues of his time (mid-nineteenth century). He advocated an income tax and redistribution of wealth. The "free" in the denomination's name refers both to Roberts's opposition to slavery and his opposition to churches charging rental for the best pews.

The FMC does not, however, recognize same-sex marriage or ordain openly gay people to the ministry or permit them to serve as leaders in the denomination or churches. It regards marriage as between one man and one woman and homosexual behavior as sinful.

For more information: www.fmcusa.org

Headquarters: 770 North High School Road, Indianapolis, IN 46214

THE SALVATION ARMY

Founded: 1880
Membership: 413,961 in 1,232 corps (congregations) (2012)

The Salvation Army (SA) and its related organizations grew out of the Methodist Church's concern for outreach to the impoverished peoples of the growing metropolises in England. In order to bring the gospel to these neglected souls, a new type of religious organization was created. It is neither a traditional denomination nor a traditional service organization but a creative union of both.

William Booth (1829–1912), an ordained minister in the Methodist New Connexion in England, left that church in 1861 to become a freelance evangelist. In 1865 he dedicated his life to the poverty-stricken unchurched masses in the slum areas of London's East End. He first planned to supplement the work of the churches, but this proved impractical because many converts did not want to go where they were sent, and often when they did go, they were not accepted. Moreover, Booth soon found that he needed the converts to help handle the great crowds that came to his meetings.

He began his work under the name "Christian Mission," and in 1878 the name was changed to the Salvation Army. Booth first organized his movement along lines of Methodist polity, with annual conferences at which reports were made and programs planned. But when the name was changed, the whole organization became dominated by the new title. Articles of War (a declaration of faith) were drawn up, and soon the mission stations became corps, members became soldiers, evangelists became officers, and converts were called seekers. Booth was designated as general, and his organization was gradually set up on a military pattern, which provided a direct line of authority and a practical system of training personnel for effective action. He reasoned that it was "just as valid to build an army of crusaders to save souls as it has been to send armies to recover a sepulchre."

While the SA has a dual function of church and social agency, its first purpose is salvation "by the power of the Holy Spirit combined with the influence of human ingenuity and love." Its social services are a means of meeting the needs of the "whole person," putting the socially disinherited—the needy both physically and spiritually—into a condition to be uplifted. The fundamental doctrines of the organization are stated in the eleven cardinal affirmations of its Foundation Deed of 1878. These statements include the Army's recognition of the Bible as the only rule of Christian faith and practice; God as the creator and Father of all humankind; the Trinity of Father, Son, and Holy Ghost; Jesus Christ as Son of God and Son of man; sin as the great destroyer of soul and society; salvation as God's remedy for human sin and the ultimate and eternal hope made available through Christ; sanctification as the individual's present and maturing experience of a life set apart for the holy purposes of the kingdom of God; and an eternal destiny that may triumph over sin and death. The Army affirms the goal and ideal of Christian individuals becoming "sanctified wholly," which justifies its inclusion in the Holiness category. Its basic theology is Wesleyan. However, even as a body of churches (corps), it does not perform outward sacraments or ordinances such a baptism or the Lord's Supper.

Administratively, the Army is under the command of a General. The primary unit of the Army is the corps, of which there may be several in a city. Each corps is commanded by an officer, ranging in rank from Lieutenant to Major, who is responsible to divisional headquarters.

The national headquarters in Alexandria, Virginia, is the coordinating office for the entire country. The national commander is the chief administrative officer, official spokesperson, and president of all Salvation Army corporations in the United States. Property and revenues are in the custody of a board of trustees, or directors, and citizen advisory boards assist in interpreting the work of the Army to the general public.

As an evangelical church, the SA includes women leaders, including officers. It does not affirm gay marriage or permit openly gay persons to lead corps (congregations) or serve as officers. As a social agency, it extends equal help to all kinds of people, including those in the gay communities, and employs gay and lesbian people, extending the same benefits to them as to heterosexual couples.

For more information: www.salvationarmy.org

Headquarters: 615 Slaters Lane, Alexandria, VA 22313

WESLEYAN CHURCH

Founded: 1968 with roots to 1843
Membership: 385,321 adherents in 1,715 churches (2012)

The Wesleyan Church (WC) was formed in 1968 through the merger of The Pilgrim Holiness Church and The Wesleyan Methodist Church. Many beliefs of The Wesleyan Church are based on doctrines set forth by the seventeenth-century Dutch theologian, Jacobus Arminius and Methodist founder John Wesley. The Wesleyan Methodist Church was the first Holiness denomination founded in the United States as a protest against slavery. Orange Scott (1800–47) was a leading abolitionist Methodist preacher, and when Methodist bishops urged silence on the subject of slavery as the country was moving toward Civil War, Orange and his associates organized a separate Wesleyan Methodist Connection. Many of the Wesleyan Methodists of that day were activists in what came to be known historically as the Underground Railway before and during the Civil War.

Following the Civil War and emancipation, the Wesleyan Methodist Connection embraced the Holiness movement, which promoted the doctrine of entire sanctification as taught by John Wesley and especially his associate theologian John Fletcher, with an uncompromising commitment to a sober and moderate lifestyle. In 1947 the word *Connection* was changed to *Church*. By the late-nineteenth century several holiness groups had formed into functioning, autonomous, ecclesiastical bodies as a result of the holiness revival that spread through much of Protestantism. In 1897 a process was begun resulting in one organized church in 1922 that adopted the name the Pilgrim Holiness Church. In 1966 the decision was made by the respective General Conferences to merge the Pilgrim Holiness Church and the Wesleyan Methodist Church as their doctrine and church polity was so similar. This merger was accomplished in June of 1968 and took place on the campus of Anderson University in Anderson, Indiana. Today, the WC has a presence in seventy-six countries with a worldwide membership of one-half million.

The WC differs almost not at all from the Free Methodist Church and both Wesleyan-Holiness denominations are headquartered in Indiana. Over the decades they have frequently discussed merger, which has been prevented so far by their differing polities and practices of baptism (the WC only baptizes believers, not infants). The Free Methodist Church has bishops; the WC does not. Like the Free Methodist Church and other Wesleyan-Holiness denominations the WC is evangelical in ethos.

The WC ordains women and has women pastors. It believes homosexual practice is sin and does not recognize or perform same-sex marriage or ordain practicing gay people to the ministry. Like most evangelical denominations its policy toward gay people is "welcoming but not affirming."

For more information: www.wesleyan.org

Headquarters: 13300 Olio Road, Fishers, IN 46037

PENTECOSTAL CHURCHES

Pentecostalism is a modern American Christian movement that emerged mostly out of the Holiness movement around the turn of the twentieth century. Two key figures in the genesis of Pentecostalism were Charles Fox Parham (1873–1929), the founder of Bethel Bible College in Topeka, Kansas, and William J. Seymour (1870–1922), an African American Holiness evangelist from Louisiana. Parham became convinced that the gifts of the Holy Spirit that were evident in apostolic times are available to Christians in modern times as well. Many Protestants believed they ceased with the end of the apostolic era of Christianity. Of particular interest to Parham was speaking in unknown tongues (languages), a phenomenon occasionally experienced among Pietist and revivalist Christians before the twentieth century. However, at Bethel Bible College in 1901 it was first interpreted by Parham as the "initial, physical evidence" of the infilling of the Holy Spirit talked about by many Holiness Christians. Five years later, Seymour, who had studied at Bethel with Parham, led a revival on Azusa Street in Los Angeles that lasted for several months. Participants experienced a "baptism in the Holy Ghost." Some were healed of illnesses, while others spoke in tongues. Thousands from across the United States traveled to the Azusa Street revival and carried the message of the "latter rain" of the gifts of the Holy Spirit back to their home churches. Many Holiness and some Pietist churches embraced the new experience and doctrine.

The movement eventually became known as "Pentecostal" because of its similarity to the first Pentecost, fifty days after Christ's resurrection, when the Spirit came upon the early Christians and enabled them to speak in unfamiliar languages (Acts 2). However, many Pentecostals themselves prefer the appellation "Full Gospel" without rejecting the Pentecostal designation. There are a great variety of Pentecostal churches, most of which are theologically and socially conservative. In general, Pentecostals are evangelical Protestants who teach that the Holy Spirit continues to act as the Holy Spirit did at the first Pentecost and among the earliest Christians. Convinced that contemporary Christians can receive the same spiritual gifts that the apostles did, many Pentecostal churches use the word *apostolic* in their names.

Seeking and receiving the gift of tongues is regarded as the necessary sign of the baptism or infilling of the Holy Spirit. Most Pentecostals do not equate this with salvation; it is viewed as a "second blessing" subsequent to conversion. Its purpose is power for Christian living and witnessing. Speaking in tongues is viewed as a "prayer language" in which the Holy Spirit prays through the person past his or her rational thought processes. Other spiritual gifts, such as healing, prophecy, and miracles, also make up Pentecostals' experience of God. Like the Baptists, many Pentecostal churches refer to rites such as baptism as "ordinances" rather than as "sacraments." Pentecostals are generally less bound to traditional forms of worship than are other churches. Pentecostals practically invented what is commonly known as "contemporary worship" using drums and other non-traditional musical instruments. "Praise and worship" chorus-singing with arms lifted in the air and sometimes "dancing in the Spirit" and even "falling in the Spirit" have spread from Pentecostalism into other evangelical traditions. The charismatic movement that sprang up among traditional denominations in the 1960s and 1970s was often called "neo-Pentecostalism" by observers. The difference was that the neo-Pentecostals often remained in their so-called mainline denominations (including the Roman Catholic Church) and did not adopt the classical Pentecostal doctrine that speaking in tongues is the *sine qua non* of Spirit baptism (or the infilling of the Holy Spirit).

In general, Pentecostal denominations are Protestant and evangelical, but many were influenced by the fundamentalist movement. They commonly hold to beliefs in original sin, salvation through the atoning blood of Christ, the virgin birth and deity of Jesus, the divine inspiration and infallibility of the scriptures, premillennialism (the return of Jesus Christ prior to his thousand-year reign on earth), and future rewards and punishments. Most Pentecostal churches practice baptism of believers by immersion and the Lord's Supper, but some of the smaller bodies also observe foot-washing. They do not consider these sacraments but ordinances; no special grace is conveyed through them.

Two deep divisions exist among Pentecostals. Some are also Holiness Christians and believe in entire sanctification and Christian perfection. Others reject that doctrine and teach the "finished work of Christ" in which sanctification is included in the atonement and worked out in the Christian's life as a process of Holy Spirit-enabled service to God without perfection. Some Pentecostals deny the doctrine of the Trinity and are known as Oneness Pentecostals or "Jesus Only." They believe Jesus is the Father, the Son, and the Holy Spirit in one person. The majority of Pentecostals, however, believe in the orthodox doctrine of the Trinity and view the Oneness Pentecostals as heretics. The two groups, trinitarian and non-trinitarian, do not have fellowship with each other.

Originally strongest among the rural peoples of the South and the Midwest, early Pentecostalism also found a home among the urban poor in the 1930s. Now the movement has spread to all fifty states and represents a cross-section of American society. Some Pentecostal bodies do not have educational requirements for clergy; anyone who manifests the "anointing" for preaching and church leadership may be ordained and pastor a church. Other Pentecostals have established Bible colleges and even seminaries for training ministers. Important for all of them is evidence of the Spirit in a preacher's life and ministry. In the 1980s and 1990s many Pentecostals in America grew prosperous and gained higher education, becoming biblical and theological scholars. The media, however, tended to focus on the travails of Pentecostal evangelists whose scandals fascinated the masses. Most of them were not affiliated with any established Pentecostal denomination but were religious entrepreneurs.

Sociologists of religion talk about the "routinization of charisma"—the tendency of enthusiastic religious movements that begin in revival fires to fall into established routines and lose their original passion. Many observers believe this has happened to American Pentecostalism; according to some scholars less than half of American Pentecostals have ever spoken in tongues or experienced prophecy, divine healing, or anything supernatural. Predictably that has given rise to new forms of Pentecostalism such as a "Third Wave" movement exemplified by the Vineyard movement and numerous independent Pentecostal and charismatic churches and ministries that do not emphasize speaking in tongues as the sine qua non of being filled with the Holy Spirit but do believe in and practice the supernatural gifts of the Spirit with emphasis on prophecy and healing.

During the latter decades of the twentieth century and first decades of the twenty-first century various forms of Pentecostalism flourished in what scholars call the Global South where the majority of humans live—especially Asia and Latin America. It also became a mass movement in Korea where the largest church in the world is a Pentecostal congregation in Seoul. Some scholars argue that Pentecostalism is not only the fastest-growing Christian movement in the world but also the largest with many Catholic Christians in Africa and Latin America adopting it as their spiritual ethos. In the first decades of the twenty-first century many non-American Pentecostal missionaries from Asia, Latin America, and Africa are coming to the United States to re-evangelize what they perceive as an increasingly secular society.

Almost without exception American Pentecostals reject same-sex marriage and ordination of gay or lesbian people to the ministry. Occasionally one hears of an independent Pentecostal church that performs gay marriages and is "welcoming *and* affirming" of homosexuals. No American Pentecostal denomination, however, does or is such. American Pentecostals tend to be very conservative in doctrine and personal ethics. Therefore, no comments will be made in individual entries here with regard to the LGBT issues of marriage and of ordination-pastoral ministry. It may fairly be assumed that none of these denominations are even struggling with those issues; they are all closed to such practices. (Some might point to the Metropolitan Community Churches [MCC], which was founded by Pentecostal and openly gay minister Troy Perry, but the MCC is not usually considered a classical Pentecostal denomination. In this *Handbook* it is included in the "Miscellaneous" category.)

Like many of the Holiness denominations, many Pentecostal ones license or ordain women to the ministry and some Pentecostal churches are pastored by women. More than one Pentecostal denomination was founded by a woman as noted in those entries here. During the first half-century of the Pentecostal movement many denominations were pacifist and had numerous women ministers and leaders. During the second half-century, however, those features of the movement tended to diminish in visibility. This change seemed to correspond with Pentecostalism's embrace by the wider American evangelical movement and its gradual but noticeable accommodations of its particularities to "generic evangelicalism."

SUGGESTIONS FOR FURTHER READING

Anderson, Robert Mapes. *Vision of the Disinherited: The Making of American Penecostalism.* New York: Oxford University Press, 1979.

Blumhofer, Edith. *Aimee Semple McPherson: Everybody's Sister.* Grand Rapids, MI: Eerdmans, 1993.

Blumhofer, Edith. *Restoring the Faith: The Assemblies of God, Pentecostalism, and American Culture.* Urbana, IL: InterVarsity Press, 1993.

Butler, Anthea D. *Women in the Church of God in Christ: Making a Sanctified World.* Chapel Hill: University of North Carolina Press, 2007.

Cox, Harvey. *Fire from Heaven: The Rise of Pentecostal Spirituality and the Shaping of Religion in the 21st Century.* Reading, MA: Addison-Wesley Publishing, 1994.

Dayton, Donald. *Theological Roots of Pentecostalism.* Grand Rapids, MI: Francis Asbury Press, 1987.

Faupel, David W. *The American Pentecostal Movement.* Wilmore, KY: B. L. Fisher Library, 1972.

Harrell, David E. *All Things Are Possible: The Healing and Charismatic Revivals in Modern America.* Bloomington: Indiana University Press, 1985.

Hollenweger, Walter. *The Pentecostals.* Minneapolis, MN: Augsburg Publishing House, 1972.

MacRobert, Iain. *The Black Roots and White Racism of Early Pentecostalism in the USA.* London: Palgrave MacMillan, 1988.

Synan, Vinson. *The Century of the Holy Spirit: 100 Years of Pentecostal and Charismatic Renewal.* Nashville, TN: Thomas Nelson, 2001.

Synan, Vinson. *The Holiness-Pentecostal Movement in the United States.* Grand Rapids, MI: Eerdmans, 1971.

Wacker, Grant. *Heaven Below: Early Pentecostals and American Culture.* Cambridge, MA: Harvard University Press, 2003.

APOSTOLIC FAITH CHURCH

Founded: 1906
Membership: est. 2,500 in 62 churches (2016)

The Apostolic Faith Church is one of the oldest Pentecostal denominations in the United States. It was founded in Portland, Oregon, by Holiness evangelist Florence Crawford and grew out of the Azusa Street Revival in Los Angeles. Today it has churches in many locations in the western part of the United States. It is both Holiness and Pentecostal with emphasis on the Wesleyan doctrine of entire sanctification and the Pentecostal doctrine of speaking in tongues as the initial, physical evidence of the infilling of the Holy Spirit. The church affirms divine healing as provided by Christ's atoning death and practices prayer for the sick with the expectation of physical healing appropriated by faith. It is evangelistic and revivalistic in ethos as well as trinitarian in doctrine. The church affirms the premillennial return of Jesus Christ. One distinctive of the denomination is the noticeable absence of offerings in worship services; members and others donate to the church through an offering box. The denomination holds weeks-long camp meetings and conferences and publishes literature disseminated throughout the world in many languages. It claims numerous churches outside the United States including six hundred in Nigeria alone.

For more information: www.apostolicfaith.org

Headquarters: 6615 Southeast Fifty-Second Avenue, Portland, OR 97206

APOSTOLIC FAITH MISSION CHURCH OF GOD

Founded: 1915
Membership: 6,880 in 16 churches (2009)

This denomination was a fruit of the Azuza Street Revival in Los Angeles and the preaching of William Seymour. F. W. Williams experienced the outpouring of the Holy Spirit during that revival and founded the Apostolic Faith Mission in Mobile, Alabama, to spread the revival. Bishop Williams incorporated the church in 1915 under the present name. The church spread to Georgia and Florida. Pastors are called bishops in this church. The headquarters is called Ward's Temple in Cantonment, Florida. The denomination ordains women and denies the orthodox doctrine of the Trinity ("Oneness Pentecostal"). For it, Jesus is the name of the Father, Son, and Holy Sprit and it recognizes only baptism in the name of the Lord Jesus Christ.

Headquarters: 806 Muscogee Road, Cantonment, FL 32533

APOSTOLIC OVERCOMING HOLY CHURCH OF GOD

Founded: 1916
Membership: 10,714 in 129 churches (2000)

Bishop W. T. Phillips (1893–1973), a former member of the Methodist Church*, became deeply concerned with the teaching of the doctrine of holiness and, after four years of study and preaching on the topic, organized the Ethiopian Overcoming Holy Church of God in 1916 in Mobile, Alabama. *Ethiopian* was later changed to *Apostolic*. Active in twenty-two states, the West Indies, Haiti, and Africa, the church's clergy, both men and women, are supported by tithes. Worship includes foot-washing and divine healing. Services generally are emotionally expressive, with participants speaking in tongues and engaging in ecstatic dances. Marriage to the unsaved, the use of tobacco, foolish talking, jesting, and use of slang are forbidden. In doctrine, sanctification and holiness are stressed, along with the deity of Christ, the final resurrection of the dead, and the punishment of evil at the time of the last judgment at the second coming of Christ. A publishing facility is located in the headquarters building in Birmingham, Alabama.

For more information: www.aohchurch.com

Headquarters: 2257 Saint Stephens Road, Mobile, AL 36617

ASSEMBLIES OF GOD

Founded: 1914
Membership: 3,192,112 in 12,897 churches (2015)

The founders of the Assemblies of God (AG) were pastors of evangelical and Pentecostal persuasion who united in the interest of doctrinal unity, more effective preaching, and an enlarged missionary crusade. The founding meeting of the AG was in Hot Springs, Arkansas, in 1914 and was in part a response to the rise of non-trinitarianism (Oneness or "Jesus Only" doctrine) among other Pentecostals. Over the century since its founding the AG has spread worldwide and become one of the largest (if not the largest) Pentecostal denominations in the United States. As of 2015 it claims to have sixty-five million adherents in the world. About twenty million are in Brazil alone. Many scholars of Pentecostalism consider the AG the "gold standard" of Pentecostalism as it has taken leadership in the American evangelical community, being the largest denomination in the National Association of Evangelicals (NAE).

Theologically, the Assemblies of God is evangelical and Arminian (after Jacobus Arminius, 1560–1609), stressing Christ's atoning death for all persons, the freedom of human will, and the need for conversion. There is also a strong belief in the infallibility and inspiration of the Bible, the fall and redemption of the human race, baptism in the Holy Spirit as a second definite "work of grace" after conversion, a life of holiness and separation from the world, divine healing, and the premillennial return of Jesus Christ. Two ordinances, baptism and the Lord's Supper, are practiced. Assemblies of God members are especially insistent that baptism in the Holy Spirit be evidenced by speaking in tongues. They hold that all the gifts of the Spirit should be evident in a church modeled after that of the New Testament.

The government of the AG is an unusual mixture of presbyterian and congregational systems. Local churches are independent in the conduct of local affairs. District officers have a pastoral ministry to all the churches and are responsible for the promotion of home missions. Work is divided into sixty-seven districts in the United States and Puerto Rico, including eleven foreign-language districts, each with a district presbytery that examines and recommends credentialing of ministers. The General Council consists of all ordained ministers and lay representatives from local churches. The biennial General Council (business meeting) elects general officers, sets doctrinal standards, and provides for church expansion and development. The General Superintendent and other general church officers serve at the national AG headquarters in Springfield, Missouri, where are also located the denomination's flagship education institutions Evangel University and the Assemblies of God Graduate School of Theology.

The AG operates several colleges and universities in the United States including North Central University in Minnesota, Southwest Assemblies of God University in Texas, and Vanguard University (formerly Southern California College) in California. The denomination licenses and ordains women to the gospel ministry and permits women to pastor churches. However, there are actually very few women lead pastors in the denomination in the United States.

For more information: www.ag.org

Headquarters: 1445 Boonville Avenue, Springfield, MO 65802

ASSEMBLIES OF THE LORD JESUS CHRIST

Founded: 1952
Membership: statistics unavailable; 420 churches (2015)

Three Oneness Pentecostal groups, known as the Assemblies of the Church of Jesus Christ, Jesus Only Apostolic Church of God, and the Church of the Lord Jesus Christ, formulated a merger in 1952, adopting the name Assemblies of the Lord Jesus Christ (ALJC). The ALJC promotes many basic Pentecostal doctrines, including the infallibility and direct divine inspiration of scripture, the fall of humankind, salvation by grace, a premillennial return of Christ, water baptism by immersion and baptism in the Holy Spirit, the Lord's Supper, the service of foot-washing, divine healing, and holiness in life.

The church teaches that the "one True God manifested Himself in the Old Testament in diverse ways, in the Son while he walked among men, as the Holy Ghost after the ascension." Baptism is in the name of Jesus only. Members are forbidden to attend dances or theatrical events, even in public schools; thus private Bible schools are preferred. Another distinctive teaching of the church is that Christians are to obey the government in all matters except for the bearing of arms. Members are thus conscientious objectors.

The Assemblies of the Lord Jesus Christ has churches in thirty-five states, with particular strength in the Midwest and the South. It maintains offices in Memphis, Tennessee. Administration includes a general superintendent and three assistant superintendents. The church maintains Parkersburg Bible College in West Virginia and the Memphis School of Ministries in Tennessee; it supports missions in eight countries outside the United States; and it carries out prison ministry, ministry to Native Americans, and church building programs throughout the United States.

Unlike some Pentecostal denominations, the ALJC does not ordain women or permit them to serve as elders or pastors.

For more information: www.aljc.org

Headquarters: 875 North White Station Road, Memphis, TN 38122

BIBLE WAY CHURCH OF OUR LORD JESUS CHRIST

Founded: 1957
Membership: est. 300,000 in 350 churches worldwide (1995)

The Bible Way Church was an organization of primarily African American Oneness Pentecostal churches formed in 1957 when Apostle Smallwood Edmond Williams led some seventy churches out of the Church of Our Lord Jesus Christ of the Apostolic Faith* to form the Bible Way Church, World Wide. The vision of the founder was to promote evangelistic goals. The church's basic beliefs include Christ's resurrection and premillennial second coming, the resurrection and translation of the saints, the priesthood of all believers, and the final judgment of humankind. Baptism is by immersion in the name of Jesus Christ, and baptism of the Holy Spirit is necessary for second birth. Foot-washing is also practiced.

Phenomenal growth was reported by the church in the late twentieth century, but precise numbers are difficult to obtain. In 1997 the denomination divided over the ordination of women. After 1997 two distinct but nearly identical denominations share the same basic name: Bible Way Church of Our Lord Jesus Christ. One prefaces that name with "International" and the other ends it with "World Wide." The International Bible Way Church of Our Lord Jesus Christ ordains women and has women pastors and district elders. The Bible Way Church of Our Lord Jesus Christ World Wide does not.

For more information: www.biblewaychurch.org and www.internationalbibleway.org

Headquarters: 261 Rochester Avenue Brooklyn, NY 11213 and Bible Way Temple, 1110 Holmes Street, Raleigh, NC 27610

CHURCH OF GOD (CLEVELAND, TENNESSEE)

Founded: 1886; 1907
Membership: 1,109,992 in 6,100 churches (2010)

The Church of God (Cleveland, Tennessee) claims the distinction of being the oldest Pentecostal body. It traces its founding to 1886 in Monroe County, Tennessee, when the Christian Union* was organized by Richard Spurling (1810–91), a Baptist,* and his son, R. G. Spurling (1857–1935). The Spurlings had been led to the Bible to stem the tide of the church's "spiritual indifference, formality, and accommodation to modern culture." In 1892 a second church was formed in Cherokee County, North Carolina, under the leadership of William F. Bryant (1863–1949); four years later, this group experienced speaking in tongues for the first time. R. G. Spurling met with the North Carolina group and others, and two more congregations were added over the next few years. The small organization was renamed the Holiness Church in 1902.

In 1903, Ambrose J. Tomlinson (1865–1943) of the American Bible Society joined the Holiness Church. In January of 1907 the name was changed once more, to Church of God, and headquarters were moved to Cleveland, Tennessee. Tomlinson was elected general overseer in 1909, and the church began publishing *The Church of God Evangel* the following year. The Church of God embraced Pentecostal practices and grew rapidly across the South and Midwest.

A crisis occurred in 1923 that raised concerns over the personal role of Tomlinson and, more important, the nature of the church's government and the leader's authority. The majority, those with whom the Church of God (Cleveland, Tennessee) is continuous, rejected Tomlinson's leadership and selected F. J. Lee as overseer. Tomlinson was then instrumental in the founding of a rival denomination known as the Church of God of Prophecy.

The church's major doctrines blend many Protestant and Holiness themes with those that are specifically Pentecostal: personal conversion (being "born again"), justification by faith, entire sanctification, baptism of the Holy Spirit signaled by speaking in tongues, fruitfulness in Christian living, and a strong interest in the premillennial return of Christ. The Church of God professes reliance on the Bible "as a whole rightly divided rather than upon any written creed." It practices divine healing; condemns the use of alcohol and tobacco; opposes membership in secret societies; and accepts baptism by immersion, the Lord's Supper, and foot-washing as ordinances. The Church of God is trinitarian and evangelical.

The Church of God elects its officers at a biennial General Assembly. The administration of the church includes a general overseer, three assistant overseers, a secretary general, and an eighteen-member International Executive Council, which is responsible for the day-to-day operations of the church. Administrative divisions include education, world evangelism, church ministries, care ministries, and support services. Pathway Press is the publishing arm of the church, producing resources for Christian education and books for ministers and laypeople. The Church of God operates Lee University and the Church of God School of Theology in Cleveland, Tennessee; a school of ministry; and a preparatory school. Its foreign missions enterprise is extensive, serving in 168 nations, with an international membership of over seven million.

For more information: www.churchofgod.org

Headquarters: 2490 Keith Street, Cleveland, TN 37320

CHURCH OF GOD IN CHRIST

Founded: 1897
Membership: est. 1,109,992 in 6,100 churches (2010)

Generally acknowledged to be the largest African American Pentecostal body in the United States, the Church of God in Christ (COGIC) was founded after ministers Charles H. Mason (1866–1961) and Charles P. Jones (1865–1949), were expelled by Baptist groups in Arkansas for what was considered an overemphasis on holiness. Together they founded the Church of Christ (Holiness) USA in 1895. This church stressed the doctrine of entire sanctification. Mason also organized a congregation in Lexington, Mississippi, in 1897, to which he gave the name Church of God in Christ. In 1907 Mason went to Azusa Street in Los Angeles, California, to observe the Pentecostal revival taking place there. While in attendance, he had his first experience of speaking in tongues.

Subsequently, Mason raised the issue of Pentecostal experience in a gathering of leaders of the Church of Christ (Holiness) USA. Charles P. Jones and others did not share Mason's enthusiasm for the Pentecostal movement and withdrew fellowship from him. Mason then called for a meeting in Memphis, Tennessee, of ministers who endorsed Pentecostal doctrine. With this group, he organized a general assembly of the Church of God in Christ, of which he was named general overseer and chief apostle. Mason remained head of the church until his death in 1961.

COGIC is trinitarian and stresses repentance, regeneration, justification, sanctification, speaking in tongues, and the gift of healing as evidence of the baptism of the Spirit. The sanctifying power of the Holy Spirit is considered a prerequisite to living a holy life, separate from the sin of the present world. Ordinances include baptism by immersion, the Lord's Supper, and foot-washing.

The Church of God in Christ is governed by executive, legislative, and judicial bodies. The executive branch is composed of the General Board, which is chaired by the Presiding Bishop. Executive officers are chosen at a general assembly that meets every four years. Clergy consist of bishops, district superintendents, pastors, evangelists, and evangelist missionaries. The denomination has its headquarters in Memphis, Tennessee, which is also the location of the publishing house and All Saints Bible College. Atlanta, Georgia, is the local of the church's Charles H. Mason Theological Seminary, which is a founding member of the Interdenominational Theological Center. The church has established ministries in over fifty countries and every state in the United States.

COGIC does not ordain women as pastors of congregations, but many congregations have an office called *Church Mother* in which a woman of the congregation leads in its spiritual life in an advisory role.

For more information: www.cogic.org

Headquarters: 930 Mason Street, Memphis, TN 38126

CHURCH OF GOD, MOUNTAIN ASSEMBLY

Founded: 1906
Membership: est. 9,000 in 103 congregations (2016)

The Church of God, Mountain Assembly (CGMA) began when a Kentucky Baptist group expelled certain ministers and members for believing in the possibility of apostasy (losing one's salvation) and for teaching entire sanctification as a second definite work of grace in a believer's life. Later the founders of the CGMA embraced the experience of Spirit baptism or infilling of the Holy Spirit together with speaking in tongues. The CGMA is a trinitarian Pentecostal denomination in the holiness tradition that believes in the premillennial return of Jesus Christ and divine healing through prayer. The denomination has a large campground near its headquarters in Jellico, Tennessee.

For more information: www.cgmahdq.org

Headquarters: 256 North Florence Avenue, Jellico, TN 37762

CHURCH OF GOD OF PROPHECY

Founded: 1923
Membership: 98,407 adherents in 1,743 churches (2010)

Church of God of Prophecy is one of the denominations that grew out of the work of Pentecostal leader A. J. Tomlinson (1865–1943) who left the Church of God (Cleveland, Tennessee) to found this denomination. At his death, his son M. A. Tomlinson was named General Overseer, a position he held until 1990.

From its beginnings, the church has based its beliefs on "the whole Bible, rightly divided" and has accepted the Bible as God's Holy Word, inspired, inerrant, and infallible. The church affirms that there is one God, eternally existing in three persons. It believes in the deity, virgin birth, sinlessness, miracles, atoning death, bodily resurrection, ascension to the Father, and second coming of Christ. The church professes that salvation results from grace alone through faith in Christ, that regeneration by the Holy Spirit is essential for the

– 227 –

salvation of sinners, and that sanctification by the blood of Christ makes personal holiness possible. The church stresses the ultimate unity of believers, based on John 17, and the sanctity of marriage and family. Other official teachings include baptism by the Spirit with the speaking of tongues as evidence; divine healing; the premillennial second coming of Christ; baptism of believers by immersion; abstinence from tobacco, alcohol, and narcotics; and holiness in lifestyle. In addition to the Lord's Supper, the church practices foot-washing.

The church is racially integrated on all levels, and women play a prominent role in church affairs, including serving in pastoral roles. The General Oversight Group consists of at least two bishops who, along with the General Overseer, are responsible for setting the vision for the entire church body. Doctrinal and business concerns of the church are addressed at the biennial General Assembly.

For much of its history the Church of God of Prophecy was perceived, rightly or wrongly, as extremely sectarian. Even other Pentecostals thought many ministers and lay-people of the Church of God of Prophecy regarded themselves, their denomination, as the only true church. Recent leaders of the denomination have worked to overcome that impression. Talks between the Church of God (Cleveland, Tennessee) and the Church of God of Prophecy have contributed to a greater mutual understanding and acceptance if not organizational reunion.

For more information: www.cogop.org

Headquarters: 2710 Keith Street Northwest, Cleveland, TN 37320

CHURCH OF OUR LORD JESUS CHRIST OF THE APOSTOLIC FAITH, INC.

Founded: 1919
Membership: est. 30,000 in 450 churches (2010)

This denomination, The Church of Our Lord Jesus Christ (as it is generally known), was organized in 1919 at Columbus, Ohio, by Robert C. Lawson as "a continuation of the great revival begun at Jerusalem on the day of Pentecost." Lawson moved to New York City later that year, where he founded Refuge Temple, which he pastored until his death in 1961. He also led the wider organization as Chief Apostle until his death. He was succeeded as pastor of the church (now Greater Refuge Temple) by William L. Bonner, who later also became Chief Apostle of the Church of Our Lord Jesus Christ of the Apostolic Faith, Inc.

Church doctrine is held to be "that of the apostles and the prophets," with Christ as the cornerstone. The basic emphases are Christ's resurrection and premillennial second coming, the resurrection and translation of the saints, the priesthood of all believers, and the final judgment of humankind. The church is non-trinitarian, maintaining belief "in the oneness of God, who was the Father in creation, the Son in redemption, and today, He is the Holy Ghost in The Church." Baptism is by immersion in the name of the Lord Jesus

Christ, and baptism of the Holy Spirit accompanied by speaking in tongues is necessary for complete second birth. Foot-washing is practiced, but not as an ordinance.

The Church of Our Lord Jesus Christ has congregations in thirty-two states; the British West Indies; Africa; the Philippines; Haiti; the Dominican Republic; and London, England. It operates a Bible college in New York City, where general offices are maintained, and carries out various ministries of caring in the communities in which it serves. A national convocation meets every year. National officers include a Chief Apostle, a Presiding Apostle, a board of apostles, a board of bishops, and a board of presbyters. Unlike some other Pentecostal groups, this one does not ordain women and even requires women to wear some kind of head covering in worship. It is a strict "holiness" denomination that emphasizes separation from all "worldliness."

For more information: www.cooljc.org

Headquarters: 943 Jefferson Avenue, Buffalo, NY 14204

CHURCH OF THE LIVING GOD CWFF
(CHRISTIAN WORKERS FOR FELLOWSHIP)

Founded: 1889
Membership: est. 42,000 in 170 temples (2006)

This denomination claims to be the first black church in the United States that was not begun by white missionaries. The Church of the Living God CWFF grew out of an organization formed in 1889 at Wrightsville, Arkansas, by William Christian (1856–1928), a former slave. At a time when many white Christians treated blacks as less than human, Christian began a group that maintained that many of the prominent people of the Bible, including Jesus and David, were black. Christian held the office of "Chief" in the new church, and was succeeded in the office by his wife and, eventually, by their son.

Christian held to trinitarian doctrine and accepted Pentecostal practices, such as speaking in tongues, without requiring that members speak in tongues. He insisted that inspired speaking must be in recognizable languages. The Church of the Living God CWFF observes three sacraments: water baptism, washing of feet, and the Lord's Supper celebrated with water and unleavened bread.

Christian also was fascinated by Freemasonry, and he developed a church structure that resembled a fraternal organization. He insisted that his "organism" be known as "operative Masonry" and characterized the three ordinances as the "first three corporal degrees." A chief bishop is the presiding officer of the organization. Members tithe their incomes to support their churches, which they call temples. The church's leaders are currently in the process of removing the Masonic aspects of the denomination.

The Church of the Living God CWFF has both male and female pastors. It publishes a quarterly newsletter entitled The Gospel Truth. Ministers are trained through the W. E.

Crumes Ministerial Institute that meets in conjunction with the denomination's conventions. Its curriculum is informed by one provided by Moody Bible Institute in Chicago. Headquarters: 430 Forest Avenue, Cincinnati, OH 45229

CONGREGATIONAL HOLINESS CHURCH

Founded: 1921
Membership: est. 29,000 in 275 churches (2013)

The Congregational Holiness Church (CHC) traces its roots to the Wesleyan Holiness revival and the Pentecostal movement of the early twentieth century. The church affirms basic evangelical, Wesleyan, and Pentecostal doctrines including salvation by grace and faith, sanctification as a second definite work of grace following conversion, the baptism of the Holy Spirit with speaking in tongues, divine healing, the imminent rapture of the church, and the premillennial second coming of Christ. The ordinances are baptism by immersion, the Lord's Supper, and foot-washing. The CHC is a trinitarian Pentecostal denomination.

The CHC emerged out of the International Pentecostal Holiness Church in 1921. The disagreements were over use of modern medicine (the founders affirmed it while many Pentecostals then avoided it) and church government. The CHC is, as its name implies, congregational, which means congregations own their own property and call their own pastors.

CHC pastors are elected by a majority vote of the congregations to which they are called. Both women and men may be ordained. In the early days of the denomination, there were no full-time elected leaders. This arrangement continued until 1935. Today a full-time elected General Superintendent, who is given the honorary and lifetime title of bishop, along with a full-time World Mission director and Mission USA administrator serve the church. A General Executive Board consisting of the General Superintendent, First Assistant Superintendent, Second Superintendent, Secretary, and Treasurer direct the monthly operations of the denomination. The local churches are now grouped into geographical districts concentrated in the southeast region of the United States as well as a Hispanic Conference that includes Hispanic congregations nationwide. Each district has a presbytery of leading ministers, which licenses and ordains ministers. Between Quadrennial General Conferences, the church is governed by a General Committee that consists of the General Executive Board, all national department heads, and district presbytery members. The General Conference is the highest ruling body of the church. *The Gospel Messenger* is the official monthly publication of the church. The denomination conducts missions in nineteen countries, primarily in Latin America. Worldwide there are about seven thousand congregations. The International Headquarters is in Griffin, Georgia.

The CHC affirms that marriage is only between one man and one woman. It also considers all forms of gambling including playing lotteries wrong. It rejects abortion except to save the life of the mother and affirms the importance of racial reconciliation.

For more information: www.chchurch.com

Headquarters: 3888 Fayetville Highway, Griffin, GA 30223

ELIM FELLOWSHIP

Founded: 1947 with roots to 1933
Membership: est. 20,000 in 103 churches (2012)

This body is an outgrowth of the missionary-oriented Elim Ministerial Fellowship, formed in 1933, and the work of graduates of the Elim Bible Institute in Lima, New York, founded in 1924 by Ivan and Minnie Spencer. The group was incorporated in 1947 as the Elim Missionary Assemblies; the present name was adopted in 1972.

Members of the Elim Fellowship hold to Pentecostal tenets of belief, beginning with affirmation of the Bible as the inspired and infallible word of God. The fellowship espouses the trinitarian understanding of the Godhead, the atoning death and resurrection of Jesus Christ, salvation, sanctification, water baptism, the celebration of Communion among believers, the baptism of the Holy Spirit as evidenced in charismatic gifts and ministries, divine healing, and resurrection of the saved and unsaved for eternal reward or punishment. One tenet that sets this group apart from other classical Pentecostal bodies is its omission from its statement of faith of the belief that speaking in tongues is the "initial, physical evidence" of Holy Spirit baptism.

The organizational pattern of Elim Fellowship is congregational, with individual churches autonomous in decision-making. An annual assembly meets in Lima, where the General Chairman maintains offices. Over eight hundred ministers have credentials through Elim Fellowship and over 150 missionaries affiliated with the fellowship are at work in Africa, Asia, Europe, and South America.

Elim Fellowship affirms that marriage is between one man and one woman and rejects homosexual behavior as contrary to God's will. The Fellowship's website speaks of "women ministers" and the importance of women's ministry.

For more information: www.elimfellowship.org

Headquarters: Elim Bible Institute, 7245 College Street, Lima, NY 14485

FELLOWSHIP OF CHRISTIAN ASSEMBLIES

Founded: 2000 with roots to the 1920s
Membership: 19,765 in 78 churches (2016)

The Fellowship of Christian Assemblies (FCA) is a fellowship of independent Pentecostal churches that traces its roots to Pentecostal revivals in Scandinavia and among

Scandinavian immigrants to the United States in the early twentieth century. It is an "association of autonomous local churches" clustered mostly in the upper Midwest. These early Scandinavian Pentecostals in the United States kept largely to themselves among other Pentecostals and were fiercely independent, rejecting denominationalism. However, in 1922 they loosely organized themselves in Saint Paul, Minnesota, under the name Independent Assemblies of God. This denomination should not be confused, however, with others that use the *Assemblies of God* moniker or with the International Fellowship of Christian Assemblies formerly known as the Christian Church of North America, an Italian-based Pentecostal denomination headquartered in Pennsylvania. This Independent Assemblies of God changed its name to the Fellowship of Christian Assemblies in 1973 but only incorporated as a denomination in 2000.

Like many other smaller Pentecostal bodies, the FCA has a most influential church—Duluth Gospel Tabernacle in Minnesota founded in 1916. That early Scandinavian Pentecostal congregation has been a focal point for the FCA throughout its history. Unlike most classical Pentecostal groups, and perhaps because of its different history (not influenced by the Azusa Street Revival of 1906), the FCA does not officially affirm the typical Pentecostal doctrine that Holy Spirit baptism, subsequent to conversion, must be accompanied by the initial, physical evidence of speaking in tongues. It does, however, affirm the subsequence of Holy Spirit baptism and the availability to Christians filled with the Holy Spirit all of the gifts of the Holy Spirit mentioned in the New Testament including the supernatural ones. It does consider speaking in tongues one of those gifts.

Local church autonomy is especially important to the FCA. On the other hand, it also considers responsibility to other FCA churches important. The FCA does permit ordination of women to the pastoral ministry and some women have served as pastors within the denomination. The denomination does not have an official position regarding openly gay or lesbian people in ministry but does affirm that marriage is only between one man and one woman.

For more information: www.fcaministers.com

Headquarters: 4909 East Buckeye Road, Madison, WI 53716

FIRE BAPTIZED HOLINESS CHURCH OF GOD

Founded: 1898
Membership: statistics unavailable, est. 198 churches (2008)

The Fire Baptized Holiness Church of God was founded by William Edward Fuller Sr. It is closely related to the International Pentecostal Holiness Church and shares a common history in southern African American Pentecostalism. Coming out of the Methodist Holiness tradition, it is an episcopal church, but in addition to baptism and Holy Communion, its members practice foot-washing. The church maintains that there is no distinction between male and female in Christ; therefore it was one of the early churches to ordain women as preachers and pastors. The church holds to basic evangelical, holiness, and Pentecostal teachings, but it also provides a list of things that it opposes. This includes Unitarianism, Mormonism, Islam, Psychics, Spiritualists, and the Seventh-Day Adventists' doctrines.

For more information: www.fbhchurch.org

Headquarters: 901 Bishop William Edward Fuller, Sr. Highway, Greenville, SC 29611

FULL GOSPEL FELLOWSHIP OF CHURCHES AND MINISTERS, INTERNATIONAL

Founded: 1962
Membership: est. 432,632 (2012) in 684 churches (2016)

This fellowship of churches was founded in Dallas, Texas, at a meeting called by Pentecostal evangelist Gordon Lindsay to support, encourage, and promote apostolic, Pentecostal ministry. As Lindsay and others envisioned it, the organization would give expression to the essential unity of those who believe in Christ and in the active work of the Holy Spirit. It was not to be a denomination as such but a fellowship of ministries. The organization also made it easier for independent churches to have tax-exempt status with the Internal Revenue Service. Gordon Lindsay was one of the most influential healing revivalists of the mid-twentieth century. He was born and raised in Zion, Illinois, when it was a town and church led by healing evangelist John Alexander Dowie. Lindsay founded a school and magazine called Voice of Healing in 1948. The school later changed its name to Christ for the Nations and still exists in Dallas, Texas.

Although individual churches or groups of churches affiliated with the Full Gospel Fellowship have doctrinal and ecclesial autonomy, certain core beliefs form the basis for fellowship. Among the suggested tenets of faith are: belief in the Bible as the inspired word of God, in the trinitarian understanding of the Godhead, in the atoning death and resurrection of Jesus Christ, in the need for personal salvation and sanctification, in the return and reign of Jesus Christ, and in heaven and hell. The fellowship strongly advocates infilling of the Holy Spirit as evidenced by the gift of speaking in tongues.

Regional conventions and an annual international convention are held; and various cooperative ministries, including curriculum development, are facilitated by the organization.

For more information: www.thefellowshipnetwork.net

Headquarters: 1000 North Belt Line, Suite 201, Irving, TX 75061

INDEPENDENT ASSEMBLIES OF GOD, INTERNATIONAL

Founded: 1922
Membership: statistics not available

This group is to be distinguished from the Assemblies of God, but it shares a common heritage in the early Pentecostal movement. In 1918, some Scandinavian Pentecostals, who were particularly concerned to preserve the principles of congregationalism, formed the Scandinavian Assemblies of God in the United States, Canada, and Foreign Lands. This group operated essentially as a fellowship of like-minded churches until 1935, when they merged with the Independent Pentecostal Churches to form the Independent Assemblies of God, International. This group shares common roots with the earlier mentioned and described Fellowship of Christian Assemblies, but they have never been organizationally one.

Doctrinally, the church's statement of faith includes the common tenets of Pentecostalism, such as belief in the Bible as the inspired and infallible word of God, in the Trinity, in the reality of Satan, and in the need for already converted Christian believers to experience the infilling of the Holy Spirit as evidenced through speaking in tongues. Ordinances include baptism by immersion and the Lord's Supper. Healing through prayer is also emphasized.

The churches in this denomination are autonomous but work together on common ministries. The leadership of the Assemblies of God International includes a General Overseer, an Assistant General Overseer, and an international mission director. The headquarters are in California, and the organization supports missionaries and national pastors in Africa, Central America, South America, Mexico, India, and the Philippines.

For more information: www.iaogi.org

Headquarters: PO Box 2130, Laguna Hills, CA 92645-2130

INTERNATIONAL CHURCH OF THE FOURSQUARE GOSPEL

Founded: 1927
Membership: 255,136 in 1,593 congregations (2016)

Founded by Pentecostal evangelist Aimee Semple McPherson (1890–1944), this church, International Church of the Foursquare Gospel (ICFG), is a tribute to the organizing genius and striking methods of its founder. Born in Ontario in 1890, McPherson was converted under the preaching of her first husband, Robert Semple, an evangelist. Semple died while they were serving as missionaries in China, and Aimee Semple returned to the United States in 1911, where she conducted evangelistic crusades throughout North America. In 1918, after her remarriage, Aimee Semple McPherson and her children, Roberta and Rolf, settled in Los Angeles. With the help of her followers, she built Angelus Temple, which was dedicated on January 1, 1923. She also founded the

Echo Park Evangelistic Association, the Lighthouse of International Foursquare Evangelism (L.I.F.E.) Bible College, and the International Church of the Foursquare Gospel.

With her speaking ability and faith in prayer for the sick, McPherson attracted thousands to her meetings. Her critics felt that the meetings were too much like a spectacle, but others appreciated her presentation. Her followers showed great interest in the sick and the poor; "more than a million and a half" are said to have been fed by Angelus Temple during the Great Depression. McPherson was president of the church during her lifetime and, together with a board of directors, oversaw the denomination's expansion. Upon her death in 1944, her son, Rolf Kennedy McPherson, became president and led the church until 1988.

The "four-fold gospel" refers to four central Pentecostal teachings that pre-date McPherson but that she popularized nationally. They are (1) salvation, (2) baptism by the Spirit, (3) divine physical healing, and (4) the second coming of Jesus Christ. The broader teaching of the church is set forth in a *Declaration of Faith* written by McPherson. It also stresses the return of Christ prior to his reign on earth, personal holiness, and the trinitarian conception of God. The Bible is affirmed as true. Baptism with the Holy Spirit, with the initial evidence of speaking in tongues, is subsequent to conversion, and the power to heal is given in answer to believing prayer. The ordinances of baptism and the Lord's Supper are observed in the church.

The official business of the church is conducted by a board of directors, a missionary cabinet, and an executive council made up of corporate officers. The highest seat of authority is the annual Foursquare Convention, which alone has the power to make or amend the bylaws of the church and that elects the president of the church to a four-year term. District supervisors are appointed for ten districts in the United States and are ratified by pastors of the respective districts every four years. Pastors are appointed by the board of directors of the denomination and are assisted by a local church council. Congregations are subordinated units of the denomination and contribute monthly to home and foreign missionary work. The official publication of the church is the *Foursquare World ADVANCE* magazine, published bimonthly.

While membership is highest on the West Coast, there are Foursquare churches in all fifty states. Overseas, the Foursquare Gospel is preached in 107 countries, with almost one million adherents. In addition to L.I.F.E. Bible College in Los Angeles, and L.I.F.E. Bible College East in Christiansburg, Virginia, the church supports numerous Bible colleges and institutes around the world. There is also an extensive youth camping program. The church sponsors radio station KFSG-FM in Los Angeles.

The ICFG ordains women and has always had women ministers. Its founder was a woman. The ICFG does not marry same-sex couples and does not credential gay or lesbian individuals to the ministry.

For more information: www.foursquare.org

Headquarters: 1910 West Sunset Boulevard, PO Box 26902, Los Angeles, CA 90026

INTERNATIONAL FELLOWSHIP
OF CHRISTIAN ASSEMBLIES

Founded: 1948
Membership: 7,200 in 96 churches (1999)

This denomination, International Fellowship of Christian Assemblies (IFCA), has had several names. From 1963 to 2008 it was known as the Christian Church of North America, but it was originally known as the Italian Christian Church. This body originated in a gathering of Italian Pentecostal ministers held in 1927 at Niagara Falls, New York. The leader was Luigi Francescon (1866–1964) who had left the Roman Catholic Church in 1892, joining the First Italian Presbyterian Church (Waldensian) in Chicago. He embraced believer's baptism in 1903 and established the first Italian American Pentecostal congregation in 1907 in Chicago. When the church was incorporated in 1948 at Pittsburgh, it took the name "Missionary Society of the Christian Church of North America." The IFCA holds to basic Pentecostal beliefs, emphasizing the infallibility of scripture, the Trinity, and salvation through faith in Jesus Christ. Although affirming the experiences of salvation and Spirit baptism, the body does not teach the doctrine of entire sanctification. Headquarters are in Transfer, Pennsylvania. The IFCA should not be confused with the similarly named Fellowship of Christian Assemblies. Attempts to gain information about current membership statistics and number of churches have been unsuccessful; 1999 is the most recent date for reliable data.

For more information: www.ifcaministry.org
Headquarters: 1294 Rutledge Road, Transfer, PA 16154-9005

INTERNATIONAL PENTECOSTAL HOLINESS CHURCH

Founded: 1911
Membership: 330,054 in 2,024 churches (2012)

The International Pentecostal Holiness Church (IPHC) traces its origins to an organization founded in 1898 at Anderson, South Carolina, by a number of Holiness associations. At that time the group was called the Fire-Baptized Holiness Church. In the same year, in Goldsboro, North Carolina, another group was organized as the Pentecostal Holiness Church. In 1907, G. B. Cashwell (1826–1916), a participant in the Azusa Street revival, led a Pentecostal revival in North Carolina and brought these two groups into Pentecostalism. The two bodies united in 1911 as the Pentecostal Holiness Church; and a third body, the Tabernacle Pentecost Church, joined them in 1915. The present name was adopted in 1975.

The theological standards and polity of Methodism prevail in the International Pentecostal Holiness Church, with certain modifications. The denomination accepts the premillennial teaching of the second coming, holding that Christ's return will precede his thousand-year reign on earth, and believes that provision was made in the atonement for healing of the human body. Divine healing is practiced, but not to the exclusion of medicine. Three distinctive spiritual experiences are taught: justification by faith; sanctification; and Spirit baptism, attested to by speaking in other tongues. Sanctification is an instantaneous work of the Holy Spirit by which a converted and Spirit-filled Christian can become entirely sanctified (made holy). Services are often characterized by "joyous demonstrations." Two ordinances are observed: water baptism and Holy Communion.

The church's general executive board is elected by a quadrennial conference. There is a General Superintendent and directors of World Missions, Evangelism, Church Education, Stewardship, and representatives from the different regions. The IPHC does have leaders called bishops who together form a governing council and who exercise some authority over local congregations. As in traditional Methodism this is called "connectionalism" with local congregations being accountable to each other and to bishops while having some autonomy as well. Twenty-eight conferences or regional judicatories cover the United States. IPHC sponsors Emmanuel College in Georgia and Southwestern Christian University in Oklahoma, both four-year accredited colleges. The church operates a children's home at Falcon, North Carolina; a children's convalescent center at Bethany, Oklahoma; and a home for the aged. Foreign mission work takes place in one hundred countries with more than 3.75 million members worldwide.

The IPHC ordains women and has women pastors of local congregations. It opposes homosexuality (as a behavior or lifestyle) and does not affirm same-sex marriage or ordination to the ministry of openly gay or practicing gay persons.

For more information: www.iphc.org

Headquarters: Global Ministries Center, 7300 Northwest Thirty-Ninth Expressway, Bethany, OK 73008

OPEN BIBLE CHURCHES, INC.

Founded: 1935
Membership: est. 22,000 in 260 churches (2016)

This association of churches (Open Bible) was originally composed of two revival movements rooted distantly in the Azusa Street Revival of 1906 but also each breaking away from pre-existing Pentecostal denominations. Bible Standard, Inc., was founded in Eugene, Oregon, by Fred Hornshuh in 1919. Hornschuh had been associated with Florence Crawford's Portland-based Apostolic Faith Mission. The other group, with which Bible Standard, Inc. merged, was Open Bible Evangelistic Association, founded in

Des Moines, Iowa, by John R. Richey in 1932. Richey had been an associate of Aimee Semple McPherson's Foursquare Gospel movement. The Pacific Coast group, with activities centered in Oregon, spread through Washington, California, and into the Rocky Mountain areas of the West; the Iowa group expanded into Illinois, Missouri, Ohio, Florida, and Pennsylvania. Similar in doctrine and government, the two groups joined on July 26, 1935, taking the combined name Open Bible Standard Churches, Inc., with headquarters in Des Moines.

The teachings of the Open Bible churches are "fundamental in doctrine, evangelical in spirit, missionary in vision, and Pentecostal in testimony." They emphasize the infallibility of the word of God, the blood atonement of Christ, baptism by immersion, personal holiness, baptism or infilling of the Holy Spirit, divine healing, and the return of Jesus Christ. Open Bible once affirmed speaking in tongues as "the initial, physical evidence" of Holy Spirit baptism or infilling, but changed its statement of faith to affirm speaking in tongues without making it the necessary sign of that experience. Open Bible churches are grouped into five geographical regions, subdivided into several districts. Individual churches are congregationally governed, locally owned, and affiliated by charter with the national organization. The highest governing body is the General Convention, which meets biennially.

Internationally, the association ministers in thirty-eight countries and sponsors ten Bible institutes serving some fourteen hundred students. Mission emphasis is on the training of nationals for ministry. Institute of Theology by Extension (INSTE), a non-traditional educational program, operates in about thirty countries with over twelve thousand students, both in Open Bible and other denominational churches. The program is translated in or being translated into ten languages. In the United States, Open Bible Churches supports New Hope Christian College in Oregon, Master's Commission discipleship and leadership development groups in Iowa and Washington, and many INSTE groups serving over fourteen hundred students studying in Spanish or English.

Open Bible has always licensed and ordained women to the gospel ministry and had women evangelists, missionaries and pastors. It does not affirm same-sex marriage or the ministry of openly gay or lesbian persons.

For more information: www.openbible.org
Headquarters: 2020 Bell Avenue, Des Moines, IA 50315

PENTECOSTAL ASSEMBLIES OF THE WORLD, INC.

Founded: 1907
Membership: est. 1,800,000 members in 2,550 churches (2012)

Tracing its origin to the Azusa Street revival in 1906, this body, Pentecostal Assemblies of the World, Inc. (PAW), is the oldest "Oneness" Pentecostal body, meaning that it denies the orthodox doctrine of the Trinity, affirming that God is one person, not three, and baptizes in the name of Jesus only. The goal of the Pentecostal Assemblies of the World, Inc., is to spread the message that Jesus Christ is Lord to all people. From its beginning, the group, including its leadership, has been interracial; however, the church is predominantly African American today. Two of its most influential leaders were G. T. Haywood, who directed the church during a period of consolidation from 1924 until his death in 1931, and Samuel Grimes, a former missionary, who led the church through a period of expansion from 1937 until his death in 1967.

Basic Pentecostal and Holiness doctrine and practice are followed, except for rejection of the trinitarian understanding of God. The church stresses holiness of life, holding that believers must be wholly sanctified to fully participate in salvation. Strict codes governing dress and leisure pursuits are maintained. Water baptism and the Lord's Supper are practiced, with wine used in the latter. Only the King James Version of the Bible is accepted as the true word of God.

The PAW hosts two major conferences annually, to which its constituents come from around the globe to worship God and to fellowship with one another. The church is headed by a Presiding Bishop who guides its members spiritually. There is also an executive board, including an Assistant Presiding Bishop, a General Secretary, a General Treasurer, and lay directors. The organization's administrator and staff handle its business affairs from general offices in Indianapolis, Indiana. This body is heavily concentrated in urban areas, such as Chicago, Detroit, and Indianapolis, but there are ministers serving in all fifty states.

The Aenon Bible College, located in Indianapolis, Indiana, serves to train Pentecostal Assemblies ministers and lay members. The college has affiliate institutes all over the United States and two foreign affiliates in Liberia: the Samuel Grimes Bible Institute and the Haywood Mission.

The PAW affirms women in ministry and rejects homosexual behavior as sinful.

For more information: www.pawinc.org

Headquarters: 3939 Meadows Drive, Indianapolis, IN 46205

PENTECOSTAL CHURCH OF GOD

Founded: 1919
Membership: 98,579 members in 1,134 churches (2012)

This body, Pentecostal Church of God (PCG), was organized in Chicago under the name *Pentecostal Assemblies of the USA* in order to better organize early Pentecostalism in the Midwest for evangelism and to preserve congregations from unethical preachers pretending to be Spirit-filled. When the church was reorganized in 1922, the name was changed to *Pentecostal Church of God*. For a number of years *of America* was a part of the name, but this was dropped in 1979. The PCG is trinitarian, evangelical, and Pentecostal in faith and practice. The doctrines of biblical inspiration and inerrancy, salvation by grace through faith, divine healing, baptism in the Holy Spirit (with the evidence of speaking in tongues), and the second coming of Christ are strongly emphasized. Ordinances include water baptism of believers, the Lord's Supper, and foot-washing.

A General Convention of the church meets biennially. Executives of the denomination include a General Bishop, a General Secretary, a Director of World Missions, a Director of home missions and evangelism, and a Director of (American) Indian missions. Headquarters are located in Joplin, Missouri. The church has six regional divisions, each presided over by an Assistant General Superintendent. Most of the divisions have annual conventions. The PCG conducts mission work in about fifty countries in Europe, Asia, Africa, and the Americas. Some five thousand churches have been established outside the United States, and over two thousand five hundred national ministers have been commissioned. The group sponsors twenty-two Bible schools, fifty-seven training centers, and fifty-one day schools across the globe. Messenger College is the PCG's sponsored school and moved from Joplin, Missouri, to Euless, Texas, in 2012. *The Pentecostal Herald* is the denomination's official publication.

For more information: www.pcg.org

Headquarters: 2701 Brown Trail, Bedford, TX 76021

PENTECOSTAL FREE WILL BAPTIST CHURCH, INC.

Founded: 1959
Membership: est. 28,000 in 148 churches (2010)

The Pentecostal Free Will Baptist Church (PFWBC) came into existence through the merging of four Free-Will Baptist conferences in North Carolina in 1959. These various groups traced their origins as Free Will Baptists to the work of Paul Palmer (d. 1750) in the Carolinas during the first half of the eighteenth century. The Pentecostal aspect of the church's doctrine was developed in response to the preaching of G. W. Cashwell (1826–1916), who had participated in the Azusa Street revival of 1906 in Los Angeles, California. Cashwell launched a series of meetings in North Carolina on New Year's Eve, 1906; in response, many Free Will Baptist individuals and churches adopted Pentecostal doctrine and practice.

The church's doctrine is a hybrid of Baptist and Pentecostal beliefs. Central affirmations include the inerrancy of the Bible, regeneration through faith in the shed blood of Christ, sanctification as a second definite work of grace (subsequent to regeneration), Pentecostal baptism of the Holy Spirit as evidenced through speaking in tongues, divine healing, and the premillennial second coming of Christ. Ordinances include baptism of believers only by immersion, the Lord's Supper, and foot-washing.

A general meeting of the PFWBC is held biennially in August; lay and ministerial representatives attend. Church officials include a General Superintendent, a General Secretary, and a General Treasurer. Offices are maintained in Dunn, North Carolina, where Heritage Bible College was established in 1971. Most of the group's churches are in eastern North Carolina; but mission work is carried on in nine foreign countries, and Bible institutes are operated in Mexico, the Philippines, and Venezuela.

For more information: www.pfwb.org

Headquarters: PO Box 1568, Dunn, NC 28355

UNITED HOLY CHURCH OF AMERICA, INC.

Founded: 1886
Membership: 544 churches (2016); number of adherents unknown*

The United Holy Church (UHC) claims to be "the oldest black Pentecostal church in America." The church was first organized in 1886 in Method, North Carolina, as a regional body. An organizing convention was held in Durham, North Carolina, in 1900. Known originally as the Holy Church of North Carolina, it was reorganized in 1918 as the United Holy Church of America, Inc. In the following decades, the church established seven districts covering different regions of the country. The church seeks to establish and maintain holy convocations, assemblies, conventions, conferences, public worship, and missionary and educational efforts. The church's famous logo features a cross in the intersection of three circles in a triangle.

Articles of faith contain statements of belief in the Trinity, the record of the revelation of God in the Bible, redemption through Christ, justification with instantaneous sanctification, baptism of the Holy Spirit, divine healing, and the future reign of Christ over the earth (premillennialism). Baptism by immersion, the Lord's Supper, and foot-washing are observed as ordinances. The UHC believes in speaking in tongues and views Spirit baptism as normative, although it shares the position held by some other Pentecostal groups that speaking in tongues is not required.

The church maintains headquarters in North Carolina, but it is now an international body with congregations in the Caribbean and Africa. The chief officer is the General President who is also the lead bishop of the denomination. Other officials include two general vice presidents, a general recording secretary, a general financial secretary, and a general treasurer. Each district has its own president. A board of bishops supervises the work of the church. The United Holy Church's primary publication is *The Holiness Union*.

For more information: www.uhcainc.org

Headquarters: 5104 Dustan Road, Greensboro, NC 27405

*The editor made several direct contacts with leaders of this denomination without ever receiving the requested current membership statistics.

UNITED PENTECOSTAL CHURCH INTERNATIONAL

Founded: 1945
Membership: 646,304 in 4,358 churches (2012)

The United Pentecostal Church International (UPCI) was founded in 1945 by the union of the Pentecostal Assemblies of Jesus Christ and the Pentecostal Church, Inc. Each of those bodies was itself the result of mergers of other Pentecostal bodies in the 1930s. All the constituent members were "Oneness" ("Jesus only") Pentecostals who withdrew from the Assemblies of God in 1916. The UPCI is, like many other Pentecostal groups, both Pentecostal and Holiness. That is, it affirms the possibility of entire sanctification.

Theologically, the UPCI is non-trinitarian. The Oneness view held by the UPCI asserts that God "revealed Himself in the Old Testament as Jehovah and in the New Testament revealed Himself in His Son, Jesus Christ." Jesus Christ is thus the one true God manifested in flesh and the Holy Ghost is the Spirit of God and the resurrected Christ. Baptism is carried out in Jesus's name only. The church embraces the Pentecostal view that speaking in tongues is the initial sign of receiving the Holy Spirit. Some UPCI ministers and laypeople believe that speaking in tongues is necessary for salvation. For the UPCI, the Bible is the inerrant and infallible word of God. Personal holiness, including modesty in appearance is stressed. For the most part women do not wear jewelry or cut their hair.

UPCI polity is essentially congregational, with autonomous local churches many of which use the word *Apostolic* in their names. The General Conference of the church meets annually to elect officials. A General Superintendent, two assistants, and a secretary-treasurer are members of a general board that also includes district superintendents, executive presbyters, and division heads. Denominational offices are located at Hazelwood, Missouri, as is World Aflame Press, the church's publishing house. The press publishes books, Sunday school materials, and a wide variety of religious literature. *The Pentecostal Herald* is the official organ of the UPCI, and there are various divisional publications. The church also sponsors "Harvest Time," an international radio broadcast.

The UPCI's foreign missions program sponsors work in 170 countries outside the United States and claims an international membership of three million. Within the United States, the church supports seven Bible colleges and Urshan Graduate School of Theology in Hazelwood, Missouri. Other UPCI ministries include children's homes in Tupelo, Mississippi, and Hammond, Louisiana; a chaplaincy program for persons in prison; and a chaplaincy program for the armed services.

The UPCI rejects homosexual behavior as sinful and does not recognize same-sex marriage as true Christian marriage. Nor does it ordain openly gay or lesbian persons to the ministry. The UPCI does ordain women to the ministry and has women pastors, but some key leadership positions in the denomination are reserved for males.

Generally speaking the UPCI is considered by other Pentecostals and evangelical Christians different because of its tendency to view salvation as linked to speaking in tongues and baptism in Jesus's name. Also its doctrine of the Godhead is widely considered heretical (viz., "modalism"). This denomination normally does not share Christian fellowship with trinitarian Pentecostal groups although some of its members participate in the Society of Pentecostal Studies. Throughout the latter decades of the twentieth century and first decades of the twenty-first century a number of UPCI ministers and congregations broke away to become independent Oneness Pentecostal churches. Some of those, while maintaining baptism in Jesus's name, have shed some of the more unorthodox beliefs and strict practices of the UPCI.

For more information: www.upci.org

Headquarters: 8855 Dunn Road, Hazelwood, MO 63402

VINEYARD CHURCHES INTERNATIONAL

Founded: 1983
Membership: 185,883 in 545 churches (2015)

The Vineyard movement began as part of the Calvary Chapel movement in California in the 1970s and grew rapidly in the late twentieth century. Kenn and Joanie Gulliksen served in a Calvary Chapel in Los Angeles, and around 1974 they began to emphasize the supernatural gifts of the Holy Spirit. In 1982, the congregation changed its name to Vineyard to distinguish it from Calvary Chapel because the Vineyard congregation promoted public expressions of speaking in tongues, healing, exorcisms, and prophecy while Calvary Chapel saw such things as private gifts of the Spirit. Another Calvary Chapel minister, the former rock musician John Wimber (1934–97), teamed up with Gulliksen to promote charismatic gifts among the younger generation. Wimber was the major public figure of the Vineyard movement until his death in 1997.

Wimber's "Signs and Wonders" course at Fuller Theological Seminary in Pasadena attracted many younger ministers to the movement despite the controversy it evoked. He called his movement the Third Wave of the modern renewal movement (the first two being Pentecostalism and the charismatic movement) and urged his followers to adopt Power Evangelism, using miracles to attract people to the faith. Christian rock music was also used effectively in evangelical outreach through recordings and radio broadcasts. The church embraces evangelical and charismatic or Pentecostal theology regarding the infallibility of scripture; the fall of the human race; the need for an experience of salvation; and the spiritual gifts of healing, prophecy, and speaking in tongues. However, unlike traditional or classical Pentecostal groups, the Vineyard has never required belief that speaking in tongues stands out as the "initial, physical evidence" of a second definite work of grace after conversion called the baptism of the Holy Spirit. The Vineyard emphasizes informal worship and has pioneered in developing contemporary Christian music and worship styles.

Contrary to the original anti-establishment character of the movement, Wimber had already begun the process of denominationalization before his death in 1997. His death was a serious blow to a movement that was centered on the idea that prayer produces healing. It has also become evident that Wimber's own personality was an important aspect of the church, and the movement has struggled to find its identity without him. However, it continues to grow as it changes; it is a dynamic movement rather than one that looks to a past tradition as authoritative.

For more information: www.vineyardusa.org

Headquarters: PO Box 2089, Stafford, TX 77497

CHRISTIAN AND RESTORATIONIST CHURCHES

With its emphasis on the Bible alone as the supreme basis of faith and practice (*"sola scriptura"*), Protestantism has always sought to remain true to the church of the apostles in the New Testament. Most Protestants have been willing to accept some historical development of the church and its doctrine in the post-biblical period (reciting the Nicene Creed, for example). There have been others, though, who have seen the history of Christianity as the story of a decline from New Testament purity. These Christians have attempted to restore "original" or "primitive" Christianity by purging the church of all non-biblical elements, including creeds and confessions of faith. The restorationist impulse has run throughout the history of Christianity, most notably, during the Reformation, among the Anabaptists.

During the Second Great Awakening of the early nineteenth century, this restorationist impulse grew particularly strong. In politics, the United States had "restored" Greek democracy; and many people thought that Americans could also restore the structure and doctrine of the original church in the new land. By returning to the New Testament alone, without recourse to creeds or rituals, the new Restorationists hoped to end fraternal strife among churches. (Here *Restorationism* and its cognates will be capitalized when referring to this particular movement growing out of the Second Great Awakening. That movement and its related denominations are not the only ones with a "restorationist" impulse, but the label *Restorationist* has been attached to it and them in a special way by scholars of American religious history.)

Thomas Campbell (1763–1854) was a Scottish Presbyterian who left his church in Ireland to come to western Pennsylvania in 1807. Campbell was convinced that the historical creeds and confessions of the church were a source of Christian division rather than union, and he preached that all Christians should share in the Lord's Supper together. When his views led to a censure from the Presbyterians* in 1809, Campbell formed the Christian Association of Washington County, Pennsylvania, and published the *Declaration and Address*, which was to become the Magna Carta of the Restorationist movement. In that document he argued that "schism, or uncharitable divisions" in the church were "anti-Christian, anti-Scriptural, and anti-natural" and "productive of confusion and every evil work." God has spoken clearly, Campbell declared, and laid down the rules for church practices in the New Testament: "We will speak when the scriptures speak, and remain silent when they are silent." With that phrase, Campbell abolished many traditional church practices, including the use of musical instruments in worship. Soon the Campbells adopted believer baptism.

Campbell's son, Alexander (1788–1866), was less scholarly than his father, but more dynamic and consistent in his application of his father's principles. He fought many public battles (by means of debates) against atheism, Mormonism, Unitarianism, creedalism, sectarianism, emotionalism, and even slavery; but he was singularly unsuccessful in bringing about church unity. His non-creedal movement to unify all Christians gave birth to one of the first denominations to be born in the United States. That is, both the movement and the denominations it spawned had and have no European roots.

The other major branch of the nineteenth-century Restorationist movement had its origins in the convictions of James O'Kelly (1757–1826), a Methodist minister; Abner Jones (1772–1841), a Baptist; and Barton Stone (1772–1844), a Presbyterian. When the Second Great Awakening swept through Tennessee and Kentucky in the early 1800s, preaching focused on the need for conversion rather than denominational or doctrinal distinctions. Barton Stone was instrumental in the famous Cane Ridge, Kentucky, revival, which began on August 7, 1801. Somewhere between ten thousand and twenty-five thousand people appeared during the weeks-long revival in which preachers from a variety of churches took part. The revival convinced Stone that salvation has little to do with church affiliation and that "deeds are more important than creeds." The egalitarian promise of the American Revolution was being felt in Cane Ridge and other Western "camp meeting" revivals, but the controversy over them led to a schism in the Presbyterian Church.

The groups led by O'Kelly, Jones, and Stone engaged in a long series of conferences that resulted in agreement on six basic Christian principles: (1) Christ, the only head of the church; (2) the Bible, sufficient rule of faith and practice; (3) Christian character, the measure of membership; (4) a right, individual interpretation of the scripture, as a way of life; (5) "Christian," the name taken as worthy of the followers of Christ; (6) unity, Christians working together to save the world.

By 1832 the "Stoneites" and the "Campbellites" had come together for a meeting in Lexington, Kentucky. Stone used the word *Christian* to designate his group, feeling that all of God's children should be known as such. Alexander Campbell used the phrase "Disciples of Christ." After 1832, some of the Christians and the Disciples of Christ merged; both names are still used. Very soon thereafter, differences arose among the Restorationists, and, over time, distinct fellowships emerged, most of which go by the name "Christian Churches" or "Churches of Christ" or both. They share a common sentiment that they are "Christians only but not the only Christians" even though some in the twentieth century did eventually begin to believe they are the only true Christians.

All the denominations described in this category are rooted in the Restorationist movement that came to be especially associated in people's minds with Campbell and Stone. Therefore, the movement and its offshoot denominations are often called "Campbellite" or "Stone-Campbell." Members prefer to be known simply as "Christians." During the twentieth century especially the Restorationist movement launched by Stone, Campbell and others fell into division. The various denominations, some of which adamantly deny being denominations at all, have little to do with each other although their scholars, historians, and theologians, are in the twenty-first century rediscovering and affirming their common heritage.

What do they all have in common? First, all have roots in the Second Great Awakening and Campbell's and Stone's (and others') desire for a church that would be only Christian and not divided by what they consider extra-biblical doctrines and practices. All have held the ideal of restoring the New Testament church in all its simplicity (restorationism). All eschew creeds and confessional statements that divide Christians from each other. Most celebrate the Lord's Supper as a memorial meal, not a sacrament, every Sunday and believe believer baptism upon confession of faith by immersion is necessary for salvation ("baptism for the remission of sins"). A person who confesses Christ as Savior and Lord is immediately baptized in water. Baptism is regarded not as a sacrament (*baptismal regeneration* is not the correct term for what these Restorationists believe), but it is regarded as an essential step in conversion to Christ. Also, in spite of their beginnings in revival, Restorationists tend not to be emotional in worship or devotion; their idea of conversion is more intellectual—a change of mind more than a change of heart (or with the heart change following the cognitive one). Some critics of the movement have seen this as evidence of influence of the Enlightenment, which placed strong emphasis on reason. Also, and finally, all Restorationist groups adopted an Arminian, as opposed to a Calvinist, view of salvation. They do not believe that God sovereignly selects certain people to be saved and draws them irresistibly to repent and believe. They believe in free will—sometimes in a way that even causes some other Arminian Protestants (e.g., Wesleyans) some degree of concern.

What sets these denominations apart from each other in spite of their common heritage and distinctives? One group eschews use of musical instruments in worship; others use them in worship. One group has cooperated enthusiastically with the ecumenical movement and adopted a more liberal stance toward the Bible and doctrine under the influence of modernity. Others reject modern biblical scholarship and theological revision and tend to think of outsiders as not fully Christian. One group in particular admits to being a denomination including having a headquarters; others do not and strongly emphasize congregational independence.

SUGGESTIONS FOR FURTHER READING

Garrison, W. E., and A. T. DeGroot. *The Disciples of Christ: A History*. Saint Louis, MO: Bethany Press, 1958.

Harrell, David E., Jr., ed. *The Churches of Christ in 20th Century America*. Tuscaloosa, AL: University of Alabama Press, 2000.

Harrell, David E., Jr. *A Quest for Christian America, 1800–1865: A Social History of the Disciples of Christ*. 2 vols. Tuscaloosa, AL.: University of Alabama Press, 2003.

Hughes, Richard T. *Reviving the Ancient Faith: The Story of Churches of Christ in America*. Grand Rapids, MI: Eerdmans, 1996.

McAllister, Lester G., and William E. Tucker. *Journey in Faith: A History of the Christian Church (Disciples of Christ)*. Saint Louis, MO: Chalice Press, 1975.

Williams, D. Newell. *A Case Study of Mainstream Protestantism: The Disciple's Relation to American Culture, 1880–1989*. Grand Rapids, MI: Wm. B. Eerdmans, 1991.

CHRISTIAN CHURCH (DISCIPLES OF CHRIST)

Founded: 1849
Membership: 689,507 in 3,731 congregations (2007)

The Disciples of Christ denomination was organized primarily by Alexander Campbell and preserves the original ecumenical aim of Campbell more fully than some other Restorationist bodies. The first national convention of the Disciples of Christ and the first missionary society (American Christian Missionary Society) were organized in 1849, but state conventions and societies had begun to meet in 1839. The group grew rapidly in the nineteenth century in the Midwest. Differences between conservatives and progressives over such matters as the organization of missionary societies and instrumental music in the churches led to the separation of the Churches of Christ* and Disciples by the end of the century.

In matters of belief, the church allows for freedom in interpretation, stemming from the conviction that there is no creed but Christ and no saving doctrines save those of the New Testament. Faith is a matter of personal conviction, but there are areas of general agreement and acceptance. The Lord's Supper is served at every Sunday service, and baptism is by immersion for adult believers. The Disciples are firm in their belief in immortality. They do not accept the doctrine of original sin, but they do teach that all people are of a sinful nature until redeemed by the sacrifice of Christ. They are not concerned with speculation about the Trinity and the nature of a triune God. They have no catechism and no set orders of worship. Faith in Christ as Lord is the only requirement.

For more than a century Disciples of Christ were strictly congregational in polity, but in the twentieth century it was felt that such an arrangement needed restructuring in the interests of efficiency and economy. A new organization was adopted at Kansas City in 1968. The whole church works under a representative government referred to as "three manifestations"—local, regional, and general. The local church is still the basic unit, and each congregation manages its own affairs, but the congregations are grouped in thirty-five regions, organized to provide help, counsel, and pastoral care to members, ministers, and congregations. The General Assembly of the church meets every two years, and the Administrative Committee, with forty-four voting members, meets twice annually. The Office of Communication is located in Indianapolis, Indiana; the church's publishing arm, the Christian Board of Publication, is in Saint Louis, Missouri.

The changes adopted in 1968 completed a long process of separation between moderates and conservatives in the Campbellite tradition. Those pastors who held to the original congregational polity and who had reservations about the liberalism of the Disciples formed a loose confederation of independent congregations known as the Christian Churches and Churches of Christ.* All three major branches of the old denomination (the Churches of Christ split in 1906) saw a severe decline in membership after the split.

There are now twenty-one colleges and seminaries in covenant relation with the Disciples, the largest of which is Texas Christian University, in Fort Worth, Texas. The church's National Benevolent Association operates eighty-three facilities and programs in twenty-two states, serving over thirty thousand people a year in residential facilities and community-based programs. True to their founding principles, the Disciples emphasize the importance of community, reconciliation, and laboring to make the kingdom of God visible in the world. Alexander Campbell was an early opponent of slavery and modern Disciples continue to oppose discrimination in its many forms.

For more information: www.disciples.org

Headquarters: PO Box 1986, Indianapolis, IN 46206-1986

CHRISTIAN CHURCHES AND CHURCHES OF CHRIST

Founded: 1830s
Membership: est. 1,439,253 in 5,471 churches (2008)

Even more so than most Baptist groups, these independent churches reject the designation as a denomination, and they do not keep denominational statistics. Until 1968, these congregations were listed as part of the Christian Church (Disciples of Christ), but the reorganization of that denomination resulted in a formal separation. The Christian Churches and Churches of Christ are more of a fellowship of independent congregations with roots in the Restorationist movement, especially the Barton Stone tradition, than a denomination. However, they do distinguish themselves from the other Churches of Christ that separated in 1906 over the issue of instrumental music.

Though the final straw for separation was the move toward centralization in the 1960s, there were theological issues involved as well. During the fundamentalist or modernist controversy in the 1920s, many Christian Churches and Churches of Christ tended toward fundamentalism and believed that the Disciples were too liberal in theology. The more evangelical pastors formed the North American Christian Convention in 1927, and this gathering served as the organizing unit of the later Christian Churches and Churches of Christ.

Key doctrines include the divinity of Christ, the authority of the Bible, the indwelling of the Holy Spirit for the believer, future reward or punishment, and God as a loving, prayer-answering deity. They baptize by immersion and observe the Lord's Supper in open Communion every Sunday. Many Christian Churches and Churches of Christ still maintain the nineteenth-century practice of the extended revival, known as the "camp meeting."

The various congregations support over twenty related colleges, most of which are preacher-training schools insulated from liberal influences. Standard Publishing, in Cincinnati, Ohio, is identified with this group as well. The North American Christian Convention, an annual preaching and teaching assembly, draws as many as twenty thousand attendees to an annual gathering each July. Active in foreign missions, with a missionary presence in about a dozen foreign countries and a domestic missionary presence as well, these churches sponsor a National Missionary Convention that meets each fall, with an attendance of between three and five thousand. The Christian Churches and Churches of Christ remains strongest in the Midwest, but grew on the West Coast toward the end of the twentieth century. There are thirty-nine colleges associated with the Restorationist movement.

For more information: www.cctoday.com

Contact: PO Box 1232 Rapid City, SD 57709-1232

CHRISTIAN CONGREGATION, INC.

Founded: 1887
Membership: 122,181 in 1,496 churches (2004)

The philosophy and work of the Christian Congregation, formed in Indiana in 1887, revolve around the "new commandment" of John 13:34-35. Unlike many other descendants of the Restorationist movement, the Christian Congregation is pacifist and opposes all war and sectarian strife. The origins of the group go back to Barton Stone, but in 1887 a number of ministers desired greater coordination of activities and formally organized a church. Inspired by the preaching of John Chapman and John L. Puckett, the church insists that "the household of faith is not founded upon doctrinal agreement, creeds, church claims, names, or rites," but solely on the relationship of the individual to God. Because of its teachings concerning the sanctity of life, the church condemns abortion, capital punishment, and all warfare. They believe that the ethical demands of the scripture transcend all national and racial barriers and should unite all persons in activism for peace.

The church remains strongest in the areas where Barton Stone preached and the original Christian Congregation groups were located: Kentucky, the Carolinas, Virginia, Pennsylvania, Ohio, Indiana, Tennessee, and Texas. The greater part of the group's work is carried on in rural and mountain areas. Polity is congregational.

Independent Christian Churches (ICC) tend to be very conservative in doctrine, Bible interpretation, and personal and social ethics. Although each church is autonomous, none ordain women or have women ministers. Similarly, none perform or acknowledge same-sex marriage or have gay elders or ministers. If there are any exceptions they (the churches) are generally regarded as outside the fellowship of ICC.

For more information: www.ccnamerica.org

Headquarters: none

CHURCHES OF GOD, GENERAL CONFERENCE (WINEBRENNER)

Founded: 1860
Membership: 29,698 in 325 churches (2016)

The Churches of God, General Conference (CGGC) has roots in the Restorationist movement but is often not included as one of the "Stone-Campbell" denominations. However, it fits that category better than others. The CGGC originated with the preaching of John Winebrenner (1797–1860) in Pennsylvania in the 1820s. Winebrenner's ministry was part of the so-called Second Great Awakening in the United States. He was ordained in the German Reformed Church but some members objected to his use of revivalistic methods. Winebrenner then adopted Arminian belief in free will, which conflicted with the Calvinism of the German Reformed Church. In 1828 he was removed from that church's ministry but continued to preach and evangelize and gathered a growing following. Soon he became convinced of believer baptism as the only true baptism and in 1830 was re-baptized by an elder of his church. He and his colleagues formed the General Eldership of the Church of God, but they were popularly known as the Winebrennerians. In 1975 the current name was adopted. This denomination should not be confused with others that use the common name Church of God.

The CGGC is different from most Baptist and Anabaptist churches because it has a presbyterian polity as opposed to a congregational one. It is organized into regions and individual congregations are accountable to each other in those connectional groups. The church recognizes three ordinances: baptism of believers by immersion, the Lord's Supper, and foot-washing. It is very evangelistic and Christocentric in piety. It encourages relevant worship, but is critical of many aspects of American culture. It teaches that believers can and should live holy lives empowered by the Holy Spirit. It is evangelical in ethos and generally conservative in both doctrine and practice.

The CGGC supports the Winebrenner Theological Seminary in Findlay, Ohio, where the denominational headquarters is located. The denomination has had women ministers since the early years of its existence. It believes marriage is the uniting of one man and one woman in covenant commitment and does not support same-sex marriage or the ordination of openly gay or lesbian people.

For more information: www.cggc.org

Headquarters: 700 East Melrose Avenue, Findlay, OH 45839

CHURCHES OF CHRIST

Founded: 1906, with roots to the 1804
Membership: est. 1,511, 747 adherents in 12,275 churches (2016)

The Churches of Christ represent the most conservative branch of the Restorationist movement. They are located throughout the nation but are concentrated in the South and the Southwest. They reject the idea of denominationalism and have no central headquarters; therefore, accurate statistics are impossible to attain, but they appear to have declined since 1970. This group has no governing bodies, but members cooperate voluntarily. This group of Stone-Campbell churches does not use musical instruments in worship and are therefore sometimes called "non-instrumental Churches of Christ."

Like other Restorationist groups, the Churches of Christ are anti-creedal and look for a Christian union based on the Bible alone. Some of the participants in the Cane Ridge revival adopted the name "Church of Christ" to emphasize their belief that they were directly descended from the original church founded in 33 CE. In the nineteenth century, the leaders of the Churches of Christ followed the more conservative Stone tradition rather than the leading of Campbell. Stressing a strict adherence to the New Testament pattern of worship and church organization, they refused to join any inter-congregational organization, such as a missionary society. Worship was simple, and they opposed the use of instrumental music on the grounds that the New Testament did not authorize it and that the early church did not use it. Those who called themselves "Disciples of Christ" adopted the use of musical instruments and encouraged ecumenical activities. Around the beginning of the twentieth century, the differences between the conservative and the more liberal wings of the restoration movements became evident, and in the 1906 there was a formal split. In the 1906 census of religious bodies, Churches of Christ were listed separately for the first time.

Key doctrines of Churches of Christ include belief in the Father, the Son, and the Holy Ghost as members of one Godhead; in the incarnation, virgin birth, and bodily resurrection of Christ; and in the universality of sin after the age of accountability. They teach that the only remedy for sin is the vicarious atonement of the Lord Jesus Christ. Strong emphasis is also laid on the church as the body and bride of Christ. A figurative, rather than literal, view is prevalent with reference to the book of Revelation. Church membership is contingent upon an individual's faith in Jesus Christ as the only begotten Son of God, repentance, confession of faith, and baptism by immersion for the remission of sins. Church attendance is stressed. Churches of Christ maintain that the final judgment of all religious groups is reserved to the Lord. This view, however, still allows for a vigorous evangelism that finds unacceptable the "doctrines, practices, names, titles, and creeds that have been grafted onto the original practice of Christianity." The Lord's Supper is observed each Sunday and baptism by immersion upon confession of faith is considered a necessary part of conversion.

The most conservative congregations tend to believe members of Churches of Christ are the only real Christians and decline all invitations to cooperate with non-Church of Christ congregations. However, in recent years some Churches of Christ have become more open to ecumenical cooperation especially with conservative churches outside the Church of Christ network and tradition. One of the best known Church of Christ ministers is Max Lucado of San Antonio, Texas, who leads a Church of Christ mega-church and has written dozens of inspirational books read by many non-Church of Christ (mostly evangelical) Christians.

Clergy in the Church of Christ, called ministers rather than pastors, are ordained rather than licensed, and they hold tenure in their pulpits under mutual agreement with the elders of the churches in which they preach. Ministerial authority is essentially moral; the actual governance of the church is vested in its elders. A vigorous missionary program is carried on in over ninety nations outside the United States, Churches of Christ support twenty-four Bible colleges, liberal arts colleges, and universities, including well-known and highly regarded Pepperdine University, and many high schools and elementary schools in the United States. They also sponsor numerous facilities for care of the aged. The church network publishes over one hundred periodicals, newspapers, and magazines.

For more information: www.church-of-christ.org and www.21stcc.com/ccusa

Headquarters: none

INTERNATIONAL CHURCHES OF CHRIST

Founded: 1979
Membership: est. 128,000 in 667 churches in the world (2016)

The International Churches of Christ (ICOC) is the most controversial body to emerge from the Restorationist movement, and many of its former members describe it in negative terms. It was founded by Kip McKean (b. 1955) while he was serving as pastor of the Lexington Church of Christ in Massachusetts. McKean was an evangelist in the Crossroads movement, which Charles Lucas began in Gainesville, Florida, in the 1960s. The ICOC utilized many of the principles of Crossroads evangelism. This included intensive recruitment of members, especially among college students and other young adults without a church community. They call their evangelical method "discipling," which means that members of the church commit themselves as a disciple and vow to bring new disciples into the fold. Discipling is based on voluntary obedience to the church-assigned "discipler." In the past, all personal decisions, including dating and marriage, were subject to the approval of the discipler. Members were expected to confess all of their sins, which could be recorded for future reference. During the 1990s and beyond these discipling methods were somewhat softened; the emphasis now is on "servant discipling" without the heavy-handedness of the past that caused some critics to call the ICOC a "cult."

Members were carefully instructed in scripture according to the interpretation provided by McKean, who served as the top of a pyramid structure of authority and obedience. The ICOC, unlike the other Restorationist churches is not congregational in polity. All congregations are linked in a pyramid structure with a Los Angeles congregation at the top. The ICOC teaches that believers' baptism by immersion is necessary for salvation. Those not baptized into the International Churches of Christ were often considered damned, and members were sometimes urged to sever ties with those not baptized. All members were expected to devote their personal time to evangelism and discipling of new members.

In the early years of the twenty-first century (circa 2002) ICOC founder and leader Kip McKean left the ICOC and after that the ICOC began to change—moving away from the very heavy-handed style of discipleship for which it was known and reaching out to other Churches of Christ for recognition and fellowship. There has been talk of the ICOC becoming a subgroup within the larger Church of Christ fellowship—which is where it began in Lexington, Massachusetts (as a Church of Christ). Meetings between ICOC leaders and mainline Church of Christ leaders at Pepperdine University and Abilene Christian University have begun to heal the rupture between the ICOC and its "mother movement" the Churches of Christ (non-instrumental).

The ICOC has "Women's Ministry Leaders" who are often wives of elders or ministers within ICOC churches. Since the ICOC does not have "pastors" in the traditional sense (leaders of congregations are elders and the one who teaches is called minister), there is a sense in which women can be and are congregational leaders, but normally that is only through their marriage to a male elder or minister.

For more information: www.icoc.org

Headquarters: 530 Wilshire Boulevard, Suite 1750, Los Angeles, CA 90010

ADVENTIST CHURCHES

Throughout the history of Christianity there have been communities and individuals who have awaited the return of Jesus Christ with eager anticipation. From the evidence of the New Testament, it appears that the expectation of the imminent return of the resurrected Christ was widespread among the first generation of Christians. As the apostolic age passed without the second coming, hope in the immediate return of Christ waned and the church adjusted to the delay of the return of Christ. In place of the earlier fervent hope in the end of history and the consummation of the messianic mission, churches Catholic, Orthodox, and Protestant placed their faith in the ongoing presence of the risen Christ through scripture, sacrament, and faith. However, when the New Testament canon was sealed in the fourth century, it included many writings about the end time, the most famous of which is the book of Revelation, also known as the Apocalypse. The symbolic language of the Apocalypse, combined with the speculations of Paul in the letters to the Thessalonians, apocalyptic statements by Jesus in the Gospels, and the Old Testament book of Daniel, gave ample scope for study about the "parousia"—return of Christ in glory—among some Christians throughout the centuries. (Scientist Isaac Newton [1643–1727] spent much of his adult life attempting to determine the year of Christ's return to earth from studying the Bible's apocalyptic literature.)

The hope that Christ would soon return to rule the world in justice and peace was particularly strong in the United States following the American Revolution. Even the phrase "the New World" conjured up images of the millennial kingdom long awaited. Ordinary farmers and merchants had defeated the world's greatest military power, had thrown off the rule of the king, and were creating a new nation. It seemed to many, even men like John Adams, that the millennial age was dawning and that Christ would soon appear to take up his rightful throne. The Second Great Awakening, a series of revivals that swept across the western frontier in the early decades of the nineteenth century, added fuel to this fire as reports about the phenomenal activity of the Holy Spirit in converting lost souls circulated around the nation.

Many American Christians both before and after the American Revolution adopted a relatively new theology about the return of Christ and the earthly kingdom of God—a utopia of peace and justice—that caught on especially among Puritans. It is called "post-millennialism" and is the belief that Christ will return *after* a thousand-year ("millennial") period of a Christianized world during which Christ's teachings will be normative for all nations and peoples. Postmillennialists such as Jonathan Edwards and John Wesley were optimistic about human history and the progress of Christianity throughout the world through missions, revivals, and social transformation.

The majority view of all this among Orthodox, Catholic, and magisterial Protestants is called "amillennialism" and is the belief that the church of Jesus Christ, however understood, *is* the kingdom of God on earth, within history, before Christ's return. According to most amillennialists, human history as we know it will end with Christ's bodily return, which will begin the universal judgment of all people and continue with a "new heaven and new earth." This view is known as "amillennialism" because it omits any belief in an earthly political messianic rule and reign of Christ for a thousand years (or any period of time within human history).

Postmillennialists especially identified the kingdom of God taught by Jesus as a Christianized world before Jesus returns. Premillennialists, however, are Christians who believe the kingdom of God in its fullness will begin only when Christ returns—at the end of a brief period of terror throughout the world in which the antichrist will persecute God's people. They also believe the kingdom of God will be a political rule of Christ himself over all the world for a thousand years after his return. The "new heaven and new earth" will begin after that.

All these views find support in scripture and ancient Christian theology. Postmillennialism, however, tended to die away during the twentieth century, which some have dubbed the "genocidal century" because of the world wars and the Holocaust. History did not seem to be progressing "upward" into a kingdom of God. During the nineteenth century in America premillennialism re-appeared very strongly. It had been a minority view called "chiliasm"—a heresy for some Christian groups—since the time of the church fathers Justin Martyr, Irenaeus, and Tertullian—all of whom were premillennialists. The resurgence of premillennialism gave birth to a new and distinctly American Christian movement called Adventism. ("Advent" here refers to the return of Christ, not his birth.) It gave rise to numerous denominations all of which are premillennial and place great emphasis on the imminent return of Christ and the study of biblical prophecy together with "reading the signs of the times" to discern the timing of the parousia. Many also adopted Saturday worship and a new emphasis on the Old Testament moral law as applying to Christians.

The Adventist movement was born out of this new emphasis on the "premillennial return of Christ" during the middle of the nineteenth century. Today regarded as conservative Protestants, Adventists were originally seen as dangerous radicals because of their intense focus on the second advent (or second coming) of Jesus Christ. By 1844, Adventist groups could be recognized as a distinct religious body separated from the traditional

Protestant churches. Modern Adventism began as an interchurch movement whose most vocal proponent was Baptist lay preacher William Miller (1782–1849) of New York, a veteran of the War of 1812. Miller had experienced conversion from skeptical deism to evangelical Christianity in 1816, during the Second Great Awakening. He became an ardent student of scripture. Miller concentrated his attention on the prophecies of the end time in Daniel and Revelation.

Accepting an interpretation that the symbolic day of Bible prophecy represents one year, Miller concluded that the twenty-three hundred days of Daniel 8:14 started concurrently with the seventy weeks of years of Daniel 9, which he claimed referred to 457 BCE, the year of the command to rebuild and restore Jerusalem. Miller believed that the twenty-three hundred "days" would end in or about the year 1843, as calculated by Jewish reckoning. Miller thought that the sanctuary mentioned in Daniel 8:14 was the earth (or the church), which would be cleansed by fire at the second advent and that this cleansing would occur sometime between March 21, 1843, and March 21, 1844.

Miller's writings struck a chord in the popular culture of the 1830s. A New England pastor published an entire hymnal, *The Millennial Harp*, devoted to the theme of the imminent return of Christ and the restoration of paradise on earth. Miller himself made speaking tours in which he used elaborate charts and chronologies to support his reading of end-time prophecies. All of his research supported his central claim that the advent would occur in the spring of 1844. Between fifty and one hundred thousand people in the United States believed in Miller's calculations and looked forward to the great day when the world would be cleansed and the righteous would meet Christ. Some even went so far as to quit their jobs and spent most of their time expecting the return of Christ in 1844.

When March and April passed, and this expectation failed to materialize, some devotees left the movement and returned to their former churches—including Miller himself. However, Miller's associates, on the basis of the study of Old Testament typology, arrived at a second date, October 22, 1844. This was to be the great Day of Atonement, prefigured in the Mosaic Law. When October 22 also passed with no second coming, vast numbers faced up to what has been termed "the Great Disappointment." Many gave up on Adventism; some gave up on the Christian faith itself; others simply gave up the desire to fix a date for the advent. Out of the ashes of the disappointment, new Adventist bodies arose, divided over the relevance of Miller's original interpretations.

The largest group of Adventists concluded that the twenty-three hundred years in the prophecy of Daniel 8 would end sometime in the unknown future. They formed a loosely knit organization in Albany, New York, in 1845, and held generally to Miller's teaching. This included the personal and premillennial character of the second advent, which means that Christ will return in person, not in spirit, before the millennial kingdom comes into being. They also taught that the resurrection of the dead happens in two stages. The faithful are to be raised at Christ's coming, but the rest of humanity will rise one thousand years later. Furthermore, the earth will be redeemed and restored as an eternal abode of the faithful. Known at first as the American Millennial Association, a portion later came to be called the Evangelical Adventist Church. That church has now dwindled to the point of obscurity. The churches discussed in this section of the *Handbook* developed out of the minority bodies that formed after the Disappointment.

Despite the differences between the various groups, Adventism as a whole is based on the conviction that the second advent of Christ is the sole hope of the world. The present age is evil and irredeemable, except through the direct action of God. Adventism holds that humanity's nature is fallen because of sin and that those who rebel against the government of God will be ultimately destroyed, while believers, by God's grace, will be saved. After that cataclysmic event, Jesus Christ will reign in triumph through the thousand-year period, or millennium, of Revelation 20:1-6.

Adventists are pessimistic about the present age, but they are filled with confidence and hope for God's future. In the meantime, they teach that God's people must be righteous, devout, and disciplined. Those who would be saved should practice a wholesome personal and family life, as well as a life of obedience to God. They should also work diligently toward the evangelization of the whole world in preparation for the return of Christ. There are still differing understandings among Adventists. Are the dead conscious or unconscious as they await the resurrection? Who are to arise: both the righteous and the wicked or only the righteous? Is there to be eternal punishment or ultimate annihilation for the wicked? What is the nature of immortality? Does the cleansing of the sanctuary in Daniel 8 refer to a sanctuary in heaven or to one on earth? Answers to these questions have served to divide various Adventist groups.

Though Adventism looks to the future, it has encouraged people to examine the Old Testament. In general, the different Adventist groups have viewed the Old Testament as prefiguring the coming millennial kingdom. Therefore it gives a reliable guide to God's will for the church. As a result, many of those influenced by Adventist teaching in the nineteenth century adopted many features of the Mosaic Law; some observe Saturday as the Sabbath.

There are many misconceptions of Adventism. Perhaps the most common one is that all Adventists belong to the largest individual denomination whose name includes the word *Adventist*, the Seventh-Day Adventist Church (or General Conference). In fact, it is only one of several Adventist denominations. Some of those spawned by the Adventist movement do not use the word at all. Among those who are aware of Seventh-Day Adventism there is the misconception that all Adventists worship on Saturday and observe it as the Sabbath. In fact, not all Adventists worship on Saturday and those who do probably borrowed the practice from the oldest continuously existing Baptist organization in North America, the Seventh Day Baptists.

The only thing all these denominations share in common is roots in the Adventist movement of the mid-nineteenth century and an intense belief in the imminent and premillennial return of Jesus Christ. The latter belief exists in many other Christian traditions including Pentecostals.

SUGGESTIONS FOR FURTHER READING

Beckford, James A. *The Trumpet of Prophecy: A Sociological Study of Jehovah's Witnesses.* Oxford, UK: Basil Blackwell, 1975.

Bull, Malcolm and Keith Lockhart. *Seeking a Sanctuary: Seventh Day Adventism and the American Dream.* San Francisco, CA: Harper Row, 1989.

Dick, Everett N. *William Miller and the Adventist Crisis, 1831–1844.* Berrien Springs, MI: Andrews University Press, 1994.

Doan, Ruth A. *The Miller Heresy, Millennialism, and American Culture.* Philadelphia, PA: Temple University Press, 1987.

Gaustad, Edwin, ed. *The Rise of Adventism: Religion and Society in Mid-Nineteenth Century America.* New York: Harper and Row, 1974.

Neufeld, Don. F., ed. *Seventh-Day Adventist Encyclopedia.* Rev. ed. Washington, DC: Review and Herald Publishing, 1961.

Penton, James. *Apocalypse Delayed: The Story of Jehovah's Witnesses.* Toronto: University of Toronto Press, 1985.

Tuveson, Ernest Lee. *Redeemer Nation: The Idea of America's Millennial Role.* Chicago, IL: University of Chicago Press, 1968.

Weber, Timothy P. *Living in the Shadow of the Second Coming: American Premillennialism, 1875–1982.* Chicago, IL: University of Chicago Press, 1987.

ADVENT CHRISTIAN CHURCH GENERAL CONFERENCE

Founded: 1860
Membership: 21,765 in 270 churches (2015)

The Advent Christian Church (ACGC) grew out of the main body of Adventists who reorganized in 1845 following the Great Disappointment. While William Miller was not directly involved in the founding of this church, his preaching and teachings concerning the second coming of Christ formed the basis for Advent Christian theological, biblical, and organizational thought. They reject the prophecies of Ellen Harmon White (see Seventh-Day Adventist) and accept the Bible as the only source of authoritative teaching. The denomination maintains no formal creedal statement, but does have a Declaration of Principles. Two ordinances are observed: baptism (of adults by immersion) and the Lord's Supper. Worship is held on the first day of the week rather than on the Sabbath. The ACGC rejects war as incompatible with Christ's teachings and its members do not participate in armed conflict.

Like several Adventist groups, the ACGC teaches the doctrine of conditional immortality, which states that only the redeemed receive everlasting life. The dead await the resurrection in an unconscious state; when Christ returns, all will rise and face the final judgment. The righteous will be given immortality, but the wicked will suffer eternal extinction (a doctrine known as "annihilationism") as opposed to eternal torment. After the final judgment and destruction of the wicked, Christ will restore the earth and make it the eternal home for the just.

The first Advent Christian General Conference in 1860 was followed closely by the founding of publications, missions societies, and Aurora University. Berkshire Christian College in Massachusetts is also affiliated with the ACGC. The denomination's publication is *Advent Christian Witness*. In 1964, Advent Christian Church merged with Life and Advent Union. Congregational in polity, the church is grouped in five regional districts in the United States and Canada. The General Conference meets every three years and maintains denominational offices in Charlotte, North Carolina, which oversee work in missions, urban ministries, church growth, Christian education, publications, administration, women's ministries, and public relations. The denomination also maintains missions in Japan, Mexico, India, Nigeria, Ghana, South Africa, Honduras, the Philippines, and Malaysia.

The ACGC is a conservative evangelical denomination and a full member of the National Association of Evangelicals (NAE). (Many people are unaware that any Adventists are fully evangelical in the doctrinal sense. Many other evangelicals disagree with its stance on conditional immortality or annihilationism, but that has not kept it from being a member of the NAE.) The ACGC does ordain women to the gospel ministry and has had women ministers. The denomination believes human sexuality is intended by God for heterosexual, monogamous marriage only and that all other sexual activities are sinful.

For more information: www.acgc.us

Headquarters: PO Box 23152, Charlotte, NC 28227

CHRISTADELPHIANS

Founded: 1844
Membership: est. 15,000 in 170 ecclesias (2000)

Though Adventist and Unitarian in theology, the Christadelphians actually have their roots in the Disciples of Christ. When John Thomas (1805–71) came to the United States from England in 1832, he joined the Disciples, but he eventually decided that the Disciples neglected many important biblical doctrines. In 1844, he founded a number of societies that preached the need for a return to primitive Christianity. Loosely organized, those various societies bore no name until the outbreak of the Civil War, when their members' doctrine of nonresistance forced them to adopt a name in order to avoid the draft. They chose the term *Christadelphians*, or Brothers of Christ.

Christadelphians reject belief in the devil and maintain that the scriptures teach that Christ was not pre-existent but was born of Mary by the Holy Spirit, that is, by the power of God. They deny the deity of Christ and the doctrine of the Trinity. They believe that humankind is mortal by nature, and Christ, the Son of God, is the only means of salvation. Eternal life comes only to the righteous.

In the United States, some Christadelphians, called *Unamended*, believe Christ will raise only those who died in the faith; all other persons will simply remain dead, without consciousness. Other Christadelphians, known as Amended, believe that Christ will raise all responsible persons, rewarding the righteous and annihilating the wicked. Both groups believe the faithful will be gathered together, and the world will be ruled from Jerusalem for a thousand years. They hold the Bible to be the inspired word of God, inerrant in its original text. Some observers consider them fundamentalists with regard to the Bible but also heretical compared with traditional, orthodox Christianity.

The church is congregational in policy; local organizations are known as ecclesias and they voluntarily choose to have fellowship with other Christadelphian ecclesias. There is no central organization of all Christadelphians. Membership in an ecclesia is by profession of faith, and baptism is by immersion. There are no paid or ordained ministers in the usual sense. Women take no part in public speech or prayer, though all vote equally in the affairs of the ecclesia. Christadelphians do not vote in civil elections or participate in war, and they refuse to accept public office. There are no associations or conventions, but there are fraternal gatherings ("fellowships") for spiritual inspiration. Many meetings are held in rented halls, schools, or private homes, though a number of ecclesias have their own buildings. Foreign missions and ecclesias are found in sixty countries.

Christadelphians are conservative with regard to sexuality and believe marriage can only be between one woman and one man; they regard homosexual behavior as sin. Only men can teach men in a Christadelphian ecclesia.

For more information: www.christadelphia.org

Headquarters: none

CHURCH OF GOD (SEVENTH DAY)

Founded: 1863
Membership: est. 11,000 in 200 churches (2012)

Like the larger Seventh-Day Adventist Church*, the founders of the Church of God (Seventh Day) believed that Christians should observe the Sabbath; however, this body rejected Ellen Harmon White's visions and prophecies (see Seventh-Day Adventist) and separated in 1858 from other Sabbath-keeping Adventists. A similar group of anti-White Sabbatarians who had organized themselves in Iowa in 1860 joined the Michigan branch in 1863. Several denominational designations were used in its early history, including

Church of Christ and Church of Jesus Christ. The present name was chosen in 1884, and the words *Seventh Day* were added in 1923.

In 1933, owing in part to disparate views on polity and administration, the church divided into two groups. An attempted merger in 1949 led to some realignment of membership and the relocation of the headquarters to Denver, Colorado. Those who did not join the merger maintained their headquarters at Salem, West Virginia, and use *7th Day* rather than *Seventh Day* in its name. The Salem body claims a membership of about one thousand in seven churches. Both groups follow basic Adventist teachings on the future millennial reign of Christ on earth and the annihilation of the wicked. In addition to baptism and the Lord's Supper, this body practices foot-washing. The Salem body also claims a "Biblical organization," which means that the numbers seven, twelve, and seventy have particular relevance in church organization. They also teach that the physical Church of God (7th Day) is the "true church." The national organization headquartered in Denver supports Spring Vale Academy, a residential high school in Michigan, and Lifespring School of Ministry in Denver.

Unlike Seventh-Day Adventists and many other Adventists, the Church of God (Seventh Day) denied the equal deity of Jesus Christ with God the Father and the Trinity as unbiblical doctrines. However, according to some sources, that unorthodox view is changing, moving toward a more traditional, orthodox doctrine of Christ's deity and the Trinity. The official Statement of Faith can be interpreted either way; it does not mention the Trinity but could possibly be interpreted as trinitarian. The Church places emphasis on Sabbath-keeping and holiness of life according to all biblical moral commandments. It rejects homosexuality as sin and rejects same-sex marriage. The Church's position on women in ministry is unknown.

For more information: www.cog7.org

Headquarters: 330 West 152nd Avenue, Broomfield, CO 80023

CHURCH OF GOD AND SAINTS OF CHRIST

Founded: 1896
Membership: est. 40,000 in approx. 50 temples or tabernacles (congregations) (2005)

The Church of God and Saints of Christ (COGASOC) is a Christian body that tries to live according to a literal understanding of Old Testament law. As such, they are sometimes called "Black Hebrew Israelites"; however, they have no direct relationship to historical Judaism. Though not properly Adventist, they do share similarities with Adventist groups that emphasize the Mosaic Law, observance of Saturday as the Sabbath, and continuing relevance of prophecy.

The church was begun by William Saunders Crowdy (1847–1908), who was born to slave parents in Maryland. After serving in the Union Army, Crowdy bought a farm near

Guthrie, Oklahoma. Active in the Baptist church, in 1893 Crowdy began having disturbing visions and hearing voices. He dreamed of tables covered in filth, each of which had the name of a denomination. Then he saw a clean table that came down from heaven; on it was the name "Church of God and Saints of Christ." Crowdy began preaching on the streets in towns and villages in the Midwest and in November of 1896 he formally organized his church in Lawrence, Kansas. Arrested numerous times because of his ministry, he made converts in prison as well.

In a vision, he received "The Seven Keys," which form the core set of doctrines: repentance of sin; baptism by burial into water upon confession of faith; unleavened bread and water for Christ's body and blood; foot-washing by elders; obedience to the commandments; the holy kiss; and the Lord's Prayer. In Philadelphia he founded a church and also several businesses; the denomination continues to stress the importance of individual enterprise and business acumen as marks of religious life.

Crowdy taught that his followers should celebrate a number of Jewish holy and feast days. Of particular importance are the observance of the Sabbath, Passover, the Day of Atonement, and the Jewish New Year. Members believe their church is built on the patriarchs and prophets of the Jewish tradition, and "Jesus the Anointed" is their chief cornerstone. They differentiate between prophetic Judaism, "which seeks to follow the living insight into the spiritual idea to its fullest implication," and "legalistic" Judaism. They accept the Decalogue (Ten Commandments) as the standard of conduct for all humankind. Men and women are instructed to wear particular clothing on the Sabbath according to the season of the year, and men are expected to wear the yarmulke and a tallith.

An executive bishop stands at the head of the church and of the bishops' council; the church maintains headquarters in Cleveland, Ohio. The *Newsletter* (Church of God and Saints of Christ), published every two weeks, serves to inform members through sermons, lectures, and announcements. An a capella choir formed of members of the church has released recordings of gospel music to critical acclaim.

For more information: www.cogasoc.net

Headquarters: 3825 Central Avenue, Cleveland, OH 44115

CHURCH OF GOD GENERAL CONFERENCE

Founded: 1921, with roots to the 1840s
Membership: 3,842 in 84 congregations 2012)

This denomination, Church of God General Conference (COGGC), should not be confused with others of similar names (such as the Winebrenner group known as the Churches of God, General Conference). It is sometimes known as The Church of God of the Abrahamic Faith and is the outgrowth of several independent local groups of similar faith, some in existence as early as 1800; others date their beginnings from the arrival of British immigrants to this country around 1847. These diverse groups shared in general Adventist theology. A national organization was instituted at Philadelphia in 1888 and 1889; however, because of strong convictions relating to congregational rights and authority, the national body ceased to function until 1921, when the present General Conference was formed at Waterloo, Iowa.

Members of the COGGC accept the Bible as the supreme and literal standard of faith. They teach that when Christ returns, he will establish a literal kingdom of God on earth. The Church of God is doctrinally Arian, teaching the absolute oneness of God and that Christ as the Son of God did not exist prior to the birth of Jesus. The Holy Ghost is the power and influence of God on earth until the return of Christ. The church also promotes the belief in the restoration of Israel as a kingdom during the millennial reign of Christ. As with many other Adventist groups, the COGGC denies the immortality of the soul. The righteous will receive their reward on earth, but the wicked will be completely annihilated in a second death. Unlike some other Adventist groups, the COGGC worships on Sundays; it is not Sabbatarian.

Due to the congregational nature of the church's government, the General Conference exists primarily as a means of mutual cooperation and development of yearly projects and enterprises. It supports Atlanta Bible College for the training of pastors; a Publishing Department; and an Outreach and Church Development Department, which promotes youth work, mission, and evangelism in preparation for the return of Christ on earth. Mission stations are located in India, Mexico, the Philippines, Malawi, Mozambique, Great Britain, and Peru.

The COGGC does have ordained women pastors. It considers homosexual behavior sin and does not ordain openly gay or lesbian people to the ministry.

For more information: www.coggc.org

Headquarters: PO Box 2950, McDonough, GA 30253

GRACE COMMUNION INTERNATIONAL

Founded: 1934
Membership: 11,000 in 300 churches (2016)

Formerly known as the Worldwide Church of God (WCG), Grace Communion International (GCI) has one of the most distinctive histories in American Christianity. The original WCG divided into several bodies in the last decades of the twentieth century. The largest group, which retained legal right to the name World Wide Church of God, has become a typical evangelical church and adopted a new name in 2006, but the Worldwide Church of God was originally characterized by the adoption of many Sabbatarian and Mosaic practices.

Originally known as the Radio Church of God, the WCG began its work in 1934 under the leadership of Herbert W. Armstrong (1892–1986) who had been a member of the Church of God (Seventh Day). The mission of the WCG was to proclaim the gospel of Jesus Christ around the world and to help members grow spiritually. The church grew rapidly from 1964 to 1974, but controversy erupted in the 1970s. Garner Ted Armstrong, the founder's son, was "disfellowshiped" on four occasions for adultery, and in 1978 he took part of the membership with him when he founded the rival Church of God International, which never flourished. The original church weathered another bitter legal battle over control of the finances, and its situation became more unstable in the 1980s. After Herbert Armstrong's death in 1986, Joseph W. Tkach became Pastor General. Tkach and his son, Joseph W. Tkach Jr., led the church through an experience nothing short of religious conversion in the late 1980s and 1990s. The church officially repudiated many of Armstrong's most distinctive teachings, which led to numerous congregations breaking away.

The elder Armstrong saw himself as the apostle-messenger of the last days and so assumed absolute authority in the organization. Congregations generally worshipped on Saturdays in rented facilities or private homes. At the time of his death, Armstrong left a church with some one hundred twenty thousand members, a budget of $200 million, and a publication, *Plain Truth*, with a circulation of eight million copies a month. His organization was a worldwide ministry, with churches in one hundred countries and territories, carried out from a headquarters in Pasadena, California.

The WCG held to some traditional Christian teachings, but it maintained several distinctive theological ideas. Accepting a number of Jewish observances as scripturally mandated, the church observed the Lord's Supper, or Passover of Jesus Christ, annually as a memorial of the death of Jesus. The Sabbath (Friday sunset to Saturday sunset) was honored as a day of worship. Seven annual holy days were kept, and certain "unclean" meats were avoided. Holidays, such as Halloween, Easter, and Christmas, were condemned as pagan. The three ordinances of baptism, the Lord's Supper, and foot-washing were practiced. Such was Armstrong's theological conviction that he did not acknowledge as Christian those who failed to keep the Sabbath.

Under the leadership of the Tkaches, the WCG made a dramatic theological turn, essentially moving to an orthodox and evangelical position. Key changes included an affirmation of the deity of Christ (equality with the Father), the Trinity (1993), and renunciation of Old Testament covenant laws (1994). The church issued formal apologies for "doctrinal errors" to the wider Christian community, and in 1997 it was accepted as a member of the National Association of Evangelicals. The wholesale conversion of the entire movement, from "an unorthodox church on the fringes of Christianity, into an evangelical church that believes and teaches orthodox doctrines," is one of the singular events in American religious history and is explained in narrative detail in Joseph Tkach's book *Transformed by Truth* (1997).

GCI is premillennial with regard to the return of Christ and his establishment of the earthly messianic reign of Christ on earth. It does not dictate belief about the conscious or unconscious state of the dead before Christ's return and their resurrection. (Many Adventist groups believe in what is termed "soul sleep.") Many GCI churches worship on Saturdays but most worship on Sundays. GCI churches baptize believers only by immersion.

The WCG changed its name to Grace Communion International to reflect its new identity and to reduce confusion with other "Church of God" bodies. The church acknowledges that it "has changed radically from what we once were to what we are today." Many adherents were disillusioned by the changes following Armstrong's death, and thousands left the church. Hundreds of staff were laid off; finances and programs were depleted; radio and television ministries were cut back; and the church's educational institution, Ambassador University, was closed. In 1996, Plain Truth Ministries separated from the WGC to form an independent nonprofit media ministry that publishes *The Plain Truth* and offers online ministry. It has no legal connection to the church. Grace Communion International publishes *Christian Odyssey* magazine and provides video programs on its website. It offers online undergraduate training through Ambassador College of Christian Ministry and graduate training online through Grace Communion Seminary.

GCI does ordain women and has women elders (pastors). Homosexual behavior is considered sin and the denomination does not ordain openly gay or lesbian people.

For more information: www.gci.org

Headquarters: PO Box 5005, Glendora, CA 91740

JEHOVAH'S WITNESSES (WATCH TOWER BIBLE AND TRACT SOCIETY)

Founded: ca. 1870

Membership: 1,184,249 in 13,021 Kingdom Halls (congregations) (2012)

The Jehovah's Witnesses (JWs) are among the most zealous religious bodies in terms of promotion of their beliefs. Meeting in kingdom halls (not in churches), members witness and publish their faith in a remarkably comprehensive missionary effort. They do not believe in a separation of clergy and laity, since "Christ Jesus did not make such a separation," and they never use titles like "Reverend." All members are expected to give generously of their time in proclaiming their faith and teaching in private homes. Called "publishers of the Kingdom," they preach only from the Bible. Pioneers, or full-time preachers, are required to give at least seventy hours per month; special pioneers and missionaries donate a minimum of 140 hours per month and are sent to isolated areas and foreign lands where new congregations can be formed. All pioneers provide for their own support, but the society gives a small allowance to some, in view of their special needs.

This missionary activity has made Jehovah's Witnesses one of the most widely known (although not widely understood) churches in the United States.

It was Adventist-influenced Charles Taze Russell (1852–1916) who established the Witnesses, and until 1931 they were known as Russellites, Millennial Dawn People, or International Bible Students. Russell, the first president, is acknowledged, not as founder (there is no human founder), but as general organizer. Witnesses claim they have been on earth as an organization for more than five thousand years (based on Isa 43:10-12; Heb 11; John 18:37).

Russell was deeply influenced by Adventist thought, which captivated American attention around the middle of the nineteenth century. He developed his own Adventist ideas based on personal study of the Bible, and his lectures attracted huge crowds. To date, some thirteen million copies of his books have been circulated, and they have profoundly influenced the Witnesses.

The first formal Russellite group was organized in Pittsburgh, Pennsylvania, in 1870, and soon after a board of directors was elected by vote of all members who subscribed ten dollars or more to support the work (a practice discontinued in 1944). In 1884, Zion's Watch Tower Tract Society was incorporated. In 1939, the name of this corporation was changed to Watch Tower Bible and Tract Society of Pennsylvania, and it remains one of the world's largest publishers. When Russell died in 1916, Joseph F. Rutherford (1869–1942), known widely as Judge Rutherford, became president. He had been a lawyer and occasionally sat as a circuit court judge in Missouri. His numerous books, pamphlets, and tracts supplanted those of Russell, but his neglect of some aspects of Russell's teaching brought dissension.

The vast literature of the Witnesses (all circulated without bylines or signatures) quotes extensively from the Bible (the JW translation known as the New World Translation) and relates the eschatological teachings of the church. Witness theology is based on the idea of theocracy, or rule of God. It teaches that there is only one God, Jehovah; Jesus is not God. In the beginning, the world was under the theocratic rule of the Almighty. At that time all was "happiness, peace, and blessedness." But Satan rebelled and became the ruler of the world, and from that moment, humankind has followed Satan's evil leading. Then Jesus, the first creation of Jehovah, came to earth as a human being, "the beginning of the creation of God" (Rev 3:14, KJV), as the prophets had predicted, to end Satan's rule.

Witnesses maintain that Jesus's heavenly rule, after he paid the ransom sacrifice of his death on earth, began in 1914. Russell had seen World War I as the final apocalyptic struggle that would usher in the return of Christ. When that did not happen, Rutherford reorganized the movement and announced in 1918 that Christ then "came to the temple of Jehovah." With Jesus now enthroned in the temple of Jehovah, the rule of Satan was nearly over, and so Rutherford began to send out his followers to preach the good news in the final days.

God, according to Witness belief, will take vengeance on wicked human beings in our time. God is now showing great love by "gathering out" multitudes of people of goodwill, to whom God will give life in the new world that is to come after the battle of Armageddon. This is to be a universal battle; Christ will lead the army of the righteous, composed of the "host of heaven, the holy angels," and they will completely annihilate the army of Satan. The righteous of the earth will watch the battle and the suffering of God's enemies, but they will not participate.

After the battle, Witnesses teach, the believers in God and God's servants will remain on the earth. Those who have proven their integrity in the old world will multiply and populate the new earth with righteous people. A resurrection of the righteous will also take place, as an additional means of filling the cleansed earth with better inhabitants. After the Great Tribulation, "righteous princes" will rule the earth under Christ, "King of the Great Theocracy." One special group—the 144,000 Christians mentioned in Revelation 7 and 14—will become the "bride of Christ" and rule with him in heaven.

The governing body today is in the hands of older and more "spiritually qualified" men who base their judgments on the authority of scripture. This is not considered a governing hierarchy, but an imitation of early apostolic Christian organization. Under direction of the leaders at headquarters in Brooklyn, New York, local congregations of Witnesses (always called congregations, never churches) are arranged in circuits, with a traveling minister who spends a week with each congregation. Approximately twenty congregations are included in each circuit, and circuits are grouped into districts, with more than forty in the United States; circuit organizations are now found in over two hundred countries and islands around the world.

The headquarters is located at Bethel Home in Brooklyn, New York. Staff engage primarily in editorial and printing work. They write, print, and distribute literature in almost astronomical proportions. The official journal, *The Watchtower*, has a circulation of many millions. More than one billion Bibles, books, and leaflets have been distributed since 1920; they are made available in nearly three hundred languages.

Although expectations of Armageddon have repeatedly been disappointed, Witnesses maintain their belief in its imminence. They have been especially active in opposing what they consider the three allies of Satan: false teachings of the churches, tyranny of human governments, and oppression by big business. This "triple alliance" of ecclesiastical, political, and commercial powers has misled humankind, the Witnesses claim, and must be destroyed at Armageddon before the new world can be born. They refuse to salute the national flag, bear arms in war, or participate in the political affairs of government, not because of pacifist convictions, but because they desire to remain apart from what they consider expressions of Satan's power over humankind.

This attitude has brought them into conflict with law enforcement agencies; they have also endured whippings, assaults by mobs, stonings, being tarred and feathered, the burning of their homes, imprisonment, and detention in concentration camps. All of this they have accepted in a submissive spirit. Their position is that they will obey the laws of the earth when those laws are not in conflict with the laws of God.

Even many other Adventists consider the JW movement and organization "cultic" in theological sense of that word (viz., radically heretical compared with orthodox Christianity). JWs, in turn, consider all churches false and members unsaved. They admit that God has always had people he favored throughout history—even before the formal organization of the Watchtower Society or JWs in the nineteenth century. However, they believe that to survive Armageddon and be taken into "Paradise Earth" (Christ's reign on earth after his return), a person must be a faithful JW.

For more information: www.jw.org

Headquarters: Watch Tower Society, 20 Columbia Heights, Brooklyn, NY 11201

PHILADELPHIA CHURCH OF GOD

Founded: 1989, with roots to 1934
Membership: est. 5000 in about 100 churches (1998)

The Philadelphia Church of God (PCG) is one of the larger groups that remained committed to the teachings of Herbert Armstrong after the Worldwide Church of God (WCG) adopted a more traditional evangelical perspective in the 1980s. George Flurry organized the PCG in 1989 to hold strictly to Armstrong's teachings, especially as outlined in the book *Mystery of the Ages*.

Armstrong held to many traditional Christian teachings, but he also promoted several distinctive theological ideas. For instance, he taught that there is one God, who is the Father. Jesus was accepted as part of God's family and is divine, but not equal with the Father as to his deity. Armstrong rejected the idea of the Trinity. The Holy Spirit was not a distinct person. Concerning human nature, the inspiration of the scriptures, Christ's bodily resurrection, and baptism, the church held traditional positions. Like many Adventist groups, the WCG took a strong stand against bearing arms and the taking of human life, and they rejected the concept of everlasting conscious torment in hell for the unsaved.

The death of Herbert Armstrong caused a crisis in the WCG, and under the leadership of Joseph Tkach the church adopted more traditional evangelical doctrines and eventually changed its name to Grace Communion International. Several splinter groups were formed to promote Armstrong's teachings. The Philadelphia Church of God holds strictly to Armstrong's teaching, including Armstrong's rejection of medical treatment. In 1995 several pastors left the PCG to form the United Church of God. The PCG broadcasts on television and radio and publishes magazines and booklets.

The PCG worships on Saturdays as did the WCG during Armstrong's life and ministry. Its views about women in ministry and homosexuality are unknown although its quite conservative approach to all matters of lifestyle, including dress, indicates it is unlikely to affirm homosexuality.

For more information: www.pcog.org

Headquarters: PO Box 3700, Edmond, OK 73083.

SEVENTH-DAY ADVENTISTS

Founded: 1863
Membership: 1,146,319 in 5,821 congregations (2016)

The Seventh-Day Adventists (SDAs) have about seventeen million members in over two hundred countries. They hold to the classical doctrine of orthodox Christianity such as the deity of Christ and the Trinity as well as the Reformation emphases of *scripture alone, grace alone,* and *faith alone.* Their understanding of biblical teachings is encapsulated in *28 Fundamental Doctrines,* which can only be modified by vote of the world assembly (called the General Conference Session), which meets every five years. The name of the church enshrines the heart of their beliefs and practices. Strongly committed to obedience to the teachings of the whole Bible, they observe the seventh day, Saturday, as the day of worship. As Adventists, they expect the soon return of Jesus to this earth. Since their organization as a church, they have distanced themselves from efforts to set a date for the second coming.

The SDA Church is the largest of the Adventist churches that arose during the upsurge in millennial anticipation in the United States in the early nineteenth century. William Miller, a farmer-preacher, predicted that Christ would return on October 22, 1844. The faithful prepared, prayed, and waited, but their hopes of seeing the returning Lord were dashed. Yet this unpromising soil provided the origin of the Seventh-Day Adventist Church. One of the small Adventist groups that emerged from the Disappointment was a seventh-day Sabbath group that reinterpreted the events of October 1844. It was not an earthly event that took place on that prophesied day, but an event in heaven itself.

As early as 1844, a small group of Adventists near Washington, New Hampshire, had begun to observe the Sabbath on the seventh day. A pamphlet written by Joseph Bates in 1846 gave the issue wide publicity and created great interest. Shortly thereafter, Bates, together with James White, Ellen Harmon (later Mrs. James White), Hiram Edson, Frederick Wheeler, and S. W. Rhodes, with the aid of regular publications, set out to champion the seventh-day Sabbath, along with the imminence of the second advent. In the 1850s they set up headquarters at Battle Creek, Michigan, and began publishing a weekly magazine called *Review and Herald.* In 1860 the name Seventh-Day Adventist was officially adopted, and in 1903 the headquarters was moved to Washington, DC. Its present location is in Silver Spring, Maryland.

Ellen Harmon White (1827–1915) was the key figure in this rejuvenation of Adventism, and the church believes that she had the gift of prophecy. When she was only in her teens, she began having visions and receiving messages from heaven. Her visions contributed to the development of the new Seventh-Day Adventist Church, doctrinally and structurally. She counseled, preached, taught, traveled, and wrote extensively (almost twenty-five million words). White believed that the Bible is the judge and test of all other revelations, but gradually Seventh-Day Adventists came to believe the Bible could only be interpreted accurately through her prophecies such as are contained in her book *The Great Controversy*.

Seventh-Day Adventists believe in creation by divine fiat (as opposed to evolution) and recognize the fall of the human race through the sin of Adam. They teach that humans are by nature mortal, but may receive immortality through divine grace and the redemption effected through the atoning work of Jesus Christ. They believe that the dead await the resurrection in an unconscious state ("soul sleep") until the whole person (body, mind, and soul) is resurrected on the last day when Christ will return in person. The righteous will then receive immortality, while the wicked are destroyed by fire (annihilationism). After Christ returns a new earth will be created out of the ruins of the old, and this will be the final home of the redeemed. Adventists practice baptism of adults by immersion and foot-washing in preparation for Holy Communion. They also encourage members to tithe their income for support of the church.

The church strongly emphasizes health and wellness, not as a means to salvation, but as a part of glorifying God in all of life. The church recommends following a vegetarian diet where this is available. Adventists own and operate numerous hospitals and nearly six hundred other medical facilities worldwide. In addition, the church operates a network of health food factories and promotes public health. The church's Loma Linda University in Southern California is noted for its medical research and medical care.

Adventists operate an extensive worldwide system of elementary and secondary schools and own more than one hundred colleges and universities. They own more than sixty publishing houses, and their radio and television broadcasts reach nearly every country. The church broadcasts twenty-four hours a day from its global satellite system: the Hope Channel. The Adventist Development and Relief Agency (ADRA) distributes food and clothing around the world, particularly when disasters strike. The organization also drills wells, educates mothers on baby care and nutrition, helps farmers become self-sufficient, and ministers to those infected with HIV and AIDS.

For many years the church has been noted for its promotion of religious liberty and the separation of church and state. Through the International Religious Liberty Association, Adventists organize symposiums, congresses, meetings of experts, and large gatherings called Festivals of Religious Freedom. Adventists have also been involved in interchurch relationship for years. They are invited as observers to the meetings of the

World Council of Churches and belong to the Conference of Secretaries of the Christian World Communions.

The church is organized in a representative form of government consisting of four steps. First is the local church made up of individual believers. Next is the local conference that covers a state or local territory. The union conference is a united body of local conferences. The General Conference embraces the worldwide church. Union conferences send delegates to the world session of the General Conference. The chaplain of the US Senate, Admiral Barry Black, is a member of the church.

The SDA Church is conservative in theology and evangelical in practice, but some evangelical (and other) Christians have questioned its doctrinal orthodoxy because of its belief in White's gift of prophecy and its traditional (but gradually dying out) belief that observance of the Sabbath and Saturday worship is necessary for authentic Christianity. More importantly, however, critics have pointed to its doctrine of the "investigative judgment" of Christ, which, traditionally, SDA people believe began in heaven in 1844. According to this unique doctrine Christ is now, between 1844 and his return, "investigating" the lives of professed Christians for their worthiness to be included in his kingdom. Again, this is a doctrine that many SDA people do not emphasize. During the latter decades of the twentieth century many evangelical critics of the SDA Church publicly changed their minds and affirmed it as an orthodox Christian denomination.

The SDA Church, like most Adventists, is strongly Arminian in its beliefs about salvation, teaching that people have free will and are not predestined to heaven or hell (as in many conservative forms of Calvinism). The Church believes a truly saved person can lose his or her salvation through "apostasy" by either rejecting Christ or living an unrepentant life of sin.

The SDA Church is generally conservative with regard to matters of gender and sexuality. It does not ordain women or have women pastors. It considers marriage between one man and one woman and condemns homosexual behavior as sinful (without singling it out as especially sinful).

For more information: www.adventist.org

Headquarters: 12501 Old Columbia Pike, Silver Spring, MD 20904

UNITED CHURCH OF GOD

Founded: 1995, with roots to 1934
Membership: 13,800 in 200 congregations (2016)

The United Church of God (UCG) is the largest denomination that still holds to the teachings of Herbert Armstrong, the founder of the Worldwide Church of God. It was founded by several leaders in the Philadelphia Church of God in 1995 who objected to the leadership of George Flurry. The United Church of God is open to the idea of salvation outside of its own denomination, and it has various accountability structures in place for finances and church administration. The church's mission is "to announce the coming of God's Kingdom, not to establish it."

Like all of the descendants of the original Radio Church of God, the UCG makes extensive use of all forms of media, especially the Internet, to promote its message, which is grounded in the thought of Armstrong. The church is strongly Adventist, believing that Christ's second coming is imminent, and it is the mission of the church to prepare people to live in the kingdom of God as godly people. This includes the adoption of many practices in the Mosaic Law, particularly the observance of Saturday as the Sabbath. The church also teaches that Anglo-Saxon peoples are descendants of the biblical patriarch Joseph, and are thus really Israelites. This is a doctrine known as "British Israelism," which was espoused by Armstrong. The church is an international fellowship that operates in over fifty countries. Its primary publication is *Good News Magazine*, which is published in four languages. As with most Adventist groups, the church believes strongly that biblical prophecies will be fulfilled in history, and it interprets contemporary events in light of prophecy.

For more information: www.ucg.org

Headquarters: PO Box 541027, Cincinnati, OH 45245

UNITARIANS AND UNIVERSALISTS

Unitarianism and Universalism represent two different religious movements that were brought together with the formation of the Unitarian Universalist Association of Congregations (UUA) in 1961. It is helpful to look at the separate history of these two movements before discussing the new institution that was established in the twentieth century and its spin-offs.

Unitarianism. The basic tenet of Unitarianism is that there is only one person who is God and Jesus was not God incarnate but a perfect man. Unitarians thus deny two key orthodox Christian doctrines: the Trinity and the deity of Jesus Christ. "Unitarian," then, does not so much refer to a desire to *unify* Christians as to *deny* the doctrine of the Trinity and affirm the absolute oneness of God as the Father only, not Jesus. Unitarians often claim that their thought reaches back into the early Christian centuries before the concept of the Trinity was developed. Unitarianism as we know it today, however, began with the Protestant Reformation, among anti-trinitarian radical reformers such as Michael Servetus (ca. 1511–53) and Faustus Socinus (1539–1604). Some Anabaptists in Switzerland, Hungary, Transylvania, Holland, Poland, and Italy held ideas similar to Unitarianism. In England Unitarianism was the religious belief of the scientist and mathematician Isaac Newton (1642–1727), the philosopher John Locke (1632–1704), and the poet John Milton (1608–1674). The first Unitarian denomination was the Polish Brethren during the Protestant Reformation; it was led by Socinus and was stamped out by Catholics and Protestants together. The first surviving, modern Unitarian denomination was then founded in England in the late eighteenth century.

American Unitarianism developed as a religious movement among New England Congregationalists who were known as "Free Thinkers." They were influenced by English Unitarians and by the cultural attitude known as the Enlightenment. The split within Congregationalism came into the open in 1805 when Henry Ware (1764–1845), a Unitarian, was appointed professor of theology at Harvard University, the bastion of Congregationalist education. The split widened in 1819 when William Ellery Channing (1780–1842) of Boston preached his famous Baltimore sermon outlining the Unitarian view. Channing defined the true church in these words: "By his Church our Savior does not mean a party bearing the name of a human leader, distinguished by a form or an opinion . . . These are the church—men made better, made holy, virtuous by his religion—men who, hoping in his promises, keep his commands." Early New England Unitarians founded Harvard Divinity College, now Harvard Divinity School, in 1816.

Eventually Unitarian Congregationalists organized the American Unitarian Association in 1825 in order to "better work for the Kingdom of God" and "and promote the interests of the religion of Jesus as love to God and love to man." Included in the plan was the expansion of liberal religion around the world. Independent local churches were grouped in local, county, district, state, and regional conferences and were united in an international association for purposes of fellowship, counsel, and promotion of mutual interests. Early American Unitarian churches were primarily former Congregational or Baptist congregations that adopted Unitarian beliefs as theirs. Some US presidents have been Unitarians including John Quincy Adams and Howard Taft.

Universalist. There are many forms of Universalism, but in general the term refers to the belief that all persons will be saved regardless of religious belief or non-belief. Universalists find evidence of their thinking and philosophy in many cultural streams, and the teaching has much in common with several religions throughout the world. Universalists claim roots in the early Christian theologians Origen of Alexandria (185–254) and Gregory of Nyssa (335–394), certain Anabaptists, and radical Pietist mystics such as Jacob Boehme (1575–1624).

In 1759, James Relly (1722–78) of England wrote *Union*, in which he opposed the Calvinistic doctrine of election of the few. Relly's conviction of universal salvation deeply influenced John Murray (1741–1815), a Wesleyan evangelist who came to New Jersey in 1770 and found groups of universalist-minded people scattered along the Atlantic coast. He became minister to one such group in Gloucester, Massachusetts, and later served briefly as a Revolutionary War chaplain in the armies of Washington and Greene. His Independent Christian Church of Gloucester became the first organized Universalist church in the United States in 1779.

A group of Universalists met at Philadelphia in 1790 to draft their first declaration of faith and plan of government. They promoted pacifism, abolition of slavery, testimony by affirmation rather than by oath, and free public education. This Philadelphia declaration was adopted by a group of New England Universalists in 1793. At about the same time, Hosea Ballou (1771–1852), a schoolteacher and itinerant preacher in Vermont, was ordained to the Universalist ministry. He broke radically with Murray's thought. His 1805 *Treatise on Atonement* gave Universalists their first consistent philosophy. In addition to the rationalist rejection of endless punishment in hell, the Trinity, and miracles, Ballou taught that God recognized humanity's heavenly nature and loved the human race as God's own offspring. The meaning of the atonement was not found in bloody sacrifice to appease divine wrath ("substitutionary atonement"), but in the heroic sacrifice of Jesus, who wanted to win all persons to God's love ("moral example atonement").

Like the Unitarians, Universalists in the nineteenth century were active very early in reform movements for prison inmates and working women. They opposed slavery, stood for separation of church and state, and have maintained a continuing interest in the fields of science, labor, management, civil rights, and human concern. Universalists founded several nonsectarian colleges and universities, including Tufts, St. Lawrence, and Goddard universities, and the California Institute of Technology.

Throughout the twentieth century Unitarians and Universalists discovered they had much in common. Both groups rejected traditional Christian orthodoxy while believing in Christ as the supreme revelation of God in humanity. (Eventually some Unitarian-Universalists would come to doubt even that opting instead for a religious pluralism or even non-theism.) Both questioned original sin, the wrath of God, and hell. Both believed in the essential goodness of human nature (humanism) and the importance of critical thinking in religion. Their merger in 1961 became inevitable. Later, however, some Unitarian-Universalists would question the religious pluralism of the new denomination and break away to return to the Christian roots of Unitarianism.

SUGGESTIONS FOR FURTHER READING

Buehrens, John A., et al. *A Chosen Faith: An Introduction to Unitarian Universalism.* Boston, MA: Beacon Press, 1998.

Robinson, David. *The Unitarians and the Universalists.* Westport, CT: Greenwood Publishing, 1985.

Williams, George H. *American Universalism: A Bicentennial Historical Essay.* Boston, MA: Universalist Historical Society, 1971.

AMERICAN UNITARIAN CONFERENCE

Founded 2000
Membership statistics not available

This organization, the American Unitarian Conference (AUC), represents a rare institutional split in American Unitarianism, and it is still unclear how this new denomination will develop as an institution. The AUC developed from Unitarian-Universalist minister Carl Scovel's concern that the Unitarian Universalist Association's (AAU's) embrace of humanism and Eastern religious beliefs was crowding out Unitarian theism, which was the traditional understanding of the denomination. The AUC remains committed to the Unitarian principle of freedom in religion and tolerating a wide variety of religious beliefs while promoting monotheism. Central to the ethos of the AUC is that faith, reason, science, and religion should be seen as collaborative rather than competitive activities. Some observers regard this movement as an attempt to get back to original Unitarianism's roots in Christian deism. However, membership is not restricted to Christians.

Among the denomination's principles are that God's presence is known in different ways and that revelation is continuing; religion should be a responsible search for meaning; that free will is a gift from God and religion should assist in the development of human ethics; that both reason and faith lead to humility and humility leads to tolerance; and finally the religious quest should lead to greater mercy and compassion in a world filled with suffering.

The AUC recognizes all member congregations as autonomous (self-governing). They may call as their ministers anyone they wish depending only on the person's character and general agreement with AUC principles.

For more information: www.americanunitarian.org

Headquarters: 6806 Springfield Drive, Mason Neck, VA 22079

UNITARIAN UNIVERSALIST ASSOCIATION

Founded: 1961
Membership: 221,367 in 1,048 congregations (2012)

In May 1961, the Unitarian and Universalist churches in the United States and Canada were consolidated as the Unitarian Universalist Association of Congregations (UUA) in North America, one of the most influential liberal churches. The two bodies had separate and interesting origins and histories (see this section's introduction above). In this association, flexibility, freedom of conscience, and local autonomy are prime values. No minister, member, or congregation "shall be required to subscribe to any particular interpretation of religion, or to any particular religious belief or creed."

The aims of the association were set forth in 1985 in a revised statement that promotes human dignity, social justice and compassion, the free and responsible search for truth, democracy, the goal of global community, and respect for the environment. Increasingly since the merger in 1961 the UUA has embraced Eastern as well as Western religious practices, beliefs, and traditions.

In recent years the Association has been heavily involved in numerous causes and concerns: the issue of racial and cultural diversity; the rise of feminist consciousness; scholarship in church history and process theology; inner-city ministries; and the rights of gay, lesbian, bisexual, and transgender persons. The Unitarian Universalist Service Committee provides leadership and materials in the field of social change. The denomination has dozens of independent affiliate organizations that advocate and provide resources for various causes.

A General Assembly, with clergy and lay representatives, is the overall policy-making body, meeting annually. The officers of the Association are elected for four-year terms and serve together with other elected members as a Board of Trustees that appoints the executive and administrative officers and generally carries out policies and directives. In 2001, the UUA elected William Sinkford as its first African American head.

UUA headquarters are in Boston, and twenty-three district offices have been established. Principal numerical strength lies in the Northeast, the Midwest, and the Pacific West Coast. Foreign work is now conducted through the International Association for Religious Freedom. Beacon Press produces many new titles each year and is one of the most distinguished independent publishing houses in the United States. There are two UUA seminaries, Meadville Lombard Theological School in Chicago and Starr King School for Ministry in Berkeley.

The UUA is noted for being liberal and pluralistic and for promoting the causes of people who consider themselves marginalized or oppressed by the wider society. It embraces within itself self-identified pagans as well as Buddhists as well as atheists as well as Christians. (Some UUA individuals and congregations form together a group within the UUA called the Unitarian Universalist Christian Fellowship, which consists of Unitarian-Universalists who feel that they are too Unitarian to be Christian and too Christian to be Unitarian.) The UUA has long ordained women and had women leaders at all levels and affirms same-sex marriage and has LGBT leaders and ministers.

For more information: www.uua.org

Headquarters: 24 Farnsworth Street, Boston, MA 02210

FUNDAMENTALIST AND BIBLE CHURCHES

Representing the most conservative form of Protestantism, both socially and theologically, Fundamentalism was one of the most potent forces within American Christianity in the twentieth century. (Here "Fundamentalism" will be capitalized when referring to the movement and not capitalized—"fundamentalism"—when referring to the distinctive ethos of the movement.) Fundamentalism, both as an ethos and a movement, is a form of conservative evangelical Protestantism, but may be distinguished from other types of evangelical churches by its intense opposition to modern philosophy, science, theology and culture. Unlike many Amish, however, Fundamentalists do not eschew technology insofar as it can be used helpfully in worship and evangelism. They do not normally separate physically from urban living, but, living among others in towns and cities, they view much of what modern, urban, industrial culture has created, including public education, as anti-Christian. Many of them "home school" their own children using fundamentalist Christian curricula that teaches, for example, that the world is only, at most, about ten thousand years old ("young earth creationism"). Fundamentalists regard modern American culture as decadent in its increasing secularity and pluralism. They also tend to regard non-Fundamentalist churches and their members as "compromised" spiritually and theologically. They do their utmost to remain separate from all "worldliness" including modern Bible translations, ecumenical cooperation, and popular entertainment that includes depictions of sex. Doctrinally, fundamentalists place great stress on the inerrancy of the Bible, its literal interpretation, conservative Protestant orthodoxy, conversion through repentance and faith, the "substitutionary atonement" of Christ (that on the cross Jesus suffered the wrath of God against sin), the miracles of the Bible including especially the virgin birth of Christ and his literal bodily resurrection, and the imminent return of Christ to judge the wicked and establish his kingdom on earth.

It is difficult to categorize and study fundamentalist churches because of the variety within Fundamentalism and the fact that fundamentalism exerts an influence beyond its membership rolls. Fundamentalist churches tend to be congregationalist and baptistic in orientation (although there are Presbyterian, Lutheran and even Methodist versions of fundamentalism); therefore, structure exists primarily on the local level. Pastors tend to found their own congregations and have fellowship and cooperation only with like-minded fundamentalists. Some preachers, like the late Jerry Falwell (1933–2007), build their congregations into major "denominetworks" of congregations that "spin off" from the original church but remain under its influence and within its orbit. Rather than having traditional denominational structures, fundamentalist churches generally establish a variety of cooperative ministry programs, such as radio and television ministries, sponsorship of foreign missions, and educational programs. Bible colleges, often associated with local congregations, are one of the backbones of Fundamentalism. Graduates of these Bible colleges often serve in denominations that are not in themselves fundamentalist and attempt to incline them toward it.

Fundamentalism grew out of late nineteenth-century American evangelicalism and revivalism. Evangelist Dwight L. Moody (1837–99), founder of Moody Bible Institute, was one of the key figures in the formation of Fundamentalist organizations, but the roots of the movement go back to the Plymouth Brethren in England. The early Brethren were disappointed with the clericalism of the "mainline" churches and encouraged all male members of their separatist, highly conservative movement of house churches to preach, evangelize, and offer the sacraments. One of the key preachers was John Nelson Darby (1800–82), who stressed the importance of biblical prophecy, especially that found in the apocalyptic books of the Bible (Daniel and Revelation), for understanding human history. Drawing on Dutch Reformed theologians of the seventeenth century, Darby taught that history was divided into seven dispensations described in the Bible. The first six ended in a cataclysm, such as the expulsion from Eden and the great flood. The seventh dispensation will be the millennial age that Christ will inaugurate after his return. Cyrus Scofield (1843–1921) made Darby's theory the centerpiece of his popular reference Bible early in the twentieth century. According to this scenario, life on earth will grow increasingly violent and sinful, as in the days before Noah's flood, until Christ "raptures" his true people from the earth. This belief system is a form of pre-millennialism but adds some details to historic pre-millennialism such as the so-called secret rapture before a "great tribulation" on earth during which a figure the Bible calls the antichrist rules the world. Then Christ will return bodily, with those he raptured into heaven, to destroy the antichrist, judge the nations, and rule and reign on earth with his true "saints" (faithful followers) for a thousand years.

This "dispensationalist" view of biblical prophecy, history, and the end times was taken up by most fundamentalists—except those who held firmly to traditional Reformed theology and its denial of a literal thousand-year reign of Christ on earth after his return (amillennialism). However, even many Presbyterian fundamentalists adopted dispensational eschatology and worked it into their otherwise Reformed theology.

Fundamentalism consciously runs counter to modern trends in biblical scholarship and scientific theories about the origin, age, and evolution of the universe. It also rejects the modern idea of social progress in favor of a view of historical decline. Since biblical truth is under attack, according to fundamentalists, true believers must defend the Bible—especially those passages that support apocalyptic eschatology and dispensationalism. *The Fundamentals: A Testimony to the Truth* was a popular pamphlet series designed to defend the Bible from critics. It appeared between 1910 and 1915 and included nearly one hundred articles that sought to defend the deity of Christ, the virgin birth, the historical resurrection, the inerrancy of scripture as the word of God, and the reality of sin and Satan against an increasing tide of "modernism" (liberal biblical scholarship and theology) within Protestant denominations. Though many of the authors of these pamphlets were conservative evangelicals rather than fundamentalists, the movement got its name from these publications. Though some fundamentalist bodies were originally connected to the Holiness movement, most have roots in the Baptist and Presbyterian churches.

World War I put the Fundamentalist controversy on hold as Christians of all kinds joined in the war effort, but by 1920, it heated up again as Baptist and Presbyterian fundamentalists fought to preserve their churches from modern theology and biblical scholarship. This early period culminated in the famous Scopes "Monkey Trial" of 1925 over the teaching of evolution in the public schools. Following that celebrated trial, fundamentalists began organizing separate congregations, schools, mission agencies, interchurch organizations, and even denominations. It appeared that the fundamentalists had lost the struggle to eject what they called "modernism" from their denominations and were retreating from society, but public ridicule merely confirmed their conviction that America was becoming an apostate nation—especially in its religious side. Throughout much of the twentieth century fundamentalist Protestants of all denominations (or none because many formed totally independent churches) encouraged their young people to attend Fundamentalist Bible colleges that taught against modern science, especially evolution, and treated the Bible, interpreted literally, as the core textbook of the entire curriculum. During the period between 1925 and about 1975 most American fundamentalists spoke very openly and critically of non-fundamentalist denominations and institutions and against secularism, religious pluralism, "godless communism" (a major enemy of fundamentalists, which they tended to see as growing everywhere including the United States), and ecumenical movements for dialogue and possible unity between other Protestants.

One man, an extremely conservative Presbyterian, emerged as a major spokesperson for all American fundamentalists in the 1930s through the 1950s: Carl McIntire (1906–2002). He was a radio preacher and founder of his own Bible Presbyterian Church—a more conservative breakaway denomination for the already very conservative Orthodox Presbyterian Church founded by earlier fundamentalists. McIntire founded a cooperative organization of fundamentalists called the American Council of Christian Churches to bring together for fellowship and mutual support and encouragement fundamentalists of different Protestant traditions. When the National Association of Evangelicals formed in 1942 McIntire declined to join it because it included too broad a variety of evangelicals including Pentecostals. When Billy Graham emerged as the figurehead leader of the neo-evangelical movement (non-fundamentalist evangelicals of many denominations) McIntire and other fundamentalists criticized him and it as not sufficiently separated from worldliness and apostate forms of Christianity (e.g., Catholicism).

By the end of the twentieth century, Protestant fundamentalists had successfully created a significant subculture in American society. World events fueled the growth of Fundamentalism. In particular, the formation of the State of Israel in 1948 seemed to confirm the fundamentalists' prediction that the Jews would return to the promised land shortly before the return of Christ. Plus, the threat of nuclear destruction during the Cold War gave renewed vigor to fundamentalist preaching and writing. A number of best-selling books, such as Hal Lindsey's *The Late Great Planet Earth*, popularized the fundamentalists' view of human history and the end of the world. The Supreme Court's decision to extend separation of church and state to the public schools (banning school-sponsored prayers and other expressions of religion) galvanized the fundamentalist movement in the 1950s. Many fundamentalists objected loudly to what they perceived as the loss of traditional Christian values and beliefs not only among non-fundamentalist religious people but also at all levels of American society.

Though prone to fractures and doctrinal disputes, fundamentalists began in the 1970s to organize to "return America to God" using political means. Fundamentalist megachurch pastor and author Jerry Falwell began calling himself and fellow fundamentalists "evangelicals" when the American media began to use "fundamentalist" to describe especially Muslim militants in the Middle East. Falwell and others like him, preferring the label "conservative evangelical" over "fundamentalist," created organizations such as the "Moral Majority" to pressure governments to adopt "family values"—a phrase they used for their own beliefs about the right ordering of society. Fundamentalism was coming out of its self-imposed inner exile and organizing to return America to what it believed was true godliness and virtue.

Membership in true, traditional fundamentalist churches may be relatively small, but the influence of Fundamentalism extends more broadly in conservative Protestantism in the United States. Pastors in many evangelical denominations have been trained in fundamentalist educational institutions, such as Dallas Theological Seminary, and the Scofield Study Bible and its descendents are widely used.

In the 1980s and 90s, fundamentalist pastors in the Southern Baptist Convention gained authority over many aspects of the denomination, including control of its theological seminaries. However, the association of the word *fundamentalist* with Islamic radicalism has led many conservative Protestants to distance themselves from the word. It is not easy to distinguish between conservative evangelicals, Holiness churches,

Pentecostals, and fundamentalists. One distinguishing hallmark of Fundamentalism, though, is "biblical separation"—a favorite doctrine and practice of true fundamentalists. It means refusal of "Christian fellowship" with people who claim to be Christian but are "infected" by modernism. Another is belief that "biblical inerrancy" is a litmus test of true, faithful Christianity. Finally, true fundamentalists interpret Genesis and Revelation as literally as possible including belief in a "young earth"—that God created the universe in six days of twenty-four hours each about ten thousand years ago—and in dispensational eschatology. Most fundamentalists admit that people who disagree with these cardinal tenets of Fundamentalism may be saved, but they view them—even fellow evangelicals—as infected with modernism and therefore not worthy of Christian fellowship.

So what do all the denominations categorized here as fundamentalist have in common? All either grew out of the Fundamentalist movement described above or have come to embrace it as their spiritual-theological ethos and brand of Christianity. Variety exists among them; there is no uniform profile that fits them all. However, it is fairly safe to say that, for example, even among fundamentalist Baptists being fundamentalist is more important than being Baptist. They will not belong, for example, to the World Baptist Alliance because they view it as infected with modernism.

The denominations named and described here do not begin to exhaust the actual numerical strength of Fundamentalism in America; many, perhaps most, fundamentalist churches are "unaffiliated"—a buzzword often used among fundamentalists (Baptists especially) for churches that do not have ties with anyone else and are not part of any denomination, association, or convention. None of these denominations ordain women or have women pastors; all regard homosexual behavior as sin and do not ordain or admit to leadership positions openly gay men.

SUGGESTIONS FOR FURTHER READING

Balmer, Randall. *Mine Eyes Have Seen the Glory: A Journey into the Evangelical Subculture of America*. New York: Oxford University Press, 1989.

LaHaye, Tim. *The Battle for the Family*. Old Tappan, NJ: Fleming H. Revell, 1984.

Lawrence, Bruce B. *Defenders of God: The Fundamentalist Revolt against the Modern Age*. San Francisco, CA: HarperSanFrancisco, 1989.

Lindsey, Hal. *The Late Great Planet Earth*. Grand Rapids, MI: Zondervan, 1970.

Longfield, Bradley J. *The Presbyterian Controversy: Fundamentalists, Modernists, and Moderates*. New York: Oxford University Press, 1991.

Marsden, George M. *Fundamentalism and American Culture: The Shaping of Twentieth-Century Evangelicalism, 1870–1925*. New York: Oxford University Press, 1980.

Marty, Martin, and R. Scott Appleby, eds. *The Fundamentalism Project*. 5 vols. Chicago, IL: University of Chicago Press, 1991–95.

Marty, Martin, and R. Scott Appleby. *The Glory and the Power: The Fundamentalist Challenge to the Modern World*. Boston, MA: Beacon Press, 1992.

Sandeen, Ernest. *The Roots of Fundamentalism*. Chicago, IL: University of Chicago Press, 1970.

AMERICAN EVANGELICAL CHRISTIAN CHURCHES

Founded: 1944
Membership: 17,400 in 192 churches (2006)*

The American Evangelical Christian Churches (AECC) calls itself a "recognized Christian denomination" and, although its statement of faith is fairly minimal (for evangelicals generally), its ethos is fundamentalist. Clergy credentialed by the AECC serve in a variety of capacities, including prison ministry, military and hospital chaplaincy, as well as outreach to truckers, bikers, and others without a permanent Christian community. Ministerial applicants must subscribe to "Seven Articles of Faith": (1) the Bible as the infallible, written word of God; (2) the virgin birth; (3) the deity of Jesus Christ; (4) salvation through the atonement of Christ; (5) the guidance of life through prayer; (6) the return of Christ; and (7) the establishment of the millennial kingdom. Upon completion of training, ministerial students are granted licenses enabling them to perform all the functions and offices of the ministry. Full ordination is withheld until the licentiate has become pastor of a regular congregation or is engaged in full-time evangelistic or missionary work. Twelve regional offices in the United States and one in Canada supervise the work of the organization.

The denomination operates the American Evangelical Bible College and Seminary headquartered in Indianapolis, Indiana, and Savage, Minnesota. It functions primarily as an off-campus, distance-learning institution and is non-accredited.

For more information: www.aeccministries.com

Headquarters: PO Box 47312, Indianapolis, IN 46227

*Like some other denominations contacted for current membership information, the AECC declined to provide current (2016) membership statistics saying that each affiliated church is so independent as to not provide the central organization with membership information.

BAPTIST BIBLE FELLOWSHIP INTERNATIONAL

Founded: 1950
Membership: est. 110,000 in 4,000 churches (2010)

Baptist Bible Fellowship (BBF) was founded by some one hundred Baptist ministers and missionaries to promote fellowship among independent Baptists in three main areas of church life: evangelism, education of church workers, and the founding of churches. Many of the founders had been part of the World Fundamental Baptist Missionary Fellowship (today known as the World Baptist Fellowship), which had roots in the Baptist Bible Union, founded in 1921. The Baptist Bible Fellowship's statement of faith was based on that of the Baptist Bible Union. It is strongly fundamentalist in character, emphasizing the inerrancy of scripture, the virgin birth, the deity of Christ, the substitutionary atonement, the resurrection of the body of Christ, biblical miracles, and the literal millennial kingdom on earth. Ministers and members of the fellowship use only the King James Version of the Bible in English-speaking churches.

The Baptist Bible Fellowship also teaches that Jesus was a Baptist in his thinking and work. They recognize baptism by immersion only, participate in Holy Communion only with members of their own church, and are adamantly opposed to dancing, drinking, smoking, movies, gambling, and sex outside of marriage. No formal membership statistics are kept, and the above figures are estimates based on attendance figures. There are churches in every state, but the greatest concentration is in the Great Lakes region and the South. Almost one third of the congregations have dual affiliation with other fundamentalist bodies.

Baptist Bible College in Springfield, Missouri, and Baptist Bible College East in Boston, Massachusetts, are owned and supported by these independent Baptists. Recently the Baptist Bible Graduate School of Theology was founded in Springfield, Missouri. Other schools supported by the fellowship are Pacific Coast Baptist Bible College and Spanish Baptist Bible Institute in Miami, Florida.

For more information: www.bbfi.org
Headquarters: 720 East Kearney Street, PO Box 191, Springfield, MO 65801

BAPTIST MISSIONARY ASSOCIATION OF AMERICA

Founded: 1950
Membership: 137,909 in 1,272 churches (2010)

Organized at Little Rock, Arkansas, as the North American Baptist Association, this group changed its name to Baptist Missionary Association of America (BMA) in 1968. It concentrates on fostering and encouraging missionary cooperation. There are workers in home missions and missionary work abroad in Mexico, Japan, Brazil, Taiwan, Portugal, Cape Verde Islands, Uruguay, Guatemala, Costa Rica, Nicaragua, Australia, Italy, France, Africa, India, Bolivia, Honduras, Korea, and the Philippines. A strong publications department issues literature for Sunday school and training classes as well as pamphlets, books, tracts, and magazines in both English and Spanish. The association also owns and operates a printing business in Brazil, where literature is printed in Portuguese for use in Africa and Europe. A worldwide radio ministry is also maintained.

The members are thoroughly fundamentalist in conviction, placing strong emphasis on the verbal inspiration and inerrancy of scripture, young earth creationism, the virgin birth and deity of Jesus, his substitutionary atonement, justification by faith alone at conversion, and the imminent, personal return of Christ to earth before his millennial reign on earth. The Lord's Supper and baptism are accepted as ordinances, and baptism is considered "alien" unless administered to believers by the divine authority as given to the Missionary Baptist churches. With its roots in the American Baptist Association, this body carries on the Landmark Baptist movement, which strongly emphasizes the nature of "church" as always and only individual congregations and holding to the historic succession of independent Baptist churches from the time of Christ.

BMA churches are completely autonomous in the Baptist tradition and, regardless of size, have an equal voice in the cooperative missionary, publication, evangelical, and educational efforts of the association. Member churches must, however, conform to the doctrinal standards of the association. Three junior colleges and several orphans' homes are maintained on a state level, and a theological seminary is located in Jacksonville, Texas.

For more information: www.bmaamerica.org
Headquarters: PO Box 1188, Conway, AR 72033

BEREAN FELLOWSHIP OF CHURCHES

Founded: 1947
Membership: est. 12,000 in 60 churches (2016)

In the mid-1930s, Dr. Ivan E. Olsen became the first pastor of the Berean Fundamental Church, an independent congregation in North Platte, Nebraska. Following the biblical principle of evangelism found in Acts 1:8, Olsen assisted in planting sixteen other churches in surrounding communities. In 1947 these churches formed the Berean Fundamental Church Council, Inc. Some time in the early twenty-first century the denomination changed its name to the Berean Fellowship of Churches (BFC) although many congregations keep the name Berean Fundamental Church. The member churches possess a common constitution, stressing the basic doctrines of orthodox

Christianity and the verbal, plenary inspiration of scripture (the inerrancy of the Bible in all matters of faith and morals); the virgin birth of Christ; the deity of Christ; the blood atonement; the bodily resurrection of Christ; and the return of Christ to earth, following the rapture and preceding the millennial kingdom. The local assemblies are also Bible centered and evangelistic. Berean Fundamental churches support a variety of independent faith missions, draw their pastors from various seminaries and Bible institutes, and freely choose their own Sunday school curricula and church literature. The denomination supports its own Maranatha Bible Camp and Conference Grounds near North Platte.

For more information: www.weareberean.org

Headquarters: PO Box 234, Broken Arrow, NE 68822

BIBLE FELLOWSHIP CHURCH

Founded: 1858
Membership: est. 7,275 in 65 churches (2015)

The Bible Fellowship Church (BFC) was formed in the 1850s when Mennonite leaders in Pennsylvania resisted the more evangelical style of some of the younger generation. The evangelical Mennonites formed their own group. Originally it was called the Evangelical Conference, but the name was changed in 1959 when a new confession of faith was adopted. The church now has a more fundamentalist outlook, but retains some of its Mennonite heritage. BFC's doctrinal emphases include salvation through the death and resurrection of Christ, transformation of life through new birth by the Holy Spirit, the authority and trustworthiness of the Bible as the word of God, the culmination of history in the second coming of Jesus (pre-millennialism), and a shared life in the church of believers, with every member being responsible for the propagation of the gospel through evangelism and missions. Churches are found mainly in Pennsylvania; New Jersey; New York; and Ontario, Canada. The churches support missions on five continents plus the Pinebrook Junior College, the Victory Valley Camp for children and youth, a home for the aging, and Pinebrook-in-the-Pines, a conference and retreat center—all in Pennsylvania.

The BFC keeps to its Anabaptist and Mennonite heritage with regard to the ordinances of baptism of believers only upon confession of faith and the Lord's Supper. It endorses and encourages the dedication of infants within the context of the family of faith but does not baptize infants. It does not require pacifism but discourages use of violence. Obedience to government, so long as it does not require violation of God's will, is affirmed.

The BFC has at its website a very detailed "Articles of Faith and Principles for Biblical Living" that indicates its fundamentalist ethos including biblical holiness and separation from all worldliness. On the other hand, many people who think of fundamentalism stereotypically might be surprised by the BGC's statements urging compassion, mercy, and justice toward all people including illegal immigrants.

For more information: www.mybfc.org

Headquarters: 3000 Fellowship Drive, Whitehall, PA 18052

GENERAL ASSOCIATION OF REGULAR BAPTIST CHURCHES

Founded: 1932
Membership: 132,700 members in 1,321 churches (2012)

Twenty-two Baptist churches of the Northern Baptist Convention (now the American Baptist Churches, USA [ABCUSA]) left that organization in May 1932 to found the General Association of Regular Baptist Churches (GARBC). Their protest was against what they considered the Northern Baptists' modernist tendencies and teachings, the denial of the historic Baptist principle of independence and autonomy of the local congregation, the inequality of representation in the assemblies of the convention, and the control of missionary work by convention assessment and budget.

Basically fundamentalist in outlook and ethos, the GARBC understands its mission as "to champion the Biblical truth, impact the world for Christ, perpetuate a Baptist heritage, and advance the Association churches." The Association subscribes to the New Hampshire Confession of Faith (1832) with a pre-millennial interpretation of the final article of that confession. It holds to the infallibility of the Bible, the Trinity, the personality of Satan as the author of all evil, humankind as the creation of God, and humankind born in sin. Doctrines deal with the virgin birth, the deity of Jesus, and faith in Christ as the way of salvation through grace at conversion. The saved are in everlasting joy; the lost are consigned to endless punishment. Civil government is by divine appointment. There are only two approved ordinances: baptism of believers by immersion and the Lord's Supper.

Any Baptist church coming into the GARBC is required to withdraw all fellowship and cooperation from any convention or group that permits modernists or modernism within its ranks ("biblical separation"). Dual fellowship or membership is not permitted. Church government is strictly congregational. Associated churches have the privilege of sending six voting messengers to an annual convention. A Council of Eighteen is elected (six each year) to serve for three years. The Council makes recommendations to the Association for the furtherance of its work and puts into operation all actions and policies of the Association. The Council's authority depends completely on the will and direction of the Association, but it does appoint a National Representative to oversee the denominational office in Illinois and to represent the Association to its churches and constituencies. The Regular Baptist Press publishes *The Baptist Bulletin*, a bimonthly magazine.

The GARBC is known among Baptists and evangelicals generally as often critical of the ministry of Billy Graham—something of a litmus test for a distinction between "neo-evangelicals" (postfundamentalist evangelicals) and fundamentalist evangelicals. Many GARBC people consider Graham too inclusive in permitting Catholics and mainline, "liberal" Protestants to cooperate in supporting his evangelistic campaigns. In 2006 the GARBC cut ties with one of its institutions—Cedarville University (Cedarville, Ohio)—for allegedly wrongly associating itself with Southern Baptists who, according to GARBC leaders, include "liberals" among their ranks. Many of the GARBC's ministers and Christian workers are educated at Faith Baptist Bible College and Seminary in Ankeny, Iowa.

For more information: www.garbc.org

Headquarters: 3715 North Ventura Drive, Arlington Heights, IL 60004

GRACE GOSPEL FELLOWSHIP

Founded: 1945
Membership: est. 60,000 in 113 churches (2016)

Dispensational and pre-millennial, the Grace Gospel Fellowship (GGF) had its beginnings as a pastors' fellowship at a conference of pastors and missionaries at the Berean Bible Church in Indianapolis, Indiana, in 1943. A year later, at Evansville, Indiana, its purpose was defined in a constitution: "to promote a fellowship among those who believe the truths contained in [our] doctrinal statement and to proclaim the Gospel of the Grace of God in this land, and throughout the world."

That doctrinal statement includes belief in the Bible as the inspired, inerrant word of God; the total depravity of the human race; redemption by God's grace through the blood of Christ by means of faith; eternal security for the saved; the gifts of the Spirit (as enumerated in Eph 4:7-16); and that the human nature of sin is never eradicated during this life. Its members believe in baptism by the Holy Spirit, without speaking in tongues, but hold that, while water baptism is biblical, it is not relevant to the present dispensation. Any church may vote to become affiliated with Grace Gospel Fellowship, provided it meets the doctrinal standards.

The GGF has sometimes been accused by critics of having a "hyper-dispensational" theology due to its belief that God's plan of salvation for Jews and gentiles are different and that they "find in Paul's writings alone the revelation, position and destiny of the Church." (For more about dispensationalism see the introduction to this section about Fundamentalist denominations.) Most dispensationalists do not go that far in distinguishing between the various dispensations (or "economies") of God in salvation history. GGF rejects the label "hyper-dispensational."

The church is present in Zaire, Puerto Rico, India, the Philippines, Australia, South Africa, Tanzania, and South America. Grace Bible College (not to be confused with Grace College in Indiana) and the headquarters of the Fellowship are located in Grand Rapids, Michigan. Closely connected to Grace Gospel Fellowship are Grace Ministries International, Grace Publications, and Grace Youth Camp in Indiana.

For more information: www.ggfusa.org

Headquarters: 1011 Aldon Street Southwest, PO Box 9432, Grand Rapids, MI 49509

GREAT COMMISSION CHURCHES

Founded: 1983, with roots to 1965
Membership: est. 25,000 regular attenders in 85 churches (2016)

In 1965 a young man name Jim McCotter set out to re-create the church of the New Testament in Greeley, Colorado. He began a house church based on the Book of Acts, and soon was attracting students from the University of Northern Colorado. McCotter's family had ties to the Plymouth Brethren and McCotter shared the Brethren's attitudes toward church discipline. The church recruited aggressively on college campuses across the United States and Canada in the 1970s in a campaign they called The Blitz. Eschewing traditional church labels, the denomination was formally organized as Great Commission International in 1983, with a focus on campus ministry and publication. Currently the organization is called Great Commission Churches.

The church is very conservative theologically and socially, especially in terms of gender roles. Over the years, McCotter's movement was frequently criticized for adopting some cult-like practices, especially alleged authoritarian leadership methods. McCotter resigned from the church in 1986 amid allegations of abusive practices in the church. In the 1980s former members of the church began Wellspring Retreat and Resource Center to assist people who felt they were victims of "religious abuse," and in 1991 the church issued a formal apology for some of its teachings and practices. Since then, it has become part of the National Association of Evangelicals.

For more information: www.gccweb.org

Headquarters: 6797 North High Street, Suite 319, Worthington, OH 43085

INDEPENDENT BAPTIST FELLOWSHIP INTERNATIONAL

Founded 1984
Membership: Unknown in 558 churches (2010)

Raymond Barber broke with the World Baptist Fellowship in 1984 after having served as president of that body. Barber was a pastor in Fort Worth, Texas, and a professor at

Arlington Baptist College, a fundamentalist school. After the split he founded Norris Bible Baptist Institute and began a publication to promote his views. The Independent Baptist Fellowship International (IBFI) is strongest in Texas and Oklahoma, but has a presence in Michigan, Ohio, and Florida, and it supports about twenty-five missionaries. Though its directory lists over almost six hundred churches, about two-thirds of them have membership in other fundamentalist associations as well.

The IBFI has two affiliated educational institutions: Crown College of the Bible and Norris Bible Baptist Seminary. The IBFI's website says these institutions are under the direction of Temple Baptist Church in Powell, Tennessee. The IBFI's Declaration of Faith includes an affirmation that the King James Version of the Bible in its 1611 or equivalent version is the only one used by the IBFI; it rejects all other translations and paraphrases of the Bible.

Norris Bible Baptist Seminary is named after famed Texas Baptist pastor and Fundamentalist leader J. Frank Norris (1877–1952), known for a fairly aggressive, separatistic form of fundamentalism.

For more information: www.ibfi.us

Headquarters: 724 North Jim Wright Freeway, Fort Worth, TX 76108

IFCA INTERNATIONAL

Founded: 1930
Membership: 61,655 in 659 churches (2012)

Originally known as the Independent Fundamental Churches of America (IFCA), the IFCA International was organized at Cicero, Illinois, to safeguard fundamental doctrines of the faith founders felt were being denied by (mostly) Congregational churches. The name was changed in the 1990s to disassociate the group from "radical fundamentalists." IFCA members must agree with doctrines of the verbal plenary inspiration and inerrancy of the Bible; the virgin birth, deity, and sinless life of Jesus Christ; the death, burial, and resurrection of Christ to provide salvation for all; the person and work of the Holy Spirit; the reality of Satan and his destructive work today; the personal and bodily return of Jesus Christ; and the bodily resurrection of all people, some to eternal life and some to "everlasting punishment."

The IFCA is less a traditional denomination than a sponsoring agency for autonomous churches and ministries. It has a strong commitment to various forms of chaplaincy, particularly military and prison ministries, and it publishes *Voice* magazine and other materials devoted to evangelical or fundamentalist ministries. The IFCA sponsors several Bible camps, Bible institutes, and children's homes. The president of the body presides over an annual conference in which the members have voting power; an executive committee of twelve serves for three years. The constituent churches are completely independent but are required to subscribe to the statement of faith of the organization in order to belong. A home office is maintained in Grandville, Michigan.

The IFCA claims as "part of its history" a long list of conservative evangelical and fundamentalist leaders including many theologians, radio preachers, and college presidents. It is a veritable "Who's Who" of mid-twentieth century conservative evangelical Protestant influencers.

The IFCA includes with its Articles of Faith and Doctrine, which emphasizes believers' separation from everything worldly, including "religious apostasy," an affirmation of dispensationalism and a list of "Movements Contrary to the Faith" including Ecumenism, Ecumenical Evangelism, Neo-Orthodoxy, and Neo-Evangelicalism.

For more information: www.ifca.org

Headquarters: 3520 Fairlines Avenue Southwest, PO Box 810, Grandville, MI 49468

INTERSTATE AND FOREIGN LANDMARK MISSIONARY BAPTIST ASSOCIATION

Founded: 1951, with roots to mid-nineteeth century
Membership: est. 14,945 in 135 churches (2000)

This association traces its origins to the Landmark controversy among Southern Baptists in the middle of the nineteenth century when James Robinson Graves, James Madison Pendleton, and Amos Cooper Dayton challenged the accepted understanding of church history. They argued that the Baptist tradition was begun during the time of Jesus and has had an unbroken history through the centuries. The individual and autonomous Baptist congregation is the only true church; therefore baptism and the Lord's Supper are only valid among Baptists. Landmark Baptists refer to non-Baptist baptism as "alien immersion" and require re-baptism for members even if they were baptized as believers by immersion before.

Landmark ideas had a strong impact on many Baptist groups in the South, especially the American Baptist Association (ABA) and the Baptist Missionary Association. The Interstate and Landmark group developed from a split within the ABA. It seeks to promote cooperation among Landmark Baptists who support their ministries only through freewill offerings rather than regular salaries. Doctrinally, they follow typical fundamentalist Baptist teachings, but they do practice foot-washing as an ordinance. They are strongest in the southern Mississippi River region but support missions in Mexico and the Philippines. They do not have salaried ministers.

For more information: www.landmarkbaptist.us

Headquarters: none

PLYMOUTH BRETHREN (CHRISTIAN BRETHREN)

Founded: 1820s
Membership: est. 42,500 in 860 congregations (2016)

"Plymouth Brethren" (PB) is a widely used, but unofficial, designation for a loose and diverse group of churches with early nineteenth-century roots in the British Isles. Within these churches, the common terminology is simply "Brethren" or "Christian Brethren," but they are to be distinguished from Brethren churches associated with the Pietist movement. Similar to the Restorationist bodies in the United States, the early Brethren envisioned a basis for Christian unity by forsaking denominational structures and names in order to meet simply as Christians. The autonomy of the local congregation or "meeting" is a strong feature of the movement.

The weekly hour-long "remembrance meeting" is probably the surest way to identify a Brethren assembly. In accordance with the meaning of "priesthood of believers," the service is unstructured and participatory. Brethren have consistently refused to restrict the administration of baptism or the Lord's Supper to ordained ministers, thus effectively eliminating a distinction between clergy and laity and the traditional concept of ordination. A preacher may serve full-time with a congregation, but will not be identified as clergy or be given control of the congregation.

The Brethren are committed to all the fundamentals of conservative Christianity, including the verbal inspiration of scripture. They emphasize gospel preaching and the necessity for personal conversion. Except for the weekly breaking of bread and the absence of collections at other meetings, their services are much like those of evangelical Baptist and Bible churches. Some PB meetings have taken the name "Bible church" as they have grown and become established congregations with their own buildings.

Among American evangelicals, Brethren have had an influence out of proportion to their numbers. Their pre-millennial theology helped to shape evangelicalism, especially in the proliferation of independent churches and mission boards. In recent years, many have responded to the Brethren emphasis on plurality of leadership and participatory worship in the local church. Brethren are also characteristically found in leadership positions in interdenominational evangelistic campaigns and the founding and operation of non-denominational Bible schools, colleges, seminaries, and parachurch organizations. They have only one multiple-year, college-level institution, Emmaus Bible College in Dubuque, Iowa.

As a result of a division in England in 1848, there are two basic types of assemblies, commonly known as "exclusive" and "open." Led in the beginning by John Nelson Darby (1800–82), the exclusive assemblies produced most of the movement's well-known Bible teachers, such as William Kelly, F. W. Grant, and C. H. Macintosh. They operated on the premise that disciplinary action taken by one assembly was binding on all. As a result, once started, a division often spreads worldwide, until by the end of the century the exclusive Brethren were divided into seven or eight main groups. Recent mergers have reduced that number somewhat, and an important American group has merged with the open assemblies.

Open assemblies were led by George Müller (1805–95), well known for his orphanages and life of faith. Their strength has always been in evangelism and foreign missions. Lacking the exclusive disciplinary premise, local disputes spread only as far as there was interest and involvement; thus open assemblies have never experienced worldwide division.

Some PB meetings are closed to non-PB visitors unless they are invited by a member. Most do not advertise themselves and neighbors may only notice a small sign outside a small, white chapel that says something like "Gospel Hall." Rarely is there mention of the appellation "Plymouth Brethren."

For more information: numerous Plymouth Brethren websites and Emmaus Bible College, 2570 Asbury Road, Dubuque, IA 52001

Headquarters: none

SOUTHWIDE INDEPENDENT BAPTIST FELLOWSHIP

Founded: 1956
Membership: at least 100,000 in 500 churches

Lee Roberson, pastor of Highland Park Baptist Church in Chattanooga, Tennessee, withdrew from the Southern Baptist Convention in 1955 and formed the Southern Baptist Fellowship the following year. In the previous decade he had established Tennessee Temple Schools, which had four campuses and which taught dispensationalist, pre-millennialist theology. (Southern Baptists have not historically emphasized pre-millennialism or dispensational theology.) In 1948 he founded the Tennessee Pre-millennial Fellowship out of which the Southwide Baptist Fellowship (SBF) developed. In 1960 he helped establish Baptist International Missions, which today includes over a thousand missionaries worldwide. The doctrine and practices of the fellowship are similar to other fundamentalist churches, and nearly half of the members are also in other fundamentalist associations. In the 1990s the denomination adopted more lenient attitudes toward dress and hairstyle. Some congregations adopted contemporary music in worship as a way to increase attendance. This may indicate a movement away from strict fundamentalism. The SBF is more of a loose confederation of churches centered around an annual convention than a denomination. However, hundreds of "independent Baptist" churches look to it as their primary affiliation.

For more information: www.southwidebaptist.org

Headquarters: none

WORLD BAPTIST FELLOWSHIP

Founded: 1932, 1950
Membership: 945 churches (2001)

One of the most famous and controversial leaders of the early Fundamentalist movement was J. Frank Norris (1877–1952) who in 1932 founded the Premillennial Baptist Missionary Fellowship, which was renamed World Baptist Fellowship (WBF) in 1950. Norris was pastor of the First Baptist Church of Fort Worth, Texas, and he led his congregation out of the Southern Baptist Convention in protest against what he perceived as liberal trends within it. He was also a vigorous proponent of dispensationalist theology, which is taught at Arlington Baptist College, the WBF's theological institution in Arlington, Texas.

The denomination does not keep statistics of overall membership, but it does list pastors who are in fellowship. About 60 percent of the congregations represented are also counted in other fellowships and associations of fundamentalist and conservative Baptist churches. The WBF officially promotes the primacy of the local church, but Norris's autocratic leadership led to splits in the WBF, the most notable being the formation of the Baptist Bible Fellowship International. The WBF continues to publish *The Fundamentalist*, a paper started by Norris in 1917 to combat modernism and promote pre-millennial dispensationalism. It also supports some 150 missionaries, primarily in Latin America.

For more information: www.wbfi.net

Headquarters: 3001 West Division Street, PO Box 13459, Arlington, Texas 76094-0459

LATTER-DAY SAINTS

Traditionally, Latter-day Saints believe that the authentic church, having gone underground for many centuries, was restored with the revelations given to their great prophet Joseph Smith Jr. (1805–44) who published the *Book of Mormon* in the 1820s. In addition to the sacred scriptures of Judaism and Christianity (the Old and New Testaments), the Church of Jesus Christ of Latter-day Saints (LDS Church), popularly known as Mormons, bases its beliefs on the *Book of Mormon* and two later works by Smith, *Doctrine and Covenants* and *The Pearl of Great Price*. However, the Mormon Church, as it is commonly called (members prefer to be called Latter-day Saints), is not the only denomination that traces its roots back to Joseph Smith and the *Book of Mormon*. It is the largest. A much smaller denomination also rooted in Smith and early Mormon history was called the Reorganized Church of Jesus Christ of Latter-day Saints; it changed its name to The Community of Christ in 2001. It has never been Mormon but was often confused with the Salt Lake City LDS Church, which led to its change of name. There are also several smaller groups of Latter-day Saints that have never been part of the Salt Lake City LDS Church called Mormons.

History. The early years of the LDS movement centered on the prophet Joseph Smith Jr., who organized the movement with six charter members at Fayette, New York, in 1830. Smith grew up in the famous "Burned-over District" of upstate New York, so called because of the frequency and intensity of the religious revivals there during the Second Great Awakening. Smith claimed to have experienced a series of heavenly visitations, beginning with the appearance of God and Jesus Christ in 1820. During these visits he was informed that all existing churches were in error and that the true gospel was yet to be restored. It would be revealed to him, and he was to reestablish the true church on earth.

According to LDS history, an angel named Moroni led Smith to a hill called Cumorah near Manchester, New York, where he found a book written on gold plates left there by an ancient prophet named Mormon. The angel also gave Smith a "seer stone" that gave him the knowledge to translate the mysterious hieroglyphic writings. The plates contained the sacred records of the ancient inhabitants of North America, righteous Jews who had fled from Jerusalem in 600 BCE and sailed to North America in a divinely designed ark. Smith returned the metal plates to the angel, but eleven other persons besides Smith claimed they had seen the book before it was returned.

The "priesthood of Aaron" was conferred upon Smith and his scribe, Oliver Cowdery (1806–50), by a heavenly messenger, John the Baptist, who instructed them to baptize each other. In 1829, a year before the founding of the church, three other divine visitors, Peter, James, and John, bestowed upon Smith and Cowdery the "priesthood of Melchizedek" and gave them the keys of apostleship.

Opposition arose as the church gained strength, and in 1831 the Mormons left New York for Ohio, where headquarters was established at Kirtland. Smith moved on to Independence, Missouri, in 1838, where he and his followers planned to build the ideal community, with a temple at its heart. Friction with other settlers there became so acute that they soon left Missouri and settled at Nauvoo, Illinois. Violence followed them and reached its peak when Joseph Smith announced his intention to run for the US presidency. He and his brother, Hyrum Smith (1800–44), were murdered by a mob at Carthage, Illinois, in 1844.

With Smith's death, the Quorum of the Twelve Apostles was accepted as the head of the church, and Brigham Young (1801–77) was made president of the Quorum. Some objected that Young was not the legal successor to Smith, and they withdrew to form other churches. Some followed James J. Strang (1813–56) to Wisconsin. The largest body of "anti-Brighamites" believed that the leadership belonged to direct descendants of Joseph Smith, and in 1847 these people, led by Joseph Smith III (1832–1914), formed the Reorganized Church of Jesus Christ of Latter-day Saints (The Community of Christ).

The majority of Saints followed Young, who had the administrative ability to save the church from disruption and further division. He led the Saints when they were driven out of Nauvoo in February 1846 and began their epic march to what is now Utah. They arrived in Salt Lake Valley in July 1847, and there they built the famous Mormon Tabernacle and Temple.

Some sources indicate that Joseph Smith Jr. informed his associates in the 1840s that polygamous marriages were sanctioned and even commanded by God. Such marriages had been contracted secretly for some time before the practice was announced publicly by Brigham Young in 1852. Following the Civil War, the United States federal government mounted an increasingly intense campaign against Mormon polygamy. In 1882, the Edmunds Act provided stringent penalties against polygamy, and in 1887 the church was unincorporated and its properties confiscated. In 1890, the church's president issued a manifesto that officially discontinued the contracting of new polygamous marriages, paving the way for Utah to be granted statehood.

Beliefs and Practices. In some respects the Latter-day Saints today resemble conservative Protestant churches; but certain aspects of their doctrines depart dramatically from traditional Christian theology. The Saints believe that before his ascension into heaven, Jesus Christ appeared in North America where he preached to the Judeans who had fled before the Babylonian Captivity in 586 BCE. The Saints teach that there are three persons who constitute the Godhead: the Father, the Son, and the Holy Ghost. But the Father and the Son have bodies of flesh and bone. It is also maintained that persons will be punished for their own individual sins, not for Adam's transgression; however, especially Mormons believe those who have died may yet be saved through the atonement of Christ.

LDS ordinances include faith in Christ, repentance, baptism by immersion for the remission of sins, the laying on of hands for the gift of the Holy Ghost, and the observance of the Lord's Supper each Sunday.

Mormon LDS also practrice baptism for the dead, which is based on the conviction that persons who died without a chance to hear or accept the gospel cannot possibly be forever condemned by a just and merciful God. They find authority for this practice in the New Testament (1 Pet 4:6). The ceremony is performed with a living person standing proxy for the dead. This and other somewhat secretive ceremonies are practiced by Mormon Saints in "temples," special buildings scattered throughout the world. Mormons consider Salt Lake City's "Temple Square" a special center for Mormonism, which they consider the "fourth branch of Christianity." (The others are Eastern Orthodoxy, Roman Catholicism, and Protestantism.) At one time especially Mormons believed they were the only true Christians, but that belief has gradually changed. They still believe the Church of Jesus Christ of Latter-day Saints is uniquely invested with authority to teach the true gospel of Jesus Christ and to embody in itself the one true church of Jesus on earth. However, in recent years, ecumenical dialogue events have been held at Brigham Young University almost every year. These events are intended to convince non-Mormon Christians that Mormons are true Christians, something many Christians have long denied, and to establish true understanding about Mormon doctrine and practice among non-Mormon Christians.

Although the LDS movement is uniquely American, it has spread throughout the world especially through the missionary activities of the Salt Lake City "Mormon" church. It is to that branch of the Latter-day Saints that most convert. There is no firm number of all LDS throughout the world, but they are in the millions. Their impact on political and social life in the United States has been increasingly significant as evidenced by the presidential candidacy of Republican Mitt Romney in 2012, which gained support from many conservative evangelical Christians.

A shadow side of the LDS movement emerged to public view in the first decade of the twenty-first century with the media and government spotlights shining on so-called fundamentalist Mormons in especially Utah and Texas. These small offshoots of the Salt Lake City LDS Church quietly practice polygamy and occasionally plural marriages of men to teenage girls. Unfortunately, much of what most American know about the Latter-day Saints comes from sensational, even salacious, cable television shows and documentaries about these groups that have no affiliation at all with the Salt Lake City LDS Church, which excommunicates them when they are discovered within it.

SUGGESTIONS FOR FURTHER READING

Allen, James B., and Glen M. Leonard. *The Story of the Latter-day Saints*. Rev. ed. Salt Lake City, UT: Deseret Book Company, 1992.

Arrington, Leonard J. *Brigham Young: American Moses*. New York: Alfred A. Knopf, 1985.

Brodie, Fawn. *No Man Knows My History: The Life of Joseph Smith, Mormon Prophet*. New York: Alfred A. Knopf, 1945.

Brooke, John L. *The Refiner's Fire: The Making of Mormon Cosmology, 1644–1844*. Cambridge, UK: Cambridge University Press, 1994.

Hansen, Klaus J. *Mormonism and the American Experience*. Chicago, IL: University of Chicago Press, 1981.

Ludlow, Daniel, ed. *The Encyclopedia of Mormonism*. 4 vols. New York: Macmillan, 1992.

Millett, Robert L. *The Vision of Mormonism*. Saint Paul, MN: Paragon House, 2007.

Musser, Donald W., and David L. Paulsen. *Mormonism in Dialogue with Contemporary Christian Theologies*. Macon, GA: Mercer University Press, 2007.

Shipps, Jan. *Mormonism: The Story of a New Religious Tradition*. Urbana: University of Illinois Press, 1985.

CHURCH OF CHRIST (TEMPLE LOT)

Founded: 1853, with roots to 1830
Membership: est. 7,630 in 32 congregations (2016)*

Though under ten thousand members, the Church of Christ (Temple Lot) denomination is included in this *Handbook* because of its significance in Saints' history. It was formed after the death of Joseph Smith Jr. in 1844, when some of the Saints who remained in the Midwest became convinced that the church leaders were advocating new teachings quite at variance with the original doctrines. The group centered in Crow Creek, Illinois, functioned under the name Church of Christ, and they returned to Independence, Missouri, in response to a revelation given in 1864 through the presiding elder, Granville Hedrick, in the "appointed year" of 1867. (In the past the movement was known by some as "Hedrickites.") They took possession of the land originally dedicated in 1831 by Joseph Smith Jr. for the building of the Lord's Temple. They believe that the church cannot build until the "appointed time," but they have a sacred obligation to "hold and keep this land free; when the time of building comes." The Church of Christ won court battles with other Saints' bodies to maintain control of these lots.

The church accepts the King James Version of the Bible and the *Book of Mormon* as its standards. It holds that all latter-day revelation, including that of Joseph Smith Jr. must be tested by these scriptures; thus it does not accept all that was given through Smith. They prefer *The Book of Commandments* to *Doctrine and Covenants*, which includes changes in the original doctrine. For this reason, the doctrines of plural marriage, baptism for the dead, celestial marriage, and plurality of gods are not accepted. However, the Church of Christ (Temple Lot) does believe and teach it is the true successor church to the ministry and leadership of Joseph Smith Jr. and that it holds the true, restored, apostolic authority given to him by God.

All the elders and apostles are men.

For more information: www.churchofchrist-tl.org

Headquarters: PO Box 472, Independence, Missouri, 64051-0472

*This membership information was provided by the Church Recorder of the Church of Christ (Temple Lot) but may include members outside the United States.

THE CHURCH OF JESUS CHRIST OF LATTER-DAY SAINTS

Founded: 1830
Membership: 6,531,656 in 12,300 wards (congregations) (2016)

The main body of Latter-day Saints is headquartered in Salt Lake City, Utah, where the Salt Lake Temple and Tabernacle are located. They believe that Christ will return to earth to rule from his capitals in Zion and Jerusalem following the restoration of the tribes of Israel. According to the LDS church, revelation is not confined to either the Bible or the *Book of Mormon*; it continues today in the living apostles and prophets of the Latter-day Saints Church (LDS Church). Members are to adhere to the official pronouncements of the living prophet (president) of the church. Subjection to civil laws and rules is advocated, together with insistence on the right of the individual to worship according to the dictates of conscience.

A distinctive teaching of LDS Church is that marriage has two forms: marriage for time and marriage for eternity (celestial marriage). Members who are married by only civil authority still remain in good standing in the church, but marriage for time and eternity in one of the church's temples is regarded as a prerequisite for the highest opportunity for salvation. There are over one hundred temples around the world, and only members of the church may enter a temple.

Latter-day Saints recognize two priesthoods: (1) the higher priesthood of Melchizedek, which holds power of presidency and authority over offices of the church and whose officers include apostles, patriarchs, high priests, seventies, and elders; and (2) the lesser priesthood of Aaron, which guides the temporal affairs of the church through its bishops, priests, teachers, and deacons. The presiding council of the church is the First Presidency, made up of three high priests—the president and two counselors. Its authority is final in both spiritual and temporal affairs. The president of the church is "the mouthpiece of God"; through God come the laws of the church by direct revelation.

Next to the presidency stands the Council of the Twelve Apostles, chosen by revelation to supervise, under the direction of the First Presidency, the whole work of the church. The church is divided into areas and stakes (geographical divisions) composed of a number of wards (local churches or parishes). Members of two quorums of seventy preside over the areas, under the direction of the Twelve. High priests, assisted by elders, are in charge of the stakes and wards.

Members of the Melchizedek Priesthood, under the direction of the presidency, officiate in all ordinances of the gospel. The stake presidents, ward bishops, patriarchs, high priests, and elders supervise the work within the stakes and wards of the church. The Aaronic Priesthood is governed by three presiding bishops, known collectively as the Presiding Bishopric, who also supervise the work of the members of the priesthood in the stakes and wards. In 1978, it was ruled that "all worthy male members of the church may be ordained to the priesthood without regard for race or color."

Mission. The church influences all aspects of the life of every member; it supplies relief in illness or poverty and assists with education and employment when necessary. This church maintains, as part of a self-help welfare system, storehouses for community food and clothing. Members operate vegetable, seed, and wheat farms; orchards, dairies, and cannery processing facilities; sewing centers; soap-processing plants; and several grain elevators. Through this system the church donates thousands of tons of surplus clothing annually to needy populations around the world and sponsors water and agricultural projects in underdeveloped countries. The welfare system also includes sheltered workshops for persons with handicapping conditions and a variety of social services, including adoption and foster-care agencies.

Over fifty thousand young persons currently serve as full-time missionaries throughout the world without compensation; they devote eighteen months to two years to spreading the teaching of their church at home and abroad at their own expense. Only about one hundred persons in full-time leadership positions receive a salary or living allowance.

The Latter-day Saints grew tremendously in the twentieth century and in the last half of the century became influential in national politics. The church is strongest in the Western United States, but now has more members outside the United States than in it. The church's largest institutions are Brigham Young University in Provo, Utah, and Brigham Young University in Rexburg, Idaho. Some five hundred twenty-five thousand secondary and post-secondary students worldwide are enrolled in seminary and institute classes, which provide religious instruction.

The doctrines of the LDS Church are stated succinctly in its Thirteen Articles of Faith, but many books written by Mormon leaders also instruct the faithful and interpret the religion for outsiders. Among common beliefs held by Mormons is the controversial one known as "eternal progression," which many believe implies that a Mormon man, and a Mormon woman in celestial marriage with a Mormon man, can attain deity in the afterlife. Many Mormons believe, although it is disputed by some LDS scholars, that "What man is, God once was; what God is, man may become." Conservative Christian critics of Mormonism point to such unorthodox beliefs to justify calling the LDS Church a "cult" (in the theological sense of that word). However, dialogues between Mormon scholars and non-Mormon Christian theologians has led to greater mutual understanding and even acceptance (which is not to imply agreement).

Whether Mormonism, the belief system of the LDS Church, is a religion or a form of Christianity is much discussed and debated among orthodox Christians. The LDS Church insists that it is the truest form of Christianity and not another religion. The LDS Church does not permit women to lead or teach doctrine to men nor does it affirm homosexuality as normal or permit gay people to lead congregations. However, the church has begun training young women to be Mormon missionaries—a role normally reserved for young men.

For more information: www.lds.org

Headquarters: Joseph Smith Memorial Building, 15 East South Temple Street, Salt Lake City, Utah 84150.

COMMUNITY OF CHRIST

Founded: 1860, with roots to 1830
Membership: 123,189 in 792 churches (2012)

Formerly know as the Reorganized Church of Jesus Christ of the Latter Day Saints, the Community of Christ (COC) claims to be the true continuation of the original church organized by Joseph Smith Jr., with leadership passing to his son Joseph Smith III in 1860. It bases this claim of succession on the book of *Doctrine and Covenants*. Court actions on two occasions, in Ohio in 1880 and in Missouri in 1894, are cited in naming it the legal continuation of the original church. It has control of the first LDS temple in Kirtland, Ohio.

The founders of the Reorganized Church rejected the claims of the group led by Brigham Young because of their abandonment of this rule of succession, along with other doctrinal disagreements. Those holding to the lineal succession eventually reorganized, and the first collective expression of this movement was a conference in Beloit, Wisconsin, in 1852. Joseph Smith III was chosen president in 1860 at Amboy, Illinois. All of his successors have been descendants of the founder. Since 1920, headquarters have been located in Independence, Missouri, where a temple was built late in the twentieth century.

The Reorganized Church held polygamy to be contrary to the teachings of the *Book of Mormon* and the book of *Doctrine and Covenants* of the original organization. It also differs from the larger body over the doctrine of the Godhead, celestial marriage, and baptism of the dead. Basic beliefs include faith in the universality of God the Eternal Father, Jesus Christ as the only begotten Son of the Father, the Holy Spirit, the worth and dignity of persons, repentance of sin, baptism by immersion, the efficacy of various sacramental ordinances, the resurrection of the dead, the open canon of scriptures and the continuity of revelation, the doctrine of stewardship, and the accountability of all people to God.

The COC considers the *Book of Mormon* canonical in a secondary sense but not as authoritative as the Bible. It does not agree with most of the distinctive doctrines of the Salt Lake City Church of Jesus Christ of Latter-day Saints such as baptism for the dead, celestial marriage, and eternal progression. In many ways the COC has evolved into a progressive Protestant denomination with its own history and culture.

The work of the COC is supported by tithes and free-will offerings. This is regarded as a divine principle, and the tithe is calculated on a tenth of each member's annual increase over needs and just wants. Church doctrines, policies, and matters of legislation must have the approval and action of a delegate conference held biennially in Independence. General administration of the church is by a First Presidency of three high priests and elders, a Quorum of Twelve Apostles who represent the presidency in the field, and a pastoral arm under the high priests and elders. Bishops are responsible for church properties, the stewardship of members, and church finances.

The COC has been active in developing ministries and understanding as it has expanded since 1960 into non-Western cultures. With work in over thirty countries, it has a worldwide membership of nearly a quarter million. It sponsors several homes for the elderly, medical clinics, and educational facilities both in the United States and abroad. It seeks to dedicate itself to the pursuit of world peace and reconciliation. The ordination of women was approved in 1984, and by 2000 more than three thousand women had been ordained to ecclesiastical orders. The COC ordains gay and lesbian people and performs same-sex marriages.

For more information: www.cofchrist.org

Headquarters: 1001 West Walnut, Independence, MO 64050-3562

FUNDAMENTALIST CHURCH OF JESUS CHRIST OF LATTER-DAY SAINTS

Founded: 1935
Membership: 6,000 (est) in 7 communities

When Mormon President Wilford Woodruff issued a manifesto banning plural marriage in the Church of Jesus Christ of Latter-day Saints in 1890, some Mormons rejected the decree and held to the older teachings of Brigham Young. The towns of Hildale, Utah, and Colorado City, Arizona (formerly known as Short Creek), were particularly resistant to the change in doctrine. Some of the residents continued to practice plural marriage despite state laws banning the practice, and in 1935 they were excommunicated from the LDS church. A number of small fundamentalist Mormon churches were formed in the 1930s and 1940s. Gradually the Fundamentalist Church of Jesus Christ of Latter-day Saints (FLDS Church), led by John Y. Barlow, emerged as the largest body.

The church insists that men and women adopt "plain dress" that covers most of the body. Women are forbidden to wear makeup or short hair. The church sells appropriate clothing online. Children are generally educated by the community, and a disproportionate number of teenage boys are excommunicated for behavior deemed inappropriate. Critics suspect this is to reduce the number of men in the community to enhance opportunities for plural marriage. In addition to plural marriage, the leader of the church assigns brides to husbands in a practice called placement marriage. The church is apocalyptic and believes that it is the righteous remnant that will survive the war between Christ and the antichrist.

In 1953, Arizona state police and National Guard troops raided the Short Creek community in an effort to stamp out polygamy. They arrested over four hundred people, including over two hundred children, but the raid backfired and generated widespread support for the polygamists. The FLDS church grew, and now there are satellite communities in Colorado, South Dakota, British Columbia, and Texas. In the 1980s Rulon Jeffs assumed leadership of some FLDS congregations and took the title of prophet. He reportedly had twenty-eight wives and over sixty children, one of whom, Warren, succeeded him in 2002.

Soon after assuming leadership Warren Jeffs was arrested on charges of being an accomplice to rape since he helped arrange the marriage of a member of the church to an underage girl. This case brought unwanted publicity to the FLDS Church, and in 2004 the church purchased about seventeen hundred acres of land near Eldorado, Texas, where they established Yearning for Zion Ranch. The ranch is nearly self-sufficient and houses over seven hundred persons. The church constructed its first Temple on the ranch, and it was dedicated by Jeffs in 2005. Reports of plural marriage and underage marriage led Texas authorities to raid the ranch and take over four hundred children into protective custody. Most of the children have been returned to their mothers, but the case raised publicly many difficult issues regarding separation of church and state. Jeffs's sermons have also been criticized for their racism and implicit call to violence. In 2011 Jeffs was sentenced to a life prison term for child sexual assault. This threw the movement into crisis but it continues. Many observers believe Jeffs still controls the church from prison.

For more information: www.flds.org (not necessarily the Jeffs group)

Headquarters: none for all fundamentalist Mormons

ESOTERIC, SPIRITUALIST, AND NEW THOUGHT BODIES

Some of the more interesting and controversial religious organizations in the United States endorse esoteric doctrines and practices. The word *esoteric* refers to hidden or secret teachings, and it is a common feature of esoteric groups that it is difficult for outsiders to gain a clear understanding of them. One needs to be initiated in order to fully learn or understand their teachings. Despite this, esoteric bodies in the United States have been able to present some of their central beliefs publicly in an effort to recruit members or defend themselves from prejudice. With the advent of the Internet, there has been an explosion of esoteric religious websites and discussion groups. Complicating study of esoteric bodies is the great diversity of groups as well as their inter-relatedness.

Many esoteric religious groups trace their origins back to the ancient world, especially to Egypt and Solomon's temple. They believe that some of the original wisdom of God was transmitted by Egyptian and Israelite priests in their temple rituals, but much of that wisdom was lost. According to esotericists, some of the important secret knowledge was passed down through various individuals and organizations, such as Hermes Trismegistus, the Templars, Paracelsus, and the Rosicrucians. Esotericism draws from Gnosticism, Renaissance Neoplatonic philosophy, medieval alchemy, and ancient magic. Some of the radical Pietist sects used esoteric thought, as did the early Freemasons, but for the most part, esotericism has been in the shadows of the greater Christian traditions. Until the rise of religious tolerance in modern times most organized esoteric religious groups were persecuted by Catholics and Protestants alike and existed secretively.

Early Christianity struggled with a particular type of religious esotericism called Gnosticism, which existed as a theology and spirituality among ancient Christians until it was forced underground by Emperor Constantine and his successors in the Christianized Roman Empire. The Gnostics claimed to be the true Christians holding higher knowledge and wisdom unknown to the masses of ordinary Christians. Those ancient Christian teachers recognized as "church fathers" by Orthodox, Catholics, and Protestants argued against the Gnostics, naming them "heretics." Among them were second century

Irenaeus, bishop of Lyons in France, and Tertullian, the most influential early Christian theologian in the Latin half of the Roman Empire.

Gnostics believed matter is evil and the creation of a lesser god, even a demented or evil god, below the one true God who is the divine fire from which every human soul is a spark. These sparks of divinity, human souls, have forgotten their true divinity and become trapped in matter. Bodies are prisons of the soul and cause sin. Salvation, the Gnostics taught, comes through knowledge (Greek "gnosis") of the divinity of the soul and ascent of the soul back into oneness with God through mystical contemplation and ultimately death followed by a spiritual progression through worlds unseen by humans trapped in matter. The Gnostics taught that Jesus was a "heavenly redeemer" of pure spirit who only appeared to be human or used a human body as a vehicle for teaching the saving knowledge. He did not really die on the cross but left the body before it died, leaving behind the secret knowledge to be communicated by a core group of disciples to others capable of understanding the esoteric truth. The Gnostics denied the resurrection of the body.

Modern Gnostics, Christian adherents of what one sociologist of religion has labeled "the alternative reality tradition in the West," esotericism, have added reincarnation to ancient Gnostic teaching. Perhaps the largest and most influential group of modern Gnostics are called Rosicrucians, but it is doubtful that they can rightly be called a denomination. Modern Gnostics prefer to call their organizations "schools of wisdom" or something similar. Some Christian groups echo some aspects of ancient Gnosticism without being "full blown" Gnostics. One Christian denomination, sometimes labeled a "cult" by critics, that openly considers the Gnostics the true Christians of the ancient world is the Church Universal and Triumphant, which, together with its older cousin the I AM Activity (Saint Germain Foundation), represents one of the purest modern American forms of Gnosticism. Few modern Gnostics would go all the way with ancient Gnosticism and say that the body or matter itself is evil, but all would emphasize the divinity or "Christ nature" of the human "Higher Self" (soul).

Already mentioned as a movement of modern Gnostics is the Rosicrucians. Closely related to them is Theosophy, or "divine wisdom." Theosophists view this divine wisdom as the universal perennial philosophy that underlies all religions. Thus it draws from both Eastern and Western philosophies and religious teachings. The chief founder of the modern theosophical movement was Helena Petrovna Blavatsky (1831–91), who was born in Russia and traveled over the world in search of "knowledge of the [spiritual] laws which govern the universe." She arrived in the United States and founded the Theosophical Society of New York in 1875. Her aim was "to form a nucleus of the Universal Brotherhood of Humanity, without distinction of race, creed, sex, caste, or color; to encourage the study of comparative religion, philosophy, and science; and to investigate the unexplained laws of nature and the powers latent in man." Blavatsky held that all religions stem from a hierarchy that includes Jesus, Buddha, and other master thinkers who have experienced a series of rebirths, or reincarnations, ultimately to attain divinity.

Reincarnation is a central theme in Theosophy. It is the method through which persons rid themselves of all impurities and unfold their inner potentials through varied experiences. Closely connected with the concept of reincarnation is that of karma, the law of cause and effect; each rebirth, then, is seen as the result of actions, thoughts, and desires brought from the past. The movement split after the death of Blavatsky in 1891. Spiritualism, a religion that centers around communication with the spirits of the dead, and Theosophy generated great excitement and controversy early in the twentieth century, but its appeal declined significantly over the course of the century. This was due in part of the spread of unlicensed mediums and psychics whose unethical practices brought the movement into disrepute. It was also due to the dramatic rise of New Age religious groups among the "baby boomers." The New Age Movement popularized, and some would say vulgarized, Theosophy.

Theosophy and esotericism influenced a number of religious thinkers and organizers, some of whom promoted less exotic and more practical versions of these beliefs. New Thought was influenced by New England Transcendentalism and draws upon both Asian and Western Gnostic traditions to help individuals learn new ways of thinking in order to realize or actualize the "divinity within." The key idea in the various forms of New Thought is that a person's physical, emotional, and spiritual health are interrelated. In another words, faith, interpreted as positive thinking, is the path to health and overall well-being. Faith, positive thinking, and prayer (positive speaking) are the spiritual practices that attune one's whole being with the universal divine being who is at the center of all being as its source. New Thought was taken up into Christianity by various alternative ministries considered unorthodox by both Catholics and Protestants. Most New Thought practitioners consider Jesus to have been the ultimate teacher of positive thinking and the one fully God-realized human being in history.

The denominations included in this category differ from each other in many ways, but all belong to the "alternative reality tradition" of Western Christianity. All claim to be "true Christianity" but are considered heretical, even non-Christian, by most orthodox Christians of all denominations. Of course they are not the only ones so considered. Jehovah's Witnesses, mentioned before under the Adventist category, and Latter-day Saints (Mormons) are usually considered heretical and even non-Christian by most Orthodox, Catholic, and Protestant Christians. For the latter diverse groups, the litmus tests for being authentically Christian are belief in Jesus Christ as uniquely God incarnate, both truly human and truly divine; different from all other humans in kind, not only in degree; and belief in the God as the Trinity of Father, Son, and Holy Spirit, three distinct persons sharing one divine essence equally. In other words, the Nicene Creed of 381, technically known to Christian theologians as the Niceno-Constantinopolitan Creed of the Council of Constantinople, is the litmus test of authentic Christian orthodoxy for Orthodox, Catholic, and Protestant Christians (even Protestants who claim to be "non-creedal"). The denominations included in this category share in common a metaphysical worldview quite different from that assumed by orthodox Christianity; they tend to blur the line between God and the human soul—a key characteristic of Gnosticism.

SUGGESTIONS FOR FURTHER READING

Albanese, Catherine L. *A Republic of Mind and Spirit: A Cultural History of American Metaphysical Religion.* New Haven, CT: Yale University Press, 2008.

Benz, Ernst. *Emanuel Swedenborg: Visionary Savant in the Age of Reason.* Trans. Nicholas Goodrick-Clarke. West Chester, PA: Swedenborg Foundation, 2002.

Braden, Charles S. *Spirits in Rebellion: The Rise and Development of New Thought.* Dallas, TX: Southern Methodist University Press, 1963.

De Witt, John. *The Christian Science Way of Life.* Boston, MA: Christian Science Publishing Society, 1971.

Ellwood, Robert and Harry Partin. *Religious and Spiritual Groups in Modern America.* 2nd ed. London: Routledge Publishing, 1988.

Esoterica. East Lansing, MI: Michigan State University.

Fuller, Robert. *Mesmerism and the American Cure of Souls.* Philadelphia: University of Pennsylvania Press, 1982.

Gibbons, B.J. *Spirituality and the Occult from the Renaissance to the Modern Age.* London, UK: Routledge, 2001.

Haller, John. S., Jr. *The History of New Thought: From Mind Cure to Positive Thinking and the Prosperity Gospel.* West Chester, PA: Swedenborg Foundation, 2012.

Jonas, Hans. *The Gnostic Religion.* Boston, MA: Beacon Press, 2001.

Nelson, Geoffrey K. *Spiritualism and Society.* New York: Schocken Books, 1969.

Toksvig, Signe. *Emanuel Swedenborg, Scientist and Mystic.* New Haven, CT: Yale University Press, 1948.

ASSOCIATION OF UNITY CHURCHES
(UNITY WORLDWIDE MINISTRIES)

Founded: 1886
Membership: est. 53,000 in 550 churches (2016)*

Unity (not to be confused with Unitarian) is a religious educational organization devoted to demonstrating that following the teaching of Jesus Christ is a practical, seven-day-a-week way of life. Unity teaches that "the true church is a state of consciousness in man." The Association of Unity Churches (here "Unity") helps provide resources for congregations dedicated to Unity teachings. Unity has been described as "a religious philosophy with an 'open end,' seeking to find God's truth in all of life, wherever it may be." Unity has no strict creed or dogma; it finds good in all religions and teaches that people should keep their minds open to receive that goodness. Unity teaches that reality is ultimately spiritual and that realization of spiritual truth will illuminate, heal, and prosper humanity. Cultivation of health-conducive emotions such as love, confidence, and joy is encouraged. Overcoming health-inhibiting emotions such as anger, hatred, and despair is also encouraged. Unity has no rules concerning health but concentrates on spiritual goals, knowing that healthful living habits will follow. Some Unity students are vegetarians in the interest of health.

Unity began in 1886 when New Thought adherents Charles Fillmore (1854–1948), bankrupt and crippled, and his wife, Myrtle (1845–1931), seriously ill with tuberculosis, discovered a way of life based on affirmative prayer ("affirmations"). They studied a variety of Christian and Eastern theosophical and esoteric systems in creating their new approach to healing. The Fillmores held that "whatever man wants he can have by voicing his desire in the right way into the Universal Mind." It is through Christ, or the Christ consciousness, that the human gains eternal life and salvation. Salvation means the attainment of true spiritual consciousness, becoming like Christ. This transformation takes place not in any hereafter, but "here in this earth" through a process of unfolding and regeneration. A person suffers no final death, but changes into increasingly better states until finally becoming like Christ. Many Unity members believe in reincarnation although that is not formally a Unity doctrine.

Prayer and meditation are suggested for every human want and illness. The Unity way of prayer and meditation involves relaxation and oral affirmation of spiritual truth to develop the consciousness of the individual and silent receptivity to the "Divine Mind" for whatever the seeker needs. The Bible is used constantly and is highly valued, but is not considered the sole or final authority in faith and practice. People must be in direct, personal communion with God, not dependent upon such secondary sources as the scriptures. Many Unity people believe the Bible can only rightly be interpreted through the Fillmore's *Metaphysical Bible Dictionary*, which explains the true meanings of biblical stories and concepts through New Thought teachings.

The Association of Unity Churches ordains ministers, provides educational and administrative support, and is self-supporting. Unity School trains ministers in a two-year program. It also educates teachers and offers retreat programs. A large staff in Unity Village, near Kansas City, Missouri, is available to pray with people day and night. Workers answer an average of one million calls and nearly two million letters annually. Most calls come from members of various Christian churches, but correspondents are never asked to leave the churches to which they belong. Unity School publishes some seventy-five million copies of booklets, brochures, and magazines annually. These materials are used by many who never contact headquarters or become members of a Unity church.

Unity leadership is not restricted by gender or sexual orientation at any level. Many people flooded into Unity, whether as members or simply followers, through the so-called New Age Movement in the late twentieth century. Some critics claim that, while Unity began as an esoteric or New Thought form of Christianity, it has become more religiously pluralistic over time. The emphasis of Unity has been not only on spiritual self-realization but also on the physical well-being of practitioners of its spiritual techniques (e.g., "affirmations"). In the past, perhaps more than the present, financial prosperity was a goal of many Unity (and other New Thought) followers through positive thinking and speaking. Some critics of the neo-Pentecostal "prosperity gospel" of health and wealth claim it is influenced by Unity or at least New Thought in general—of which Unity is probably the most important organized form in America.

For more information: www.unity.org

Headquarters: 1901 Northwest Blue Parkway, Unity Village, MO 64065

*It is unclear whether these statistics refer to Unity worldwide or only in the United States.

CHURCH OF CHRIST, SCIENTIST
(CHRISTIAN SCIENCE)

Founded: 1879
Membership: approx. 1,153 churches*

The Church of Christ, Scientist (popularly known as "Christian Science" and not to be confused with other religious groups that use the word *science* or some derivation thereof) is one of the few denominations founded by a woman, and for a time it was very influential in American society. Generally described as "a religious teaching and practice based on the words and works of Christ Jesus," Christian Science was regarded by the founder, Mary Baker Eddy (1821–1910), as "the scientific system of divine healing," the "law of God, the law of good, interpreting and demonstrating the divine Principle and rule of universal harmony." Eddy believed that God is "the Principle of all harmonious Mind-action." Eddy's *Science and Health with Key to the Scriptures* (1875, 1883) and the Bible are the twofold textbooks of Christian Science. Christian Scientists believe the Bible cannot be correctly understood without Eddy's book.

Christian Science originated from Eddy's personal experience. Eddy had suffered from a form of paralysis much of her life until 1866 when, after reading the account of Christ's healing of a man with a form of palsy (Matt 9:1-8), she recovered almost instantly. Convinced that God was the source of her healing, Eddy found confirmation of her ideas in the writings of both Emanuel Swedenborg and Phineas Quimby, perhaps the first New

Thought teacher in America. She became an advocate for spiritual causation and mental healing, and she quickly demonstrated a rare ability to recruit and organize followers. Under her direction, the Church of Christ, Scientist was established in her hometown of Lynn, Massachusetts, in 1879. In 1892 she built a large "Mother Church" in Boston, which became the headquarters for her rapidly expanding denomination.

Christian Science teaches that God is the only "Mind"; God is "All-in-all"; the "divine Principle of all that really is"; "the all-knowing, all-seeing, all-acting, all-wise, all-loving, and eternal; Principle; Mind; Soul; Spirit; Life; Truth; Love; all substance; intelligence." The Bible is seen as sacred scripture and the church proclaims faith in the Father, Son, and Holy Spirit. The crucifixion and resurrection of Jesus are held as serving "to uplift faith to understand eternal Life, even the allness of Soul, Spirit, and the nothingness of matter." Jesus Christ is thought of by Christian Scientists as the perfect Christian Science Practitioner.

The "allness" of spirit and "nothingness of matter" involve the basic teaching of Christian Science concerning reality. As *Science and Health* explains, "All reality is in God and His creation, harmonious and eternal. That which He creates is good, and He makes all that is made. Therefore the only reality of sin, sickness, or death is the awful fact that unrealities seem real to human, erring belief, until God strips off their disguise. They are not true, because they are not of God."

In Christian Science belief, God forgives sin through destroying it with "the spiritual understanding that casts out evil as unreal." The punishment for sin lasts as long as one's belief in sin endures. Adherents of Christian Science do not ignore what they consider "unreal"; rather, they seek to forsake and overcome error and evil through Christian discipleship, prayer, and progressive spiritual understanding of God's "allness" and goodness; they strive to see the spiritual "body," created in God's likeness, as the only real body.

Christian Scientists commonly rely wholly on the power of God for healing rather than on medical treatment. Healing is not held to be miraculous but divinely natural. Disease is understood to be basically a mental concept that can be dispelled by active Christian discipleship, spiritual regeneration, and application of the truths to which Jesus bore witness. Prayer is "an absolute faith that all things are possible to God—a spiritual understanding of Him, an unselfed love." Baptism is not observed as a traditional ceremony, but is held to be a continuing individual spiritual experience, "a purification from all error."

The local Churches of Christ, Scientist employ their own forms of democratic government within the general framework of bylaws laid down by Eddy in the *Manual of the Mother Church*. Reading rooms, open to the general public, are maintained by all churches. The affairs of the Mother Church are administered by the Christian Science Board of Directors, which elects a president and other officers of the church.

There are two Readers in each branch church, usually a man and a woman, who are elected by the church members. In all services on Sundays and Thanksgiving Day, they read alternately from the Bible and from *Science and Health*. The "lessonsermons" of Sunday services are prepared by a committee and are issued quarterly by the Christian Science Publishing Society.

Christian Science "Practitioners" devote their full time to healing and are listed in a directory in the monthly *Christian Science Journal*. A board of education consists of three members: a president, a vice president, and a teacher of Christian Science. Under the supervision of this board, a normal class is held once every three years. Teachers are duly authorized by certificates granted by the board to form classes. Women practioners outnumber male practioners ten to one. Since World War II, the denomination has experienced a significant decline in membership and a corresponding increase in average age of membership.

Critics of Christian Science, from Mark Twain to evangelical "anti-cult" writers, claim it is false. Many evangelical and other orthodox Christian critics claim it is "pantheistic," blurring the boundary between God and creation. Secular critics add that, especially in the past, some children have been denied needed medical care by their Christian Science parents. Most Christian Scientists, however, will avail themselves of professional medical care when necessary in addition to "prayer" led by a Christian Science Practitioner. They believe the mind, when attuned to the all-Mind of God, has power to heal the body and even to overcome death. Traditionally, Christian Science teaches that everything negative, including sin, sickness, and death, is unreal except in terms of wrong thought and belief. Most Christian Science apologists, however, claim that critics simply do not understand it.

The Church of Christ, Scientist takes no position regarding homosexuality or same-sex marriage. All levels of leadership are open to women and the majority of Christian Science Practitioners are women.

For more information: www.christianscience.com

Headquarters: 210 Massachusetts Avenue, Boston, MA 02115

*The Church of Christ, Scientist churches are technically branches of the "Mother Church" in Boston but with a degree of self-governing power. The denomination does not publish membership statistics. Traditionally many scholars have estimated there to be about four hundred thousand members in the United States, but other scholars think that number is outdated and that actual membership is now closer to one hundred thousand.

THE GENERAL CHURCH OF THE NEW JERUSALEM (SWEDENBORGIAN)

Founded: 1897
Membership: est. 25,000 in 85 churches (2016)

One of the primary figures in both Spiritualism and Theosophy was Emanuel Swedenborg (1688–1772). He was born in Stockholm, Sweden, and was an Enlightenment-era scientist distinguished in the fields of mathematics, geology, cosmology, and anatomy before he turned seriously to theology. Although certain he was divinely commissioned to teach the doctrines of the "New Church," Swedenborg never preached or founded a church. His followers, however, felt that the need for a separate denomination was implicit in the new revelation given in Swedenborg's monumental work *Arcana Celestia*, in which, they believed, he unlocked the hidden meaning of scripture and recorded his conversations with great figures long dead including Jesus and his apostles.

The Swedenborgian church centers its worship on the risen and glorified present reality of Christ and looks for the establishment of the kingdom of God in the form of a universal church on earth. In this new church all people will strive for peace, freedom, and justice. Swedenborgian bodies have often used the name "Churches of the New Jerusalem" to indicate the in-breaking of the eschatological reality described in the New Testament. The most famous Swedenborgian evangelist in America was John Chapman (Johnny Appleseed), and today J. Appleseed & Co. distributes books and pamphlets based on Swedenborg's writings.

Swedenborgians believe that the Bible has both a literal, historical meaning and a deeper, spiritual ("esoteric") meaning. The church teaches that there is one God, known by many names, and that the Christian Trinity denotes aspects of this God. Human beings are believed to be essentially spirits clothed in material bodies, which are laid aside at death; the human spirit lives on in a spirit world, in a manner determined by its attitudes and behavior on earth.

The Faith and Aims of the church state that the "Lord Jesus Christ has come again, not in a physical reappearance, but in spirit and in truth; not in a single event only, but in a progressive manifestation of his presence among men." Adherents claim that tokens of Christ's coming appear in the burst of scientific development, the rise of the spirit of inquiry, the progress toward political and intellectual freedom, and the deepening sense of national and international responsibility that has characterized the modern era.

The New Church as an organization arose in London in 1783 when Robert Hindmarsh (1759–1835), a printer, gathered a few friends to discuss the writings of Swedenborg. They formed a general conference of their societies in 1815. The first Swedenborgian Society in the United States was organized at Baltimore, Maryland, in 1792, and in 1817 the General Convention of the New Jerusalem in the USA was established. It was incorporated in 1861.

The General Church of the New Jerusalem broke away from the original Swedenborgian body in 1890. It shares many of the doctrines of The New Church, but teaches that the writings of Swedenborg are divinely inspired. The General Church built a cathedral in Bryn Athyn, Pennsylvania. There are Swedenborgian theological schools in Newton, Massachusetts, and Bryn Athyn. The Swedenborg Foundation is in West Chester, Pennsylvania. At the end of the twentieth century, a new Swedenborgian church, the Lord's New

Church, was established in South Africa and now has a handful of congregations in the United States. Perhaps the most celebrated Swedenborgian in America was Helen Keller.

Swedenborg was controversial in his own lifetime and since the rise of churches based on his visions and writings Christian critics have claimed he was a heretic and his writings more Gnostic than Christian in any orthodox sense. His followers, those devoted to the truth of his visions, claim that he was a "seer," a prophet, and a religious reformer. While Swedenborg himself was not a medium and did not hold traditional "séances," many Spiritualists in Great Britain and the United States based some of their religious beliefs and teachings on his experiences and writings. Some scholars of modern alternative religions in the West believe Swedenborg's influence on European and American religious life has been greatly underestimated.

The General Church of the New Jerusalem is the more conservative of the two main Swedenborgian bodies in the United States and does not ordain women or gay or lesbian people. The New Church ordains women and gay and lesbian people to the ministry.

For more information: www.newchurch.org; www.swedenborg.org

Headquarters: 1100 Cathedral Road, PO Box 743, Bryn Athyn, PA 19009

THE I AM ACTIVITY AND THE CHURCH UNIVERSAL AND TRIUMPHANT

Founded: 1930s (I AM Activity) and 1975 with roots to 1958 (CUT)

Although they are not organizationally related, the I AM Activity and the Church Universal and Triumphant (CUT) are so historically and religiously similar as to justify treating them here together. The I AM Activity, also known as the Saint Germain Foundation, is somewhat esoteric and does not generally communicate about itself with investigators merely seeking information. Membership statistics are unavailable to outsiders. Attempts to establish contact with leaders for research purposes often go unanswered. There are I AM Sanctuaries and Reading Rooms in many American cities, but they do not advertise or list themselves under "churches" in such listings. Inquirers may make contact with the group through its website or by mail and take correspondence courses that include reading the founders' books. Eventually they may be invited to attend an I AM meeting, which are generally not open to the public.

The I AM Activity and the Saint Germain Foundation are rooted in the teachings of founders Guy Ballard (1878–1939) and Edna Ballard (1886–1971) who together claimed to "channel" a group of spiritual beings called Ascended Masters and especially Saint Germain who they claimed is the present Master overseeing the spiritual development of humanity. Guy Ballard, whose spiritual name was Godfre Ray King, wrote many volumes of spiritual teachings based on revelations he received from the Ascended Masters. Some scholars believe he was inspired by the teachings of Theosophy but blended them with American nationalism and Christian Gnosticism.

Many religious observers consider both the I AM Activity and CUT modern forms of ancient Christian Gnosticism with reincarnation added. Both claim to be Christian because they believe Jesus Christ was a teacher of great spiritual wisdom who resides now among the Ascended Masters. And they both believe in and promote the reality of a Christ-spirit in everyone as their "higher self," a spark of the divine.

Both the I Am Activity and CUT teach a spiritual technique known as "decreeing," which involves chanting, individually and in groups; affirmations (possibly to burn off "karmic debt"); and increase realization of the higher self, which is regarded as a divine spark of God.

When the I Am Activity began in the 1930s it included large rallies that intermingled pro-American nationalism and messages from the Ascended Masters through the Ballards. It then had as many as a million followers although actual membership in the group was probably much smaller. After founder Guy Ballard's death his wife and son Donald led the I Am Activity from a headquarters and sanctuary in Santa Fe, New Mexico. Due to public ridicule and legal problems, the group went partially underground, becoming more esoteric than exoteric in its public presence. One of its largest sanctuaries stands in downtown Chicago where visitors may view the ground floor Reading Room but not the Sanctuary. The I Am Activity produces an annual play about Christ near Mount Shasta in northern California, which is where Guy Ballard claimed to have first encountered an Ascended Master and been assigned to teach.

The CUT is widely regarded by scholars who study American new or alternative religions as a different organization with strikingly similar teachings and practices as the I AM Activity. It began in the 1950s when founder Mark Prophet (1918–75) formed a group devoted to the Ascended Masters known as Summit Lighthouse. Prophet's message included teachings about the divinity of the human soul or "higher self" and the need and ability for each human person to self-realize his or her true divinity or "Christ consciousness within" through following the teachings and spiritual techniques of Summit Lighthouse. The main such spiritual technique was and remains chanting "decrees." Summit Lighthouse eventually evolved into the CUT led by Prophet's widow Elizabeth Clare Prophet (1939–2009) whom followers called "Guru Ma." Prophet moved the group's headquarters to a large ranch in Montana where many observers believe it became something of a survivalist group. Prophet traveled the United States and the world teaching the same basic message as the I AM Activity about the Ascended Masters and especially "El Morya" titled the "Master of God's Will." Under Prophet CUT claimed to be a revival of both the ancient wisdom underlying all major world religions and ancient Gnostic Christianity. Prophet claimed the Gnostics were the true Christians who believed, as she did, in reincarnation.

Some critics believe both the Ballards and the Prophets were inspired more by esoteric religions such as Theosophy and Rosicrucianism than by orthodox Christianity. Both, however, have always claimed to be revivals of true Christianity. Some critics have called both groups "cults" in the theological sense. The I AM Activity remains mostly esoteric while CUT became more exoteric in its public meetings to which visitors were often welcome as "Guru Ma" channeled the Ascended Masters.

Both the I AM Activity and CUT have women leaders; their attitudes and policies toward homosexuality is unknown.

For more information: www.saintgermainfoundation.org; www.summitlighthouse.org

Headquarters: The I AM Activity of Saint Germain Foundation: 1120 Stonenedge Drive, Schaumburg, IL 60194; The Church Universal and Triumphant: 63 Summit Way, Gardiner, MT 59030

LIBERAL CATHOLIC CHURCH

Founded: 1916
Membership: 5,800 in 21 churches (2012)

This church was founded in London by J. I. Wedgewood. It traces its holy orders to an apostolic succession that runs back to the Roman Catholic Church under the reign of Pope Urban VIII (1568–1644). The Liberal Catholic Church (LCC) aims at a combination of traditional Catholic forms of worship with the utmost freedom of individual conscience and thought. The church adopted the name Liberal Catholic Church, Province of the United States in the 1940s during a dispute with what is now called the Liberal Catholic Church International (LCCI). As with the Old Catholic churches, Liberal Catholic priests and bishops may marry, and they exact no fee for the administration of the sacraments; LCC priests are employed in secular occupations, but LCCI churches may offer a salary to their priests if financially able. The church endorses the Nicene Creed, and its Statement of Principles outlines additional theosophical principles, such as reincarnation. Clergy are expected to be in general agreement with the Statement, but laity are free to accept or reject these beliefs. The church also encourages members to adopt a vegetarian and alcohol-free lifestyle. The LCC, Province of the United States is in communion with the worldwide LCC headquartered in London. The denomination is governed by a General Episcopal Synod made up of thirty bishops from around the world.

Although the LCC claims apostolic succession and true catholicity, it is in no way related to the Roman Catholic Church led by the pope, the bishop of Rome. Its theological roots lie deep in esoteric Christianity and especially Theosophy, the "mother religion" of most American and European esoteric religious groups. One of the movement's founders was C. W. Leadbeater (1854–1934) who was by most accounts an avid follower of

Theosophy. He simply wanted to discover a more Christian form of Theosophy and thus the founding of the Liberal Catholic Church.

For more information: www.thelccusa.org

Headquarters: 1502 East Ojai Ave., PO Box 598, Ojai, CA 93024

NATIONAL SPIRITUALIST ASSOCIATION OF CHURCHES

Founded: 1893

Membership: est. 3,000 in 144 churches (2008)

Spiritualism, generally understood as the practice of communication with the dead through "mediumship" in séances, has had a broader impact on American culture than is evident from its institutional forms. The Spiritualist movement in the United States began in 1848 with the activities of Margeretta and Kate Fox in Hydesvill, New York. The sisters claimed that they had succeeded in contacting the dead who communicate through strange "rappings." Central to the beliefs and practices of Spiritualism in its many forms is the ability to communicate with the spirits of those who have departed this earthly life. This may be done through such things as mediums, séances, and mystical rites. In recent years there has been greater interest in psychic experiments and extrasensory perception. Many modern Spiritualists hold to a belief in reincarnation and seek to reconnect with past-life experiences. During the twentieth century organized Spiritualism seems to have fallen under the influence of Theosophy and was given a boost by the New Age Movement that swept the United States in the 1980s and 1990s.

The older Spiritualist organizations in the United States remain closer to the Abrahamic tradition than the more recent New Age spiritual movements. In traditional Spiritualism, Christ is often regarded as a master medium; the annunciation is seen as a message from the spirit world; the transfiguration was an opportunity for materialization of the spirits of Moses and Elias; and the resurrection was evidence that all people live on in the spirit world but can communicate with the living.

Spiritualists often call the soul the "astral body." At death the material body dissolves, and the soul, or the body of the spirit, progresses through a series of spheres to a higher and higher existence ("spiritual evolution"). In two lower spheres, persons of bad character or sinful record are purified and made ready for higher existences. Most of the departed are to be found in a third sphere, the "summer land." Beyond this are the philosopher's sphere, the advanced contemplative and intellectual sphere, the love sphere, and the Christ sphere. All reach the higher spheres eventually; Spiritualists do not believe in heaven or hell or that any are ever lost. Many traditional beliefs of American Spiritualism derive from the writings of nineteenth-century Spiritualist writer and lecturer Andrew Jackson Davis (1825–1911) who was, in turn, influenced by Immanuel Swedenborg and possibly the budding Theosophical movement.

Spiritualists in general profess belief in Infinite Intelligence (God) and that natural phenomena are expressions of that Intelligence. True religion includes a correct understanding of the expressions of the Infinite Intelligence and learning how to live in accordance with the Infinite Intelligence. The personality of each individual lives on after death, which is just a change in state, and that the living can and do contact those who have passed beyond. The moral code of Spiritualism is Jesus's Golden Rule, and happiness or unhappiness depends on whether people obey or disobey Nature's physical and spiritual laws. Spiritualism, like Pentecostalism, believes that prophecy and healing are still spiritual gifts.

Services, usually including séances, are held in private homes, rented halls, or churches. Most Spiritualist churches have regular services with prayer, music, selections from writings by various spiritualists, a sermon or lecture, and spirit messages from the departed. Churches and ministers are supported by free will offerings; mediums and ministers also gain support from classes and séances in which fees are charged. Attendance at church services is usually small, averaging twenty to twenty-five.

Administration and government differ slightly in the various groups, but most have district or state associations and an annual general convention. All have mediums, and most have ministers in charge of the congregations. Most of the ministers are also mediums. Requirements for licensing and ordination also differ between Spiritualist groups, but a determined effort is being made to raise the standards of education and character in the larger groups.

The National Spiritualist Association of Churches (NSAC) is the largest Spiritualist denomination and was organized in Chicago around the time of the World's Parliament of Religions, which had heightened American interest in Eastern religions and esoteric philosophies. The NSAC furnishes literature for the whole American Spiritualist movement. In 1994, the Association established the Center for Spiritual Studies, NSAC in Lily Dale, New York, the most important center of Spiritualism in America. It offers a course of study for members, licentiates, healers, mediums, National Spiritualist Teachers, and ordained ministers, leading to an Associate of Arts in Religious Studies.

The National Spiritualist Alliance (TNSA) separated from the NSAC in 1913 in a dispute over reincarnation. TNSA is primarily located in New England, but its influence is broader than its membership. The alliance stresses paranormal manifestations of and intercommunication with the spirit world. A board of directors steers the work of ministers and certified mediums; college training is not required, but a minister must have passed a course of study arranged by the alliance. Mediums may baptize, but only ministers may officiate at ceremonies of ordination and marriage. A distinctive feature of the Alliance is its Psychic Fairs, held in various locations, which display psychic literature and phenomena.

The NSAC remains the largest and most influential of all Spiritualist denominations and networks in the United States. Its churches often use names that do not include

"Spiritualist" such as "Church of Universal Life." Women have always played central roles of leadership in Spiritualism including the NSAC. The current president of the organization is a woman. The NSAC's position regarding homosexuality, same-sex marriage, ordination of gay or lesbian people, and so on, is unknown.

For more information: www.nsac.org

Headquarters: NSAC, PO Box 217, Lily Dale, NY 14752-0217

MISCELLANEOUS DENOMINATIONS

There are numerous denominations in the United States that do not fit any of the traditional categories used by scholars of American religion; most of them have no clear historical roots in common with other denominations. Many were simply started by someone who did not begin by trying to reform another denomination or tradition or take a group of congregations out of one. Some of them were begun by independent congregations finding each other and deciding to form a network, which then evolved into a new denomination. What these Christian denominations have in common is simply not fitting into any historical-theological category. Another thing many of them have in common is reluctance to share information about themselves—especially membership statistics—with researchers.

ACTS 29 NETWORK

Founded: 2007
Membership: Unknown in 288 churches (2014)*

The Acts 29 Network (Acts 29) was started by Mark Driscoll who was twenty-five years old when he began the Mars Hill Church in his apartment in Seattle, Washington. From the beginning Driscoll's church was directed at the so-called Generation X, which was born after the "Baby Boom." Driscoll's preaching was modeled on the style of aggressive stand-up comedians, like Chris Rock, and he spoke in the vernacular used by the disaffected youth of the Northwest. As a result, he was sometimes referred to as "the cussing preacher." Despite his "grunge" persona, Driscoll's preaching was grounded in traditional evangelical systematic theology with a Calvinist interpretation. Because of Driscoll's sometimes aggressive style of communication and his tendency to speak very directly into controversial issues in a provocative style the magazine *Christianity Today* labeled him "Pastor Provacateur." Driscoll became a prolific author and spiritual mentor—through Internet podcasts—to thousands of "young, restless, and reformed" Christians including especially young men who liked his "macho" style.

The Mars Hill Church has an extensive educational program to promote its conservative theology, particularly in regard to gender roles in the church, family, and society. The church has a very web-based ministry, and Driscoll's blogs are read by as many as one hundred thousand people each week. In 2003, the church opened its first satellite congregation, and now has seven locations. Services are often very lively, and Driscoll has had to employ bodyguards because of threats against him. In 2007, the church reorganized, making Jamie Munson the lead pastor and Driscoll the preaching pastor. In 2014 the boards of Mars Hill Church and Acts 29 removed Driscoll from his leadership roles amid controversies about his allegedly authoritarian leadership style. Both the church and the network, however, continue under the leadership of Texas mega-church pastor Matt Chandler.

The Acts 29 Network is dedicated to planting new churches on the Mars Hill model, and it conducts "bootcamps" to train church planters. The denominetwork promotes Calvinist theology. It distinguishes itself from both fundamentalists and liberals, and believes that there are demonic forces in the world that must be overcome by prayer. There are twenty-eight chapters in the Book of Acts in the New Testament, which tells of the spread of Christianity and it ends with the Apostle Paul going to Rome. "Acts 29" refers to the mission of the church beyond the New Testament into the whole world. Acts 29 places great emphasis on church planting and has achieved much success in that endeavor. It is a conservative evangelical denominetwork that attracts many younger Christians disillusioned with traditional evangelical church life.

Under Driscoll's leadership Acts 29 was "complementarian" with regard to male and female roles both in family and in church. Women were not allowed to lead and were encouraged to live in submission to men. Acts 29 is a conservative evangelical network and does not condone same-sex marriage within itself or permit openly (practicing) gay men to lead in congregations.

For more information: www.acts29.com

Headquarters: 2111 Justin Road, Suite 106, Flower Mound, Texas 75028

*Acts 29 declined to provide membership statistics other than numbers of churches. The number provided is for North America; most of them are in the United States.

ALLIANCE OF RENEWAL CHURCHES

Founded: 1980s
Membership: Unknown in est. 40 churches (2016)

The Alliance of Renewal Churches (ARC)* is one of the fastest growing new youth-oriented evangelical denominetworks. It began in a series of events throughout the 1980s in which a previous denominetwork known as the Assembly of Covenant Churches collapsed as a result of controversies over gender roles in the home and the church (and other disagreements among members and leaders). The ARC emerged as the main successor to the Assembly and describes itself as a network of non-exclusive churches (members can belong to other denominations as well as ARC) distinguished by the equal inclusion of three streams of Christianity: evangelical, sacramental, and charismatic. The deep background of ARC theology is Lutheran, but leaders insist one does not have to have that background or theology to belong to ARC. ARC's theology is rooted in the ancient ecumenical creeds of Christianity including the Apostles' Creed and the Nicene Creed especially. It is generally conservative with regard to doctrine but contemporary with regard to worship and organization.

ARC's positions on women in ministry and gay and lesbian members and leaders is unknown. However, many churches affiliated with the Evangelical Lutheran Church of America (ELCA) have affiliated with ARC because of their opposition to the ELCA's opening to gay clergy.

For more information: www.allianceofrenewalchurches.org

Headquarters: PO Box 270083, Vadnais Heights, MN 55127

*The acronym ARC can also refer to the Association of Related Churches, which is also included in this category; they are not related but only share the same initials.

APOSTOLIC NETWORK OF GLOBAL AWAKENING

Founded: 1994
Membership: 142 churches*

The Apostolic Network of Global Awakening (ANGA) was founded in 1994 by evangelist Randy Clark who was instrumental in the so-called Toronto Blessing that drew thousands of people to the Toronto Airport Christian Fellowship in the 1990s. Like many other newer denominetworks, the ANGA is non-exclusive; it does not require members or churches to leave their previous denominations to join its renewal program. The ANGA is influenced by the teachings of C. Peter Wagner, long time professor of evangelism at Fuller Theological Seminary and promoter of the renewal of the office of apostle among contemporary Christians ("New Apostolic Reformation" movement). The ANGA sponsors the Wagner Leadership Institute, a non-accredited, distance-learning school in Colorado Springs, Colorado, as a training organization for men and women seeking to minister with the ANGA. The primary purpose of the ANGA is to promote apostolic and prophetic Christian ministry throughout the world. It places great emphasis on supernatural signs and wonders such as healing prophecy. It is not, however, precisely Pentecostal or charismatic. Some religion scholars would label it "renewalist" or "Third Wave" in terms of its ethos.

For more information: www.globalawakening.com

Headquarters: 1451 Clark Street, Mechanicsburg, PA 17055

*An e-mail received from the ANGA provided the number of affiliated churches in the United States but stated "350 total members within the U.S." This must have been in error.

ASSOCIATION OF RELATED CHURCHES

Founded: 2000
Membership: Unknown in est. 500 churches*

The Association of Related Churches (ARC) (not to be confused with the Alliance of Renewal Churches whose acronym here is also ARC) was founded by a group of six pastors meeting in 2000. It is, therefore, one of the newest denominations in this *Handbook*. The founding pastors had a vision for planting new churches, which is the focus of ARC as an organization. It exists to help "couples" start new churches that will bring the "hope of Jesus" to their cities. The Billy Hornsby Center for Church Planting in Birmingham, Alabama, is an important part of the denomination's purpose and work. It is named after the founding lead pastor who passed away in 2011. Its policies regarding women in ministry can only be guessed at from the language of "couples," which implies that husbands and wives can be co-pastors. No information about ARC's policy, if any, regarding homosexuals was found or forthcoming from phone calls and e-mail inquiries.

For more information: www.arcchurches.com

Headquarters: unknown

*Unknown is whether these churches are all in the United States or also elsewhere. Attempts to obtain information from this denomination were not successful (beyond its website's "500 churches").

CALVARY CHAPELS

Founded: 1968
Membership: statistics not available, but at least 500,000 in 700 churches (2004)*

The Calvary Chapels, known collectively as the Calvary Chapel Association (CCA), began as a single Calvary Chapel in Costa Mesa, California, in 1965 and has grown to over seven hundred related congregations, most of them also named Calvary Chapel, across the nation. The founder and head of Calvary Chapels is Chuck Smith (1927–2013), who began his ministry career in 1946 in the International Church of the Foursquare Gospel. Frustrated with the restrictions of that and other denominations, Smith went independent in the early sixties, with a focus on campus ministry. His focus was on addressing the everyday needs and concerns of his listeners. Two years after taking over the twenty-five-member Calvary Chapel, he had increased attendance to over two thousand worshippers. Soon they built a much larger facility, which regularly has over twenty-five thousand worshippers. It is the fountainhead for the Calvary Chapel network, which took on the name CCA.

One of the hallmarks of Smith's ministry in the 1960s was reaching out to the "hippies" and drug users of the California beach culture. He was a leader of the "Jesus Freak" movement that encouraged people to "turn off to drugs and on to Jesus." Smith founded over one hundred "community houses" modeled on the original "House of Miracles" for recent converts who needed a supportive environment.

Smith was a pioneer in the adaptation of secular rock and roll music for Christian worship. He established the Maranatha Music and Calvary Chapel recording companies, which have had a major impact on contemporary Protestant music. This "praise music" uses guitar and piano rather than traditional church instruments and has an upbeat tempo that has become very popular on Christian radio stations. This informal, lively music corresponds to the practice of wearing casual clothing, and following very informal worship. Worship, fellowship, and study times may be very emotional since members are encouraged to express their love for Christ, love for one another, and offer their personal testimonies of salvation.

CCA and its Chapels emphasize evangelism, conversion, and personal experience of the Holy Spirit, but try to do so in an invitational rather than confrontational way. Slightly fewer than 15 percent of the members report that they had no previous church connection before joining a Calvary Chapel.

CCA may be classified as "renewal" or "Third Wave" churches by sociologists of religion; they are conservative evangelical in theology and neo-Pentecostal or charismatic in spirituality with emphasis first on the Bible as the inerrant word of God and second on the supernatural gifts of the Holy Spirit. But they do not teach that speaking in tongues is necessary for the infilling of the Holy Spirit, which is an experience subsequent to conversion. Calvary Chapels do not baptize infants; they baptize believers upon confession of faith (conversion) by immersion. The denomination (which prefers to call itself a fellowship of churches) believes strongly in the "pretribulational rapture" and pre-millennialism (dispensational eschatology).

The CCA, or Calvary Chapels, operates Calvary Chapel Bible College in Murrieta, California. Calvary Chapels are led by pastors on what has been called the "Moses model," which points to authority; the CCA is led by a council of twenty-one leading pastors from regions around the country. The CCA website refers to "pastor's wives," which indicates that women cannot lead churches as pastors. The Calvary Chapel movement is very conservative theologically and culturally; it is highly unlikely that any openly gay person could serve in a leadership role.

For more information: www.calvarychapel.com

Contact: 3800 S Fairview Street, Santa Ana, CA 92704

*Statistics for the United States Calvary Chapels are difficult to come by; the CCA claims seventeen hundred affiliated churches worldwide. An e-mail from CCA headquarters said that they do not collect data on individual congregations as to attendance.

INTERNATIONAL COUNCIL OF COMMUNITY CHURCHES

Founded: 1950
Membership: 68,300 in 148 churches (2012)

Not a denomination in the traditional sense, the International Council of Community Churches (ICCC) provides services to several hundred independently organized and operated community churches in the United States and around the world. The stated purposes of the council are (1) to be an answer to Christ's prayer: "That they may all be one" (John 17:21 NRSV); (2) to affirm the worth and dignity of every person; (3) to attend to human need and suffering throughout the world; (4) to seek and share the truth; and (5) to build toward a new world of peace. The ICCC has no binding statement of doctrinal beliefs.

The current organization resulted from a 1950 merger of two other councils: one composed of predominantly black congregations, the other of churches with predominantly white memberships. The council holds an annual conference to which every member church can send two voting members, at least one of which must be a layperson. This conference elects a president, an executive director, a board of trustees, and other officers who carry on the business of the Council between conferences. The executive director and a small staff oversee the projects of the Council on a daily basis; headquarters are in Frankfort, Illinois.

The Council's services include ecclesiastical endorsement, personnel placement, continuing education, direct and brokered consultation for help in various areas, and supportive networks for clergy and their spouses and children. Publications include *The Christian Community*, a monthly newspaper; *The Pastor's Journal*, a quarterly for professionals; and materials from the Community Church Press.

It should be noted that many of the Council's member churches do not use the word *Community* in their names. Moreover, many churches that do include this term in their names are affiliated with a denomination, are members of a national organization outside the historic movement, or are independent congregations.

The ICCC is a diverse and inclusive network of independent churches most of which are liberal-leaning in theology and social justice issues. Some even function out of a "mystical and esoteric Christian" tradition. It affirms women in ministry.

For more information: www.icccnow.org

Headquarters: 21116 Washington Parkway, Frankfort, Illinois 60423

LOCAL CHURCHES

Founded: 1962
Membership: est. 25,000 in 300 churches (2016)

The Local Churches movement (LCM) began in China with the ministry of Chinese Christian Watchman Nee (1903–72), author of many books of evangelical Christianity widely read in English translations in the United States. Nee, a Free Methodist, was also influenced by the Plymouth Brethren. In 1934 his friend Witness Lee (1905–97) joined Nee in forming a new Christian movement without a specific name; others called their churches "Local Churches" due to the emphasis on "localism"—that there should be one Christian church in each city. By the 1940s there were about seven hundred Nee and Lee influenced churches throughout China. Nee was imprisoned by the Chinese communist government in 1952; he died in prison but the movement had spread to Taiwan and other places in the Far East.

Witness Lee brought the movement begun by Nee to America in 1962 where he built on Nee's fame as a Christian author especially among evangelical young people. Lee and his followers established a publishing house known as Living Stream Ministry that publishes over seven hundred titles by Nee and Lee. Lee died in California where his LCM began in America in 1997. His American followers established a network of American local churches that spread across the United States with the intention of having one Christian church in each city. Churches that belong to the movement, sometimes called "The Lord's Recovery," are often known simply as "The Church in Houston" or "The Church in Minneapolis." Some have grown very large and rented or purchased used facilities in which to meet. Others are smaller and meet in homes ("house churches").

The local churches of the LCM emphasize superfluous following a system very close to that of the Plymouth Brethren without clergy and with unprogrammed meetings for Bible study and worship. They are trinitarian in theology and center their faith and devotion on the person and work of Christ, committed to the authority of the Bible. They emphasize evangelism and discipleship.

During the 1970s through the 1990s some critics claimed the LCM was a cult. They pointed to certain unusual beliefs and practices that, according to the LCM, they misinterpreted. Most notable among the claimed controversial beliefs was that of Christians being able to become part of God's family. The LCM claimed that this was misunderstood and that they never have believed in Christians, their followers, or anyone else, becoming God as God is God. Some critics also claimed that the LCM taught exclusivity—that only they were true Christians and that other churches were false. This was later cleared up as the LCM emphasizes inclusivity of all true believers in Jesus Christ in one worldwide body of Christ.

Eventually, after some turmoil and controversy, the LCM emerged vindicated as an evangelical Christian group and is now widely accepted as such. The LCM, through

Living Stream Ministry, publishes a scholarly journal called *Affirmation and Critique* that explains their beliefs and explores a wide variety of issues in theology.

The LCM affirms women's leadership in some areas but the eldership or oversight of a local church is assigned to men only. The LCM holds to the view that biblical marriage is only between a man and a woman and that all sexual activity outside such marriage is forbidden.

For more information: www.localchurches.org

Headquarters: For information: Living Stream Ministry, PO Box 2121, Anaheim, CA 92814-0121

MESSIANIC JEWISH ALLIANCE OF AMERICA

Founded: 1915
Membership: est. 100,000 in 200 congregations (2010)

Founded as the Hebrew Christian Alliance of America, the Messianic Jewish Alliance of America (MJAA) is one of several networks of "Messianic Jews" that blend Judaism with Christianity. Generally speaking they are all more acceptable to Christians, because they believe in Jesus Christ as the Son of God, than to Jews. Most of them also include gentile Christians who are attracted to the idea that Christianity was never meant to "supersede" but only to fulfill Judaism. Also many "Christian Zionists" are attracted to Messianic Judaism because of its strong emphasis on God's providential restoration of Israel as a Jewish land and nation. (Christian Zionism is a feature of much evangelical and fundamentalist Christianity in America; "dispensational" theology usually includes some element of Christian Zionism.)

The MJAA is decidedly Christian in doctrines while adhering to many practices of orthodox Judaism; Messianic Jews and gentile members of messianic synagogues worship Jesus as not only the Jewish messiah but also as the Son of God and God incarnate. On the other hand, they observe many traditional holy days, feasts, and traditions of Judaism (such as observing Friday sundown to Saturday sundown as the Sabbath). The MJAA is also evangelical in its Christian ethos, believing in born again experience (conversion by faith in Jesus Christ) and the Christian canon, including the New Testament, as the inspired word of God written.

Messianic Judaism is controversial; some Jews and others consider it anti-Semitic. On the other hand, it rejects "replacement theology" or "supersessionism," which is the belief of much traditional Christianity that Christianity wholly replaced Judaism and the church replaced the synagogue, as "God's people," with the death and resurrection of Jesus Christ and the Day of Pentecost.

For more information: www.mjaa.org

Headquarters: PO Box 274, Springfield, PA 19064

– **329** –

METROPOLITAN COMMUNITY CHURCHES

Founded: 1970
Membership: 15,666 in 115 churches (2012)

The Metropolitan Community Churches (MCC) is unique among Christian bodies in that it was founded specifically to reach out to and affirm LGBT persons. The church holds the belief that theology is the basis to present the good news of God's love to a segment of society often excluded from participation in church life. This awareness prompted Troy D. Perry (1940–) to create a denomination in which such marginalized people could find genuine acceptance in a context of Christian worship and service. Perry had been discharged from the Church of God (Cleveland, Tennessee) after his bishop discovered that Perry was gay. He called a congregation into being in Los Angeles, and soon churches were organized in other cities. In the summer of 1970, the first general conference was held.

Heterosexuals may and do belong to the MCC, but a large percentage of the membership is homosexual. The church faces the controversial nature of its existence by stating that its members accept homosexuality as "a gift from God," just as heterosexuality is "a gift from God." Nonetheless, it holds that "our sexuality is not and should not be the focal point of our lives. The MCC emphasizes that everything in our life, including our sexuality, must center on our relationship with God, through faith in Jesus Christ." The denomination describes its ministry as a shared one—lay and clergy, women and men, privileged and underprivileged, lesbian, gay, and heterosexual. About half of its clergy are women.

The MCC professes traditional Christian theology on such doctrines as scripture, the Trinity, and the sacraments. The Bible, "interpreted by the Holy Spirit in conscience and faith," is the guide for faith and discipline. Since its members come from all types of Christian churches, the worship style, liturgy, and practice of congregations are eclectic and varied. Some congregations are more or less Pentecostal while others are very liturgical. Baptism and Holy Communion are the sacraments.

The membership of this denomination is active in a variety of ministries, reflecting its primary orientation to the social gospel and liberation theology. In particular, it has sought to address the needs of the hungry, the homeless, and the powerless. It supports a freeze on nuclear weapons and is committed to eradicating sexism in its theology and in society at large. The civil rights of all people are a major concern. It also addresses the AIDS epidemic as a major social issue, partly because incidences of the disease are so prevalent among its own membership.

The government of the MCC is vested in a Board of Elders, which includes the Moderator and six regional elders. The denomination was restructured in 2002, and subsequently decentralized its offices. The church is an international body, with a strong presence in Canada and Australia.

Obviously the MCC welcomes and affirms LGBT people at all levels of membership and leadership and, as stated, has women ministers. Although the MCC continues to meet the spiritual needs of the LGBT communities, its uniqueness in that regard is lessening as other Protestant denominations become "welcoming and affirming" of LGBT people.

For more information: www.mccchurch.org

Headquarters: PO Box 50488, Sarasota, FL 34232

NEW APOSTOLIC CHURCH USA

Founded: 1863
Membership: 30,619 members in 228 churches (2016)

The New Apostolic Church of North America (NACNA) is part of an international Christian church that developed from the Catholic Apostolic Church—a precursor of Pentecostalism led by Presbyterian pastor Edward Irving (1792–1834) in nineteenth-century Great Britain. It is led by apostles and its foundation is the Holy Scriptures. The New Apostolic Church recognizes three sacraments: baptism, Holy Sealing, and Holy Communion. They practice believer's baptism with water. Through the act of Holy Sealing, the baptized believer is filled with the Holy Spirit through prayer and laying on of the hands of an apostle. The idea of the return of Christ "to take home his bride," the church, is a central component of New Apostolic doctrine. The church also emphasizes the importance of personal accountability of its members for their actions. The gospel of Christ and values inherent in the Ten Commandments provide orientation for behavior.

The NACNA, like its worldwide affiliate church of which it is simply the American branch, is a hybrid of Catholic and Protestant theologies and practices. Its basic doctrinal standard is the Apostles' Creed; it is sacramental and episcopal in polity. And it holds to the basic beliefs about salvation expressed in the Protestant Reformation. Its belief about the pre-millennial return of Christ is especially important. Around the world the New Apostolic Church has about eleven million members.

LGBT persons cannot serve in ministry, but they are welcomed as members and have access to pastoral care including a prayer of blessing for their committed relationships. The church does not recognize same-sex marriage, but neither does it condemn people who enter into lifelong, committed same-sex relationships. The NACNA does not ordain women or have women pastors or apostles.

For more information: www.nac-usa.org

Headquarters: 6005 Perry Highway, Erie, PA 16509

TWO BY TWOS
(CHRISTIAN CONVENTIONS, THE TRUTH)

Founded: 1897
Membership: est. 41,000 (2016)

Some have called this network of congregations the largest Christian house-church movement in the United States if not the world. It is also noted among scholars of American religious groups as the Church with No Name. It is known to outsiders by various titles such as Two by Twos, Go-Preachers, the Workers, and Cooneyites. Members refer to their faith simply as The Truth or The Way and to each other as friends. Although it has existed for over a century, this network has no national or international headquarters but is led by regional Overseers. The label *Christian Conventions* was used by members to register with governments for tax purposes and so that young male members could register as conscientious objectors with the Selective Service.

The movement was founded by William Irvine (1863–1947) in Ireland and spread quickly to Great Britain and from there to Europe and the United States. Irvine was inspired by the Faith Mission movement in Ireland and Great Britain, which was Restorationist in ethos—intending to restore the primitive church or the New Testament. Irvine was deposed as leader of the movement in 1914 and succeeded by a group of men known as Overseers. The name Two by Twos, never accepted by the members, was applied to the movement by outsiders who noticed that unmarried Workers evangelized for the movement in same-gender couples who owned no property but traveled and stayed with members.

Reliable information about the movement has always been difficult for outsiders to obtain as little is published by the movement itself. Circular letters and annual regional conventions, often held on farms, form the communications among the scattered house churches and workers. Workers and Overseers keep some records; members always know where to find a house church when they travel. Evangelism is mostly by Gospel Meetings held by Workers in rented spaces.

Most information about the teachings of the movement are available only from ex-members, many of whom have created websites some of which are informational about the movement and some of which are anti-Two by Twos. It is extremely difficult for researchers to know what information is reliable as leaders of the movement generally do not communicate about it with scholars, researchers, or journalists.

Members of The Truth, Two by Twos, are conservative as to lifestyle and strongly committed to the movement as the only true form of Christianity. They do not believe that Jesus Christ was God incarnate but only the Son of God, not equal with the Father. They do not believe in the Trinity. Salvation is by dedication to the way of life of The Truth. Baptism is by immersion upon confession of faith. Services are held on Sundays and Wednesday evenings in homes of elders. Workers and Overseers have degrees of authority over house churches.

According to the best sources consulted, only men can serve as Overseers and elders but many Workers are women. It is highly unlikely that any openly gay person could serve in any leadership capacity. All publicly available websites related to this group are hosted by ex-members.

Headquarters: none

UNIFICATION CHURCH

Founded: 1954
Membership: est. 10,000

One of the most controversial churches born in modern times is the Unification Church (UC) founded by Sun Myung Moon (1920–2012) whom many members hailed as the "Lord of the Second Advent"—a prophetic precursor of the return of Jesus Christ to earth if not the return of Jesus Christ himself (a second incarnation). This church originated in Korea and burst upon the American scene in the 1970s. Its teachings are a blend of Eastern traditional philosophy and evangelical Christianity. Members hold that Satan distorted the original harmony of creation, but through the sacrifice of Jesus and revelations given to the Reverend Moon that harmony is being restored. Central to Moon's teaching is that God is a balance of masculine and feminine traits (basically the Yin and Yang of Taoism) and that humans can restore this harmony of polarities through spiritual marriage. Humans can also connect with the spiritual world and experience spiritual growth through proper actions, attitudes, and devotions that blend Eastern and Western elements.

Moon was born in 1920 in Korea and studied at a Confucian school. Around 1930, his parents became fervent Presbyterians, and the young Moon became a Sunday school teacher. At Easter 1935, as he was praying in the Korean mountains, Moon had a vision of Jesus who asked him to continue the work Jesus had begun on earth nearly two thousand years before. Moon studied the Bible and many other religious teachings in order to unravel the mysteries of life and human history. Embracing asceticism, he came to an understanding of God's own suffering and longing to be reunited with God's children.

By 1945, Moon had organized the teachings that came to be known as the *Divine Principle*, and he began his public ministry. On May 1, 1954, in Seoul, Moon founded the Holy Spirit Association for the Unification of World Christianity, popularly called the Unification Church. Despite opposition from other churches and the government, including imprisonment of Moon and other leaders, the church quickly spread throughout South Korea. In 1959, the first missionaries arrived in the United States.

Marriage is central to the teachings of the church, and the wedding of Moon to Hak Ja Han in 1960 was seen by his followers as the marriage of the Lamb foretold in the book of Revelation, marking the beginning of the restoration of humankind back into God's lineage. Moon and Hak Ja Han established the position of True Parents and are considered the first couple to have the complete blessing of God and to be able to bring forth children with no original sin. The church teaches that all people, whether previously married or single, can receive the blessing of God upon their marriages through the Moons' standing as the True Parents. The number of couples who have received this blessing in large wedding ceremonies was three hundred sixty thousand by 1995.

In 1971, Moon expanded his ministry by coming to the United States. He conducted a "Day of Hope" speaking tour throughout the United States in the early 1970s with the purpose of reviving traditional Judeo-Christian values. He was invited to the White House, where he met with President Richard Nixon. On two occasions, Moon addressed members of the United States Congress in both the House and the Senate. In 1975, Reverend Moon sent missionaries to 120 countries, making the Unification Church a worldwide faith. Controversy followed Moon and his followers, however, and in the 1980s he was convicted of tax evasion and imprisoned in the United States for thirteen months.

In 1992 Moon declared that he and his wife are the Messiah and True Parents of all humanity. For adherents, this marks the beginning of the Completed Testament Age. Since then, Mrs. Moon has taken a more active role in the worldwide work of the church. In a speech at a United States Congressional reception in 2004 Moon was officially crowned, and he then declared that he "is none other than humanity's Savior, Messiah, Returning Lord, and True Parent." Moon's organization owns the *Washington Times* newspaper in the nation's capital.

Over the years the UC has adopted several names including the previously mentioned Holy Spirit Association for the Unification of World Christianity. Another one is the Family Federation for World Peace and Unification—USA. The UC, under whatever name, has never been fully accepted by most traditional Christian groups as authentically Christian; many have called it a "cult"—a word widely discarded by religion scholars except for religious groups with violent and criminal tendencies. Most religion scholars in the United States consider the UC an "alternative religion" or "new religious movement" rather than a cult as it is peaceful.

Moon's death in 2012, together with some public statements about the group by ex-members and even by some Moon family members, led to turmoil within the UC. Moon was succeeded as leader of the UC by his son Huyng Jin Moon. The UC places strong religious value in heterosexual, monogamous marriage and does not permit openly gay persons to serve as leaders. The church's position on women in religious leadership is unknown. However, Moon's daughter In Jin Moon was appointed by her father as CEO of the American branch of the church in 2008. She resigned that position in 2012. Her brief tenure of leadership of the American Unification Church indicates that women can be leaders of the church.

For more information: www.unification.net and www.familyfed.org

Headquarters: 481 Eighth Avenue, Box A-12, New York, NY 10001

UNITED HOUSE OF PRAYER FOR ALL PEOPLE

Founded: 1927
Membership: est. 27,500 in 145 churches (2016)

The United House of Prayer for All People (TUHOPFAP) was founded by Charles Manuel Grace, an immigrant to the United States from the Cape Verde islands, first in Massachusetts and then in Washington, DC where its headquarters stands. Known to his many followers as "Sweet Daddy Grace," the founder appointed himself bishop of his churches and served as the denomination's sole leader until his death in 1960. Grace led an almost exclusively black Christian movement while emphasizing racial reconciliation and justice for all people. Especially during the Great Depression of the 1930s the TUHOPFAP served the poor by providing jobs and food. "Daddy Grace" was looked to by many of his followers as a kind of contemporary apostle. Some critics claimed the movement was a cult of personality and that the movement's teachings were unorthodox especially with regard to the Trinity ("Oneness Pentecostalism"). However, the church's creed and statement of "Our Faith" do not reflect that. They are very simple statements of orthodox Christianity except for one: "We believe in one leader as the ruler of the kingdom of God." Who is the "one leader" is left unstated; some critics have claimed it refers to the current bishop of TUHOPFAP, but TUHOPFAP does not say that.

TUHOPFAP is noted for loud musical parades and "shouting" events led by "shout bands," which draw attention and celebrate its past and present bishops. It has been known to perform large "street baptisms" sometimes with hoses. TUHOPFAP endeavors to provide for the material needs of its members as well as others through its own welfare programs including low-income housing, job training, and small businesses that provide work for members. However, the bishop of TUHOPFAP is the sole trustee of the organization's properties and appoints all ministers.

For more information: www.tuhopfap.org
Headquarters: 601 M Street Northwest, Washington, DC, 2001

VOLUNTEERS OF AMERICA, INC.

Founded: 1896
Membership: 16,000 employees, 80,000 volunteers, 2 million served (2016)

Volunteers of America (VOA) is a Christian church and a human-service organization founded in 1896 by Ballington (1857–1940) and Maud (1865–1948) Booth, son and daughter-in-law of William Booth, founder of the Salvation Army. The mission of VOA is to reach and uplift all people, bringing them to the immediate knowledge and active service of God. VOA is one of the largest and most financially efficient service organizations in the world. Over 85 percent of its multi-million dollar budget goes directly to those whom it serves. It is present in communities across the United States, providing over 160 different human-service programs and opportunities for individual and community involvement. From rural areas to inner-city neighborhoods, VOA engages tens of thousands of professional staff and volunteers in operating programs that deal with today's most pressing social needs. It responds to individual community needs to help abused and neglected children, youth at risk, the frail elderly, the disabled, homeless individuals and families, and many others. Each year, it helps more than 1.8 million people in need.

Volunteers of America adheres to a defined set of beliefs, or Cardinal Doctrines, that conform to biblical teaching and traditional Christian thought and practice. Individuals who are commissioned as VOA ministers (having met all requirements for religious study and spiritual formation) become fully accredited clergy and may perform sacramental and evangelical functions. Volunteers of America is governed by both a religious body, the Grand Field Council, and a corporate body, the National Board of Directors. The Council is made up of all VOA clergy and represents the membership of the organization. The Council is responsible for framing the articles of incorporation, constitution, bylaws, and regulations and for electing its president. The National Board of Directors consists of thirty-one volunteer members and is responsible for the direction and effective functioning of the organization. The National Ecclesiastical Board is a smaller body of VOA clergy charged with ministerial affairs. The chief officer of Volunteers of America, Inc., elected for a five-year term, is president of the corporation as well as head of the church. The national office, in Alexandria, Virginia, provides technical and administrative support to local VOA programs and directs other strategic initiatives to address the organization's mission.

Although the VOA is a service organization, like the Salvation Army (from which it evolved), it is also a church. The VOA has thirty-four "Affiliates," also known as "Posts," each led by a "Minister in Charge," which may be either a man or a woman. The VOA has a total of 450 active ministers (2016). Worship is held in each Post and the VOA considers itself interdenominationally Protestant in tradition and theology. It is an inclusive "church without walls" that welcomes all people as children of God.

For more information: www.voa.org

Headquarters: 1660 Duke Street, Alexandria, VA 22314

APPENDICES

Appendix 1:
Foreign Missionary Churches
in the United States

The presence in the United States of churches populated mostly by immigrants and aliens (legal, illegal, permanent, temporary), pastored by missionaries from other countries, is not new. Many established American churches and denominations were originally founded by immigrants and missionaries to the United States. However, most of those eventually settled in and became, for better or worse, "American churches." Most of them either created a distinctly American denomination with a headquarters in the United States or joined an already existing American denomination. Many examples could be cited. Nineteenth-century Swedish Baptist immigrants to the United States brought Swedish pastors, based in Sweden, to pastor their churches and preach. Gradually they sent some of their own people to American seminaries and brought most of their churches under the "umbrella" of the Northern Baptist Convention (now the American Baptist Churches, USA). Eventually, however, many of them banded together to create their own distinctly American Baptist denomination called the Swedish Baptist Conference and then the Baptist General Conference and now "Converge Worldwide" with headquarters in Arlington Heights, Illinois. This has been the usual pattern for Christian immigrants to the United States.

In recent years, however, many immigrants to the United States virtually bring their home-based churches with them or create offshoots of foreign-based denominations with no apparent intention of joining an American denomination or creating an American-headquartered denomination of their own. The nineteenth and early twentieth century immigrant ideal of becoming American, of blending in and adopting American ways, is not as strong as before.

All that is simply to say that, scattered across America and more densely clustered in certain especially coastal cities, one now finds small and large churches filled with immigrants to the United States who look to their home-based denominations and church networks to supply them with pastors who then become a new kind of missionaries to the United States. These "foreign missionary churches" are different from those in the past in that they do not intend to adapt to American Christianity. Usually they keep to themselves, create their own networks of ethnic and foreign-based churches, and worship and practice Christianity in the ways they did in the countries from which they came.

Another pattern is for foreign denominations and churches to send missionaries to the United States to evangelize immigrants who speak their language and even, often, to bring them into the embrace of a foreign-headquartered denomination—with no intention of facilitating their "Americanization."

For example, in large American cities especially on the West Coast it is common to see seemingly independent churches whose worship, witness, published material, church signs, and websites are all in Korean. Most of these Korean churches look across the Pacific Ocean to Korea for their "headquarters" (if any). While individuals and their families may be becoming Americanized through popular culture, jobs, and public education, their churches have no intention of ever becoming Americanized. And their networks of churches look to no American-based headquarters. Everything they do is linked to a home base in Korea. Any evangelizing they engage in is focused primarily on Korean immigrants to the Unite States.

None of this description is meant as criticism. The only point is to say that it is extremely difficult, sometimes impossible, for an American researcher or reporter to study them. They (and by "they" we mean all kinds of churches and networks of churches in the United States like this) may never establish an American headquarters. If they do it may be nothing more than an office and annual convention to facilitate networking among them. These Christian groups who still, and perhaps always will, look back to a headquarters in their home country and who resist becoming Americanized in any way (in terms of their worship, witness, and church practices) have become so common in large American cities that they constitute a new kind of phenomenon for students of American Christianity and a real challenge for categorizing and describing them.

This writer is very familiar with a loose network of Ukrainian Pentecostal churches in the Upper Northwest of the United States. They have no "connective tissue" among themselves other than being Ukrainian and Pentecostal Christian (and, of course, friends). They do not seem to care about other Pentecostals in the United States—in terms of discovering common bonds and creating any "connective tissue" with them. They have and intend to maintain their own distinctively Ukrainian Pentecostalism. They look back to Ukraine and a Pentecostal denomination there for their loyalty and leadership. Will this group eventually establish an American denomination—even with distinctively Ukrainian practices? I think that is less likely in the twenty-first century than it was in the nineteenth and early twentieth centuries. Again, no criticism or judgment is implied in this description and prediction. The only point being made here is that the multiple presence of such churches and networks of immigrant churches within the United States creates a new challenge for handbooks like this and for researchers into American Christianity.

There exists, and has long existed, an organization of professional researchers, whose self-assigned task is to track and describe American religious bodies, called the Association of Statisticians of American Religious Bodies. The members work to discover and publish information about American denominations and networks of churches. (So far they tend to focus primarily on Christian religious bodies in the United States as this *Handbook* does.) One reason for their existence as an organization of researchers is the federal government's decision to drop questions about religious affiliation in the once-every-decade censuses. (The organization existed before that but was given special, new impetus by it.) These researchers, of which this writer is one, find the increasing existence of immigrant churches with no US headquarters challenging (to say the least).

If the pattern of the past holds, these immigrant, "missionary" churches in the United States will eventually evolve into American Christian denominations. Until that happens, however, they will remain largely a challenge to researchers due to the lack of any American headquarters.

Appendix 2:
Interdenominational Agencies

Especially during the twentieth century many American Christian denominations began to form transdenominational "umbrella" organizations to create or enhance dialogue and cooperation among themselves. Such organizations are sometimes called "ecumenical," but that term came to be associated with attempts to unite all Protestant, if not Christian, denominations into one church visibly and institutionally. The organizations and agencies described here do not all have that goal. Listed and described here will be trans- and interdenominational organizations and agencies that bring together diverse denominations for cooperation, dialogue, and fellowship. These are parachurch organizations, but there are many other parachurch organizations that do not belong in this list because they do not serve the purpose of trans- and interdenominational cooperation, dialogue, and fellowship. For example, many parachurch organizations that serve denominations and whose boards include representatives of different denominations exist for purposes of missions, Bible translation, charity, community development, and so on. They are far too numerous to be included here. Here only those parachurch organizations that explicitly exist to promote trans- and interdenominational cooperation, dialogue, and fellowship among American denominations will be listed and described. Even they are too numerous for all to be included; only the major, larger ones will be listed and described here.

AMERICAN COUNCIL OF CHRISTIAN CHURCHES

Founded 1941
Fundamentalist Protestant

The American Council of Christian Churches (ACCC) was founded in 1941 by influential fundamentalist Presbyterian minister Carl McIntire (1906–2002). McIntire was part of the conservative exodus from Princeton Theological Seminary led by J. Gresham Machen who founded the Orthodox Presbyterian Church and Westminster Theological Seminary. However, McIntire became dissatisfied with Machen's moderate conservatism and founded his own separatist denomination, the Bible Presbyterian Church, and seminary, Faith Theological Seminary (Baltimore, Maryland). McIntire envisioned an umbrella organization for fundamentalist Protestants to rival the Federal Council of Churches (later the National Council of Churches). The ACCC was and remains anti-ecumenical in the sense of resisting any vision of a visibly and institutionally united Christian church. It also rejects Roman Catholicism, liberal Protestantism, and neo-evangelicalism. Churches affiliated with the National Council of Churches or the National Association of Evangelicals may not join the separatistic ACCC, which insists on doctrinal purity for fellowship (although it permits differences of doctrine among members over secondary matters such as baptism and the Lord's Supper). The ACC provides various opportunities for interaction, support, and fellowship for fundamentalist, non-charismatic Protestants.

Member denominations:

Appalachian Independent Minister's Fellowship
Faith Presbytery, Bible Presbyterian Church
Association of Ministers of the Reformed Faith
Evangelical Methodist Church, The
Fellowship of Fundamental Bible Churches
Free Presbyterian Church of North America
Fundamental Methodist Church
Independent Baptist Fellowship of North America
Independent Churches Affiliated
    For more information: www.accc4truth.org
    Headquarters: PO Box 628, Orwell, OH 44076

CHRISTIANS TOGETHER IN THE USA

Founded: 2001–06
Catholic, Eastern Orthodox, Protestant

About twenty-seven and then thirty-two American Christian leaders met in three stages beginning in 2001 to discuss the need for a place, or organization, where American Christians of diverse traditions could meet, have conversations, and cooperate for Christian mission. The first meeting was in Baltimore and the second was in Chicago. The felt need was to expand and broaden fellowship, unity, and witness among the diverse expressions of Christian faith. The final organized expression of this group was held in Atlanta in 2006 where a constitution and bylaws were finalized.

At the 2002 meeting the founders of this group promulgated "The Chicago Statement" decrying divisions among Christians and setting forth a belief basis around which Christians can cooperate in spite of continuing differences. This basic belief basis is: "Christian Churches Together in the U.S.A. gathers together those churches and Christian communities which, acknowledging God's revelation in Christ, confess the Lord Jesus Christ as God and Savior according to the Scripture, and in obedience to God's will and in the power of the Holy Spirit commit themselves to seek a deepening of their communion with Christ and with one another; to fulfill their mission to proclaim the Gospel by common witness and service in the world for the glory of the one God, Father, Son and Holy Spirit."

Member Denominations:

American Baptist Churches, USA
Antiochian Orthodox Christian Archdiocese
Archdiocese of the Syriac Orthodox Church of Antioch
Armenian Orthodox Church in America
Christian Church (Disciples of Christ)
Christian Reformed Church in NA
Church of God (Anderson, IN)
Church of the Brethren
Cooperative Baptist Fellowship
Coptic Orthodox Church
Episcopal Church
Evangelical Covenant Church
Evangelical Lutheran Church in America
Free Methodist Church
Greek Orthodox Archdiocese of America
International Council of Community Churches
International Pentecostal Holiness Church
Korean Presbyterian Church in America
Mennonite Church USA
Moravian Church
National Baptist Convention of America
National Baptist Convention, USA
Orthodox Church in America
Polish National Catholic Church
Presbyterian Church USA
Reformed Church in America
Salvation Army
United Church of Christ
United Methodist Church
U.S. Conference of Catholic Bishops
Vineyard USA
Wesleyan Church, The
    For more information: www.christianchurchestogether.org
    Headquarters: PO Box 4963, Louisville, KY 40204

NATIONAL ASSOCIATION OF EVANGELICALS

Founded: 1942
Evangelical Protestant

The National Association of Evangelicals (NAE) is an association of about forty evangelical Protestant denominations and more than one hundred other organizations, including parachurch ministries and academic institutions. NAE members adhere to a basic statement of faith that contains commonly held evangelical theological commitments. The NAE's mission is to foster cooperation among its member groups in missions, ministry, and political action, and to provide a representative voice for evangelicals in matters of public importance. The association maintains a government affairs office in Washington, DC; it is the largest endorsing body for chaplains in the United States armed forces, and provides its member bodies with a variety of services, including human resources consulting and medical insurance for long and short-term missionaries.

The NAE is one of the largest and most prominent representative voices for evangelical Protestantism in the Unites States. Founded in 1942, the NAE represents one of the earliest and most enduring attempts by evangelical Protestants to reengage society following Protestant fundamentalism's retreat from the public square in the early twentieth century. After a number of losing battles over denominational leadership and subsequent denominational splits, by the 1940s evangelical Protestants were searching for a source of religious identity beyond their denominational affiliation. The NAE purposed to fill this void, offering an institutional expression of evangelical identity and a conservative alternative to the more liberal National Council of Churches (NCC) and its predecessor, the Federal Council of Churches, as well as to fundamentalist Protestantism.

The NAE has long struggled with its identity. In an attempt to distance itself from its fundamentalist predecessors, the NAE intended to present a positive vision for evangelical Protestantism. But the NAE spent much of its early existence countering the activities of the NCC. In response to the NCC's representation of America in the World Council of Churches, the NAE worked to resurrect the World Evangelical Alliance in 1951. When the NCC released the *Revised Standard Version* of the Bible, the NAE helped to organize a translation more agreeable to conservatives, the International Bible Society's *New International Version*. Not until the rise of the Religious Right in the late 1970s did the NAE develop a social and political vision for the organization distinct from its progressive counterpart.

During the 1980s, NAE membership and influence increased significantly, but the association never fully freed itself from its identity crisis. In the late 1990s and 2000s the NAE attempted to expand evangelical political concerns beyond the Religious Right's traditional focus on opposition to abortion and LGBT rights by emphasizing environmental concerns, social justice, and human rights, which incited a backlash from certain evangelical leaders in the Religious Right. Its president, Minnesota mega-church pastor Leith Anderson, has helped to refocus the NAE on its founding mission to present a positive vision for evangelical Protestantism.

Member denominations:

Advent Christian General Conference
Anglican Mission in America
Assemblies of God
Brethren Church, The
Brethren in Christ Church
Christian and Missionary Alliance
Christian Reformed Church in North America
Christian Union
Church of God (Cleveland, Tennessee)
Church of the Nazarene
Conservative Congregational Christian Conference
Converge Worldwide (Baptist General Conference)
ECO: A Covenant Order of Evangelical Presbyterians
Elim Fellowship
Evangelical Assembly of Presbyterian Churches
Evangelical Church, The
Evangelical Congregational Church
Evangelical Free Church of America
Evangelical Friends Church International
Evangelical Presbyterian Church
Every Nation Churches
Fellowship of Evangelical Bible Churches
Fellowship of Evangelical Churches
Foursquare Church, The
Free Methodist Church USA
Grace Communion International
Great Commission Churches
International Pentecostal Church of Christ
International Pentecostal Holiness Church
Missionary Church, Inc.
North American Baptist Conference
Open Bible Churches
Presbyterian Church in America
Primitive Methodist Church USA
Royalhouse Chapel International

Salvation Army, The
Transformation Ministries
United Brethren in Christ
U.S. Conference of the Mennonite Brethren Churches
Vineyard USA
Wesleyan Church, The
  For more information: www.nae.net
  Headquarters: PO Box 23269, Washington, DC 20026

NATIONAL COUNCIL OF CHURCHES OF CHRIST IN THE USA

Founded: 1950 (predecessor founded in 1908)

The National Council of Churches in Christ in the USA, commonly known as the National Council of Churches (NCC), is an association of thirty-five denominations including Protestants, Anglicans, American branches of Eastern Orthodoxy, and historically black denominations. The organization's major foci are facilitating dialogue and cooperation among its member groups; advancing various social and political initiatives; and promoting theological and Biblical scholarship, including the translation of the *Revised Standard Version* and *New Revised Standard Version* of the Bible. The NCC maintains five commissions to carry out its mission and offices in New York City and Washington, DC. The organization is led by an annual General Assembly and a Governing Board composed of elected officers and other representatives from the organization.

The NCC is the successor organization to the Federal Council of Churches, founded in 1908 as an expression of the trans-denominational ecumenical movement of the early twentieth century. The thrust of the ecumenical movement was to stress the commonality of different Christian denominations rather than their differences. Since the mid-1800s, trans-denominational organizations had formed in both Europe and America to promote missionary, social, and political causes. By focusing on causes shared across denominations, the organizations of the ecumenical movement fostered a sense of common cause and shared identity among its members despite their denominational differences. The Federal Council of Churches focused largely on missionary activities and activism in line with the Social Gospel.

In 1950, twenty-five Protestant and four Orthodox bodies inaugurated the NCC as a larger and more robust version of its predecessor. Organized like the United Nations, the NCC would focus on missions and social activism by providing a locus of trans-denominational cooperation and offering denominations a means to influence public policy. It would also represent the United States in the World Council of Churches. Often viewed as politically progressive, the NCC was active in the civil rights movement, taking part in the 1963 March on Washington and supporting the Civil Rights Act of 1964 and the Voting Rights Act of 1965.

The NCC went through a difficult period of budget cuts and restructuring during the 1990s due in large part to the decline in mainline Protestant denominations. Today, the NCC remains a leading progressive religious voice, most known for its social and political advocacy for the environment, social welfare causes, and international justice. Some of this advocacy has created controversy within its member churches. The NCC also promotes interfaith dialogue through the Faith and Order Commission, which includes participants that are not member churches of the NCC, most notably Roman Catholics and evangelicals. One of the most successful endeavors of the NCC is the annual Crop Walk to raise money for hunger relief.

Member denominations:

African Methodist Episcopal Church
African Methodist Episcopal Zion Church, The
Alliance of Baptists
American Baptist Churches in the USA
Armenian Church of America, Eastern and Western Dioceses
Assyrian Church of the East
Christian Church (Disciples of Christ) in the United States and Canada
Christian Methodist Episcopal Church
Church of the Brethren
Community of Christ
Coptic Orthodox Archdiocese of North America
Ecumenical Catholic Communion
Episcopal Church (USA), The
Evangelical Lutheran Church in America
Greek Orthodox Archdiocese of America
Hungarian Reformed Church in America
International Council of Community Churches
Korean Presbyterian Church Abroad
Malankara Orthodox Syrian Church, American Diocese
Mar Thoma Church
Moravian Church in America, Northern and Southern Provinces
National Baptist Convention of America, Inc.
National Baptist Convention, USA, Inc.
National Missionary Baptist Convention of America
Orthodox Church in America
Patriarchal Parishes of the Russian Orthodox Church in the USA
Polish National Catholic Church

Presbyterian Church (USA)
Progressive National Baptist Convention, Inc.
Reformed Church in America
Religious Society of Friends, Friends United Meeting
Religious Society of Friends, Philadelphia Yearly Meeting
Serbian Orthodox Church in North and South America
Swedenborgian Church of North America, The
Syrian Orthodox Church of Antioch, Archdiocese of the Eastern United States
Ukrainian Orthodox Church of the USA
United Church of Christ
United Methodist Church, The
  Information: www.nationalcouncilofchurches.us
  Contact: 475 Riverside Drive, Eighth Floor, New York, NY 10115

PENTECOSTAL AND CHARISMATIC CHURCHES OF NORTH AMERICA

Founded 1994 (predecessor founded 1948)
White, African American, Hispanic, and Other "Renewalists"

The Pentecostal movement is generally believed to have begun, as a movement, with the Azusa Street Revival in Los Angeles, California, in 1906. It has precursors such as events at the Bethel Bible College in Topeka, Kansas, in 1901 and nearly simultaneous outbreaks of speaking in unknown tongues ("glossolalia") among Scandinavian Pietists and Southern revivalists in the late nineteenth century. The leader of the Azusa Street Revival was an African American holiness evangelist named William Seymour (1870–1922). Soon after that weeks-long revival, however, in which speaking in tongues was interpreted as the sign of a new outpouring of the Holy Spirit, racial and other divisions began to appear among Pentecostals. Numerous denominations sprang into existence out of the early Pentecostal movement. Some held the same doctrinal beliefs and practices but differed about church government. Others disagreed with fellow Pentecostal groups about whether a Spirit-filled Christian can attain "Christian perfection" (entire sanctification) before death. Other issues that kept Pentecostal denominations apart included women's roles in leadership and the doctrine of the Trinity. No issue seemed as divisive, however, as that of race. African American and Caucasian Pentecostals went their separate ways, forming different denominations that had little or no contact with each other.

In 1948 a group of white Pentecostal denominational leaders met in Des Moines, Iowa, the headquarters of one Pentecostal group, to form the Pentecostal Fellowship of North America (PFNA)—an "umbrella" organization of trinitarian Pentecostals uniting for cooperation and fellowship. The various denominations, including the Assemblies of

God, the Church of God (Cleveland, Tennessee), and the International Church of the Foursquare Gospel, had no intention of uniting institutionally, but they began holding annual meetings together. The PFNA largely healed a divide among Pentecostals over sanctification; they agreed to disagree and made it no obstacle to fellowship and cooperation. The PFNA, however, excluded African American Pentecostals who probably made up about half of all Pentecostals in the United States. The Church of God in Christ, one of the oldest Pentecostal bodies, was not invited to the founding PFNA meeting.

In 1994 white PFNA leaders voted to dissolve the organization because of what they regarded as its racist beginnings. They determined that the founders consciously excluded African American Pentecostals and that the only remedy for that was to disband and invite African American Pentecostals to form a new umbrella organization. The change was formally celebrated with an event called "The Memphis Miracle" in which the Church of God in Christ, headquartered in that Tennessee city, took the leadership in the formation of the new racially inclusive organization. It eventually settled on the name Pentecostal and Charismatic Churches of North America (PCCNA). As of 2016 the PCCNA includes about forty distinct Pentecostal and charismatic organizations (including some headquartered in Canada) including African American, Hispanic, and Caucasian. Still excluded from the organization are the so-called Oneness Pentecostal groups that doctrinally reject the traditional doctrine of the Trinity (Nicene) in favor of belief in "Jesus Only." The "Jesus Only" belief is that Jesus is the Father, the Son, and the Holy Spirit. Trinitarian Pentecostals are traditional evangelical Protestant Christians with the addition of belief that speaking in tongues, prophecy, divine healing, and miracles are gifts of the Holy Spirit for all times and did not cease with the deaths of the apostles or the completion of the canon of scripture.

The PCCNA promotes fellowship and cooperation among trinitarian Pentecostals and charismatics regardless of race or ethnicity and includes both "Holiness" and non-Wesleyan Pentecostals who regard sanctification as a process and not an event-experience resulting in Christian perfection.

Member denominations (includes Canadian and Mexican):

Apostolic Church of Pentecost of Canada
Assemblies of God
Canadian Assemblies of God
Capitol Hill Full Gospel
Church of God (Cleveland, TN)
Church of God in Christ
Church of God Mountain Assembly
Church of God of the Apostolic Faith
Church of God of Prophecy
CMI Global

Coastal Church
Elim Fellowship
Foursquare Church, The
Full Gospel Fellowship
Grupo de Unidad Cristiana de Mexico AR
Iglesia Evangélica San Pablo
Independent Assemblies of God Int'l
Independent Assemblies of God Int'l (Canada)
International Center for Spiritual Renewal
Intimate Life Ministries
Int'l Fellowship of Christian Assemblies
Int'l Pentecostal Church of Christ
Int'l Pentecostal Holiness Church
NHCLC (National Hispanic Christian Leadership Conference)
Open Bible Churches
Open Bible Faith Fellowship
PCCNA Memphis Chapter, Rising Sun Outreach Ministries
Pentecostal Assemblies of Canada
Pentecostal Assemblies of Newfoundland
Pentecostal Church of God
Pentecostal Free Will Baptist Church
Pentecostal Holiness Church of Canada
Reformed Churches of God in Christ International
United Evangelical Churches
United Holy Church of America
    Information: www.pccna.org
    Contact: 8408 131st Street Court East, Puyallup, WA 98373

Appendix 3: Denominations, Headquarters, Websites

Acts 29 Network	1411 NW 50th Street, Seattle, WA 98107	www.acts29network.org
Advent Christian Church General Conference	PO Box 23152, Charlotte, NC 28227	www.acgc.us
African Methodist Episcopal Church	500 8th Avenue South, Nashville, TN 37203	www.ame-church.com
African Methodist Episcopal Zion Church	3225 Sugar Creek Road, Charlotte, NC 28269	www.amez.org
African Orthodox Church	122 West 129 Street, New York City, NY 10023	www.netministries.org
Albanian Orthodox Archdiocese in America	533 East Broadway, South Boston, MA 02127	www.orthodoxalbania.org
Alliance of Baptist Churches	3939 LaVista Road Suite E-122, Atlanta, GA 30084	www.allianceofbaptists.org
American Association of Lutheran Churches	TAALC, 921 East Dupont Road #920, Fort Wayne, IN 46825	www.taalc.org
American Baptist Association	4605 North State Line, Texarkana, TX 75503	www.abaptist.org
American Baptist Churches in the USA	PO Box 851, Valley Forge, PA 19482-0851	www.abc-usa.org
American Bible Society	1865 Broadway, New York, NY 10023.	www.americanbible.org
American Carpatho-Russian Orthodox Church	312 Garfield Street, Johnstown, PA 15906	www.acrod.org
American Catholic Church in the United States	5595 Rivendell Place Frederick, MD 21703-8673	www.accus.us
American Evangelical Christian Churches	PO Box 47312, Indianapolis, IN 46277	www.aeccministries.com
American Unitarian Conference	6806 Springfield Drive, Mason Neck, VA 22079	www.americanunitarian.org
Amish Churches	PO Box 398 Valdese, NC 28690	www.waldensian.org
Anglican Church in North America	800 Maplewood Avenue, Ambridge, PA 15003	www.anglicanchurch.net
Anglican Province of America	3348 West State Road 426, Oviedo, FL 32765	www.anglicanprovince.org
Antiochian Orthodox Christian Archdiocese of North America	PO Box 5238, Englewood, NJ 07631-5258	www.antiochian.org
Apostolic Catholic Assyrian Church of the East, North American Diocese	7201 North Ashland, Chicago, IL 60626	www.news.assyrianchurch.org
Apostolic Christian Churches of America	10699 Steiner Road, Rittman, OH 44270	www.apostolicchristian.org
Apostolic Episcopal Church	8046 234th Street, Queens, NY 11427	www.apostolicepiscopalchurch.org
Apostolic Faith Church	6615 Southeast Fifty-Second Avenue, Portland, OR 97206	www.apostolicfaith.org

Apostolic Faith Mission Church of God	806 Muscogee Road, Cantonment, FL 32533	www.apostoliclutheran.org
Apostolic Lutheran Church of America	PO Box 2996, Battle Ground, WA 98604	www.aohchurch.com
Apostolic Overcoming Holy Church of God, Inc.	2257 Saint Stephens Road, Mobile, AL 36617	www.armenianchurch-ed.net
Armenian Churches	630 Second Avenue, New York, NY 10016	www.ag.org
Assemblies of God	1445 Boonville Avenue, Springfield, MO 65802	www.aljc.org
Assemblies of the Lord Jesus Christ	875 North White Station Road, Memphis, TN 38122	www.arpchurch.org
Associate Reformed Presbyterian Church	One Cleveland Street Suite 110, Greenville SC 29601	www.aflc.org
Association of Free Lutheran Congregations	3110 East Medicine Lake Boulevard, Plymouth, MN 55441	www.arbca.org
Association of Reformed Baptist Churches of America	401 East Louther Street Suite 303, PO Box 289, Carlisle, PA 17013	www.unity.org
Association of Unity Churches	1901 Northwest Blue Parkway, Unity Village, MO 64065	www.bbfi.org
Baptist Bible Fellowship International	720 East Kearney Street, PO Box 191, Springfield, MO 65801	www.bgct.org
Baptist General Convention of Texas	7557 Rambler Road Suite 1200, Dallas, TX 75231	www.bmaamerica.org
Baptist Missionary Association of America	PO Box 1188, Conway, AR 72033	www.beachyam.org
Beachy Amish Mennonite Churches	3015 Partridge Road, Partridge, KS 67566	www.weareberean.org
Berean Fellowship Church	PO Box 234, Broken Bow, NE 68822	www.mybfc.org
Bible Fellowship Church	3000 Fellowship Drive, Whitehall, PA 18052	www.biblemethodist.org
Bible Methodist Connection of Churches		www.biblewaychurch.org
Bible Way Church of Our Lord Jesus Christ World Wide, Inc.	4949 Two-Notch Road, Columbia, SC 29204	www.biblewaychurch.org and www.internationalbibleway.org
Bible Way Church of Our Lord Jesus Christ	261 Rochester Avenue, Brooklyn, NY 11213 and Bible Way Temple, 1110 Holmes Street, Raleigh, NC 27610	www.brethrenchurch.org
Brethren Church (Ashland)	524 College Avenue, Ashland, OH 44805	www.bic-church.org
Brethren in Christ Church	481 Grantham Road, Mechanicsburg, PA 17005	www.bulgariandiocese.org/
Bulgarian Eastern Orthodox Church	Diocese of the USA, Canada and Australia, 550-A West Fiftieth Street, New York, NY 10019	www.calvarychapel.com
Calvary Chapels	3800 South Fairview Street, Santa Ana, CA 92704	www.usccb.org
Catholic Church in the United States, Roman Catholic Church	United States Conference of Catholic Bishops, 3211 Fourth Street, Washington, DC 20017	www.christadelphia.org
Christadelphians		www.cmalliance.org
Christian and Missionary Alliance	8595 Explorer Drive, Colorado Springs, CO 80929	

Christian Church (Disciples of Christ)	PO Box 1986, Indianapolis, IN 46206-1986	www.disciples.org
Christian Churches and Churches of Christ	PO Box 1232 Rapid City, SD 57709-1232	www.cctoday.com
Christian Congregation, Inc.		www.ccnamerica.org
Christian Methodist Episcopal Church	4466 Elvis Presley Boulevard, Memphis, TN 38116	www.thecmechurch.org
Christian Reformed Church in North America	2850 Kalamazoo Avenue Southeast, Grand Rapids, MI 49560	www.crcna.org
Church Communities International	Woodcrest, 2032 Route 213, Rifton, NY 12471	www.bruderhof.com
Church of Christ (Holiness) USA	PO Box 3135, Jackson, MS 39207	www.cochusa.org
Church of Christ (Temple Lot)	PO Box 472, Independence, MO 64501-0472	www.churchofchrist-tl.org
Church of Christ, Scientist	210 Massachusetts Avenue, Boston, MA 02115	www.tfccs.com
Church of God (Anderson, IN)	PO Box 2420, Anderson, IN 46018-2420	www.chog.org
Church of God (Cleveland, TN)	2490 Keith Street, Cleveland, TN 37320	www.churchofgod.org
Church of God (Holiness)	Kansas Christian College, 7401 Metcalf, Overland Park, KS 66204	www.cogh.net
Church of God (Seventh Day)	330 West 152nd Avenue, Broomfield, CO 80023	www.cog7.org
Church of God and Saints of Christ	3825 Central Avenue, Cleveland, OH 44115	www.cogasoc.net
Church of God General Conference	PO Box 2950, McDonough, GA 30253	www.coggc.org
Church of God in Christ	930 Mason Street, Memphis, TN 38126	www.cogic.org
Church of God in Christ, Mennonite	Information and Gospel Publishers, CGIC, Mennonite, PO Box 230, Moundridge, KS 67107	www.cogicm.org
Church of God of Prophecy	2710 Keith Street Northwest, Cleveland, TN 37320	www.cogop.org
Church of God, Mountain Assembly	256 North Florence Avenue, Jellico, TN 37762	www.cgmahdq.org
Church of Jesus Christ of Latter-day Saints	15 East South Temple Street, Salt Lake City, UT 84150	www.lds.org
Church of Our Lord Jesus Christ of the Apostolic Faith	943 Jefferson Avenue, Buffalo, NY 14204	www.cooljc.org
Church of the Brethren	1451 Dundee Avenue, Elgin, IL 60120	www.brethren.org
Church of the Living God (Christian Workers for Fellowship)	430 Forest Avenue, Cincinnati, OH 45229	
Church of the Lutheran Brethren of America	1020 West Alcott Avenue, PO Box 655, Fergus Falls, MN 56538	www.clba.org
Church of the Lutheran Confession	501 Grover Road, Eau Claire, WI 54701	www.clclutheran.org
Church of the Nazarene	17001 Prairie Star Parkway, Lenexa, KS 66220	www.nazarene.org

Appendices

Organization	Address	Website
Church of the United Brethren in Christ	302 Lake Street, Huntington, IN 46750	www.ub.org
Churches of Christ		www.church-of-christ.org
Churches of Christ in Christian Union	1553 Lancaster Pike, Circleville, OH 43113	www.cccuhq.org
Churches of God, General Conference (Winebrenner)	700 Melrose Avenue, PO Box 926, Findlay, OH 45839	www.cggc.org
Community of Christ	1001 West Walnut, Independence, MO 64050-3562	http://cofchrist.org
Congregational Holiness Church	3888 Fayetteville Highway, Griffin, GA 30223	www.chchurch.com
Congregational Methodist Church	PO Box 9, Florence, MS 39073	www.cm-church.org
Conservative Baptist Association of America	3686 Stagecoach Road Suite F, Longmont, CO 80504	www.cbamerica.org
Conservative Congregational Christian Conference	8941 Thirty-Third Street North, Lake Elmo, MN 55042	www.cccusa.org
Conservative Mennonite Conference	9910 Rosedale-Milford Center Road, Irwin, OH 43029	www.cmcrosedale.org
Continuing Anglican Churches		www.anglicansonline.org
Converge Worldwide	2002 South Arlington Heights Road, Arlington Heights, IL 60005	www.converge.org
Cooperative Baptist Fellowship	160 Clairemont Avenue, Decatur, GA 30030	www.cbf.net
Coptic Orthodox Church	427 West Side Avenue, PO Box 4397, Jersey City, NJ 07304	www.coptic.org
Cumberland Presbyterian Church	8207 Traditional Place, Cordova, TN 38016	www.cumberland.org
Cumberland Presbyterian Church in America	226 Church Street, Huntsville, AL 35801	www.cpachurch.org
Eastern Rite Catholic, Uniate Churches		
ECO: A Covenant Order of Evangelical Presbyterians	5638 Hollister Avenue Suite 200, Goleta, CA 93117	www.eco-pres.org
Ecumenical Catholic Church+USA	Vilatte Institute, 1100 Whispering Pines Drive, Dardenne Prairie, MO 63368-6958	www.ecc-usa.org
Ecumenical Catholic Churches in the USA		
Ecumenical Catholic Communion	483 East Lockwood Avenue Suite 3, Webster Grove, MO 63119	www.catholiccommunion.org
Elim Fellowship	Elim Bible Institute, 7245 College Street, Lima, NY 14485	www.elimfellowship.org
Episcopal Church	815 Second Avenue, New York, NY 10017	www.episcopalchurch.org
Ethiopian Orthodox Christianity in the United States		
Evana (Evangelical Anabaptists)	104 South Main Street, Goshen, IN 46526	www.evananetwork.org
Evangelical Association of Reformed and Congregational Churches	9051 Watson Road #241, Saint Louis, MO 63126	www.evangelicalassociation.net

Organization	Address	Website
Evangelical Church of North America	15 Eighty-Second Drive Suite 140, Gladstone, OR 97027	www.theevangelicalchurch.com
Evangelical Congregational Church	100 West Park Avenue, Myerstown, PA 17067	www.eccenter.com
Evangelical Covenant Church	8303 West Higgins Road, Chicago, IL 60631	www.covchurch.org
Evangelical Free Church of America	901 East Seventy-Eighth Street, Minneapolis, MN 55420-1300	www.efca.org
Evangelical Friends Church, International	PO Box 2079, Yorba Linda, CA 92885	www.friendschurchsw.org
Evangelical Lutheran Church in America	8765 West Higgins Road, Chicago, IL 60631	www.elca.org
Evangelical Lutheran Synod	6 Browns Court, Mankato, MN 56001	www.els.org
Evangelical Methodist Church		www.emchurch.org
Evangelical Presbyterian Church	17197 North Laurel Park Drive Suite 567, Livonia, MI 48152-7912	www.epc.org
Fellowship of Christian Assemblies	4909 East Buckeye Road, Madison, WI 53716	www.fcaministers.com
Fellowship of Evangelical Churches	1420 Kerrway Court, Fort Wayne, IN 46805	www.feministries.org
Fellowship of Grace Brethren Churches	PO Box 386, Winona Lake, IN 46590	www.charisfellowship.us
Fire Baptized Holiness Church of God	901 Bishop William Edward Fuller, Sr. Highway, Greenville, SC 29611	www.fbhchurch.org
Free Methodist Church of North America	770 North High School Road, Indianapolis, IN 46214	www.fmcusa.org
Friends General Conference	1216 Arch Street #2B, Philadelphia, PA 19107	www.fgquaker.org
Friends United Meeting	101 Quaker Hill Drive, Richmond, IN 47374-1980	www.fum.org
Full Gospel Baptist Church Fellowship International	1691 Phoenix Boulevard Suite 370, Atlanta, GA 30349	www.fullgospelbaptist.org
Full Gospel Fellowship of Churches and Ministries, International	1000 North Belt Line Suite 201, Irving, TX 75061	www.thefellowshipnetwork.net
Fundamentalist Church of Jesus Christ of Latter-day Saints		www.flds.org
General Association of General Baptists	100 Stinson Drive, Poplar Bluff, MO 63901	www.generalbaptist.com
General Association of Regular Baptist Churches	3715 North Ventura Drive, Arlington Heights, IL 60004	www.garbc.org
General Church of the New Jerusalem (Swedenborgian)	1100 Cathedral Road, PO Box 743, Bryn Athyn, PA 19009	www.newchurch.org
Grace Communion International	PO Box 5005, Glendora, CA 91740	www.gci.org
Grace Gospel Fellowship	1011 Aldon Street Southwest, PO Box 9432, Grand Rapids, MI 49509	www.ggfusa.org
Great Commission Churches	6797 North High Street Suite 319, Worthington, OH 43085	www.gccweb.org
Greek Orthodox Archdiocese of America	8 East Seventy-Ninth Street, New York, NY 10021	www.goarch.org

Organization	Address	Website
Hutterian Brethren		www.hutterites.org
I Am Activity and the Church Universal and Triumphant	1120 Stonenedge Drive, Schaumburg, IL 60194	www.saintgermainfoundation.org
IFCA International	3520 Fairlines Avenue Southwest, PO Box 810, Grandville, MI 49468	www.ifca.org
Independent Assemblies Of God, International	PO Box 2130, Laguana Hills, CA 92645-2130	www.iaogi.org
Independent Baptist Fellowship International	724 North Jim Wright Freeway, Fort Worth, TX 76108	www.ibfi.us
International Church of the Foursquare Gospel	1919 West Sunset Boulevard, PO Box 26902, Los Angeles, CA 90026	www.foursquare.org
International Churches of Christ	530 Wilshire Boulevard Suite 1750, Los Angeles, CA 90010	www.icoc.org
International Communion of the Charismatic Episcopal Church	50 Thomas Place, Malverne, NY 11565	www.iccec.org
International Council of Community Churches	21116 Washington Parkway, Frankfort, IL 60423-3112	www.icccnow.org
International Fellowship of Christian Assemblies	1294 Rutledge Road, Transfer, PA 16154-9005	www.ifcaministry.org
International Pentecostal Holiness Church	Global Ministries Center, 7300 Northwest Thirty-Ninth Expressway, Bethany, OK 73008	www.iphc.org
Interstate and Foreign Landmark Missionary Baptist Association	PO Box 7895, Madison, WI 53707	www.intervarsity.org www.landmarkbaptist.us
Jehovah's Witnesses (Watch Tower Bible and Tract Society)	20 Columbia Heights, Brooklyn, NY 11201	www.jw.org
Korean American Presbyterian Church	309 State Street, Hackensack, NJ 07601	www.kapc.org
Latvian Evangelical Lutheran Church in America		www.dcdraudze.org
Liberal Catholic Church	1502 East Ojai Avenue, PO Box 598, Ojai, CA 93024	www.thelccusa.org
Local Churches	PO Box 2121, Anaheim, CA 92814-0121	www.localchurches.org
Lutheran Church—Missouri Synod	1333 South Kirkwood Road, Saint Louis, MO 63122-7295	www.lcms.org
Lutheran Congregations in Mission for Christ	7000 North Sheldon Road, Canton, MI 48187	www.lcmc.net
Malankara Orthodox Syrian Church and Mar Thoma Orthodox Syrian Church (India Orthodox)	Malankara Diocesan Center, 270 Whippany Road, Whippany, NJ 07981. Sinai Mar Thoma Center, 2320 South Merrick Avenue, Merrick, NY 11566	www.malankaraorthodoxchurch.in; www.marthomanac.org
Mennonite Church USA	3145 Benham Avenue Suite 1, Elkhart, IN 46517	www.mennoniteusa.org
Messianic Jewish Alliance of America	PO Box 274, Springfield, PA 19064	www.mjaa.org

Organization	Address	Website
Metropolitan Community Churches	PO Box 50488, Sarasota, FL 34232	www.mccchurch.org
Missionary Church	3811 Vanguard Drive, Fort Wayne, IN 46809	www.mcusa.org
Moravian Church	101 Center Street, PO Box 1245, Bethlehem, PA 18016-1245	www.moravian.org
National Association of Congregational Christian Churches	8473 Howell Avenue, PO Box 288, Oak Creek, WI 53154	www.naccc.org
National Association of Free Will Baptists	PO Box 5002, Antioch, TN 37011-5002	www.nafwb.org
National Baptist Convention of America, Inc.	777 S. R. L. Thornton Freeway Suite 210, Dallas, TX 75203	www.nationalbaptist.com
National Baptist Convention USA, Inc.	1700 Baptist World Center Drive, Nashville, TN 37207	www.nationalbaptist.com
National Missionary Baptist Convention of America	6925 Wofford Drive, Dallas, TX 75227	www.nmbca.com
National Primitive Baptist Convention USA.	PO Box 17727 Tallahassee, FL 32522	www.natlprimbaptconv.org
National Spiritualist Association of Churches	PO Box, 217 Lily Dale, NY 14752	www.nsac.org
Netherlands Reformed Congregations	1233 Leffingwell Northeast, Grand Rapids, MI 49505	www.netherlandsreformed.org
New Apostolic Church USA	6005 Perry Highway, Erie, PA 16509	www.nac-usa.org
North American Baptist Conference	1219 Pleasant Grove Boulevard, Roseville, CA 95678	www.nabconference.org
North American Lutheran Church	3500 Mill Run Drive, Hilliard, OH 43026	www.thenalc.org
Old Catholic Churches	Saint Willlibrord Court, 180 Candy Road, Mohnton, PA 19540	www.occus.org
Old German Baptist Brethren		
Old Regular Baptists		www.oldregularbaptist.com
Open Bible Churches, Inc.	2020 Bell Avenue, Des Moines, IA 50315	www.openbible.org
Original Free Will Baptist Convention	201 West James Street, Mount Olive, NC 275776	www.ofwb.org
Orthodox Church in America (Russian Orthodox)	PO Box 675, Syosset, NY 11791-0675	www.oca.org
Orthodox Presbyterian Church	607 North Easton Road, Building E, Box P, Willow Grove, PA 19090-0920	www.opc.org
Pentecostal Assemblies of the World, Inc.	3939 Meadows Drive, Indianapolis, IN 46205	www.pawinc.org
Pentecostal Church of God	2701 Brown Trail, Bedford, TX 76021	www.pcg.org
Pentecostal Free Will Baptist Church, Inc.	PO Box 1568, Dunn, NC 28355	www.pfwb.org
Philadelphia Church of God	PO Box 3700, Edmond, OK 73083	www.pcog.org

Plymouth Brethren (Christian Brethren)	2570 Asbury Road, Dubuque, IA 52001	
Polish National Catholic Church of America	1004 Pittston Avenue, Scranton, PA 18505	www.pncc.org
Presbyterian Church (USA)	100 Witherspoon Street, Louisville, KY 40202	www.pcusa.org
Presbyterian Church in America	1700 North Brown Road Suite 105 Lawrenceville, GA 30043	www.pcanet.org
Primitive Baptists		www.oldschoolbaptist.org
Progressive National Baptist Convention, Inc.	601 Fiftieth Street Northeast, Washington, DC 20019	www.pnbc.org
Progressive Primitive Baptists		www.progressivepb.org
Protestant Reformed Churches in America	4949 Ivanrest Avenue, Grandville, MI 49418	www.prca.org
Reformed Catholic Church	PO Box 28710, Columbus OH 43228	www.reformedcatholic.org
Reformed Church in America	475 Riverside Drive, Eighteenth Floor, New York, NY 10115	www.rca.org
Reformed Church in the United States	407 West Main Street, Grass Valley, CA 95945	www.rcus.org
Reformed Episcopal Church	4142 Dayflower Drive, Katy, TX 77449	www.rechurch.org
Reformed Presbyterian Church of North America	7408 Penn Avenue, Pittsburgh, PA 15208	www.reformedpresbyterian.org
Romanian Orthodox Churches (The Romanian Orthodox Episcopate of America)	PO Box 309, Grass Lake, MI 49240	www.roea.org
Russian Orthodox Church outside of Russia	79 East Ninety-Third Street, New York, NY 10128	www.synod.com
Salvation Army	615 Slaters Lane, PO Box 269, Alexandria, VA 22313	www.salvationarmy.org
Schwenkfelder Church	105 Seminary Street, Pennsburg, PA 18073	www.schwenkfelder.com
Separate Baptists in Christ	905 South Main Street, Edinburgh, IN 46124	www.separatebaptist.org
Serbian Orthodox Church in the USA	2311 M Street Northwest Suite 402, Washington, DC 20037	www.serborth.org
Seventh Day Baptist General Conference	PO Box 1678, Janesville, WI 53547-1678	www.seventhdaybaptist.org
Seventh-Day Adventist	12501 Old Columbia Pike, Silver Spring, MD 20904-6600	www.adventist.org
Society of Pius X	Regina Coeli House, 11485 North Farley Road, Platte City, MO 64079	www.sspx.org
Southern Baptist Convention	901 Commerce Street Suite 750, Nashville, TN 37203	www.sbc.net
Southern Methodist Church	541 Broughton Street, Orangeburg, SC 29115	www.thesmc.org
Southwide Independent Baptist Fellowship		www.southwidebaptist.org

Organization	Address	Website
Syrian (Syriac) Orthodox Church of Antioch (Archdiocese in the USA and Canada)	55 West Midlands Avenue, Paramus, NJ 07652	www.syrianorthodoxchurch.org
Transformation Ministries	970 South Village Oaks Drive Suite 101, Covina, CA 91724	www.transmin.org
Two by Twos (Christian Convention)		
US Mennonite Brethren Churches, Mennonite Brethren, US Conference	1701 Signal Ridge Drive Suite 140, Edmond, OK 73013	www.usmb.org
Ukrainian Orthodox Church of the USA	PO Box 495, South Bound Brook, NJ 08880	www.uocofusa.org
Unification Church	481 Eighth Avenue, Box A-12, New York, NY 10001	www.unification.net
Unitarian Universalist Association	24 Farnsworth Street, Boston, MA 02210	www.uua.org
United American Free Will Baptist Church	110 West Seventh Street, Lakeland, FL 33805	www.uafreewillbaptconf.org
United Church of Christ	700 Prospect Avenue, Cleveland, OH 44115	www.ucc.org
United Church of God	PO Box 541027, Cincinnati, OH 45245-1027	www.ucg.org
United Holy Church of America, Inc.	5104 Dustan Road, Greensboro, NC 27405	www.uhcainc.org
United House of Prayer for All People	601 M Street Northwest, Washington, DC, 2001	www.tuhopfap.org
United Methodist Church	PO Box 320, Nashville, TN 37202-0320	www.umc.org
United Pentecostal Church International	8855 Dunn Road, Hazelwood, MO 63042	www.upci.org
United Reformed Churches in North America	227 First Avenue Southeast, Sioux Center, IA 51250	www.urcna.org
Vineyard Churches International	PO Box 2089, Stafford, TX 77497	www.vineyardusa.org
Volunteers of America, Inc.	1660 Duke Street, Alexandria, VA 22314-3421	www.voa.org
Wesleyan Church	13300 Olio Road, Fishers, IN 46037	www.wesleyan.org
Wisconsin Evangelical Lutheran Synod	N16 W23377 Stone Ridge Drive, Waukesha, WI 53188	www.wels.net
World Baptist Fellowship	3001 West Division Street, PO Box 13459, Arlington, TX 76094-0459	www.wbf.net

INDEX

Ababa, Addis, 30
Abernathy, David Ralph, 181
Abraham, 208
Abrahamic faith, xxxi, 264
Abrahamic theme, 5
Abrahamic tradition, xxxi, 6, 319
Absoluters. *See* Predestinarian Primitive Baptists (Absoluters)
Acts 29 Network, 322–323, 353
Adams, John, 256
Addai, Saint, 24–25
Adler, Randolph, 74
Advent Christian Church General Conference, 260, 353
Adventism, 7, 257–259, 271
Adventist churches, 256–259; Advent Christian Church General Conference, 260, 353; Christadelphians, 261–262, 354; Church of God (Seventh Day), 262–263, 266, 355; Church of God and Saints of Christ, 263–264, 355; Church of God General Conference, 264, 355; Grace Communion International, 265, 357; Jehovah's Witnesses (Watch Tower Bible and Tract Society), 267, 358; Philadelphia Church of God, 270, 273, 359; Seventh-Day Adventists, 261, 271–273, 233, 360; United Church of God, 270, 273–274, 361
Adventist Development and Relief Agency (ADRA), 272
African Americans. *See* black churches and organizations
African Methodist Episcopal Church, 190–193, 195, 349, 353
African Methodist Episcopal Zion Church, 190, 194–195, 349, 353
African Orthodox Church, 20–21, 353
AIDS, 170, 181, 272, 330

Albanian Orthodox Archdiocese in America, 21–22, 353
Albanian Orthodox Diocese of America, 22
Albright, Jacob, 66, 146, 191
Alliance of Renewal Churches, 323–325
Allen, Horace Newton, 106
Allen, Richard, 193–194
Alliance of Baptist Churches, 160–161, 170, 353
Almen, Lowell G., 84
Amana Business Society, 141
Amana Church Society, 141
American Anglican Council, 67
American Association of Lutheran Churches, 81, 353
American Baptist Association, 156, 161–162, 287, 293, 353
American Baptist Churches in the USA, 158, 162–164, 349, 353
American Baptist Convention, 163
American Baptist Home Mission Society, 162, 168
American Baptist Missionary Union, 162
American Bible Society, 225, 353
American Carpatho-Russian Orthodox Church, 22–23, 353
American Catholic Church in the United States, 51, 353
American Christian Missionary Society, 248
American Council of Christian Churches, 282, 343–344
American Episcopal Church, 67–68, 70
American Evangelical Christian Churches, 285, 353
American Evangelical Lutheran Church, 84
American Friends Service Committee (AFSC), 134

Index

The Fundamentals: A Testimony to the Truth, 282
Garvey, Marcus, 20–21, 195
General Association of General Baptists, 171–172, 357
General Association of Regular Baptist Churches, 289–290, 357
General Church of the New Jerusalem, 314–316, 357
General Conference Mennonite Church, 128
General Eldership of the Church of God, 251
General Missionary Convention of the Baptist Denomination in the United States of America for Foreign Missions, 157, 162
German Baptist Brethren, 141, 144
German Brethren, 5
German Evangelical Lutheran Synod of Wisconsin, 90
German Reformed Church, 94–95, 251
Gibbons, James, 49, 54
Global Ministries, 116
Gnosticism, 307–308, 310, 317
Grace, Charles Manuel, 335
Grace Communion International (Worldwide Church of God), 265–267, 270, 347, 357
Grace Gospel Fellowship, 290–291, 357
Graham, Billy, 9, 283, 290
Grant, F. W., 294
Graves, James Robinson, 156, 293
Great Commission Churches, 291, 347, 357
Great Depression, 235, 335
Grebel, Conrad, 118
Greek Orthodox Archdiocese of America, 31, 345, 349, 357
Greek Orthodox Church, 31
Gregory, Brother, 150
Gregory of Nyssa, 276
Gregory the Illuminator, Saint, 26
Grimes, Samuel, 293
Grundorf, Walter, 68
Gulliksen, Joanie, 243
Gulliksen, Kenn, 243
Hak Ja Han, 333–334
Harding, William, 59
Harms, Lawrence J., 52
Harris, Barbara C., 73
Hawaweeny, Raphael, 23
Haywood, G. T., 239
Hedrick, Granville, 300
Heidelberg Catechism, 92, 100, 108, 112–113

Heidelberg Confession of Faith, 91, 111, 114, 117
Helwys, Thomas, 171
Henry, Patrick, 64
Henry VIII, 63
Hermes Trismegistus, 307
Hicksites, 133
Hindmarsh, Robert, 315
Hines, John, 72
Hip-hop churches, xxx
Hodur, Francis, 60
Hoeksema, Herman, 112
Holiness churches, 192, 202–204, 283; Apostolic Christian Churches of America, 204–205; Bible Methodist Connection of Churches, 205–206; Christian and Missionary Alliance, 206–207; Churches of Christ in Christian Union, 212; Church of Christ (Holiness) USA, 207–208; Church of God (Anderson, Indiana), 208–209; Church of God (Holiness), 210; Church of the Nazarene, 210–211; Free Methodist Church of North America, 212–213; New Apostolic Church of North America, 331; The Salvation Army, 213–215; Wesleyan Church, 215–216
Holiness Church of Christ, 210
Holiness Methodist Church, 197
Holiness movement, 202–203, 208, 212, 215, 217, 282
Holy Catholic Church (Anglican Rite), 59–60
Holy Church of North Carolina, 241
Holy Spirit Association for the Unification of World Christianity, 333–334
Holy Ukrainian Autocephalic Orthodox Church, 70
Hooker, Richard, 63–64
Hornshuh, Fred, 237
human rights, 8, 107, 201, 346
humanism, 277
Hungarian Reformed tradition, 116
Hungarian Reformed Church in America, 349
Hus, John, 44, 150, 152
Hutter, Jacob, 127
Hutterian Brethren, 127–128, 358
Hutterites, 127–128
I AM Activity and the Church Universal and Triumphant, 308, 316–318, 358
IFCA International, 292–293, 358
Ignatius of Antioch, 43

– **372** –

Ukrainian Catholic Church, 56
Ukrainian Orthodox Church of America, 40
Ukrainian Orthodox Church of the USA, 40, 350, 361
Unamended Christadelphians, 262
Uniate churches, 14, 56–57, 356
Unification Church, 333–334, 361
Union Church of Africans, 190
Unitarianism, 233, 246, 275, 277–278
Unitarians and Universalists, 275–279
Unitarian Conference, American, 277–278, 353
Unitarian Universalist Association, 275, 277–278, 361
United American Free Will Baptist Church, 361
United Brethren Church, 140, 146–147, 191, 200
United Brethren in Christ, 146, 191, 348, 356
United Church of Christ, 8, 115–116, 345, 350, 361; Alliance of Baptist Churches and, 161; Evangelical Association of Reformed and Congregational Churches and, 105; Evangelical Lutheran Church in America and, 85; National Association of Congregational Christian Churches and, 107; Reformed Church in America and, 113; Reformed, Presbyterian, and Congregationalist Churches and, 95
United Church of God, 270, 273–274, 361
United Episcopal Church, 70
United Holy Church of America, Inc., 241, 352, 361
United House of Prayer for All People, 335, 361
United Reformed Churches in North America, 116–117, 361
United Methodist Church, 8, 188, 191–192, 199–201, 345, 361; American Methodist Episcopal Zion Church and, 195; Brethren and Pietist churches and, 140, 146; Church of the United Brethren in Christ and, 146; Evangelical Church of North America and, 197; Evangelical Congregation Church and, 146;
United Missionary Church, 129
United Pentecostal Church International, 242–243, 361
United Presbyterian Church in the USA, 109

United Presbyterian Church of North America, 110
United Synod of the Presbyterian Church, 97
Unity Churches, 310–312, 354
Universalist Primitive Baptists (No-Hellers), 181
Universalists, 275–279; See also Unitarians and Universalists
Universal Negro Improvement Association, 20
Urban VIII, Pope, 318
United States Conference of Catholic Bishops, 56, 345
Uskokovich, Archmandrite Mardary, 38
US Mennonite Brethren Churches, 130–131, 361
Varick, James, 194
Vilatte, Joseph René, 21, 59
Vineyard Churches International, 243–244, 361
The Vineyard movement, 69, 219, 243
Vladimir of Kiev, 33
Vladimir the Great, Saint, 40
Volunteers of America, Inc., 335–336, 361
voting rights, 8
Voting Rights Act of 1965, 349
Wagner, C. Peter, 324
Wagner Leadership Institute, 324
Waldensian, 236
Walters, Alexander, 195
Walther, C. F. W., 87
Ware, Henry, 275
Warner, Daniel S., 208
Washington, Booker T., 175
Washington, George, 64
Watch Tower Bible and Tract Society of Pennsylvania, 267–268, 358
Watts, Isaac, 189
Webb, Thomas, 189
Webber, Robert, 68, 74
Wedgewood, J. I., 318
Weir, Moses T., 103
Wellspring Retreat and Resource Center, 291
Wenger Amish, 122–123
Wesley, Charles, 189
Wesley, John; Adventist movement and, 257; Churches of Christ in Christian Union and, 212; Congregational Methodist Church and, 197; Episcopal and Anglican churches and, 70; Holiness movement and, 202; Methodism and, xxvii,